A CULTURAL HISTORY OF FURNITURE

VOLUME 1

A Cultural History of Furniture
General Editor: Christina M. Anderson

Volume 1
A Cultural History of Furniture in Antiquity
Edited by Dimitra Andrianou

Volume 2
A Cultural History of Furniture in the Middle Ages and Renaissance
Edited by Erin J. Campbell and Stephanie R. Miller

Volume 3
A Cultural History of Furniture in the Age of Exploration
Edited by Christina M. Anderson and Elizabeth A. Carroll

Volume 4
A Cultural History of Furniture in the Age of Enlightenment
Edited by Sylvain Cordier, Christina M. Anderson, and Laura Houliston

Volume 5
A Cultural History of Furniture in the Age of Empire and Industry
Edited by Catherine L. Futter and Christina M. Anderson

Volume 6
A Cultural History of Furniture in the Modern Age
Edited by Claire I.R. O'Mahony

A CULTURAL HISTORY OF FURNITURE

IN ANTIQUITY

Edited by Dimitra Andrianou

BLOOMSBURY ACADEMIC
LONDON • NEW YORK • OXFORD • NEW DELHI • SYDNEY

BLOOMSBURY ACADEMIC
Bloomsbury Publishing Plc
50 Bedford Square, London, WC1B 3DP, UK
1385 Broadway, New York, NY 10018, USA
29 Earlsfort Terrace, Dublin 2, Ireland

BLOOMSBURY, BLOOMSBURY ACADEMIC and the Diana logo are
trademarks of Bloomsbury Publishing Plc

First published in Great Britain 2022

Series design: Raven Design.
Cover image: A young woman arranging clothes in a coffer, fifth century BCE terracotta
plaque, Epizephyrioi Locroi (Magna Graecia) (© Museo Archeologico Nazionale, Taranto,
Puglia, Italy / Bridgeman Images)

A catalogue record for this book is available from the British Library.

A catalog record for this book is available from the Library of Congress.

ISBN: Pack: 978-1-4725-7789-4
         HB: 978-1-4725-7776-4

Series: The Cultural Histories Series

Typeset by Integra Software Services Pvt. Ltd.
Printed and bound in Great Britain

To find out more about our authors and books visit www.bloomsbury.com
and sign up for our newsletters.

CONTENTS

LIST OF ILLUSTRATIONS

PLATES

FIGURES

TABLE

BOXES

CONTRIBUTORS

Ilias Anagnostakis is Research Director Emeritus at the Institute of Historical Studies, National Hellenic Research Foundation, Athens. He is the program supervisor of "Everyday and Social Life in Byzantium" (NHRF). His publications include the edited volumes *Flavours and Delights: Tastes and Pleasures of Ancient and Byzantine Cuisine* (2013) and *Animals and Environment in Byzantium, 7th–12th Centuries* (2011), and the monograph *Wine Culture in Byzantium: The Bithynian Example* (2008, in Greek).

Dimitra Andrianou is Senior Researcher at the Institute of Historical Studies, National Hellenic Research Foundation, Athens. She holds a Ph.D. in Classical Archaeology from Bryn Mawr College. She is the author of *The Furniture and Furnishings of Ancient Greek Houses and Tombs* (2009; winner of the Academy of Athens Prize Award) and *Memories in Stone: Figured Grave Reliefs from Aegean Thrace* (2017). She has published articles on various aspects related to ancient furniture. As a member of the EuroWeb Cost Action (CA19131-Europe Through Textiles: Network for an integrated and interdisciplinary Humanities), her current research focuses on furniture textiles through the archaeological and textual evidence.

Athina Chatzidimitriou is Curator in the Archaeological Service of the Hellenic Ministry of Culture and Sports. She holds a Ph.D. in Classical Archaeology from the University of Thessalonica (1999). Her published dissertation "*Παραστάσεις εργαστηρίων και εμπορίου στην εικονογραφία των αρχαϊκών και κλασικών χρόνων*" (2005) deals with the workshops and commerce in the iconography of the Archaic and Classical period. Her publications deal with iconographical themes of Attic vase painting and generally the iconography of the Classical period.

Stefan Feuser is Temporary Professor of Classical Archaeology at Christian–Albrechts University Kiel. He is the author of *Der Hafen von Alexandria Troas* (2009), *Monopodia—Figürliche Tischfüße aus Kleinasien. Ein Beitrag zum Ausstattungsluxus der römischen Kaiserzeit* (2013) and *Hafenstädte im östlichen Mittelmeerraum vom Hellenismus bis in die römische Kaiserzeit* (2020).

Geoffrey Killen is an ancient furniture historian, technologist and Egyptologist. He studied Design and Technology at Shoreditch College, a Constituent College of the University of London, before being awarded his PhD from the University of Liverpool, where he specialised in Ramesside woodworking. He has written four major works on his specialism. He is a contributor to both Nicholson and Shaw's: '*Ancient Egyptian Materials and Technology*' (2000) and Redford's: '*The Oxford Encyclopedia of Ancient Egypt*' (2002). He has studied the collections of ancient Egyptian furniture at most of the major world museums and has lectured and given practical demonstrations of ancient woodworking processes and techniques in Egypt, Israel, Switzerland, United States of America and Britain.

Maria Leontsini is Senior Researcher at the Institute of Historical Research, National Hellenic Research Foundation, Athens. She has published on the reign of Constantine IV, as the last emperor of the Early Byzantine period (2006). Her articles, reviews, and chapters follow her wide interests across the historical geography of Byzantium, as well as daily life and the ways and means of living in the urban and rural environment.

Stephan T.A.M. Mols is Associate Professor in Classical and Roman Archaeology at Radboud University, Nijmegen, the Netherlands. He works on Greek and Roman architecture, interior decoration, and furniture. He is the author of *Wooden Furniture in Herculaneum: Form, Technique and Context* (1999). He has written several contributions on Roman wall painting including *La Villa della Farnesina: Le pitture* (2008, with Eric Moormann) and "L'edificio romano sotto S. Maria Maggiore a Roma e le sue pitture: proposta per una nuova lettura" (*Römische Mitteilungen*, 116 [2010]: 469–506, with Eric Moormann). He is currently project leader of the multidisciplinary research project *Mapping the Via Appia*, writing a cultural biography of a section of the queen of roads.

Vassilis Petrakis is Assistant Professor of Prehistoric Archaeology at the National and Kapodistrian University of Athens. He holds a Ph.D. in Archaeology from the University of Athens. He works on the archaeology of Aegean Prehistory, Aegean scripts, and Minoanization and Mycenaeanization as historical processes. His current involvement in field projects includes the excavations of the Bronze Age settlement of Koukonisi on Lemnos, the study of material from the Minoan palace of Kato Zakros in east Crete and the Mycenaean palatial site of Ayios Vasileios in Laconia.

Platon Petridis is Professor of Byzantine Archaeology at the National and Kapodistrian University of Athens and the Director of the Museum of Archaeology and Art History. His publications include *La céramique protobyzantine de Delphes: Une production et son contexte* (2010, winner of the Prix Gustave Mendel of the Académie des Inscriptions et Belles Lettres), *Early Byzantine Pottery in Greece* (2013), and *Delphes de l'Antiquité tardive: Le Secteur au Sud-Est du Péribole* (2014, with V. Déroche and A. Badie). His research interests lie in the area of late Roman/ early Byzantine archaeology and history of art.

Elizabeth Simpson is Professor Emerita at the Bard Graduate Center, New York, and Consulting Scholar at the University of Pennsylvania Museum, Philadelphia. She holds a Ph.D. in Classical Archaeology from the University of Pennsylvania. She directs the project to study, conserve, reconstruct, and publish the ancient furniture and wooden artifacts from Gordion, Turkey. Her publications include *The Spoils of War* (1997), *Gordion Wooden Furniture* (1999), *The Gordion Wooden Objects 1: The Furniture from Tumulus MM* (2010), *The Adventure of the Illustrious Scholar: Papers Presented to Oscar White Muscarella* (2018), and *The Gordion Wooden Objects 2: The Furniture and Wooden Artifacts from Tumulus P, Tumulus W, and the City Mound* (forthcoming).

†**Barbara Tsakirgis** was Associate Professor of Classical and Mediterranean Studies and History of Art at Vanderbilt University. She earned her Ph.D. from Princeton University and was a long-time member of the excavation and research teams at the Hellenistic city of Morgantina in central Sicily and the Athenian Agora. She published widely on the elements of Greek houses and households, including the decorated pavements at Morgantina and the remains of the Greek and Roman houses excavated at both sites. Along with Allison Glazebrook she was the editor of the *Houses of Ill Repute: The Archaeology of Brothels, Houses and Taverns in the Greek World* (2016).

Jean MacIntosh Turfa holds a Ph.D. in Classical and Near Eastern Archaeology and Latin from Bryn Mawr College. She was a consultant for the permanent reinstallation of the Kyle M. Phillips Etruscan Gallery of the University of Pennsylvania Museum, where she has been a Rodney Young Research Fellow and is now a Consulting Scholar. She has published extensively on various topics of Etruscan culture. Her books include *A Catalogue of the Etruscan Gallery of the University of Pennsylvania Museum* (2005), Etruscan catalogues of the Manchester Museum and Liverpool Museum of World History, and *Divining the Etruscan World: The Brontoscopic Calendar and Religious Practice* (2012). She is the editor of *The Etruscan World* (2013).

SERIES PREFACE

A Cultural History of Furniture is a six-volume series examining the changing cultural framework within which furniture was designed, produced, and used, as well as the cultural construction of furniture itself, from antiquity through to the present day in the Western tradition. All the volumes follow the same structure: an editorial overview of the historical context of the period under consideration is followed by chapters written by specialists that each correspond to one of the following themes: design and motifs; makers, making, and materials; types and uses; the domestic setting; the public setting; exhibition and display; furniture and architecture; visual representations; and verbal representations. The configuration of the series means that readers can use the material synchronically or diachronically: an individual volume provides a thorough grounding in the furniture of a particular period while following one distinct theme across all volumes presents the reader with the evolution of a specific aspect of furniture over time. The six volumes divide the history of furniture in this way:

Volume 1: A Cultural History of Furniture in Antiquity (From the beginnings to 500 CE)

Volume 2: A Cultural History of Furniture in the Middle Ages and Renaissance (500–1500)

Volume 3: A Cultural History of Furniture in the Age of Exploration (1500–1700)

Volume 4: A Cultural History of Furniture in the Age of Enlightenment (1700–1800)

Volume 5: A Cultural History of Furniture in the Age of Empire and Industry (1800–1900)

Volume 6: A Cultural History of Furniture in the Modern Age (1900–twenty-first century)

Christina M. Anderson
General Editor

Introduction

DIMITRA ANDRIANOU

At the beginning of the twentieth century and in one of the seminal studies on ancient furniture, Caroline L. Ransom introduced the subject by admitting that "the monumental evidence [on ancient beds] is far from satisfying .... There are fundamental problems of form and construction to which the ancient sources, literary and monumental taken together, do not furnish adequate answers" (Ransom 1905: 13–14). The ancient material that Ransom had at her disposal in 1905 amounted to a bronze Etruscan bed from the seventh century BCE and another from about 200 BCE, "possibly the only one from the second century" (14). She noted numerous beds dating from the centuries immediately before and after Christ, followed by a break in the second century CE. With the then available amount of excavated furniture pieces she stressed that discussions should depend upon relief sculpture, wall paintings, and vase decorations in which beds appear. In her time, Greek reliefs, Etruscan wall paintings, and vase paintings of the sixth and fifth centuries BCE along with wall decorations of Roman date were the principal source of information in regard to ancient beds.

Twenty years after Ransom's study, Gisela M.A. Richter, for many years Curator of Greek and Roman Art at the Metropolitan Museum in New York, published a meticulous study on various kinds of *Furniture of the Greeks, Etruscans and Romans* (1926) with more excavated material on which to base her findings. An appendix by Albert Baker provided about twenty drawings of Greek types. Richter later revised her work in 1966 adding material and illustrations, creating a superb reference for an overlooked category of ancient material. A brief account of earlier Aegean furniture was added, along with references to furniture on Linear B tablets. The classification developed in 1926, in which each type of furniture is studied separately, was still used and further expanded in this study. New material in the Greek section of her book included a discussion of the evidence for the use of shelves and cupboards, although with the material evidence available at the time, she was not convinced that the latter appeared before the Hellenistic period; this is nowadays refuted by the findings from the second millennium BCE at Akrotiri on the island of Thera. Her revision coincided with (or perhaps was the result of) a renewed interest in ancient furniture created by an exhibition of Greek furniture reproductions designed by an American furniture designer, T.H. Robsjohn-Gibbings, and manufactured by a Greek furniture maker, E. Saridis, in 1961. Robsjohn-Gibbings and Saridis worked from representations in sculpture, paintings, and pottery and copied models of ancient Greek furniture. "Clean-lined grace and delicate proportions" were among the comments praising the pictures that accompanied the exhibition in contemporary media. Richter underlined the fact that ancient furniture techniques have influenced household equipment ever since and are indeed of significance to modern designers.

Also in 1966, at the same time as Richter's revised edition, Hollis S. Baker, a prosperous furniture manufacturer from the American midwest with firsthand technical knowledge of furniture manufacture and a primary interest in the history of furniture design, published a volume on the origins and evolution of furniture in the ancient world. He attempted to consider ancient furniture as a whole and to compare the types that evolved in the different civilizations of the ancient world. According to Baker, the attention given to the subject of ancient furniture by furniture historians was usually limited to a brief summary prior to a discussion of "period" or "modern" furniture. As he readily admitted in his introduction, it was the outward appearance of furniture rather than its function that was his main concern (Baker 1966).

Since 1966 the subject of ancient furniture has piqued scholarly interest, and studies on specific types of furniture and more concise periods and geographical regions have appeared (Kyrieleis 1969; Killen 1980; Gubel 1987; Herrmann 1996b; Allison 1999; Mols 1999; Croom 2007; Lavan, Swift, and Putzeys 2007; Andrianou 2009; Simpson 2010; Naeh and Gilboa 2020). Use rather than strict typology or art appreciation is one of the main focuses of current studies that concentrate on actual furniture rather than furniture depicted in other media. Building on the previous knowledge regarding types and styles acquired through the work of scholars such as Richter, we are now in a position to understand pressing issues such as use, function within the household, status, and display, and consequently to study furniture within its context and not solely as art. The following chapters on furniture aim to give an overall picture of the scholarly work that has been achieved since Richter's revised edition.

The earliest furniture can perhaps be seen as an attempt by humans to enhance their comfort, safety, and social standing. For millennia they had been sitting and sleeping on the ground with skins, brushwood, and perhaps rugs to comfort them, but chairs support an aching back, and beds improve the quality of sleep. Protection against snakes, scorpions, and other creatures at ground level may have been the motivation for the creation of chairs. Once chairs were produced, tables were necessary to bring food up to the level of the seated individual so as to reduce exertion.

Although one might assume that furniture began to be produced as soon as permanent human settlements appeared in the Neolithic period, around 10000 BCE, the relationship between the two is not straightforward. The archaeological record suggests that a long time intervened between the beginning of the Neolithic and the date of the earliest known actual furniture (3500–2500 BCE), when our volume begins. The oldest extant pieces of furniture betray remarkable sophistication, hardly representative of a craft in its formative stage. This lacuna between the earliest permanent human settlements and the earliest extant furniture pieces reflects issues that permeate the study of furniture as a whole, namely the incomplete nature of the surviving archaeological record and the difficulty of understanding the use of early furniture in various contexts. Scholarship traces ancient furniture in domestic, funerary, and sacred contexts. Serving as ancillary sources are the depictions of furniture on vases and in sculpture and the references to furniture in texts and inscriptions. All these sources have their limitations, as we will see below, but their careful combination may answer questions on the cultural history of furniture.

EVIDENCE FROM ARCHAEOLOGICAL EXCAVATIONS

Ancient furniture, being made of perishable materials, has largely not survived in the archaeological record. The preservation of furniture is thus affected both by social custom and by climate. Egypt is a good example of this, giving it an enviable role that dominates most discussions of early furniture. Egyptian traditions of equipping the dead for the afterlife, with wood and textiles often being superbly preserved by the country's dry climate, have made Egyptian evidence fundamental for understanding the history of technology in both Egypt and western Asia. In addition to the extant pieces of furniture, numerous tools have been preserved, and paintings on the walls of tombs show carpenters at work. Actual organic materials have survived alongside ample documentation regarding the production and use of these items.

Excavations in Egypt have unearthed a wealth of Early Dynastic furniture from Naqada, Saqqara, Abydos, and Hierakonpolis. The preserved fragments indicate that the Egyptian upper class already enjoyed a high standard of luxury in the third millennium BCE. The set of furniture of Queen Hetepheres, wife of the first pharaoh of the Fourth Dynasty, discovered in a pit near the pyramid of Khufu at Giza, included two armchairs, a carrying-chair, a bed with a footboard, a headrest, and a collapsible canopy, along with storage boxes for toilet articles and jewelry.

Since Egypt was in contact with the Levant and technology traveled widely, we can assume that carpentry techniques attested in Egypt were also employed in woodworking centers in areas of western Asia, a vast region that stretches from the shores of the Mediterranean to the Indus River and from the Karakum desert to Arabia. Elsewhere, and particularly in the Greek world, extant furniture is found only occasionally in domestic and funerary contexts. Natural disasters, such as the devastating volcanic eruptions that buried Akrotiri on the island of Thera (1650–1600 or 1550–1500 BCE) or Pompeii near Vesuvius (79 CE), created near-perfect conditions for the preservation of organic material or the valuable imprints of furniture made of this material in a pumice matrix. For example, at Akrotiri a shelf at a height of 1.85 meters above the floor was found running along the west wall in the room of the Spring Fresco (Delta 2), and a cupboard in the West House (room 5) was plastered, painted red, and had at least two superimposed wooden shelves (Palyvou 2005: 152–3). Were it not for the destruction and subsequent preservation of the material we would have only hypothesized about the possible uses of shelves and cupboards in houses at such an early date.

In Asia Minor, furniture, and indeed of wood, was excavated at Gordion (Phrygia). A large collection of furniture, household objects, and miniature sculptures was excavated at the site between 1956 and 1961. Approximately thirty-seven pieces of furniture and fifty-six wooden objects were found in three royal tombs, while many carbonized fragments were unearthed in the destruction level of the city mound. All date to the eighth century BCE, the period of King Midas and his predecessors, when the power and influence of the Phrygian capital was at its height. Various types of wood were used to make the carved and inlaid furniture from Gordion, the largest and best-preserved collection of ancient furniture to survive from the ancient Near East. This unique discovery was the focus of an exemplary study and conservation project undertaken by Elizabeth Simpson and Krysia Spirydowicz (1999).

In addition to the fragmentary nature of the archaeological record, there are lacunae in the scholarship, created by the way furniture has been presented in published reports. The nineteenth- and twentieth-century excavations of major sites with ample domestic contexts, such as Delos and Olynthos (Greece), produced volumes dedicated to various types of objects, one of them being furniture. Although furniture was featured in volume eighteen of the *Delos* series by Waldemar Déonna (1938) and received the attention it deserved, it was presented among lists of "minor objects." The system of publication directly from field notes has created a certain scholarly mentality where "minor objects" are usually given in a catalog format disassociated from their primary contexts, such as the rooms in which they were found. It is thus often impossible to tell whether an artifact was found on the floor or in some other context, information critical for reconstructing the interior of a room. In addition, many older publications have focused on a select group of finds, recorded as "minor objects," which included only objects made of precious or well-preserved materials (ivory, bronze, glass). As a result, traces of wooden furniture frequently went unnoticed or unmentioned by the excavators.

Another major domestic site that produced furniture in Greece is Olynthos (Macedonia). Its unique history, extensive excavation (which uncovered more than a hundred houses), and full publication make Olynthos the best-documented site for the study of household and urban organization in Classical Greece. Thanks to Olynthos, we can now consider not only the "typical house" but also a range of variations among contemporary houses and their contents, including furniture. David M. Robinson and J. Walter Graham's publication (1938), and Nicholas D. Cahill's subsequent revision of the remains (2002), reveal a much richer corpus of domestic implements than at any other Greek site, and indeed one that belongs largely to a single destruction level. Cahill's exemplary study strove to assign rooms to the domestic finds, and thus examine furniture in its primary context, by reevaluating the excavation notebooks. He used the assemblages of artifacts to investigate how different activities and parts of the Greek house were organized (i.e., preparation of food, food storage, weaving, and entertainment in *andrones*) and stressed the fact that architecture alone does not tell the whole story, but rather the distribution of artifacts in a house may indicate the diverse patterns of household organization.

In Italy the famous excavations of Pompeii and Herculaneum gave archaeologists another welcome assemblage of preserved furniture. We have a detailed account of the disaster recorded by Pliny the Younger, who interviewed survivors and recorded events in a letter to his friend Tacitus. Little wooden furniture was preserved in Pompeii; a larger group was found in Herculaneum, where about forty pieces of wooden furniture have been preserved (Mols 1999) leading scholars to reevaluate the older assumption that Roman houses were sparsely furnished.

In reading through the chapters of this volume, one should, therefore, keep in mind that we lack much information concerning the main body of furniture in household, sacred, or funerary assemblages. This must be considered when attempting to compare furniture from various sites or to use statistical analysis to draw conclusions about the use of furniture in antiquity. Different cultural processes (destruction versus simple abandonment of a site, for example) have a major impact on the amount, location, and state of preservation of furniture in ways that were not always immediately understood by excavators or researchers.

FURNITURE IN DOMESTIC SETTINGS

House contents, the "nonfixed–feature" elements (Rapoport 1990: 96–101) that are not part of the architecture, but are evidently part of the household, constitute a major contribution to insights into household behavior and relationships between social action and material (Allison 1999: 6). Such holistic approaches to the archaeological record and specifically to the distribution of household artifacts within houses, from which the field of furniture study can only benefit, were first addressed in the 1970s and in the dissertation studies of Olynthos (Cahill 1991), Pompeii (Allison 1992), and Halieis (Ault 1994). Household material culture provides information on domestic behavior that may elucidate, be contradictory to, or alternatively not be evident in related textual and visual material. Certain scholars (Goldberg 1999) have even highlighted the adaptability of domestic space and indeed furniture to argue that investigation of architecture alone is misleading regarding household behavior.

It is widely accepted that domestic interiors of antiquity, the context where furniture is expected to be found, were not as elaborately appointed as modern interiors. The amount of modern furniture is dictated by various needs that did not exist in the ancient world. Privacy, for example, is largely a modern prerequisite and results in various kinds of similarly furnished rooms within a house (bedrooms). Ancient households did not maintain the same degree of privacy, and thus furniture, when not built-in, was portable and could be moved from one room to another, or from the interior of the house to the exterior courtyard, where many activities took place (daily chores such as weaving, for instance, when the weather permitted). Use-specific rooms, such as *andrones* (for entertainment), first appear in late Classical and Hellenistic private houses and palaces, later adopted in Roman and late Antique villas. They were distinguished from other rooms by their size and wealth of decoration. Their floors were laid with tiles or mosaics, and they were typically furnished with permanent installations, such as *klinai*, for *symposia*. By the Late Antique period, the walls and ceilings of these rooms could also be richly decorated.

One important reason for the need for portable furniture and multifunctional spaces was the source of light. During daylight hours, the rooms of the house that were better lit attracted most of the domestic activities and thus furniture, whereas later in the day that same furniture was apparently moved to rooms that were better ventilated and/or lit. In the same sense, furniture changed function. Thus, the modern notion of furniture being used for specific purposes inside well-defined rooms is far from the ancient practice of furniture use in multifunctional areas. Adaptability and mobility are thus two key issues to consider; some furniture was easy to dismantle or folded to facilitate storage and transportation. Folding stools and light, small tables designed to fit under a couch are a few of the extant examples.

FURNITURE IN FUNERARY SETTINGS

Furniture is also found in funerary contexts, and in fact it often survives better here because of more favorable conditions of preservation. The use of furniture in tombs occurs cross-culturally and can be associated with aspects of funerary ritual, as in the case of Hellenistic Macedonian tombs, or beliefs regarding sustenance in the afterlife, as in the case of Egypt. Royalty and members of the nobility went to their graves accompanied by fine pieces of furniture. Mortuary meals or exposition of the deceased required certain types of furniture, such as *klinai* (beds), chairs, and tables. The role of wooden funerary biers in ritual mourning and funerary processions is equally important, judging from the visual representations of such scenes.

Besides full-sized furniture, reduced-scale models of terracotta or metal were also deposited for reasons of economy or for ideological purposes (as in the case of Archaic Sindos, northern Greece). Furniture may have been unaffordable or, more likely, furniture models were seen to suffice for the use of the deceased in the afterlife, much like the depictions of banquets on tombstones that accompany the deceased in the Hellenistic period. Such depositions presuppose still remotely understood mortuary rites tightly connected to social and political competitions or the negotiation of identities. In certain cases, the analysis of organic residues from bronze and pottery vessels has enabled researchers to recover much information about pertinent funerary banquets, for which these pieces of furniture were possibly originally intended.

Both Egypt and the Near East have yielded evidence for the deposition of furniture as part of elite mortuary ostentation. In the eighth-century BCE Tumulus MM, the so-called Midas Mound at Gordion, where favorable conditions aided the preservation of furniture, nine tray-top banquet tables, two serving stands, two stools, and a chair accompanied the deceased, who was certainly of royal status. The king had been laid out on a large uncovered log coffin for display at a lavish funeral banquet, and he was then buried with the remains of the banquet including the furniture, food, and drink. Similar ostentation is observed in the fourth-century BCE Tomb II at Vergina, the so-called Tomb of Philip, where the cremated ashes of the two occupants of the tomb were placed in two separate gold boxes (*larnakes*), each stored inside a marble chest, and in one case the remains were covered by a textile woven with gold (Drougou 2018). A wooden *kline* with exquisite ivory, gold, and glass decoration and possibly another piece of wooden furniture were placed in the middle of the main chamber of the tomb for the arrangement of vessels (Andronikos 1984).

A logical question that arises from the deposition of furniture in tombs is whether these were made specifically for the journey of the deceased to the otherworld or whether they had been used during life and then, as beloved (and precious) objects, accompanied the deceased as burial goods. This is a vexing question that is hard to answer conclusively, and scholarship tends to favor the second hypothesis, although burial practices differ from one site to another, and one theory will likely not suffice for all examples.

FURNITURE IN THE VISUAL ARTS

The gaps in our knowledge left by the paucity of excavated furniture are partly compensated for by depictions of furniture on vases and in wall paintings, sculptures, and mosaics, as well as by administrative or cultic inventories. This is a large body of evidence, worthy in its own right. In western Asia, depictions of furniture begin to occur with regularity on Sumerian cylinder seals of the mid-fourth millennium BCE. Gisela Richter's seminal study based its typology on depictions of furniture found largely on ancient Greek and Etruscan vases. Visual representations of furniture may convey the uses of furniture in domestic contexts, a body of evidence that has been lost, along with the types of furniture used in these contexts.

Caution, however, should be exercised with visual depictions: ancient imagery often depicted *topoi* or conventions that were rooted in tradition and did not necessarily reflect contemporary reality. At the very least, vase painting in particular shows the way furniture was used, although the variety of types and the richness of materials depicted cannot be treated as "photographs" of upper-class houses. The various containers and types of chairs depicted in "bridal" scenes, for example, do not necessarily represent pieces of furniture customarily used by brides. Iconography is rarely objective, but consistently representative of the specific sociopolitical conditions of its production and consumption. The visual arts may equally be (deliberately?) anachronistic, as in the case of the so-called funerary banquet iconography with males reclining on a couch while females are seated on either side of it, often seen on Hellenistic and especially Roman funerary reliefs. This particular iconography (rich in the depiction of *klinai*, tables, stools, footstools, or more elaborate seats and cupboards) became with time a fixed formula, an artistic cliché, reproduced in areas such as Gallia and the northwestern provinces of the Roman Empire at a time when other depictions and literary references generally indicate that women were allowed to recline as well.

FURNITURE IN TEXTUAL SOURCES

Our earliest written documentation of furniture comes from the early states developed in Egypt and the Near East, including Hittite Anatolia in the second millennium BCE. Although this is a large source of information regarding furniture in terms of records of transactions and inventories, it is seldom descriptive. Records are records, with minimal information on all the aspects of furniture that interest us (shapes, sizes, functions). Their main aim was to archive pieces of furniture for various purposes. Second-millennium BCE dowry inventories from the ancient Near East, for example, include a fair amount of elite domestic furniture intended for the king's daughters. Diplomatic letters from Tell el-Amarna also dating to the second millennium BCE include descriptions of furniture sent as diplomatic gifts. At the so-called Palace of Nestor at Pylos, clay tablets list inventories of furniture and other utensils apparently used during a palace banquet. Classical inventories from the sanctuary of Athena on the Acropolis at Athens record the property of the sanctuary, possibly the dedications of pious guests, while the so-called *Attic Stelai* also from Athens record the confiscated, private property of Alcibiades and his followers, wealthy Athenians who possessed luxurious furniture in their private houses.

Other than archives, furniture looms large in literary texts, although daily life in a house is not detailed in any text. Vergil, in the first century BCE, described the poor home of Evander on the Palatine and the couch of leaves covered by a Libyan bearskin upon which "towering Aeneas" slept (*Aeneid* 8.359–69). Homer, on the other hand, gives us the famous description of Odysseus' bed, whose construction included a secret known only to the married couple, namely, that the bed had been carved from the trunk of a living olive tree still in place. Homer used the bed as a symbol par excellence of wedded life and as a powerful metaphor for the solidity of Odysseus' household.

Plato used the bed as an example of a simple, physical object in his theory of Forms (*Republic* X, 596–8). In this particular passage, Socrates drew a distinction between a universal Form (the Platonic ideal) and the particular things that participate in that Form, using as an example beds and tables. Socrates, who ostensibly condemned artists, maintained that craftsmen could only make the *appearance* of things but not the things themselves as they truly are (596e). The Form is the bed a God makes, a particular bed is the bed a craftsman makes, and an appearance or imitation of a bed is the bed a painter makes. In other words, a painter is an imitator, one whose product is once removed from the natural one, and twice removed from the truth, which is the Form (597e). So painters or poets, though they may paint or describe a carpenter or any other maker of things, know nothing of the carpenter's (the craftsman's) art, and though the better painters or poets they are, the more faithfully their works of art will resemble the reality of the carpenter making a bed, nonetheless the imitators will still not attain the truth (the God-made Form). The bed made by a craftsman demonstrates a kind of productive knowledge possessed by its creator, which is useful to human well-being. It is thus understood that an item of furniture required technical knowledge of how these pieces were supposed to join and work, and it is this very knowledge that raises craftsmanship above painting.

Contemporary Xenophon stated that

in small towns the same workman makes chairs and doors and ploughs and tables, and often the same artisan builds houses, and even so he is thankful if he can only find employment enough to support him … In large cities, on the other hand, inasmuch as many people have demands to make upon each brand of industry, one trade alone, and very often even less than a whole trade, is enough to support a man.

(Cyropaedia 8.2.5)

Other writers described (mythical) works of art that impressed them because of their rich figural decorations, such as Pausanias' description of Daidalos' folding stool, whereas fourth-century New Comedy writers mentioned furniture almost exclusively in the context of cooking and the humorous cooks attending to dinners and setting tables. Yet other writers, such as fifth- to sixth-century CE Hesychios and tenth-century CE Suidas, compiled a thesaurus of furniture terms, a text that reads like a dictionary but is worthy from a linguistic point of view.

Notwithstanding the wealth of information on shapes, names, and component materials of furniture and furnishings preserved mainly in the Classical and Hellenistic sources, one should keep in mind that the pairing of ancient Greek terms with excavated pieces of any period is problematic. The issue of nomenclature is especially difficult to solve since later sources quote earlier sources or identify furniture types with a variety of terms. The use of different names for one and the same type of furniture is not infrequent in the Greek world, as in the case of most of the names under which ancient containers have come down to us. Literary and epigraphic sources enhance our understanding of most of the furniture types but do not come with pictures. Conversely, visual representations show the use of furniture but do not come with inscriptions that give their names.

What furniture can tell us about the past

Despite the often problematic nature of excavated evidence or scholarly publications, ancient furniture undoubtedly offers opportunities for understanding human behavior, values, and thought. Furniture implies a level of culture, and indeed a settled existence. Furniture was apparently inherited, as literary evidence for dowries suggests. Power and status were expressed through furniture. In the early examples of the Neolithic period throughout the Mediterranean and the Near East, terracotta figurines show voluptuous figures seated on stools, something that may suggest age or high rank. Expensive or imported materials signify the well-to-do. Was the first furniture invented and developed for elite use alone? Inherent biases in our extant sources tend to show less interest in the lifestyle of common people, where the absence of actual wooden furniture at Neolithic settlements may suggest that permanent installations, such as plastered benches or wall niches, fulfilled the function of tables, beds, or chairs.

Furniture alludes to gender issues. It is by now well established that ancient Greek women were not kept in seclusion in women's quarters, nor do our texts (despite the mention of the *gynaikonitis*) provide evidence for a fixed space for women. On vase paintings we see women who are surrounded by part of their movable furniture and furnishings that tell the story of what some women did when they gathered. Furniture here acts as a visual clue for women and their lives. In texts we read of household furniture among descriptions of dowries. Although ancient Greek writers and artists were predominately male, we can definitely observe the activities and hear the voices of women. We know of objects that women dedicated at sanctuaries, and we have works of art that were intentionally created to please women, as for instance wedding gifts. While spinning, weaving, and performing household tasks, women used furniture. At the same time, metaphors explicitly connected to women incorporate furniture, as with the myth around Pandora's *box*, a mistranslation of the original *pithos* (Hesiod, *Works and Days* 94) by sixteenth-century writer Erasmus. Boxes, chests, and other containers occupy a place in a woman's world, where utilitarian objects and symbolic values are kept. François Lissarrague (1995) in his pioneering article draws upon three myths that pertain to females, where chests and boxes play an essential visual and metaphorical role: Danae is kept in a box as a form of confinement by her father Akrisios; female curiosity opened the box in which Erechthonios had been secretly placed by Athena; and a box of seductions was placed in Polynikes' hands in order to bribe Eriphyle with a necklace. Containers seem to be tied to female space in Greek thought, sometimes to conceal or to hoard, "to exercise a control over an indoor private space, where women are themselves detained" (Lissarrague 1995: 93). Containers are metaphorically interpreted as signifiers pointing to a woman's role in managing the material goods of the *oikos*. The cover of the present volume depicts just that: a woman is arranging textiles in a richly decorated chest on a terracotta *pinax* from Epizephyrian Locris (Taranto, Museo Nazionale). Boxes of various sizes are depicted in the hands of women or in female scenes. A bride is often surrounded by female companions who bring all sorts of baskets and chests, probably containing wedding gifts. In other instances, they hold fabrics, jewelry, or musical instruments. A *kalathos* in a funerary context may signify the *oikos* and the female virtues associated with it: when presented as a grave marker it may signify the (female) deceased. Equally in iconography, *klinai* may be tied to a man's space, if we consider the symposion rooms where only male participants were allowed to recline. However, as everyday objects, both boxes and *klinai* were certainly used by both sexes in real life.

Fine furniture is appreciated as art. Throughout furniture history, great care has been exercised in the production of certain pieces by specialized craftsmen. From the very beginning craftsmen strove to create what to them was beautiful as well as useful. The famous inlaid table from Tumulus MM at Gordion was made of three kinds of wood (boxwood for the frame and legs, juniper for the inlay and walnut for the table top). Applied decoration on furniture often surprises us, and scholars have hypothesized that specialized craftsmen of ivory or gold were involved in the decoration of fine pieces of furniture. Funerary *klinai*, for example, in Hellenistic tombs were decorated with gold, ivory, and glass inlays. Wood, the leading material of furniture in antiquity, was readily available and generally considered cheap. However, a certain type of wood, the citrus-wood, was an exception and became the shorthand cliché for extravagant furniture in the Roman period. The most expensive woods often had elaborate grain patterns. Likewise, ivory was used as an expensive luxury material for inlays while bone was its cheap alternative. The furniture of wealthy Romans and Byzantines incorporated veneers, plating, and inlays to display a much richer and more decorative effect than solid timber. In addition to different types of woods, furnishings such as pillows, cushions, and valances often added color and fabrics to the way materials were blended in a domestic or funerary interior to create ambiance not easily grasped by our fragmented notion of such interiors. A remarkable example is the bedding appearing in the funerary banquet depicted on the frieze of the Agios Athanasios tomb in Macedonia, where the sheets and the blanket on the bed are color-coordinated.

Furniture, being a valued gift, was used in diplomacy. It was exchanged by monarchs and received as tribute. One such exchange described in the Amarna Letters, the diplomatic archive between the Pharaoh of Egypt and Asiatic kings dating to the fourteenth century BCE, records the request of the Kassite king of Babylon for Egyptian furniture. Elite gift exchange is evidenced in the Bronze Age, especially in the cosmopolitan environment of the Late Bronze Age eastern Mediterranean (*c.* 1400–1200 BCE). Fine furniture was among the most valuable of possessions, the prerogative of wealth and status, an attribute of royalty and divinity throughout the ancient world (Simpson 1995: 1669–70). The aristocratic classes of Latium, Caere, Tarquinia, Vulci, and other cities in Etruria evidently obtained Oriental luxuries in order to show off their wealth and status in the first millennium BCE. Similarly, the quality and quantity of furniture in a Roman house depended considerably on the wealth of the family. Pliny's description of his Laurentine villa, for example, mentions at least twenty-seven rooms. Here multifunctionality is gone, since wealth is demonstrated by duplicate rooms or suites of rooms to provide variety for both the owner and his guests.

Furniture is recorded as booty. Less peaceful than the diplomatic gifts, some exchanges involved the wholesale removal of furniture from defeated cities, as recorded in detail on the reliefs of the Assyrian kings and Livy's accounts of Roman triumphs in Asia Minor in the second and first centuries BCE (Andrianou 2006: 225). Both booty and diplomatic gifts, as well as regular commercial trade, doubtless had an effect on fashion and techniques, while other traditions remained independent. Along with furniture pieces, manufacturing techniques, designs, and their makers migrated.

Human behavior and social context are also evidenced through furniture. Couches in western Asia were used in a different way than in other, earlier regions: to recline on at dinner, as well as to sleep on. Ashurbanipal is depicted feasting in the royal gardens, after defeating the king of Elam, reclining on a high couch with a table beside him, while his queen sits nearby in an armchair with her feet on a footstool. In the Greek world reclining on a couch is a male prerogative during a symposion, while in Thrace (Kazanluk) a man and woman are depicted seated before a table laden with food. In Etruria a couple is reclining, side by side, on a couch. A regular change from reclining to sitting during banquets in the western part of the Roman Empire must have started in the fourth century CE (Dunbabin 2003: 89–91), whereas in the eastern part of the Empire the reclining position apparently remained stable until the sixth century CE (141–74). Similarly, and regarding gender issues, male participants are customarily allowed to recline during a banquet in the Greek world, whereas in the Etruscan and Roman world women reclined as well. Thus, different cultures embraced different attitudes and uses for furniture. Throughout the ancient world, supreme authority, sacred or secular, has more often been represented seated rather than standing: the throne may symbolize or even personify the power of the state or the divinity. On the other hand, in a funerary context, the seated female in a two-figure composition on a stele is often interpreted as the venerated dead for whom the stele was made.

Furniture is neither purely practical nor purely ceremonial. Social habits, such as eating and sleeping, are inculcated from our earliest years and rarely change. Certain types of furniture, such as the three-legged table, are considered to be more stable on uneven ground, and thus some types possibly evolved from particular needs in domestic use. In the houses of ordinary people, furniture was most probably stored in a way that would not impede daily life, with smaller tables or stools stored under larger tables. Unusual or rare items are major ceremonial pieces of furniture, as for example the platforms supporting the royal throne on the reliefs at Persepolis and the *automata* in the palace of Constantinople (singing birds, roaring lions, and the imperial throne raised into the air together with the Emperor, details mentioned by Constantinus Porfirogenitus in the *De Ceremoniis*) (Brett 1954: 477–87).

When there was not enough furniture for a particular occasion, more was brought in from a different location, as for instance in a well-known Assyrian text from Nineveh, where tables and chairs are brought in from an adjacent store for a banquet. Similarly, furniture is borrowed from wealthier neighbors when needed, as in the case of the Thracian slave Getas who asks peevish Knemon (the bad-tempered man) to contribute cooking pots, seven tripods, twelve tables, a bronze wine krater, nine rugs, and a woven barbarian curtain a hundred feet long to his master's banquet (Menander, *Dyskolos* 920–45). In paintings and reliefs, furniture is transported by servants, as is the case in the palace of Sargon at Dur Sharrukin/Khorsabad and the red-figured *pelike* (jar) made by the so-called Pan Painter (*c.* 480 BCE) depicting a couch and table being carried on the back of a nude youth, during either the preparations for or the clean-up after a drinking party (*ARV*² 555, no. 87).

Furniture in early, strictly hierarchical societies may signify honor and status, as in the case of the Persian Empire, where King Darius is enthroned while the rest of his attendees are standing. In Egypt, by contrast, convivial banquet scenes depicted in tomb paintings show a party of revelers seated on chairs. In the Greek world, Zeus may be seated on a throne or a simpler seat next to Hera. On the Parthenon frieze, the Gods are depicted seated on simple stools, whereas a throne is mentioned among the *private* belongings of Alcibiades' confiscated property. Thrones were carved in Hellenistic and Roman Greek theaters for the seating of magistrates and other important people.

Throughout furniture history, luxurious furniture was a prerogative of the wealthy. Furniture made of expensive materials or imported is known throughout antiquity. A few very fine pieces of furniture found in two princely Praenestine tombs were imported from the same workshop that produced some of the Nimrud ivories in the possession of the Assyrian kings. Equally, some early Etruscan furniture seems to have been inspired by Near Eastern prototypes. Itinerant craftsmen, native to North Syria, or their apprentices may have been responsible for some of the carved ivories found in Etruria. Public royal processions that were deliberately performed and recorded for political reasons as an enactment of the ostentation of the king and the glory of his state, such as the one by Philadelphus in Alexandria, exhibited luxury through expensive materials and the amount of furniture displayed. Wealthy individuals, such as Cicero, paid half a million sesterces for a table of Mauretanian citrus wood and ivory (Pl., *HN* XIII.29.95), whereas imported furniture remained through the Late Roman and Byzantine times a main source of individual self-esteem and social recognition.

The desire for imported luxury items and the extent of the ancient furniture trade is further evidenced by shipwrecks of the late Hellenistic and Roman periods. The Mahdia shipwreck, for example, found five kilometers off the Tunisian coast, is an especially valuable source of information for a relatively early stage of Greek influence on elite Roman interior design and decoration: the cargo, wrecked in the early first century BCE, included high-quality architectural elements, works of art, and consumer goods, which the ship was carrying to Italy from Athens, where most of the items seem to have been made. Furniture fittings, beds, and candelabras were transported to decorate rich Italian villas and fine houses.

Ultimately, furniture assists our understanding of cross-cultural ties. Roman furniture, for example, seems to have taken formal and decorative elements from Greece and Etruria, but also from further afield, such as Egypt and to a lesser extent the Near East. Pieces of furniture traveled in peace and during war, furniture makers traveled to find appropriate orders, and thus furniture types influenced cultures and peoples far beyond their original places of manufacture.

Similarly, manufacturing techniques loom large in cross-cultural discussions: the forerunners of Roman cabinetmakers are Egyptians and Greeks. The Romans refined earlier techniques, combining them with the skills already at hand in the Apennine peninsula. Technical skill reached a high level in the Roman period and remained almost unchanged until the Industrial Revolution (Mols 1999: 273).

Since Richter's seminal study, excavations have brought to light various contexts in which furniture was used, symbolically or practically: tombs of various periods and areas, sanctuaries with furniture and dedications, and house complexes with traces of furniture or extant furniture pieces. Our knowledge regarding ancient furniture has significantly increased over the last decades through detailed excavation records and improved conservation techniques. This knowledge allows us to visualize certain Greek houses with a significant variety and quantity of furniture, which were perhaps not as bare as Richter once thought, and at the same time appreciate the use of furniture in diverse public or private contexts. Furniture used for the storage of manuscripts, for instance, in Roman and Byzantine libraries is now better understood through excavated finds and visual evidence.

In the following chapters, we present an overview of the scholarly discussions on ancient furniture design, form, and techniques, along with the evidence of excavated furniture from domestic, funerary, and sacred contexts covering a wide geographical area that stretches from Central Asia to Italy and from the Donau River to Egypt. Not everything can be covered in a volume of furniture dedicated to antiquity with predetermined specifications, but the most important material evidence is included and the most important questions to be asked are addressed. In certain cases, answers are hampered by our incomplete evidence or the still largely unknown symbolism that follows some of these pieces in funerary contexts and the afterlife. There is still great value in the literary and epigraphic sources from antiquity, which are presented here in a concise overview for the first time.

Finally, a general timeline has been composed with the most important events and historical periods, in an effort to provide the reader with a broad overview regarding the historical events that run parallel to the use and production of furniture from the Neolithic period to 500 CE. The timeline is followed by a brief glossary of the technical terms mentioned in this volume.

TIMELINE

The Neolithic period

c. 10000–4000 BCE	NEOLITHIC PERIOD (permanent human settlement, agriculture, livestock breeding)
7100–5900 BCE	Settlement at Çatalhöyük (East Mound) in Central Anatolia

Sixth–fifth millennium BCE	Lakeside settlement of Dispilio (northern Greece)
Late fifth millennium BCE	Furniture models of terracotta from the settlement of Ovcharovo (northeastern Bulgaria)
Late fourth millennium BCE	Stone-built fixed furniture at the settlement of Skara Brae (Orkney, Scotland)
3500–2500 BCE	Earliest surviving remains of furniture items (Egypt and western Asia)

Egypt

c. 5500–3100 BCE	PREDYNASTIC (NAQADA III) PERIOD
c. 3100–2686 BCE	EARLY DYNASTIC PERIOD
c. 3100–2890 BCE	First Dynasty
c. 2890–2686 BCE	Second Dynasty
c. 2686–2181 BCE	OLD KINGDOM OF EGYPT
c. 2667–2648 BCE	Reign of Djoser (Third Dynasty)
c. 2613–2494 BCE	Fourth Dynasty
c. 2589–2566 BCE	Reign of Khufu or Cheops
c. 2494–2345 BCE	Fifth Dynasty
c. 2345–2181 BCE	Sixth Dynasty
c. 2278–2184 BCE	Reign of Pepi II
c. 2055–1650 BCE	MIDDLE KINGDOM OF EGYPT
c. 2055–1985 BCE	Eleventh Dynasty
c. 1985–1795 BCE	Twelfth Dynasty
c. 1650–1550 BCE	SECOND INTERMEDIATE PERIOD (OR HYKSOS PERIOD)
c. 1550–1069 BCE	NEW KINGDOM OF EGYPT
c. 1550–1295 BCE	Eighteenth Dynasty
c. 1352–1336 BCE	Amarna period (later part of the reign of Akhenaten, formerly Amenhotep IV)
c. 1336–1327 BCE	Reign of Tutankhamun
c. 1295–1069 BCE	Ramesside period of the New Kingdom (Nineteenth–Twentieth Dynasties)
c. 1295–1186 BCE	Nineteenth Dynasty
c. 1279–1213 BCE	Rameses II
c. 1186–1069 BCE	Twentieth Dynasty
c. 1184–1153 BCE	Rameses III
c. 1000 BCE	"Tale of Wenamun" (Egyptian fictional story)

Western Asia

c. 6500–3800 BCE	Ubaid period
c. 3800–3100 BCE	Uruk period
c. 3100–2900 BCE	Jemdet Nasr period
c. 2900–2300 BCE	Early Dynastic period in Mesopotamia
Mid-third millennium BCE	Royal Cemetery of Ur
c. 2500–2300 BCE	Palace G at Ebla (present-day Tell Mardikh, Syria)
c. 2300–2154 BCE	Akkadian period
c. 2154–2112 BCE	Gutian period
c. 2112–2004 BCE	Ur III period
c. 2047–2030 BCE	Reign of Ur-Nammu, king of Ur
c. 2030–1982 BCE	Reign of Šulgi (son of Ur-Nammu), king of Ur
c. 2004–1596 BCE	Isin-Larsa period (Mesopotamia)
c. 1953–1925 BCE	Reign of Išbi-Irra, king of Isin (Mesopotamia)
c. 2000–1600/1850–1550 BCE	Old Babylonian period
c. 1728–1686 BCE	Reign of Hammurabi, king of Babylon
Nineteenth–eighteenth centuries BCE	Acemhöyük palace (Acemhöyük level III, central Anatolia)
Sixteenth–fifteenth centuries BCE	Pella palace (Jordan)
Seventeenth–sixteenth centuries BCE	Middle Bronze Age in Palestine (Jericho extramural cemetery)
c. 1700–1550 BCE	Miletos phase IVa (peak of Minoan cultural influence at the site)
c. 1775–1762 BCE	Reign of Zimri-Lim at Mari (present-day Syria)
c. 1762 BCE	Babylonian conquest of Mari by Hammurabi
c. 1600–1500 BCE	Hittite Old Kingdom (Anatolia)
c. 1550–1155 BCE	Kassite period in Mesopotamia
c. 1430–1180 BCE	Hittite New Kingdom (Anatolia)
c. 1400–930 BCE	Middle Assyrian period
c. 1400–1200 BCE	Floruit of Ugarit (modern Ras Shamra in present-day Syria)
c. 970–930 BCE	Reign of Solomon, king of Israel
1200–1100 BCE	Megiddo Level VIIA
c. 1180–700 BCE	Syro-Hittite or Neo-Hittite period (small principalities in Anatolia and Syria)
911–609 BCE	Neo-Assyrian period in Mesopotamia

Ninth–seventh centuries BCE	Floruit of the kingdom of Urartu (centered around Lake Van in Armenia)
Eighth century BCE	Monumental burial mounds at Gordion (capital of ancient Phrygia, Anatolia)
744–727 BCE	Reign of Tiglath-Pileser III, king of Assyria
722–705 BCE	Reign of Sargon II
c. 653 BCE	Assyrian conquest of Elam
c. 650–645 BCE	Construction of North Palace of Ashurbanipal at Nineveh
609–539 BCE	Neo-Babylonian period in Mesopotamia
587 BCE	Babylonian conquest of Jerusalem
Fourth–third centuries BCE	Pazyryk barrows (Siberia)
550–330 BCE	Achaemenid period

Etruscans

c. 1100–900 BCE	Proto-Villanovan period
c. 900–700 BCE	Villanovan period
c. 700–600 BCE	Orientalizing period
c. 600–479 BCE	Archaic period
479–323 BCE	Classical period
323–31 BCE	Hellenistic period

The Aegean and Cyprus

c. 3000–1100 BCE	AEGEAN BRONZE AGE
c. 2800–2300/2200 BCE	Early Cycladic marble figurine production
c. 2400–1900 BCE	Early Cypriot period
1650–1600 or 1550–1500 BCE	Theran eruption and abandonment of settlement at Akrotiri on Thera (Cyclades)
Late seventeenth–sixteenth centuries BCE	Grave Circles (Shaft Graves) of Mycenae in the Argolid
c. 1450 BCE	Collapse of Minoan centers; end of the Neopalatial period on Crete; probable takeover of Knossos and other Cretan sites by Greek-speakers
Late fifteenth–early fourteenth centuries BCE	Consolidation of Mycenaean power in the southern Aegean
c. 1400–1200 BCE	Heyday of Mycenaean palatial power; use of the Linear B script for the earliest known inscriptions in the Greek language

c. 1400–1250 BCE	Probable dates of the various groups of Knossos Linear B tablets (successive destructions of the palace complex)
c. 1250–1170 BCE	Destructions and eventual collapse of Mycenaean palaces
c. 1200–1170 BCE	Destruction of the Palace of Nestor; Linear B tablets accidentally fired and preserved
c. twelfth century BCE	Postpalatial Bronze Age
c. 1100–1050	Bronze Age collapse: beginning of the Greek "Dark Age" (Geometric) period
c. 1100–800 BCE	GEOMETRIC PERIOD IN GREECE; Cypro-Geometric period in Cyprus
760–700 BCE	Late Geometric period (pictorial pottery flourishes in Attica); bronzes deposited at the Idaean Cave on Crete
Late eighth century BCE	Royal burial at Salamis, Cyprus
c. 700–600 BCE	ORIENTALIZING PERIOD IN GREECE
657–627 BCE	Reign of Kypselos (b. *c.* 690–670 BCE), son of Periander and tyrant of Corinth
c. 600–480 BCE	ARCHAIC PERIOD IN GREECE; Cypro-Archaic period in Cyprus
480–323 BCE	CLASSICAL PERIOD IN GREECE
431–404 BCE	Peloponnesian War-Pericles
323–31 BCE	HELLENISTIC PERIOD IN GREECE (see Macedonia)

Macedonia

413–399 BCE	Reign of Archelaos
360–336 BCE	Reign of Philip II
336–323 BCE	Reign of Alexander the Great
318–297 BCE	Rule and Reign of Cassander
294–286 BCE	Reign of Demetrius I Poliorcetes
277–239 BCE	Reign of Antigonos II Gonatas
239–229 BCE	Reign of Demetrios II
229–221 BCE	Reign of Antigonos III Doson
221–179 BCE	Reign of Philip V
179–168 BCE	Reign of Perseus
167 BCE	Macedonia divided into four districts subject to Rome
148 BCE	Macedonia becomes a Roman province
146 BCE	Destruction of Corinth-Greece under Roman rule

Rome

88 BCE	First Mithridatic War
83 BCE	Second Mithridatic War
73 BCE	Third Mithridatic War
44 BCE	Assassination of Julius Caesar
31 BCE	Battle of Actium
27 BCE–14 CE	Reign of Emperor Augustus
2 CE	Augustus acclaimed *Pater Patriae* by Senate
27 BCE–68 CE	Julio-Claudian Dynasty
68–96 CE	Flavian Dynasty
96–192 CE	Nerva-Antonine Dynasty
193–235 CE	Severan Dynasty
235–285 CE	Crisis of the Third Century
284–364 CE	Tetrarchy and Constantinian Dynasty
324 CE	Constantine the Great transports the capital of the Roman Empire from Rome to Constantinople
364–392 CE	Valentinian Dynasty

Theodosius I was the last person to rule both halves of the Roman Empire, splitting it between his sons Arcadius and Honorius on his death.

395 CE	Roman Empire is divided into the Eastern and Western Section
Early Byzantine period	Fourth–sixth centuries CE
Middle Byzantine period	Seventh–twelfth centuries CE
Late Byzantine period	Thirteenth century–1453 CE

Greek and Latin authors

900–700 BCE	Most likely dates for the formation of Homeric epics
Seventh century BCE	Alcman (Greek lyric poet)
484–425 BCE	Herodotos (Greek historian)
c. 460–*c.* 400 BCE	Thucydides (Greek historian)
446–386 BCE	Aristophanes (Greek comic poet)
430–354 BCE	Xenophon (Greek historian and philosopher)
384–322 BCE	Demosthenes (Greek orator and statesman)
c. 371–287 BCE	Theophrastos (Greek philosopher)
Third century BCE	Theocritus (Greek poet)

106–43 BCE	Cicero (Roman politician and orator)
23–79 CE	Pliny the Elder (Roman naturalist and writer)
c. 110–180 CE	Pausanias (Greek traveler and geographer)
c. 46–120 CE	Plutarch (Greek biographer and essayist)
Late second–early third century CE	Athenaeus (Greek grammarian)
Third century CE	Porphyry (Greek Christian author)

GLOSSARY OF TECHNICAL TERMS

Butterfly cramp A type of interlocking scarf-joint.

Butt-joint A method of joining two pieces of wood by placing their flat finished faces together without any special shaping, relying exclusively upon mechanical (pins, dowels, thongs) or adhesive (glue) reinforcement means.

Cupping A distortion of the shape of a sawn wooden board caused by shrinkage of the timber while drying.

Gesso A binder of animal glue, white pigment, and chalk, often used as a primer substrate to receive applied paint.

Mortise-and-tenon joint This method of joining wooden members comprises two components: the mortise opening or hole and the tenon "tongue." Such joints are often employed between members joined at a right angle. The tenon is formed at the end of a member and is inserted into the mortise hole (often of rectangular or square shape) of the corresponding member. To be locked in place, the tenon should be cut to fit the mortise hole exactly; for the same securing purposes, it often has shoulders that seat when its full length enters the mortise hole. Further support may be provided by adhesive (glue) or mechanical means (wedges, pins).

Scarf-joint   A method of joining two members end to end through attached faces (interlocking or not) aided by adhesive or mechanical fastening.

"Through-and-through" cutting   A method of cutting timber where the cutting implement (usually a saw or axe) passes through the entire length of the log several times in order to produce several boards.

CHAPTER ONE

Design and Motifs

ELIZABETH SIMPSON AND GEOFFREY KILLEN

EGYPT

The topic of ancient furniture design covers several thousand years, with many types and styles produced over a wide region. Furniture types and their uses are discussed in Chapter 3 in this volume, where the reader may turn for a general history. Here, design and motifs are addressed specifically, with reference to works from Egypt, the Near East, and the Classical world. A large variety of well-preserved organic materials survives from Egypt, due to the dry climate, yielding unparalleled evidence for furniture design and construction beginning in its earliest stages. In ancient Egypt before the Early Dynastic Period (*c.* 3100–2686 BCE), the design of furniture focused on using tree branches to make bed frames that were lashed together with plant fibers. Other examples used the natural structure of the tree to create functional design forms; a unique three-legged stool preserved in the Petrie Museum of Egyptian Archaeology at University College London, for instance, is made from the roots and base of a tree trunk (Petrie 1913: 11; Killen 2017a: 65, plate 68).[1]

Low block stools were hewed from stone or timber using simple stone tools. Originating as a design form during the Predynastic Period (*c.* 5500–3100 BCE), stone stools continued to be manufactured throughout the Dynastic Period, albeit of better quality because of the introduction of copper and later bronze tools. Such stools were designed to stand on short legs or pairs of runners, their seats often shaped to provide a recess for a cushion.[2] A fine example of a four-legged stool in the Manchester University Museum is cut from a single rectangular block of timber and has four rounded legs[3] and a thin dished seat.

The entire surface of this stool has been worked to shape with an adze (Killen 2017a: 59, plates 45–6).

By the beginning of the Early Dynastic Period (c. 3100 BCE) copper woodworking tools allowed timber and ivory to be worked accurately into individual elements and rendered into sculptured forms. Egyptian carpenters began to employ a sophisticated measuring system when designing furniture. The standard unit of linear measurement used by carpenters was the "cubit," based on the length of a man's forearm from the elbow to the tip of the middle finger. This measurement was standardized by the Early Dynastic Period.[4] The "royal cubit" (524 millimeters) was subdivided into smaller units comprising seven palm widths, with each palm subdivided into four finger-sized digits. Carpenters placed great importance on measurement to ensure accuracy and uniformity of construction.[5]

Although the majority of Egyptian furniture was of plain utilitarian form, there was an expectation that furniture designed for the royal, noble, and middle classes should reflect and draw on Egypt's distinct cultural and religious identity. This is seen as early as the Early Dynastic Period, where bed frames and stools were supported on legs fashioned in bovine form. The use of zoomorphic features to enhance furniture designs entered the ancient Egyptian design canon at this time and was practiced throughout the remaining Dynastic Period. The complex relationship between animal forms and their use in furniture goes beyond the need to design furniture simply to evoke the qualities of a particular animal. This animal imagery gave ancient Egyptians a mechanism to promulgate their belief systems.

On a basic level, bovine legs on a piece of furniture elevated the owner to a position above those animals the Egyptians lived among; however, their use has a deeper symbolic meaning. There were many bull cults in practice during the Early Dynastic Period, and a bull's attributes—virility, power, and fighting spirit—were recognized and linked to the pharaoh through association. Indeed, the bull also became associated with protection for the deceased, and therefore it is unsurprising that bed frames and stools from Early Dynastic burials might be furnished with legs of bovine form.[6] Similarly, the lion became a symbol of kingship whose close connection with the pharaohs of the New Kingdom (c. 1550–1069 BCE) resulted in chair and stool legs of leonine form.

In one interesting example, a three-legged stool from the tomb of Tutankhamun has highly stylized curved legs with feline or canine feet (Eaton-Krauss 2008: plates LXI–LXIII). The legs are attached to the seat by means of cylindrical projections or "collars" carved from the underside (see below). The seat is carved in openwork, depicting a pair of lions lying head to tail and bound by their legs. Around the edge of the seat is a spiral motif suggesting Aegean influence, perhaps indicating the growing commercial, diplomatic, artistic, and political ties these two regions enjoyed during the late second millennium BCE.[7]

Some folding stools were also designed with lion legs.[8] However, the majority of extant examples have duck-head terminals carved at the bottom of the crossing legs, the bird's tongue forming the tenon that locates in a mortise in the floor rail, joining the two parts. Inlaid in the duck's head are imitation feathers and eyes made from ivory.[9] The decoration applied to the legs of some round-legged stools consists of bands of ivory petal shapes and droplets; the horizontal stretchers below the seat that brace the legs are often capped with papyrus-shaped ferrules made of ivory.[10]

To protect women during childbirth, images of the hippopotamus goddess Taweret and the dwarf god Bes were used to embellish bed frames, either painted or carved as an openwork panel incorporated into the bed's footboard. These deities were also carved from wood to form the supporting legs of the bed frame. Such bed legs are significantly different in both character and purpose than typical domestic-type bed legs. An ostracon (a limestone flake) preserved in the Medelhavsmuseet, Stockholm, illustrates a maternity scene, where a bed frame with Bes-shaped legs played a significant part in the act of labor and gave protection to both the mother and baby (Peterson 1973: 103, plate 69).

A pair of similar Bes-shaped bed legs is preserved in the Rijksmuseum van Oudheden, Leiden.[11] Their plumed headdresses form the legs' tenons, which would have located in mortises chopped in the underside of the bed frame's side rails. After birth, women returned to using normal domestic bed frames, and evidence shows that infants and often an older child shared the domestic bed. Preserved in the British Museum is the figure of a naked woman with a child sleeping together on a single bed.[12] The bed frame is shown to be made from timber rails, including a cross rail that supports the lumbar region of the woman's back; her feet rest against a vertical footboard.

The design of boxes, chests, and cabinets developed from simple rectangular coffin construction, where Egyptian carpenters already in the Early Dynastic Period were able to join flat boards with a wide range of ingenious edge- and corner-joints to manufacture a rigid wooden carcase or box.[13] Early box design follows this concept but on a smaller scale (Killen 2017b: 14–16, figs. 15–16, plates 5–8). Boxes illustrated in Old Kingdom tomb reliefs show a wide range of types with lids manufactured with pent (angled), barrel, and shrine-shaped profiles, the last having a rounded front connected to a sloping back board (11–22).

Two design features were employed to lock such boxes. The first was a molded rail under the back edge of the lid that fit into an adjacent groove in the top inner edge of the box's back board. The second was the actual means of securing the box, achieved by wrapping a cord around a pair of mushroom-shaped knobs on the lid and box and then sealing the cord with wax. Various permanent and temporary design solutions developed from these concepts to provide additional security features. One method employed to lock boxes was to place a pair of molded runners along the top long edges of the box. These would slightly overhang its interior, while on the underside of the lid a further pair of sliding rails was attached that allowed the lid to slide onto the box. Once the lid was in position, a latch would swing and drop from a rectangular hole set in the lid's front panel and lock the box (Killen 2017b: 49–51, fig. 53, plates 29–34).

A box has also been discovered with a rotary lock that operated by turning a mushroom-shaped knob on the box's lid. An *ankh* symbol (the ancient Egyptian symbol of life, resembling a cross but with a loop at the top) was engraved on the knob to indicate the point to which it should be turned to achieve a locking position (Aldred 1954: 695, fig. 496b). Deposited in the tomb of Tutankhamun were a number of boxes and cabinets that were fitted with pairs of gold hinges that provided another way of attaching the lid to the box (Killen 2017b: 78–9, fig. 68, plate 54).

As with constructional design, those motifs applied to embellish Egyptian furniture conveyed a dual purpose, being employed as a decorative convention and also a symbolic mechanism that projected the Egyptians' core cultural and religious beliefs. Utilitarian furniture manufactured by workmen for their own personal use was usually left undecorated. Some of the earliest furniture decoration consisted of ivory strips used as veneer to cover or edge a wooden carcase or frame. These veneer strips are found with incised diagonal, crossing, zigzag, nail-head, or concentric circle motifs, the incisions being stained black to highlight the design (Killen 2017b: 5–6, fig. 6).

An important furniture fragment comprising two joining pieces was discovered in the Early Dynastic cemetery at Abydos, deposited as funerary material in the tomb of King Semerkhet (*c.* 2900 BCE). The fragment is carved along its top edge and at one end with an imitation basketwork pattern that had been covered with fine linen as a base for gilding. Small pieces of gold can still be seen impressed into the basketwork pattern. Framed by the border on one side is a design formed by inlaid triangles of blue and green faience, together with pieces of dark-colored wood. The other side is carved with a royal *serekh*, a motif representing a gated palace façade surmounted by the falcon god Horus, enclosed within a *ka* sign (two upraised arms) and flanked by *was* scepters (a staff with an abstract canine head) and *tyet* signs (resembling an *ankh* but with downturned arms).[14]

The use of hieroglyphic signs such as these to decorate furniture was well established by the Third Dynasty (*c.* 2686–2613 BCE), the most commonly applied signs being the *tyet*, *djed*, *ankh*, *was*, and *neb* (basket). Two of these signs—the *tyet* (known also as the Isis knot and translated as "life" and "welfare") and the *djed* (a column imitating a bundle of stalks, bound together at the top and translated as "stable" and "enduring")—are found on four boxes shown in a painted wall scene in the tomb of Hesyra (*c.* 2686–2613 BCE) at Saqqara (Killen 2017b: 6–7, fig. 7).

Two boxes discovered in the tomb of Tutankhamun (*c.* 1336–1327 BCE) employ the motif of repeating signs placed between the bottom horizontal frame rails of the box and stretcher rails that brace the slender square legs. The frieze applied to one box comprises groups made up of a single *ankh* sign ("life") flanked by a pair of *was* signs ("dominion"), which stand on a row of repeating *neb* signs ("all"). Here the meaning can be read, "All life and dominion." The *ankh* signs are carved from African Blackwood (*Dalbergia melanoxylon*) and the *was* and *neb* signs are gilt wood.[15] The second box is similarly treated with groups comprising a single polished African Blackwood *tyet* sign, flanked by a pair of gilt *djed* signs that stand on a row of gilt *neb* signs (Figure 1.1). The meaning here reads, "All enduring life."[16]

FIGURE 1.1 Box with hieroglyphic sign decoration, Tomb of Tutankhamun (*c.* 1336–1327 BCE). Egyptian Museum, Cairo, JE 61447. Photograph courtesy of the Griffith Institute, University of Oxford.

Apart from the use of repeating hieroglyphic signs that convey a clear meaning as well as a simple visual motif, furniture was also used to provide the medium by which a reoccurring literary theme could be delivered. The Egyptian language created a complex narrative that provided the cultural, political, and religious cohesion the Egyptian state wished to propagate. This special blending of ideas is beautifully illustrated in the decoration applied to a cedar throne buried with the pharaoh Tutankhamun (Figure 1.2). In terms of design it is not unusual, with its lion legs standing on gilded ribbed drums and its double-cove seat. However, its embellishment exemplifies the power that language and symbolism can play in support of the ruling class's perspective of their nation's identity.[17]

FIGURE 1.2 Cedar throne, Tomb of Tutankhamun (c. 1336–1327 BCE). Egyptian Museum, Cairo, JE 62029. Photograph courtesy of the Griffith Institute, University of Oxford.

The central image of this cedar throne is the openwork back support, which displays the figure of the god *Heh* (the god of eternity), who kneels with one knee raised on a *nub* sign ("gold"); in each hand he holds a palm branch, and on his right arm hangs an *ankh* sign. This motif embraces the concept of Tutankhamun's endless reign. Above the god's head is a solar disk flanked by a pair of royal cobras (*uraei*). Emblazoned upon the top rail of the throne's backrest is a gilded winged solar disk and *uraei* with a pair of cartouches at each wing tip. The cartouche formed part of the royal titulary employed to legitimize a monarch's reign and, by the Middle Kingdom (*c.* 2055–1650 BCE), consisted of five names, all of which occur on this cedar throne. Two forms of Tutankhamun's name are found in these cartouches: the king's throne name (praenomen) "Nebkheperure" and his personal/birth name (nomen) "Tutankhamun." These names are again found on small panels together with the king's royal titles to each side of the god's head. He faces the king's praenomen; behind his head is the king's nomen.

Two falcons wearing the double crown of Upper and Lower Egypt are perched upon two large inscribed rectangular panels that bear the king's Horus name, "Mighty bull, perfect of birth." The carved scene is enclosed by the frame of the throne's backrest, which displays a band of hieroglyphic inscriptions that promulgate the king's legitimate right to rule, in his relationship to the gods Amun, Atum, Re, and Horakhty and his role as protector of the sacred center of Heliopolis. At the rear of the backrest are similar bands of hieroglyphic inscriptions that declare again the king's Horus name together with his Nebty (two ladies) name, "Whose perfect laws pacify the two lands," and his Horus of Gold name, "He who wears the crowns, who satisfies the gods." Below the throne's seat was placed a motif, now largely missing, that is commonly found on royal furniture: a *sema* sign (only this remains), once bound by the heraldic plants of Upper and Lower Egypt. Belonging to this chair is a footstool made of cedar boards that have been edge-jointed together. Its top surface, on which the king would have placed his feet, is carved with an impressive scene showing four prostrate Asiatic and four Nubian captives, the traditional enemies of Egypt, with their arms tied behind their backs; between each pair is an archer's bow, a common motif found in Egyptian art.[18]

Much surviving Egyptian furniture derives from a funerary context. On the death of the owner some furniture that had been in daily use was customized and placed in the tomb; other pieces were designed exclusively for the tomb, depicting scenes that illustrate images of the afterlife. Some of the furniture manufactured for the tomb was of poorer constructional quality, as its painted decoration was judged to be of greater significance. Much of this decoration was personalized, evoking the individual's life and lacking the symbolism seen on royal furniture. Some of the best examples of painted funerary furniture are boxes that relate stylistically to those from the tomb of Tutankhamun. These royal boxes were elaborately decorated, with their panels edged with strips of ivory and African Blackwood set into the timber carcase, forming bands of stringing often accompanied by rows of squares of faience and carnelian (a semiprecious stone). The legs of some royal boxes were inlaid with small pieces of ivory and African Blackwood, alternating to produce a decorative comb pattern; these techniques were replicated in paint on boxes of lesser quality. Common motifs applied to the central panels of these painted boxes include scenes of the deceased sitting before an offering table, heaped with food, being mourned by the family. The end panels of such boxes could be painted with a motif showing a pair of antelopes, standing on their hind legs, eating foliage from an exotic tree.[19]

The design of furniture in ancient Egypt developed from very primitive forms to examples that were sophisticated in both a technological and creative way. Although most furniture was utilitarian in character and devoid of decoration, high-status furniture and that destined for the tomb was replete with symbolic imagery that transmitted to people within and without Egypt's borders the cultural, religious, political, and social values of that civilization.

THE ANCIENT NEAR EAST

Early furniture in the Near East was simple in form and design, like that of Predynastic Egypt. Evidence from the Neolithic East Mound of Çatalhöyük in modern-day Turkey suggests that people used built-in furniture in the eighth and seventh millennia BCE, along with small stools that were surely portable. There are signs, however, that furniture could be more elaborate. A clay statuette from Çatalhöyük shows a voluptuous female figure seated on a stool flanked by felines (Simpson 1995: fig. 1). Whether part of the stool or attributes of the figure, the felines add to the grandeur of the composition and serve to identify this woman as important—and very probably a goddess with animals among her domain (see Figure 5.1). Her stool, or throne, is the first in a long series of furniture forms incorporating animal elements, which served to convey power and status through association.

By the mid-third millennium BCE, seats with bull's legs appear prominently in the Near East, depicted on Sumerian objects from the Royal Cemetery at Ur in southern Mesopotamia and elsewhere. The banqueters on the Standard of Ur (c. 2600 BCE) sit on square backless stools, with the seat supported by vertical legs and struts, including a bull's leg near the front (Baker 1966: plate XII; Simpson 1995: fig. 5). The banqueters are serenaded by a musician playing a lyre with a bull's head projecting at the front. Actual lyres were found in the Royal Cemetery, with bull's head attachments of gold, silver, or copper (Baker 1966: figs. 247–8). A chair with a low back and a bull's leg at the rear is shown on a neo-Sumerian seal (c. 2100 BCE) in the British Museum

(Simpson 1995: fig. 6). The bull was associated with deities in Mesopotamia (the storm god Adad or the moon god Nanna-Suen), making bull's legs and other attachments appropriate for royal and religious furniture.

Lions also appear on Near Eastern furniture in the third millennium BCE, decorating the side panels of stools and shown on a footstool flanking a rosette (Baker 1966: figs. 259, 265; Simpson 2010: plate 116b). Lion heads adorned a wooden sledge (or chariot) found in the tomb of Queen Puabi in the Royal Cemetery of Ur (PG 800), and the rosette occurs throughout the finds from the Ur tombs. The lion and rosette were associated with the goddess Inanna/Ishtar (and her counterparts) in early Mesopotamia and Iran, and these motifs would persist on Near Eastern furniture through the next two millennia.

A fine chair or throne from Acemhöyük in Turkey, which can be reconstructed in drawings, shows an imaginative use of ivory lion legs in the nineteenth–eighteenth century BCE (Simpson 2013). Four sphinxes stood on the ground, with four lion legs on top of the sphinxes; these composite legs supported the corners of the seat (Figure 3.1). Both motifs (sphinx and lion leg) can be called "Egyptianizing"—deriving ultimately from Egypt but not replicating Egyptian styles or types; the composite legs are not Egyptian but Anatolian. Numerous Egyptianizing ivory plaques are associated with this chair and must have decorated the backrest and other areas. This kind of reference to Egypt—direct but not exact—is found in Near Eastern furniture design and decoration throughout the second millennium and into the first millennium BCE.

Extensive remains of wooden furniture from the Middle Bronze Age tombs at Jericho (Palestine) and Baghouz (Syria) provide evidence for a variety of types—tables, beds, stools, and boxes—as well as interesting design features (Parr 1996). The tools used to make these pieces were like those in the Egyptian repertoire (Ricketts 1960: fig. 227). Simple four-legged stools had round legs joined at their tops by seat rails, which were strung with webbing for the seat; four stretchers connected the legs lower down. Mortise-and-tenon joinery was used, with through tenons at the ends of the seat rails, and sometimes half-lap joints (Ricketts 1960: fig. 229:4; Simpson 1995: fig. 9:4).[20] Stools of this design were found at both sites and were surely used throughout the Near East. A second type of stool (or bench) found at Jericho had square legs with scroll feet raised on flaring bases—highly simplified versions of Egyptian lion-paw feet (Ricketts 1960: fig. 229:3). Bed frames were rectangular (with cross stretchers for added strength at Jericho) supported by four simple legs (at Baghouz).

Tables from Baghouz had round tops with upturned rims and three removable legs. The legs were wooden rods that were gathered at the center in a ring, splaying out to fit into slots cut in the underside of the tabletop. This produced three feet below the ring that rested on the ground. The top formed a tray, which could be used to transport food and might be set up, with its legs, where convenient. The three legs assured the table's stability on any type of surface. Tray tables were also found at Jericho, although their design was somewhat different. The Jericho tables were generally low, with rectangular tops with upturned rims (or added borders). The tables typically had three legs, attached to the table tops with mortise-and-tenon joinery. Tenons were carved at the tops of the legs, which passed up through cylindrical "collars" that extended down from the underside of the table tops (Ricketts 1960: fig. 229:2; Simpson 1995: fig. 9:2).[21] At Jericho, the tenons were secured in the collars with wood pins. The legs might curve out, ending in feet resembling boots, ram's heads, or duck's feet. The Near Eastern three-legged tray table had a long history and wide geographical range in antiquity, in use from Etruria to Siberia by the first millennium BCE.

Hundreds of ivory fittings from Near Eastern sites show that carved struts or supports of various styles and types adorned luxury furniture in the Late Bronze Age, much in the manner of the hieroglyphic motifs on the box of Tutankhamun (Figure 1.1). Ivories from Megiddo (Israel, fourteenth–twelfth century BCE) include plaques in the form of trees and floral motifs, as well as sphinxes, griffins, and hieroglyphic signs (Loud 1939). Many of these have tenons at the top and bottom, suggesting that they were elements of openwork friezes on furniture. The earliest instance of such decoration comes from Palace G at the site of Ebla (Tell Mardikh) in Syria, destroyed by fire in the third millennium BCE. Carbonized remains include fragments of a wooden table with a rectangular top with a raised rim, supported from below by openwork scenes of animals in combat, heroes dominating animals, and warriors in battle (Simpson 1995: 1652). This indicates that not only ivory but also wooden strutwork was used as furniture decoration—although wood rarely survives in archaeological contexts from the Near East. One of the Megiddo ivories depicts a king seated on a throne with a high back and a large sphinx at the side, with wings outstretched to cover the area below the armrest.[22] This Late Bronze Age throne design recalls the seat on top of the Ark of the Covenant, flanked by sphinxes (cherubim), on which the Lord was said to have been invisibly enthroned (Simpson 1995: 1656, 1659; see Chapters 3 and 9).

Carved struts and plaques continued in use on sumptuous furniture into the first millennium BCE, appearing on tables and thrones shown in Assyrian palace reliefs (Curtis 1996: plates 45a–c, 50c, 51a,c). Small standing male figures support the seats and armrests of thrones and decorate the backrests, and rows of floral struts support the tops of tables. Lion-paw feet occur on what are apparently three-legged tables, and also on four-legged tables (and footstools), where the paws point in opposite directions (to the front and back). These feet rest on bases of tapering cones, which are often found on Assyrian royal furniture (see Chapter 3). Syrian- or Phoenician-style plaques and a carved stretcher are shown on the couch of Ashurbanipal (r. 668–627 BCE) on a relief from Nineveh—famous for its depiction of the reclining banquet, long considered the first evidence for this custom from the Near East.[23] The bed has a high curving headboard, against which the king leans while drinking from a bowl (Plate 14; Curtis 1996: plate 46b).

Syrian and Phoenician ivory attachments were found in large numbers at Assyrian sites, notably the site of Nimrud (Kalhu) (Simpson 1995: 1658–60). The "Layard series" of ivories from Nimrud includes Egyptianizing ivory furniture fittings carved in styles that have been attributed to Phoenician workshops. The "Loftus group" includes fittings carved in Syrian style. Additional ivories were excavated in Fort Shalmaneser, the arsenal of Nimrud, with Room SW7 yielding the remains of nineteen ivory chair backs in situ. These chairs can be divided into five types, associated with furniture in "regional styles" depicted on north Syrian stone reliefs (Herrmann 1996a). Motifs on the Nimrud ivories include a variety of culturally significant images: animals, sphinxes, griffins, winged disks and scarabs, Egyptianizing cartouches and deities, floral tendrils and friezes, fanciful trees, seated or standing figures, and also the furniture on which the figures sit. Structural elements of ivory include stretchers, feet with floral decoration, and lion legs and paw feet.

Elaborately carved and decorated wooden furniture was found in three Phrygian royal tumulus burials at Gordion, Turkey, dating to the eighth century BCE (Simpson 1996).[24] The burial chambers were covered with huge mounds of earth, keeping the humidity constant inside the chambers and preserving the wooden objects in good condition. The largest, Tumulus MM, is thought to be the tomb of the Phrygian king Midas or his father. The king was found lying on the remains of his log coffin, along with fourteen pieces of fine furniture: nine three-legged tables, two serving stands, two stools, and a chair (Simpson 2010). The contents of the burial were the remains of a funeral and feast, placed in the tomb after the ceremony (Plate 6, and see Chapter 3).

Eight of the tables were plain but beautifully carved, with boxwood (*Buxus*) legs and walnut (*Juglans*) tops (Figure 1.3).[25] The legs were curved (carved from curved branches), with simple pad feet. The table tops were tray shaped with upturned rims, attached to the legs with collar-and-tenon joinery as at Jericho, approximately nine hundred years earlier. The collar-tenon construction—as well as the three legs—contributed strength and stability, essential for tables that were used to transport food (Simpson 2010: 57–64).

The ninth table was extremely ornate, carved and inlaid with geometric patterns (Plate 6, foreground). The tabletop was walnut, and the legs and frame were boxwood, inlaid with juniper (*Juniperus*). The square tabletop was tray shaped with a raised rim; the curved legs were attached to the top with collar-and-tenon joinery. The top was supported by eighteen carved struts in the form of stylized trees, set into inlaid panels of the square frame. At the corners, the struts took the shape of handles for carrying. From the three legs rose fanciful

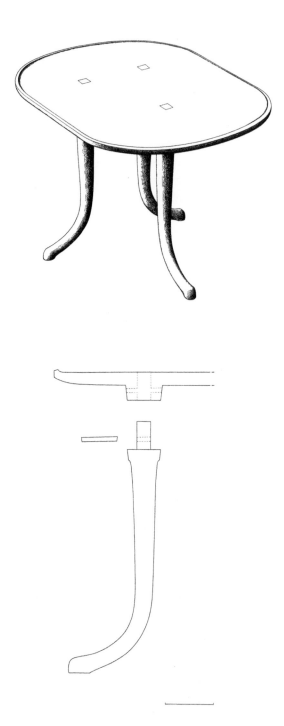

FIGURE 1.3 Table 5, Tumulus MM (5202 W 78), Gordion, eighth century BCE. Reconstruction and leg-top assembly. Drawings © Elizabeth Simpson, 2010.

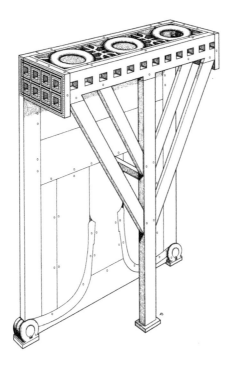

FIGURE 1.4 Serving stand A, Tumulus MM (5229 W 81), Gordion, eighth century BCE. Front face and back construction. Drawings © Elizabeth Simpson, 2010.

struts, designed to support the four corners of the frame. The feet of the table were stylized lion paws, rendered in an abstract version characteristic of Phrygian furniture. The inlaid motifs were much more than geometric patterns: these included swastikas, mazes, and "genealogical patterns"—magical signs associated with fertility, abundance, and protection, relating to the Phrygian mother goddess Matar (Simpson 2010: 31–56).

The two serving stands were made of boxwood with juniper inlay and walnut top pieces; the top pieces were carved with open rings to support round-bottomed bronze cauldrons, ten of which were found in the tomb (Figure 1.4 and Plate 6, background). The front faces were inlaid with geometric designs relating to the Phrygian goddess, as with the inlaid table. Set into each face was a large inlaid rosette with a raised, beveled border, supported from below by two curved legs with abstract lion-paw feet. The rosette complex was embedded in a grid of inlaid square designs surrounded by thousands of inlaid diamonds and triangles. The rosette was a symbol of the goddess Matar, as with Inanna/Ishtar in Mesopotamia. Like those goddesses, Matar was associated with lions, symbolized on the stands by the curved lion legs supporting the rosette. This interpretation is affirmed by Phrygian rock monuments, which show Matar, flanked by lions, at the door of her shrine (Simpson 2010: plates 120–1a). The Tumulus MM serving stands, with their rosettes and lion legs, were surely portable shrines of the Phrygian goddess. The square designs on the stands' faces have a special type of symmetry, such that a small number of patterns could be rotated and flipped to create great variety. Taken together, the total number of square designs in the main fields of both stands (364 or 365) suggests the number of days in a year—giving rise to the theory that the two stands comprised a kind of cosmic metaphor relating to the realm of the goddess (Simpson 2010: 65–110). As in Egypt, furniture with magical and religious imagery was used by the kings of Phrygia to enhance their power and prestige.

Tumulus P at Gordion, the tomb of a young prince, had also contained spectacular furniture, although in fragmentary condition. The burial goods included approximately fifty small wooden artifacts and twenty-one pieces of fine furniture: an inlaid serving stand (with a rosette supported by lion legs on the front face), an inlaid table ("Mosaic Table"), a large carved table with exceptional glued joinery ("Tripod Tray Table"), two plain tray tables, ten stools, two footstools, and an inlaid bed. Tumulus W had contained a serving stand, carved in openwork and studded with bronze tacks. Such extraordinary furniture, in terms of design and decoration, indicates the magnitude of our loss of organic remains—and wooden furniture in particular—from the archaeological record.

Assyrian furniture design was emulated by the Urartians (of the kingdom of Urartu in eastern Anatolia), Babylonians, and Persians to evoke the wealth, power, and taste of the great Assyrian kings (Simpson 1995: 1666–8). Particularly noteworthy is the Persian royal furniture shown on the reliefs of Persepolis, which includes thrones and monumental stools with lion-paw feet, pointing to the front and rear in Assyrian fashion. Amazingly well-preserved wooden furniture and other wooden objects were excavated from the frozen tombs of Pazyryk and Ukok in Siberia (fourth–third century BCE). Wooden stools (or pillows) of simple block type were found along with wooden tray tables or their legs. The Pazyryk tables had dished tops and four legs, attached with the collar-and-tenon method as at Gordion and Jericho. On two of these tables (Barrow 2), instead of lion legs or curved legs with lion-paw feet, the felines themselves occur, standing on their hind legs to support the collars (Rudenko 1970: 65–8, plates 50–1). The tenons were not pinned in the collars, allowing the legs to be removed, so the tables could be broken down and transported.

This long-lasting table design—beginning in the Middle Bronze Age (*c.* 2000–1550 BCE) or earlier and lasting through the third century BCE—surely owes its longevity to its efficiency and suitability for its purpose: the conveyance and service of food. This overrode the cost of materials and labor, which must have been significant, since the tabletop was made from a thick slab of wood, carved away extensively on the underside, leaving only the collars (Ricketts 1960: fig. 228). Such tables, along with other kinds of Near Eastern furniture, were used in daily life and also buried with their owners—deposited as grave goods for use in the hereafter, as gifts for deities, and as remnants of the funeral and feast.

THE AEGEAN BRONZE AGE AND THE CLASSICAL WORLD

Evidence for simple furniture exists in the Greek Neolithic period (*c.* 6500–3300 BCE), of the sort found in early Egypt and the Near East. By the third millennium BCE, complex designs were in use in the Aegean, if one can judge from the furniture depicted in Cycladic sculpture. Seats for harpists can be simple four-legged stools or more elaborate chairs (Baker 1966: figs. 377–83). The chair of the famous harpist from Keros in the Athens National Museum has curved legs with struts rising from the feet to support the seat; at the back the struts extend up to become the chair back, which ends at the top in a gentle arc (Richter 1966: plate 34). This Cycladic chair design is unlike those of Egypt or western Asia in the third millennium BCE.

The unusual character of Aegean furniture is further indicated by the gypsum throne from the Palace of Knossos (fourteenth century BCE) and the casts of wooden furniture made at the site of Akrotiri on Thera, which was buried in a volcanic eruption (*c.* 1550–1500 BCE or earlier). The Knossos throne has a tall back with undulating profile, and a dished seat supported on a block-like base (Baker 1966: fig. 385; Richter 1966: plate 1). Carved in relief on the block are four legs, along with stretchers at the sides connecting the front and back legs. In front view, the legs form an arch, carved with striations and tapering toward the bottom; below the arch is a pendant swag carved on the block in relief. Adventurous design of this sort is also seen in the casts of two tables from Thera, Building Complex Delta, which were made by pouring plaster into the void left in the volcanic ash by the disintegrated wooden originals (see Chapter 4). A three-legged table from Room Delta 1 has tapering legs, carved on the front face with three tiers of swag-like decoration (Muhly 1996: fig. 7). A second table (Room Delta 18) has even fancier legs, with streamers at the top, a wavy molding further down, and feet in the form of three-tiered pendant blossoms (Figure 4.2 a-b).

A Mycenaean ivory furniture leg from Thebes in Boeotia is likewise unusual by Egyptian and Near Eastern standards (Richter 1966: plates 4–5). The upper section is carved as four adjoining cylinders with two through mortises and a boss on top; the four-cylinder motif continues below, decorated with a wavy pattern at the middle, and ending in four tiers of petals at the bottom. Mycenaean footstools were fitted with ivory plaques carved with Aegean motifs, including miniature shields, helmeted heads of warriors, running spirals, and volutes (spiral scrolls) at the ends (Sakellarakis 1996). Highly ornate furniture—including footstools associated with thrones—is described in the Linear B texts, although the technical vocabulary has presented problems for translation (see Chapter 9).

Simpler furniture was also in use, as shown by the remains of two small wooden tray tables from Shaft Grave V at Mycenae (*c.* sixteenth century BCE). One of these was sufficiently preserved for its form to be reconstructed (Muhly 1996: figs. 2–3). This table (NM 890) had three legs and a dished top with upturned rim, as with its Near Eastern counterparts (see Figure 6.1). The legs were flat and wide, tapering toward the edges. Tenons extended up from the tops of the legs, inserted into mortises cut directly into the tabletop and secured with wood pins. Plain wooden furniture of this sort must have continued in use after the fall of the Mycenaean palaces at the end of the Bronze Age (*c.* 1200 BCE), when there was no longer a demand for elaborate royal furnishings.

Greek furniture

Examples are lacking following the collapse of the Mycenaean centers, and furniture reappears only later in the form of depictions on Greek Geometric vases (eighth century BCE). These are schematic representations of funerary scenes (*prothesis* and *ekphora*), showing the deceased lying on a couch or bed (*kline*); mourners may be seated on stools or, on a vase in New York, a chair with footstool.[26] Furniture legs are rendered in silhouette, giving the appearance of turned legs with a clearly defined top section, although they may have been carved instead (see Chapter 8). Greek Geometric furniture appears as rudimentary in these depictions, although this may not have been the case. Contemporary wooden furniture fragments from the Sanctuary of Hera, Samos, are decorated with incised patterns such as those on Geometric vases (Richter 1966: plate 280). Passages in the *Odyssey* describe luxury furniture such as the bed of Odysseus (23.190–201) and the chairs and tables of Circe and Penelope (10.314–15; 10.352–70; 19.53–8), which perhaps reflect aspects of fine furniture of the period. Certainly, royal Phrygian furniture, with its sophisticated design and ornamentation, was known to the Greeks in the eighth century BCE.[27]

Little actual furniture survives from ancient Greece, in comparison with the great collections of Egypt and the Near East—no doubt because most of it was made of wood. Nonetheless, depictions in art are plentiful beginning in the seventh century BCE, providing a basic understanding of Greek furniture design and decoration—although not always of materials and construction. Gisela Richter's masterly treatise, *The Furniture of the Greeks, Etruscans, and Romans* (1966), organized by types and styles, has provided the basis for study, augmented and updated by other scholars (e.g., Andrianou 2009; Baughan 2013). By the sixth century BCE, to judge from illustrations on vases and in sculpture, furniture was widely available in a variety of designs (see Chapter 8). In the twentieth century, T.H. Robsjohn-Gibbings gave form to these depictions, reproducing all types of ancient Greek furniture in wood, inspired by Greek vases and sculpture. These fine reproductions were made for sale and display, and published in photographs (Robsjohn-Gibbings and Pullin 1963), providing access to Greek furniture design in three dimensions.

Forms and motifs were adopted from elsewhere, modified to become typically Greek. Lion legs were utilized for chairs and thrones (*thronoi*), sometimes using entire legs of the animal in the Egyptian manner, but ordinarily with the front and back feet pointing outward in opposite directions, as found on Assyrian and Persian furniture (see, e.g., Richter 1966: plates 40, 42, 46). Exceptions were chairs from the Greek region of Laconia with both legs facing the front (Richter 1966: plate 52). Chests could have lion-paw feet, as could three-legged tables; folding stools featured stylized legs of lions or bulls, pointing either outward or inward (Richter 1966: plates 237–49). Standing figures and rampant animals decorated thrones, supporting the seat or armrests. Chairs and stools (*diphroi*) could also have "turned" legs, a term used by Richter to denote legs that look as though they were turned on a lathe. Perhaps the most famous seats with "turned" legs are those of deities on the Parthenon frieze (Richter 1966: plates 70, 204). Block stools and thrones with solid sides occur as well.

A highly individual type of carved leg occurs as early as the sixth century BCE and is found on thrones, couches, and stools—called "rectangular" by Richter, although this term is not particularly apt. These legs were tall and flat, as though made from "rectangular" boards, with "carved-out incisions" in Richter's terminology, or cut-out sections at the sides near the bottom. A couch with such legs is well illustrated on the red-figure side of a fine bilingual vase in Munich showing Herakles reclining at a banquet on Mount Olympus (Figure 1.5). This scene was painted by the Andokides Painter around 520 BCE (Simpson 2002).[28] The features of the couch are meticulously detailed, including the tall bases of the legs, the cut-out sections and bosses with palmettes above and below, the stars near the top of the legs, the Aeolic capital on the leg at the head of the couch, and the swastikas and stars on the long side rail. Near the top of both legs is a flat short strip, painted with interior hatching, a telling detail regarding the painter's expertise. This represents the ends of through tenons extending out from the cross rails at the head and foot, located in mortises cut in the legs—the hatching indicates the end grain on these tenons, as it would have actually appeared.

A table stands in front of the couch, laden with food and drink. This is a three-legged Greek banquet table (*trapeza*) with lion-paw feet. The leg seen at the left faces outward and is shown in side view; the bracket behind the leg top served to increase the bearing surface of the leg. The leg at the right faces front, one of two legs at this end of the table. A few such legs have survived in metal and stone, showing that the painter was correct in his depiction of this table, as he was with the couch (Simpson 2002: plate 81a–b). Elements of a *kline* with "rectangular"

FIGURE 1.5 Attic bilingual amphora (Munich 2301), red-figure side by the Andokides Painter, *c.* 520 BCE. Photograph by Renate Kühling. Courtesy of Staatliche Antikensammlungen und Glyptothek, München.

legs have survived from a grave in the Kerameikos cemetery, Athens (Simpson 2002: figs. 1–2).[29] The wood of the couch had disintegrated, but its ivory, bone, and amber fittings were preserved, in the form of volutes, palmettes, stars, and rosettes (see Figure 6.2). Such legs were a tour de force of Greek woodworking— meant to look vulnerable although they were stable and strong[30]—indicating that Greek furniture was no less accomplished than its predecessors.

Perhaps the most characteristically Greek piece of furniture was the *klismos* (Figure 1.6). This was a lightweight wooden chair with a high back and wide top rail that curved to accommodate the sitter's back; the rail was supported on incurving stiles that extended up from the back legs at the level of the seat. Below the seat, the back legs curved out toward the rear of the chair, producing a graceful reverse curve from bottom to top. The front legs curved out toward

FIGURE 1.6 Tombstone of the shoemaker Xanthippos, *ca.* 430–420 BCE. From Athens. British Museum, Townley Collection GR 1805,0703.183. Photograph courtesy of Wikimedia Commons. Photographer Marie-Lan Nguyen (2007).

the front, creating a stable base for the delicate chair (Richter 1966: plates 169–97). Since *klismos* chairs are known only from depictions, it is not clear just how the wooden legs were made. They were likely cut from curved branches, with the grain following the curve of the legs, providing the requisite strength.[31] The *klismos* is shown on black-figure vases (sixth century BCE) and remained popular for hundreds of years, still used by the Romans (Richter 1966: plate 513). It was these Roman versions, depicted in sculpture, that were seen by Grand Tourists in the eighteenth century, leading to a neoclassical revival of the form.

Etruscan furniture

The *klismos* and other Greek furniture designs were adopted and adapted by the peoples of Italy, culminating in the fine furniture of the Romans, depicted in paintings and in sculpture, and represented by extant examples of furniture and fittings in stone, metal, and wood. However, the earliest furniture from Italy is not Greek in style, but Etruscan or Villanovan, combining aspects of Near Eastern design and construction with forms native to the region. Several rich Orientalizing tombs of the seventh century BCE—the Regolini-Galassi, Barberini, and Bernardini tombs—contained Etruscan, Greek, and Near Eastern objects along with furniture and fittings. Most famous is the "Barberini throne," a wooden throne with a cylindrical base and curved back, covered with bronze plates worked in repoussé (relief hammered from the reverse side) with rosettes, guilloches (resembling braided ribbons), dotted circles, birds, human figures, and quadrupeds (Richter 1966: plate 427). The Regolini-Galassi tomb contained a bronze bed with webbing of bronze strips, as well as bronze attachments for a chair or throne (Richter 1966: plate 432; Haynes 2000: fig. 59).

Extensive remains of wooden furniture and other objects have been excavated from tombs at the site of Verucchio, near Rimini, dating to the eighth–seventh centuries BCE. Eleven tombs yielded evidence for thrones similar in style to the Barberini example, the most elaborate being a wooden throne from Tomb 89, Lippi necropolis (Von Eles 2002). The backrest of the throne is carved with schematic depictions of buildings; men riding in horse-drawn carts, shearing goats, and engaged in woodworking tasks; and women spinning and working at upright looms (Haynes 2000: fig. 29a–b). The women are seated on chairs placed on stands or tables, with footstools of the type found in the tomb. The footstools terminate at the ends in volutes, which serve as the feet—much like the design of Mycenaean footstools. A simpler wooden throne of the same form was found in Tomb 85, along with a footstool and three wooden tables. The tables had round tops and curved legs ending in carved, lyre-shaped feet; the legs were attached to the table tops with a version of collar-and-tenon joinery.

By the sixth century BCE the reclining banquet had reached Etruria, and diners are shown on couches of increasingly Greek form. Terracotta plaques from Murlo (in the province of Siena) dating to the early sixth century BCE show couches with what may be "rectangular" legs with cut-out sides, along with tables laden with food. Two magnificent terracotta sarcophagi from Cerveteri show this type of couch in three dimensions (Haynes 2000: figs. 105, 176a). Couches with "turned" legs and Greek-style tables are rendered in detail in the fifth-century Tomb of the Triclinium (Tarquinia) and Tomb of the Diver (Paestum). The Murlo plaques also show an Etruscan throne with cylindrical base, footstools, and folding stools that appear to have hoof feet (Haynes 2000: fig. 106). Etruscan folding stools are like their Greek counterparts but with special significance, as the Romans believed that the *sella curulis* had its origins in the Etruscan form (see Chapter 8).

Roman furniture

The *sella eburnea* (ivory stool), a term that came to denote the Roman *sella curulis* (curule stool), was said to have been adopted from the Etruscans along with other royal insignia. This special folding stool was used from early times as the seat of office for Roman kings, retained during the Republic for the most important magistrates, and later used as a seat of honor by Roman emperors (Wanscher 1980: 121). Roman folding stools were also used in domestic contexts, and legs of such stools have been preserved in bronze and ivory (Richter 1966: plate 527). Also adopted from the Etruscans was the throne with cylindrical base, resulting in refined Roman versions such as the marble Corsini Chair, dated to the first century BCE. These types notwithstanding, it was Greek furniture that formed the basis for much Roman furniture design. Greek-style thrones, chairs, stools, footstools, tables, chests, couches, and beds all found their way into the Roman repertoire, either via Etruscan versions or directly inspired by Greek examples. Roman furniture was not copied from the Greek, however, but was modified to suit Roman needs and tastes, and new types and styles were developed.

Extensive evidence for Roman furniture exists in ancient texts as well as painting and sculpture (see Chapters 8 and 9), and actual furniture has survived, in whole or in part. Roman marble thrones of several types have been found in Greece, in theaters and other contexts, with lion legs or winged sphinxes supporting the seats. Thrones (*solia*) with "rectangular" legs and cut-outs at the sides are found in marble, and marble legs in this style survive from couches (Richter 1966: plates 482–3, 562). Roman beds and couches (*lecti*) have been reconstructed from their metal (and ivory) fittings, including legs, rails, corner pieces, and *fulcrum* ornaments—curved plaques that attached to the sides of the armrests (*fulcra*) at the ends of the platform.[32] A fine example is the couch from Amiternum in the Capitoline Museum, dating to the first century BCE or first century CE (Plate 1). The couch had legs and attachments of bronze inlaid in silver and copper with floral motifs and figural scenes; the fulcrum plaques end at the top in horses' heads, with small busts in roundels below. This couch was restored wrongly as a bench (*bisellium*) in the nineteenth century by Augusto Castellani, and has since been reconstructed correctly. Roman couches of this type derive from Greek prototypes with "turned" legs, in their later Hellenistic versions.

Three-legged Roman tables (*mensae*) were used as banquet tables, for indoor or outdoor dining; these also derive from Hellenistic prototypes and, ultimately, from their Near Eastern predecessors (Richter 1966: plates 374–7, 570–2, and others). Fancy versions had legs with lion-paw feet and protomes (busts) of lions or other figures at the top. Bronze tripod braziers might have very ornate legs based on this form, such as examples from the House of Julia Felix (Pompeii) with satyrs at the top of the legs, and from the Temple of Isis (Pompeii) with seated sphinxes (Richter 1966: plate 567).[33] This leg type was also used for folding tables with four legs, such as a table from Pompeii with bronze lion legs featuring babies holding rabbits issuing from acanthus leaves (Richter 1966: plate 563). This inventive use of the lion leg was a Roman stylistic development. Additional Roman designs include marble pier tables with wide carved supports on the short sides, and tables with a single central leg supporting the tabletop (Livy's *monopodium*).

Perhaps the most remarkable collection of Roman furniture is the wooden furniture from Herculaneum, preserved by the eruption of Vesuvius in 79 CE. Wooden doors, shutters, shelves, and household furnishings were carbonized in situ by the heat of the pyroclastic material that buried the town, providing a rare view of Roman furniture design in its domestic and civic context (Mols 1999). Wooden three-legged tables had round tops and legs ending in lion-paw feet with various kinds of decoration on the upper part of the legs: feline protomes (Casa dell'Atrio Corinzio), garlanded male heads (Casa del Bel Cortile), volutes (Casa del Mobilio Carbonizzato), or dogs charging up the legs (Collegio degli Augustali). A small square stool was inlaid on top with a star design. Wooden benches (*subsellia* or *scamna*) had supports at both ends, showing a reverse curve at the front, in an abstract rendering of the lion legs of three-legged tables. Wooden bed or couch frames were preserved with bronze-sheathed legs suggesting turning (Casa del Tramezzo di Legno) and wood panels extending up at the sides and back (Casa del Mobilio Carbonizzato). Of particular interest is the wooden storage furniture, including chests and cupboards of panel construction; some cupboards included a top tier in the form of a small shrine (*aedicula*) for statuettes of the household gods (see Plate 29). Although the wooden furniture from Herculaneum was not ostentatious, it was well made and, in some cases, finely detailed and quite handsome.

The history of ancient furniture design is a complex tale involving numerous types, styles, techniques, and kinds of decoration, covering several millennia and a wide geographical area. It is clear from this account that furniture design and motifs depended on region and period as well as cultural practice and religious belief. Nonetheless, certain designs persisted—in varied forms—due to their usefulness and according to custom. Motifs were transferred and translated, carrying with them the tastes and requirements of other times and places. Within these currents new styles emerged and themselves became influential.

CHAPTER TWO

Makers, Making, and Materials

VASSILIS PETRAKIS AND MARIA LEONTSINI

MAKERS

By and large, furniture makers were expert carpenters, working alongside leather-workers, reed-workers, goldsmiths, or craftsmen for attached decoration (ivory, semiprecious stones, etc.). Stuffing with soft materials is not attested in ancient furniture; furnishings were, however, added to furniture for comfort (Andrianou 2009: 90–8; 2021). The status of the specialized craftsman is a problematic issue in most ancient contexts. Although it is relatively safe to infer that most ancient craftsmen were of moderate social status, belonging in some "middle class" and receiving payment in the form of food rations, it must be stressed that their standing was very diverse, depending on their skill and the sociopolitical environment in which their work was accomplished and "consumed".

Availability of raw material is essential to every craft. To secure access to good timber or other structural materials, Bronze Age craftsmen often had to attach themselves to institutions that would guarantee such a flow. "Independent" production, resembling what we could call a "private" enterprise, is largely invisible in our extant Egyptian, Near Eastern, and Aegean documentation. Yet, some freelance work would have been possible in all periods and regions: some *ostraca* (inscribed pottery sherds) from Deir el-Medîna are marked with sketches of furniture types, indicating transactions outside strict state control (Killen and Weiss 2009).

In Egypt the entire process of furniture production was under tight supervision: every movement of material and all stages of the work were monitored by inspectors and overseers, all working under the patronage of the nomarch. Artisan communities, largely associated with specific royal projects, resided in special workmen's villages, such as the ones excavated at Kahun (El-Lahun) or Deir el-Medîna (western Thebes). Although most of the industrial production in these artificial communities was state-commissioned, artifacts recovered in small amounts, such as furniture from the southern suburb of Amarna, suggest "small-scale domestic production that can only have realistically functioned within a tight interdependent network of families, supplying one another's needs" (Shaw 2012: 149).

In early Mesopotamia, non-private or institutional workshops employed a variety of specialists, whose skills were combined to produce commissions often made by the ruling elite. Just how "dependent" these workers really were on central institutions like the palace or temple is, however, difficult to assess, because ancient sources are very eclectic and record the activity of craftsmen only in the context of specific transactions. The earliest image of a Near Eastern woodworker—a man seated on a stool carving a table leg with an adze—occurs on an Old Babylonian terracotta plaque in the Louvre (c. 2000–1600 BCE; Simpson 1995: 1653, fig. 8).

The cuneiform documents comprising the "craft archive" from Isin in Mesopotamia (c. 2000 BCE) exemplifies what a "multitask" workshop was like. It involved at least four artisan groups: carpenters, felters, leather-workers, and reed-workers, which produced furniture that necessitated a combination of their skills: leather cushions stuffed with wool were used with chairs made of a wooden frame and reedwork. Silver decoration was made in collaboration with a different workshop (van de Mieroop 1987: 39). Although some of the furniture was of such outstanding quality as to be intended for the dowry of the king's daughter, this same workshop produced a diverse range of items, including shields, doors, musical instruments, and footwear.

Carpenters are among those receiving rations from the Ebla palace (in modern-day Syria), and a separate "house [workshop] of carpenters" is also mentioned (Peyronel and Vacca 2013: 442). Also informative on furniture production are certain administrative texts from Mari (also in modern-day Syria) related to projects during the reign of Zimri-Lim, last king of Mari (1775–1762 BCE).

Mycenaean Greek records (c. 1400–1200 BCE) mention a number of specialists including chair-makers (*thronoworgoi*). Besides carpenters (*tektones*; cf. later Greek τέκτων) and wood-cutters or tree-cutters (*drutomoi*), the description of some fairly elaborate items indicates that *khrusoworgoi* (goldsmiths), *khalkēwes* (coppersmiths/bronzesmiths working with either copper or alloyed bronze), *kuwanoworgoi* (workers of glass-paste), and perhaps *kowiloworgoi* (hollow-makers, engravers) or *aitēres* (inlayers?) may also have been involved in furniture production. Knossian and Pylian *prihestēres* (sawyers) may have been specialized in cutting particular materials, probably ivory or horn, but possibly precious timber as well. A record from Pylos refers to sawyers in the context of a building project (Nakassis 2015: 595)

The demise of Aegean palatial administrations *c.* 1200 BCE resulted in a lack of both demand and, consequently, sustainability of such specialized craftsmanship. Craft terminology that continued in later Greek, therefore, seems to be associated with industries relatively less dependent on the palaces (Morpurgo-Davies 1979). The continuous use of τέκτων (also attested in the compound δομοτέκτων) as the main term for carpenters in the first millennium BCE fits this pattern well. Specialization was also high among later Greek furniture makers. Demosthenes refers to κλινοποιοί (couchmakers) (*Against Aphobus* I 27.9) and Plutarch informs us of a street where κιβωτοποιοί (chestmakers) resided in Athens (*De Genio Socratis* 580e). Ancient terminology and descriptions of woodworking cannot always be attributed to specific fields of production. Nonetheless, the term *κλινοποιός* and the related craft *κλινοποιική* describe a discrete set of skills for the making of beds or recliners, as indicated in the *Onomasticon* of Pollux (VII, 159.4; Bethe 1967: 95; Grosdidier de Matons 1979a: 363–73; Andrianou 2009: 22, 31–3). In Latin this artisan was called *faber lectarius* and was engaged in the manufacture of both the *lecti cubiculares* and *lecti tricliniares*. These joiners were proficient in operating a lathe and experts in creating decorative veneer inlays. Specialization became even more systematic by the Late Roman Period.

There are well-known carpenters in Greek mythology, such as Daidalos (the maker of Pasiphae's wooden cow) or Epeios (the maker of the Trojan Horse) (Richter 1966: 127–8). Daidalos, the archetypal itinerant artisan, was credited with the invention of woodworking itself and the rudimentary carpenter's toolkit (*HN* 8.198), while more sophisticated inventions, such as the lathe, were attributed to Theodoros of Samos (perhaps an early sixth-century BCE figure) (Rackham 1969: 640–1; Miller 1972: 422–3; Acton 2014: 172; Lapatin 2015: 122–3).

Craftsmen were patronized by the goddess Athena. Harmonides, a legendary Homeric artisan, for example, is reported as "exceedingly loved" by Athena (*Iliad* 5.61). Greek appreciation of craftsmen is well reflected in the Homeric passage where Eumaios responds to Antinoos' protest that a beggar was admitted in Odysseus' hall: "who would invite a stranger … unless he be one of those who can provide public service, such as a seer, a healer, a carpenter or a bard who may bring joy to us with his singing? Because such men are welcome all over the infinite world" (*Odyssey* 17.382–6; author's translation). Odysseus himself appears to be a very skilled carpenter, able to fit an olive trunk into a bed frame, which he further embellished with gold, silver, and ivory (*Od.* 23.195–201).

In the Roman period rich references to specialists engaged in woodworking reflect different stages of both furniture production and the processing of wood. Epigraphy from the environs of Nicomedia (İzmit, northwest Asia Minor), for example, provides such references for the trading of timber until at least the sixth century, as shown by the funerary inscriptions of a woodworker (ξυλογλύφος in the third century CE and a ξύλεργος), as also of a ξυλέμπορος, a trader of wood (timber merchant), and of a ξυλόκαρος, a wood cutter. The term ξυλικάριος mentioned in funerary inscriptions from Cilicia (Diokaisareia, Seleucia, and Korykos, fifth to sixth century CE), would also refer to carpenters or joiners (Robert 1966: nos. 4, 337–9; 1978: 413–19; Corsten 1991: nos. 149, 176; Kiourtzian 2003: 53; Feissel 2006: no. 553, p. 176).

Working with the lathe and woodcarving were skills acquired by Alexander, son of Perseus, the king of Macedonia (c. 212–166 BCE; Plutarch, Aem. Paul. 37.4), indicating the high regard of this occupation. The term used for joiners was tekton leptourgos (τέκτων λεπτουργός), while craftsmen working on wood were called xylourgoi (ξυλουργοί; Orlandos and Travlos 1986: 167, 185–6). The terminology was yet diverse and even the generic terms τέκτων and τεχνίτης were sometimes referring to specialists working on wood and/or marble (Kazhdan and Cutler 1991b: 382–3). Tekton was listed in the second-century Onomasticon of Julius Pollux, as a term referred to the manufacturers of beds and doors as well of tables, tripods, stools, thrones, and benches (VII.111.1–2; VII.112.4, Bethe 1967: 83).

More specialized were the fabri citrarii occupied with the inlays of exotic woods such as citrus or thyine wood (Greek θύον, see below). Artisans involved in ivory carving were called ἐλεφαντουργοί, a classical term, still in use, responding to the term fabri eborarii, or eburarii mentioned in inscriptions of Rome and also to an epistle of Horace (first century BCE; Epist. ii, 1, 96). The term κεραοξόος, known already in the Iliad (4.110), describes the craft of scraping horns, or bones, later called κερατουργός or κερατογλύφης (Pseudo-Zonaras, K1185.22; Tittmann 1967: 1185).

Luxurious furniture was decorated with veneers and inlays of ivory or shell, and perhaps bone applied to wooden surfaces. Lucian (Πῶς δεῖ ἱστορίαν συγγράφειν, 27, second century CE) relates that Pheidias (480–430 BCE), the architect whose statue of Zeus at Olympia was one of the seven wonders of the ancient world, and the famous Attic sculptors Alkamenes (second half of the fifth century BCE) and Praxiteles (fourth century BCE) all had the skill to saw, polish, glue, and align ivory (Lapatin 2001: 170). Thus, the ancient author viewed ivory application as an art. The politor eborarius, an ivory polishing specialist and ἐλεφαντοτόμος, referred to by (Pseudo-)Oppian, the third-century CE Greco-Roman poet, has been understood to refer to a cutter of inlays (Calabi Limentani 1960; Neesen 1989: 197; Cutler 1994: 20; St. Clair Harvey 2003: 10–12, 34–7; Ulrich 2007: 8; Verboven 2007: 884). The first stage of ivory processing also required specialized skills, as illustrated by a miniature in the eleventh-century richly illuminated manuscript created for the didactic poem

Kynegetica (On Hunting) by (Pseudo-)Oppian, which shows an ivory carver working on the tusk of an elephant, seated on a bench and holding an adze (Marcianus Graecus Z 479 col. 881; Spatharakis 2004: 107–8, and fig. 72).

Since antiquity ivory craftsmanship was considered comparable to the high level of skill required of goldsmithing. According to Themistios, a philosopher and member of the fourth-century Byzantine court, both crafts were connected to the imperial household (Downey and Schenkl 1965: 324). The exploitation of ivory, ranked among imperial privileges, is illustrated in the bottom panels of the *Barberini* and the *Murano* ivory diptychs, now in the Louvre in Paris and the Muzeo Nationale in Ravenna, respectively, where ivory tusks were brought as tribute to triumphant emperors (Breckenridge 1979: no. 28, pp. 33–5; Dinkler 1979: fig. 59, p. 403).

Carpenters and joiners often practiced more than one specialty; for example, an *arcularius* was specialized in manufacturing boxes and chests (*armaria*) of wood and/or ivory (Neesen 1989: 191, 259; Ulrich 2007: 8–9). A fully working furniture workshop was pictured on a marble relief, today in the Capitoline Museum (Montemartini, Rome, inv. 2743, late first century CE; Ulrich 2007: 11). The relief belonged to an altar dedicated to Minerva, the patroness of the *collegium fabrum tinguariorum* (carpenters' association) and represented furniture construction and its related equipment, like the frame saw, attached to an apparatus, the carpenter's square (*norma*), large calipers (*circinus*), the bucksaw, and possibly a lathe (Ulrich 2007: 10, 11, fig. 2.3). Furniture made of stone or marble was produced in marble workshops. A scene carved in relief on the bottom edge of a second-century CE sarcophagus, found at Ephesos, shows a rather young craftsman polishing a marble table leg on a large wooden bench (Claridge 2015: 114–15).

Many of the same skills and joinery techniques were employed in the making of tables and benches so it is possible that the *faber lectarius* was fully capable of producing all such wooden equipment (Neesen 1989: 197; Ulrich 2007: 8–11, 232). On the other hand, highly skilled artisans involved in carpentry cooperated with metalworkers or specialists in bone and ivory carving. Couches used for reclining at meal times were portable or in some cases built against the walls of the *triclinia* (Balty 1984: 476–8, 496; Ellis 1997: 46–50; Croom 2007: 46–50; Putzeys 2007: 54–6; Vroom 2007: 318–25; Mols 2007–8: 145–60; Petridis 2008: 247–58; Andrianou 2009: 35).

Luxurious furniture was made from a range of high-cost materials, such as marble, ivory, and bone, and could be decorated with inlays and metallic components (Plate 2). Examples include a pair of silver furniture ornaments from the Esquiline Treasure (second half of the fourth century CE, now in the British Museum) and *Tychai* or female personifications representing Rome, Constantinople, Antioch, and Alexandria (Loverance 2004: 10–11, 93, nos. 5, 7, 43, 93; Croom 2007: 23–30, 35–7, 71–2, 110–12; Ulrich 2007: 44,

219, 222). A multifunctional team had presumably manufactured a sumptuous altar of gold and precious stones destined for liturgical use that, according to the historian Sozomenos (IX.1.4, Hansen and Bidez 1960: 390–1), was dedicated to Hagia Sophia of Constantinople by Princess Pulcheria, the sister of the emperor Theodosios II (408–450) (Mango 1972: 51). The production of fine furniture was well established in Constantinople after the fourth century CE, as proven by the majestic imperial carriage with a jewel-encrusted golden throne used for transporting the relics of saints Andrew, Luke, and Timothy in Constantinople referred to in the *Chronography* of Theophanes Confessor (Mango, Scott, and Greatrex 1997: 331).

Imperial factories or state workshops (*fabricae*, ἐργαστήρια βασιλικά) fabricated such items of precious and luxurious furniture. Craftsmen engaged in marble carving, carpentry, metalwork, and goldsmithing or silversmithing operated under the particular legislative framework of an association (Cutler 1994: 66–71, 233; Baldini Lippolis 1999: 22). It is not clear though whether the activities of joiners or other craftsmen related to furniture makers had to be within associations or whether they could be performed by private arrangement or contract. In any case, state supervision guaranteed quality and reliability with regard to orders. The state support of craftsmen was essential for the protection of the transmission of technical skills to apprentices; specialized artisans, except in certain flourishing cities, were coerced to adjust their techniques to the needs of the countryside, a condition imposed by the difficult circumstances of late antiquity (Ward-Perkins 2001: 172).

Furniture makers were thus associates of large groups, but could also work in independent workshops. In general, artisans involved in furniture making worked in small family enterprises, providing their products for a plurality of consumers. The setting for their work took place in the ἐργαστήριον, which commonly functioned as both a workshop and salesroom (Kaplan 1999: 158–60). The transmission of technical skills and inheritance of workshop equipment, including drawings, were dealt with in special legislative provisions of the edicts issued by Constantine I in 334 and 337 CE. Practitioners and craftsmen who produced such luxury furnishings were exempt from taxes, assessments, and public services on condition that they devoted their time to the instruction of their craftsmanship.

Thus, the imperial legislation should have motivated artisans both to be proficient themselves and further to promote their skills by training their sons. In the appended list of crafts in the *Codex Theodosianus* (*De excusationibus artificium*, *Codex Theodosianus* XIII.4; *Codex Justinianus* X.66.1–2), as earlier in the edict of Diocletian, joiners (*intestinarii*; Lauffer 1971: 7, 3, 118–19) were ranked once more among the most highly specialized artisans, like architects, makers of panelled ceilings (*laquearii*), plasterers, carpenters, sculptors, or mosaicists (Mango 1972: 14–15; Stern and Hadjilazaro Thimme 2007: 207). These long-standing protective measures for the promotion of technical expertise were again incorporated in the later regulations of the *Prefect Book* (Τὸ ἐπαρχικὸν βιβλίον) and in the legal collection of *Basilika* of Leo VI (886–912) (Koder 1991: 22, 138–40; Kolias and Chroni 2010: 286–7). As the number of skilled workers continued to decline, carpentry and furniture craftsmen were hired to build defense equipment (Claude 1981: 204–66; Dennis 1985: 12.22; 44.29; Aufleger 1996: 599–604; Henning 2007: 10–11; Petersen 2013: 74, 120–2, 377).

Although skilled craftsmen never belonged to the upper classes, artisans with expertise and talent enjoyed a respectable position and enhanced the prestige of their patrons. Indeed, a craftsman is pictured as a peripheral figure in a miniature in the Dioscorides' illuminated manuscript, offered to the imperial princess Juliana Anicia in about 515 CE (Österreichische Nationalbibliothek in Vienna, Codex Vindobonensis med. gr. 1, f. 6v). Similarly, a carpenter planing a board is depicted on an ivory fragment of the third to fourth century CE from Alexandria (Princeton Art Museum inv. y1956-105; Weitzmann-Fielder 1979: no. 254, p. 278; Kazhdan and Cutler 1991a: 196; 1991b: 382–3; Ayalon 2005: 157–9; Putzeys and Lavan 2007: 106). The woodcarver Gerontios (second quarter of the fifth century CE), moreover, was sent to the Sophist Isokasios in Antioch by his master Theodoretos, the influential theologian and bishop of Cyrrhos (Κύρρος, situated north of Aleppo). Theodoretos described Gerontios as a prominent professional and a specialist in carving various figures of animals and trees (Azéma 1955: 1:102.22–103.2; Mango 1972: 51–5; Ulrich 2007: 12).

MAKING

The basic tools and techniques of ancient carpentry (see Glossary of Technical Terms) seem to have been much the same throughout ancient western Asia and the Mediterranean (Figure 2.1). The limited availability of wood determined the development of ancient furniture production; strict control over the use of raw materials, for example, is evident throughout the ancient Near East. This contributed greatly to the early and rapid development of skills and ingenuity in furniture-making techniques. Certain regions where good timber was more abundant and therefore less exploited, such as the Aegean, may have followed different patterns. The relatively easy accessibility of wood in Crete, for example, suggests that wooden furniture must have been widely employed in non-elite households.

After trees were carefully chosen to avoid any defects in the heartwood or dense inner part of the tree trunk, felling was done with axes composed of stone or metal blades attached to shafts of strong wood (ash was preferred in Egypt). Then, to facilitate transportation and further processing, felled trunks were cut into logs with an average length of 1.7 meters, close to the average height of adult male workers fit for the task (Killen 1994b: 12). Longer lengths of timber could be produced by scarf-jointing shorter ones and securing the joint with a butterfly cramp (Killen 1994b: 15, fig. 13).

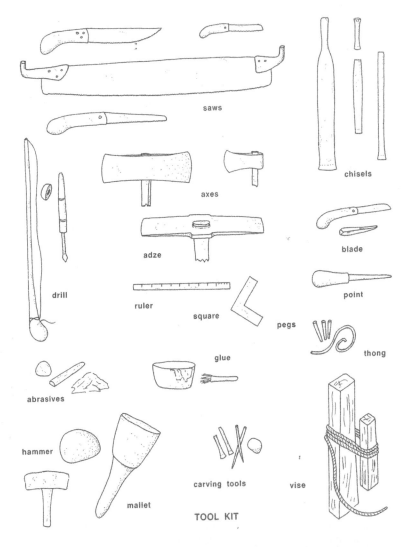

FIGURE 2.1 The toolkit of Bronze Age carpenters, including makers of wooden furniture. *Source:* Evely 1993–2000: 532, fig. 219. Courtesy of Don Evely.

An early but so far isolated use of plywood (a technique of gluing thin sheets or "plies" of timber in cross-grain fashion) can be found in an Egyptian coffin panel dating to the reign of Djoser (Third Dynasty, mid-third millennium BCE) (Lucas 1936; Gale et al. 2000: 356–7, fig. 15.19) (Figure 2.2). The lack of other ancient examples suggests that this technique had no follow-ups until its modern (apparently independent) reinvention. Logs lashed to the aforementioned sawing

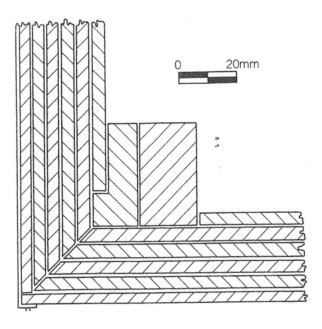

FIGURE 2.2 Plywood construction from an Egyptian coffin found in a gallery under the step pyramid of Djoser at Saqqara, Third Dynasty. *Source:* Killen 2000: fig. 15.19. Courtesy of Geoffrey Killen.

posts could be ripped down into boards while still "green" (i.e., not yet dried) with metal pullsaws. We must assume that bark and sapwood would have been removed by axe or adze beforehand.[1] While converting a log into boards, "through-and-through" cutting alongside the log was practiced. This minimized waste, but the resulting boards were subject to cupping because of tangential shrinkage. Slow seasoning was therefore crucial, since the quick evaporation of timber moisture would result in splitting or further shrinkage: wet, "green" boards must have been exposed to some controlled conditions, perhaps under a tent, covered by reed mats or probably stacked in wigwam fashion to allow air to circulate freely among them (Killen 1994b: 13–14, figs. 8–10).

Woodworking involved a certain range of tools. The transition from flint to copper (mostly strengthened with arsenic) as a tool material in the Late Predynastic/incipient Early Dynastic Period (*c.* 3100–2686 BCE) was profoundly important, and it was only bettered by the introduction of tin bronze during the Middle Kingdom (*c.* 2055–1650 BCE; Killen in Gale et al. 2000: 354). Tomb 3471 (*c.* 3100–3000 BCE) from Saqqara in Egypt yielded a considerable collection of copper tools, with copper saws, adzes (used much like modern planes), and both mortise and firmer chisels already developed. Wooden mallets and thin blade awls (for piercing holes) were also extant by that time. Notably, ancient saws had a uniform "set" (all teeth of the blade were punched from the same side; Killen 1994b: 20, fig. 21). Bow-drills must already have been introduced by that time too, as indicated by the thong-holes in First Dynasty bed frames, although the earliest illustration of the bow-drill occurs in a painting from the Fifth Dynasty (mid-third millennium BCE) Tomb of Ty at Saqqara (Killen 1994b: 33–4). Painted depictions of carpenters from the Tomb of Rekhmire at Thebes show that, by the New Kingdom, carpenters had expanded their toolkit with more specialized implements, such as the straight edge and cubit rod, the try square, the marking knife, and the miter block (Killen 1994b: 44, fig. 51) (Figure 2.3: *top*).

A lively and illuminating image of a contemporary carpenter's workshop is found in the tomb of the treasurer Meket-Rē at Sheikh Abd el-Qurna (Eleventh Dynasty; *c.* 2055–1985 BCE): woodworkers work mostly in the shade, under a tent, with the sawing post placed amidst a small open courtyard (Winlock 1955: 89–90) (Plate 3).

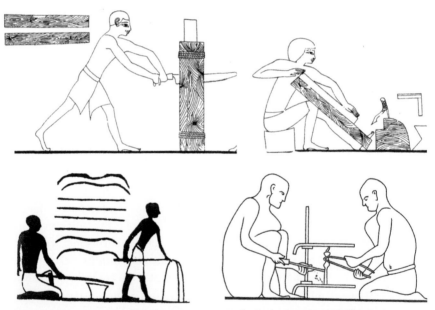

FIGURE 2.3 Top: Images of Egyptian carpenters from the Tomb of Rekhmire at Thebes. Eighteenth Dynasty Egypt. Top left: A worker makes planks with a pullsaw. Top right: Carpenter using the straight edge, try and miter squares to prepare wooden parts to be joined. Both images drawn and rearranged by Vassilis Petrakis after N. de G. Davies, *The Tomb of Rekh-Mi-Re at Thebes* (New York, 1943), plate LV. Bottom left: Workers steam-bending bows of timber. Sketch of a scene from the tomb of Amenemhat at Beni Hasan, Middle Kingdom, Twelfth Dynasty. *Source:* Killen 2000: fig. 15.20. Courtesy of Geoffrey Killen. Bottom right: Carpenters turning wood on a lathe. Sketch of a scene from the early Ptolemaic tomb of Petosiris at Tuna el-Gebel. Fourth Century BCE. *Source:* Killen 2000: fig. 15.21. Courtesy of Geoffrey Killen.

Joinery must have developed at the same time as woodworking itself. Various types of joints (of which butt-joints with leather thongs through perforation holes was the most popular) are known from Predynastic Egypt (Killen 1994b: 14–15, figs. 11–12) (Figure 2.4). Alongside scarf-joints with butterfly cramps

FIGURE 2.4 Various types of joints, as attested in extant ancient Egyptian furniture. From left to right, top to bottom: butt, edge (tied), edge (with loose tenon), edge (dowelled), coopered, half-lap, housing, bridle, dovetail, lapped dovetail, common through dovetail, simple plain miter, shoulder miter, double shoulder miter, butt surmounting long plain miter, half dovetail surmounting long plain miter, scarf with "butterfly" cramp locking piece, tied hooked scarf, spliced scarf. *Source:* Killen 2000: figs. 15.23–15.29, 15.31, 15.37–15.48. Courtesy of Geoffrey Killen.

used to produce longer rails of timber, revolutionary mortise-and-tenon joinery is also found. First Dynasty Egyptian bed frames and luxury furniture (table and chairs) from Ebla (Palace G, room 2601) in northwest Syria already display this technique, which is also seen among the furniture in the Middle Bronze Age tombs at Jericho. Throughout the first millennium BCE, mortise and tenon is ubiquitous in surviving furniture.

Intricate joints, such as the so-called "dovetail," which has been identified on a bed frame canopy from the Fourth Dynasty tomb of Queen Hetepheres I (mother of Khufu or Cheops; d. *c.* 2590–2560 BCE) at Giza (Killen 1994b: 16, figs. 14–15), could only be fashioned with one-hand pullsaws made of metal, such as those available from the First Dynasty onward. From the Second Dynasty (*c.* 2890–2686 BCE) onward, wooden dowels and nails were combined with many types of joints providing extra support, while the added application of adhesives provided further integrity.

Elaborate joinery must also have been employed in Bronze Age Cretan furniture, as suggested by the employment of wood in architecture, evident from holes for dowels and clamps on stone blocks (Evely 1993–2000: 531–4, fig. 220). Evely has interpreted the relative scarcity of metal nails as an indication for the wide application of various joints (534–5, fig. 221). In a wooden table from Shaft Grave V at Mycenae, for example, small pegs were used to secure the tenon into the mortise slot (Muhly 1996: 198–200, fig. 3).

The collar-and-tenon system is mostly found joining tabletops and legs at Jericho, Gordion, and Pazyryk in Siberia (Simpson 1995: 1668; Muhly 1996: 203). Since this joinery facilitated reassembly and portability, Elizabeth Simpson suggests that it may have originally been developed for the needs of a nomadic lifestyle. However, the only evidence for its use by nomads comes from the late Pazyryk barrows (fourth to third century BCE). Furthermore, portability does not necessarily imply nomadism: bronze hinges belonging to collapsible furniture were found at Nimrud, probably so that pieces could accompany the Assyrian king and his court on outdoor activities, campaigns, or travels (Curtis 1996: 179).

Steam-bending of timber was a simple technique with impressive results. A board (preferably unseasoned) was held above a pot of hot water and the evaporating steam penetrated the cellular structure of the wood, softening it so that it could be bent into the desired shape. Perhaps this practice originated in fourth-millennium BCE Mesopotamian wheel-making, but paintings from the Old Kingdom tomb belonging to the physician Hesire at Saqqara also depict bed legs that may have been steam-bent. Illustrations of the technique itself come from Middle Kingdom wall paintings from Beni Hasan in Middle Egypt (Killen 1994b: 8, fig. 1; Gale et al. 2000: 357, fig. 15.20) (Figure 2.4 *bottom left*), and it has been suggested that the elegantly sweeping legs of the Classical Greek *klismos* chairs were similarly fashioned (Richter 1966: 125). However, caution is necessary with this interpretation because curved boxwood legs from the inlaid table from Gordion Tumulus MM (eighth century BCE), originally interpreted as steam-bent, were shown to have been made of naturally bent or trained branches (Simpson 2010: 199–200).

The early use of the lathe (Greek τόρνος), either vertical or horizontal, has been intensely debated. Simpson has identified clear evidence for an advanced use of the lathe in wooden plates from Tumulus W at Gordion, the capital of ancient Phrygia (eighth century BCE) (Simpson 1999). It is remarkable that the Gordion plates were made of different boards glued together before they were turned, indicating the high quality of the adhesives employed (Simpson 1999: 784). Earlier than this, there is also evidence for the use of some kind of turning device in certain stool legs from New Kingdom Egypt: the unevenness of the marks notwithstanding, Killen has identified grooves, which do suggest turning, even if the legs were finished manually (Killen 1997: 14–17; Simpson 1999: 783; Gale et al. 2000: 358, fig. 15.22). Similar evidence for the use of the lathe has been found in wooden furniture from the Middle Bronze Age (seventeenth to the sixteenth century BCE) tombs near Jericho (Simpson 1999: 784, plate 174d; Cartwright 2005: 107–8, fig. 5, 125). Simpson also records a possibly "turned" stool leg from a nineteenth- to eighteenth-century BCE context at Acemhöyük in central Anatolia (1999: 784).

It would be interesting to know where the Aegean Bronze Age stands in all this, but the paucity of archaeological evidence impedes further discussion. It has been hypothesized that the Mycenaean Greek spellings *qe-qi-no-to* and *qe-qi-no-me-no* found in descriptions of elaborate furniture (tables and chairs) and raw ivory on Linear B tablets from Pylos, may indicate "turned" pieces. However, the exact meaning of these terms is still obscure.

In any case, in the Aegean, the lathe was used on wood at least from the seventh- sixth century BCE onwards, as a stool leg fragment from the Heraion on Samos suggests (Simpson 1999: 781–2). The earliest depiction of a lathe in use comes from the tomb of the priest Petosiris at Tuna el-Gebel in Egypt (late fourth century BCE; Killen 1994b: 54–5, fig. 21; Figure 2.3 *bottom right*), but it is uncertain whether a vertical or horizontal lathe is depicted (cf. Simpson 1999: 782).

We should not be quick to interpret the absence of the lathe from certain contexts as evidence of primitiveness or technological inferiority. In the Gordion tumuli—including Tumulus MM—Simpson found that nearly all woodwork was hand-carved (1999: 783). Handmade production, despite being more labor-intensive and time-consuming (or perhaps because of it), increased the perceived value of an artifact. Additionally, we need to consider that certain materials were easier to "turn" than others. Boxwood, for instance, was particularly suitable for the lathe (Vergil, *Georg.* 2.449).

Veneering (the application of thin layers of precious materials over less costly ones) was widely practiced. In New Kingdom Egypt, for instance, ebony veneers were particularly popular (Killen 1994b: 16–17). When applying veneers, the substrate timber had to be strong, while veneers themselves needed to be dense and consistent. Veneering was also known in ancient Greece, but references to it are scarce and it certainly ran counter to the anti-exhibitionist classical ethos that intensely criticized luxury (τρυφή) (see Chapter 9). The χάμευνα παράκολλος from the *Attic Stelai* listing confiscated property from rich Athenian households of the late fifth century BCE (see Chapter 9) is translated as "veneered low couch/bed." This item must have been highly valued because the price listed on the inscription is double that of an average bed (Pritchett 1956: 231–2).

Inlay decoration, in either organic (ivory,[2] bone, even precious timber) or inorganic materials (precious metals, faience, glass-paste, precious or semiprecious stone or shell) is also very widespread, and the contrast of hues would have played an important role: the combination of light-colored materials such as ivory, boxwood, or bone with darker ones such as ebony was utilized throughout Egypt and the Near East, even as far away as the Aegean. Unlike veneer, inlay leaves much of the wood exposed and was therefore preferred with better quality timber.

The Pylos Ta tablets (*c.* 1200 BCE), written in the Mycenaean Linear B script, include some detailed descriptions of elaborate furniture that unfortunately has no surviving archaeological counterpart. The word *a-ja-me-na* (perhaps *aiāimenā*?) is consistently accompanied by names of precious materials in the Instrumental case (e.g., *kuwanōi*, "*with* [blue] glass-paste").[3] The context of use of the term strongly suggests that it refers to inlaid or applied decoration, while the combination of certain materials mentioned in these records (namely, ivory, glass-paste, and gold) occurs elsewhere in Minoan and Mycenaean art, especially jewelry. Understandably, items from Tutankhamun's tomb are hardly representative of average Eighteenth Dynasty craftsmanship, but they do illustrate that even in the most lavish royal burial inlays mattered more than the actual structural material that supported them. A particularly ornate casket inlaid with ebony and ivory, for instance, with over 45,000 small pieces arranged to produce intricate abstract and floral designs, was made of humble native tamarisk (Hepper 2009: 40). A popular and more affordable substitute for veneering was painting over poor quality timber that had been covered with a thin layer of gesso. This material was also used to apply gold leaf to produce gilt wood.

Although animal glues were used in wood structures throughout antiquity, gesso must have been the primary adhesive used in Egypt before the introduction of organic glues made of animal fat, skin, and bone boiled together. It was used, often in combination with nails for extra safety, from the Fifth Dynasty onward (Killen 1994b: 17–18; Newman and Serpico 2000). At Gordion, in addition to glue residue in the corner joints of the Tumulus MM inlaid table, the top of the Tripod Tray Table from Tumulus P shows boxwood boards butted edge to edge and glued without any other support, suggesting strong clamping mechanisms (Simpson 2010: 31, n. 3, 68–9, n. 25). Oil-based varnish and beeswax were already used in New Kingdom Egypt and throughout antiquity; they were perhaps employed on Philoxenus' "shining table" (Athenaeus, *Deipn.* 4.146).

The (admittedly scarce) representations of furniture makers and their tools in Archaic and Classical Greece have not yielded any surprises in the range of the tools used. In fact after the introduction of copper, and later, bronze woodworking tools the design and woodworking techniques employed by carpenters remained similar and constant until iron tools were fully developed during the Roman period. A long-handled adze (σκέπαρνον) is depicted on a fifth-century BCE red-figure cup, a jagged saw with a curved handle (πριών) on a fourth-century BCE Campanian bell-crater, while a drill-bow (τρύπανον) is depicted in mythological scenes of the Classical period showing the manufacture of the chest where Danae is to be placed (see Chatzidimitriou 2005, 102, 217, nos. X1, 2, 4, pl. 38; Chapter 8 in this volume).

A representative inventory of carpentry tools in the Hellenistic period, drawn in a sepulchral epigram, composed by Leonidas, a Greek epigrammatist from Taranto (300–250 BCE), was saved in the Greek Anthology (a collection of ancient and Byzantine epigrams). The listed tools in poetic format, being indicative of the equipment found in a carpenter and a joiner's workshop of all periods, belonged to a carpenter called Leontichos and were dedicated to the goddess Athena as a compensation for the auspices to the craft. This poetic list included the grooved file, the plane (called the "rapid devourer of wood"), the cord, the hammer that strikes with both ends, the rule stained with red chalk (*sanguine*), the drill-bow, and the rasp, while a heavy axe with its handle was characterized as the chief tool of the craft; the list encompasses also the augers, the gimlets, four screwdrivers, and also the double-edged adze (Paton 1969: VI. no. 103, 354–5; no. 205, 404–5).

Tools discovered in excavations testify to the common use of similar equipment, allowing quite an instructive picture of the technical procedures in woodworking and furniture making to be drawn (Russel 2000: 80–6, 136; Decker 2008: 49). On top of this, artistic representations and the literary record help to complete our knowledge of the set of specialized instruments and tools for the drawing, measurement, and construction of furniture. Experts such as the τορευτής (*tornator*), who owned a lathe and knew how to shape wood, may have been able to serve more than one workshop (Goodman 1964: 9–11, 452–3; Weitzmann-Fielder 1979: no. 259, 281–2; Ginouvès and Martin 1985: 65–78; Ulrich 2007: 10, 15–51; Cholakov 2010). The measuring and marking devices included rulers, compasses, bobs, squares, levels, and chalk lines. Clamping devices were necessary for setting the glue between joints and although examples of clamps are nonextant, their use is assumed by the evident joining techniques of furniture known from texts and excavations dating to the Roman period (Ulrich 2007: 51–8). Late antiquity was crucial for the improvement of ancient woodworking methods, as attested by furniture illustrations becoming more common on silver plate, sarcophagi, funerary reliefs, mosaics, ivory reliefs, and in texts (literary, legal, official, and private documents), offering possible interpretations, though not always accurate, of the pictorial evidence found in manuscripts and wall paintings (Allison 2001: 181–208; Parani 2003: 159–87; Stern and Hadjilazaro Thimme 2007: 205–6; Decker 2008: 496–7; Zimmermann 2010: 622, plate 6).

MATERIALS

Optimal preservation conditions and meticulous discussion of the evidence (see Gale et al. 2000) have propelled Egypt to a position of paramount importance in the study of ancient woodworking and furniture production, although extrapolations to other ancient traditions should always be viewed with caution. Native Egyptian trees (acacia, tamarisk, willow, sidder, or sycamore fig) could be used for general construction and had been exploited since the Predynastic Period (i.e., before c. 3100 BCE), but restricted resources and the growing demand for high-quality woods that could express prestige within the incipient state made timber import imperative already in the Early Dynastic Period. From the middle of the third millennium BCE until Roman times, the timber trade had been of great importance to the Egyptian political economy: it is, for example, the backbone of the fictional "Tale of Wenamun" (c. 1000 BCE), in which the king of the Phoenician city of Byblos in present-day Lebanon appears keen on what is described as a regular business involving woodcutters, laborers, and livestock for the cutting and carrying of thousands of logs to the port (Egberts 2001). The significance of the lumber trade was great, as indicated by relief representations of the transport of timber in the Assyrian palace of Sargon II at Dur-Šarrukin (c. 716–705 BCE), present-day Khorsabad in northern Iraq. In southern Mesopotamia, in fact, wood was so scarce that not only furniture but also wooden doors and roof-beams appear in inheritance records (McIntosh 2005: 158). This is unlike western Syria, where such natural resources were rich and readily exploited. At the late third or second millennium BCE site of Ebla (modern Tell Mardikh, Syria), for instance, extensive charcoal analyses indicate the concurrent use of many kinds of timber, including fruit trees (particularly wild cherry), ash, and olivewood for both ordinary and elite furniture manufacture (Caracuta and Fiorentino 2013).

The Greek climate has not favored the preservation of wooden artifacts. Instead, we rely primarily on written sources for understanding ancient Greek furniture manufacture that are unsurprisingly biased toward the fashionable, the luxurious, and the extravagant and less interested in recording the materials of the ordinary furnishings of their time. This applies to Greek and Roman *testimonia* (including the Mycenaean palatial records using the syllabic Linear

B script, *c.* 1400–1200 BCE), as well as Near Eastern sources. Again, information on materials and craftsmanship recovered from the studies of wood remains from such elite contexts as the burial of Tutankhamun (Hepper 2009: 37–49) represent the exceptional rather than average.

The strength and pale color tones of boxwood (Greek πύξος/πύξον; Latin *buxus/buxum*; Akkadian *taskarinnum*) made it particularly attractive to furniture makers who would use it both as a structural and as a decorative material (for inlay or veneer), contrasting with darker woods such as African Blackwood (*Dalbergia melanoxylon*, widely and inaccurately cited in earlier scholarly literature as "ebony"). Boxwood might have reached Egypt from Syria through middlemen from Byblos in Ugarit, an ancient port city in present-day northern Syria, as indicated by complaints addressed to the pharaoh by the governor of Byblos (Moran 1992: 205–7). Turning to the Aegean, a Linear B tablet from Pylos (*c.* 1200 BCE) describes two tables made of yew or ash "with two supports of boxwood." The combination of boxwood with darker woods is also seen in the inlaid table and serving stands ("screens") from Gordion Tumulus MM in Turkey, where boxwood had received inlays of darker juniper (Simpson 2010: 19, 31, 65–6, 70–1).

African Blackwood was a highly valued wood in antiquity. Its logs are mentioned as exotic gifts of the highest level in the correspondence from Amarna, the Egyptian capital established by Akhenaten around 1350 BCE (Moran 1992: 101, 106). African Blackwood and cedar logs have been found in a contemporary cargo of this correspondence that sank off Uluburun (southwest Anatolia), probably en route to some Aegean destination(s) (Figure 2.5).

As accounts of gifts exchanged at top levels indicate, African Blackwood was combined with materials of a contrasting brighter hue, such as boxwood, ivory, and gold (Moran 1992: 10–11). Echoes of this apparent fondness for color contrast can also be found in the description of luxury furniture from Pylos (*c.* 1200 BCE). There, a dark wood that may be laburnum (Mycenaean Greek *kutesos*, later Greek κύτισος, *Laburnum* sp.) is mentioned as the main material of chairs, footstools, and tables alongside ivory inlays. On one entry in this set of Linear B tablets, a stone tabletop is described "with supports of laburnum and ivory." There are Near Eastern parallels for such contrast of hues, but these need not indicate that the Pylian items were imports; rather, such similarities point toward the existence of certain shared fashions (a sort of artistic *koine*) elements among Eastern Mediterranean polities of the late second millennium BCE (cf. Feldman 2006: 120), possibly generated and maintained through elite level contact.

African Blackwood, the true ancient ebony, continued to enjoy a high profile throughout antiquity. Classical Greece made limited use of it, and then often in a religious context (e.g., Pausanias 5.11.2 refers to ebony decoration of Pheidias' throne of Zeus in Olympia). Secular usage occurred more often in Near Eastern or Egyptianizing contexts, such as in the procession of Ptolemaios Philadelpheus (between 280 and 270 BCE), where two thousand ebony logs were carried by

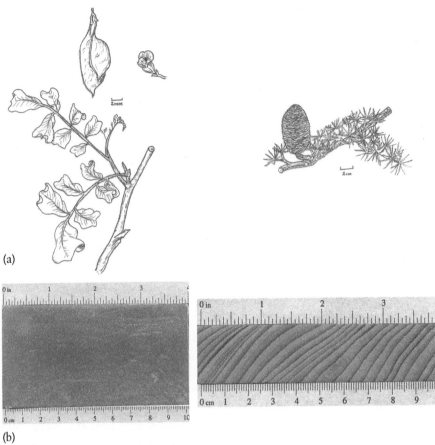

FIGURE 2.5 (a) (Left) The African Blackwood (*Dalbergia melanoxylon*) and (right) the Lebanese cedar (*Cedrus libani*). Drawn by Vassilis Petrakis after Gale et al. 2000: figs. 15.5, 15.13. Courtesy of Vassilis Petrakis. (b) Textures of African Blackwood (left) and Lebanese cedar (right). *Source:* https://www.wood-database.com. Courtesy of Eric Meier.

Aethiopian δωροφόροι (tribute-bearers) alongside ivory tusks, gold, and silver (Athenaeus, *Deipn.* 5.201a). This is also the case in depictions from the Mortuary Temple of Hatshepsut at Deir el-Bahri, across from Luxor in Egypt, advertising the marvels brought from the Land of Punt (perhaps a region in the Horn of Africa).

Citrus (Greek θύον; Latin *citrus/citrum*), was an aromatic wood much sought after by wealthy Romans of the Late Republican or Early Imperial period (see below). There is little evidence of it being used for furniture before this time, the earliest Greek mentions of citrus wood seeming to refer to its aromatic properties. A Linear B tablet from Pylos mentions *tu-wo*, perhaps *thuwon* "citrus-wood," among other substances that may also be aromatic; in Homer, Calypso burns θύον with cedar (*Od.* 5.60) and θυώδης already indicates "fragrant" in Homer (*Od.* 4.121, 5.264, 21.52).

Maple trees (Greek σφένδαμνος, ζυγία; Latin *acer*) produce a hard, strong wood that would have been used where stress to the material was expected, including joinery. Its sturdiness is well echoed in Aristophanes' designation of Marathon veterans as σφενδάμνινοι "[tough as] maple" (*Acharnians* 180–1), as well as its employment for the manufacture of tables and couches (Cratinus frag. 301; Theophr., *Hist. pl.* 5.7.6).

Cedar (Greek κέδρος; Latin *cedrus*; Egyptian ꜥš; Akkadian *erenu*) and cypress (Greek κυπάρισσος; Latin *cyparissus* or *cypressus*; Akkadian *šurminum*) were also well known and valued for their durability, longevity, and strength. Commonly associated with the Mount Lebanon range, *Cedrus libani* is also found in mountainous regions in Anatolia (Taurus), Syria (Amanus), and Cyprus (Troodos). Praise of its physical properties is found abundantly in the Old Testament, and control of the Lebanese timber trade was pivotal in shaping Egypt's Mediterranean policy (Meiggs 1982: 63–8). Cedar wood, either in the form of logs or as finished wooden artifacts, was intensely traded in the second millennium BCE, principally through a direct coastal route from Lebanon to Egypt (Lev-Yadun et al. 1996; Gale et al. 2000: 349–50; Hepper 2001; Lev-Yadun 2007: 152–3). This route also involved southwest Anatolia and Cyprus and reached as far as the Aegean (Asouti 2003). *C. libani* has been identified as the material of the shafts of bronze double-axes from a large ritual deposit found in the Arkhalokhori cave on Crete and two funerary beds from Poros near Herakleion, also on Crete (Netolitzky 1934; Muhly 1996: 209–10, respectively).

The preference for fragrant cedar wood for funerary furniture, documented in Egypt (Davies 1995; Gale et al. 2000: 368), at Gordion in Turkey (Simpson 2010: 119–25), and on Crete (see above), may indicate some ritual significance for this material. A fragrant chest of cedar is mentioned in a mortuary context in Theocritus (*Idyll* 7.80–1). The seventh-century BCE Corinthian tyrant Kypselos dedicated an elaborate chest (also made of cedar) at Olympia (Pausanias 5.17.5). In addition, cypress was used for the coffins of the cremated remains of the Athenian dead during the first year of the Peloponnesian War (Thuc. 2.34.3) and for the fourth-century BCE Scythian royal coffin found at the Kul-Oba tumulus near Kerch in the Crimea (ancient Panticapaeum).

Beech (Greek ὀξύα, φηγός/φᾱγός; Latin *fagus*) is known as a strong, easily worked, and aesthetically pleasant wood widely used for furniture (Theophr., *Hist. pl.* 3.10.1). The scarcity of references to beech in Greek literature may be due to its limited accessibility and to competition from other woods with similar properties, such as maple. Beech as well as yew (Greek τάξος; Latin *taxus*) was imported to the island of Thera during the mid-second millennium BCE, as charcoal analysis from Akrotiri, a town with a strong Minoan influence, suggests (Asouti 2003).

Oak (Greek δρύς; Latin *quercus*) provided durable timber. The evergreen valonia oak (*Quercus aegilops*) was imported into Egypt, where it has been identified as the material for a dowel and tenons from some shrines (containers of sarcophagi and other valuable items) in Tutankhamun's burial (Hepper 2009: 38, 48). Unfortunately, oak-wood decays quickly, so archaeological evidence for its use is scarce. In the Greco-Roman world, however, where oak was far more accessible (and affordable), oak furniture is barely mentioned in the written sources either. From Cicero, who mentions the use of oak benches as an example of laudable Spartan austerity as opposed to contemporary Roman taste (*Mur.* 74), we may infer how biased these literary references actually are: unpretentious timber attracted much less interest (Meiggs 1982: 295).

The wooden base of furniture was frequently embellished with other materials, often with the goal of bringing together contrasting hues. As previously noted, precious metals, ivory, vitreous materials, or other wood could all be used as ornamentation. The decoration of furniture's wooden surface appears to have been a very widespread fashion, and furniture partly or entirely covered with gold or silver leaves or sheets, or decorated with other precious materials already existed in late fourth-millennium BCE Mesopotamia (see the deliberately burned "chest" or seat from the Riemchen Building in the Eanna district of Uruk IV *c.* 3300–3100 BCE in present-day Iraq) as well as Early Dynastic Egypt.

The scarcity of timber in Egypt and especially south Mesopotamia made wickerwork a welcome substitute (Wendrich 2000) (Figure 2.6). Egyptian Early

FIGURE 2.6 Left: weaving patterns on ancient Egyptian furniture matting. *Source:* Wendrich 2000: fig. 10.4. Courtesy of Willemina Wendrich. Right: Bronze model of plaited chair (with a variant of Wendrich's pattern b), accompanied by a footstool, from Enkomi, Cyprus (Late Bronze Age). Redrawn by Vassilis Petrakis from Laser 1968: plate III:b. Courtesy of Vassilis Petrakis.

Dynastic evidence shows that rush seats were considered prestigious enough to be depicted in statues of important officials, such as Ebikhil, superintendent of the Temple of Ishtar at Mari (Early Dynastic Period, *c.* 2900–2300 BCE).

Although evidence for ancient woodworking outside Egypt is quite sparse, patterns and forms that may have been used can be gleaned from the assumed influence of carpentry on the working of other materials, such as metal or stone. A "translation into stone" of wooden structural details, analogous to that in the entablatures of the Doric and Ionic orders, is quite common in furniture, as suggested by gypsum examples that survive in Bronze Age Crete. For example, the curved "strut" shown in relief at the front of the solid block constituting the permanent Knossos "throne" from the eponymous "Throne Room" in the West Wing of the palace, as well as the relief cross-bars on its sides, obviously imitate wooden prototypes (Evans 1935: 914–19, figs. 890, 893). A bench from the so-called Country House at Myrtos Pyrgos on Crete (Neopalatial period, *c.* 1700–1450 BCE) also bears elegant triglyph decoration in obvious imitation of carved woodwork (Cadogan 1976: 151, plate 47).

In the Roman world the selection of timber suitable for making different types of furniture must have been an additional expertise of skilled craftsmen (see above). Hardness and density were the main qualities that determined the suitability of particular types of wood for woodworking. Ebony (*ebenum/hebenus*) and boxwood were considered the best for woodworking according to Theophrastos and Pliny (see above). Among the species of timber used by Roman woodworkers for household objects and furniture, although mentioned only for shipbuilding and architecture, was silver fir wood and oak (*quercus*). Silver fir wood covered a high percentage of samples among the wood found in Pompeii and Herculaneum. The wood of acer (maple) was valued as a furniture wood, *buxus* (box tree) and *terebinthus* (turpentine-tree) were assessed for their veneer and resisting properties. *Iuglans* (walnut), and the more extravagant citrus wood, which was always reckoned very valuable, were famous for the circular tabletops of the popular *mensae delphicae* and precious tables, enlisted in the fortunes of the consul and orator Cicero, the king Ptolemy, and the Roman emperor Tiberius (14–37 CE). *Cupressus* (cypress) was used for statues, sarcophagi, and doors, such as the fifth-century CE Santa Sabina on Aventine Hill; however, it is not common in the furniture samples found at Pompeii and Herculaneum. *Fagus* (beech) was the most common type of wood according to textual evidence and archaeological finds, especially for bedsteads. The species used for the particular woodworking items were certainly, based on the possibility of on-site supply, but some kinds were also traded (Ginouvès and Martin 1985: 13–22; Simpson, Spirydowicz, and Dorge 1992; Mols 1999: 81, 82; Croom 2007: 19–21, 25, 68, 70, 110; Ulrich 2007: 239–60, 318–31).

Joinery pieces recovered at Tossal de les Basses in southeast Spain, dating from the fourth century BCE until Roman times, consist of various timber species: 50 percent of the squared pieces/boards and 40 percent of the joinery pieces are of pine, juniper, or cypress. The latter was frequently imported in the Roman period but was used and probably traded four hundred years before, as the Iberian findings prove (Croom 2007: 19–21, 25, 68, 70, 110; Ulrich 2007: 239–60, 318–31; Carrión and Rosser 2010: 755–62). Olive wood was documented in almost 20 percent of the pieces (Croom 2007: 19–21, 25, 68, 70, 110; Ulrich 2007: 239–60, 318–31; Carrión and Rosser 2010: 755–62). The local origin of wood was also crucial for the choice of materials, as proven by findings of palm wood in Egypt (Dautermam Maguire, Maguire, and Duncan-Flowers 1989: no. 29, 92–3).

Metal, bone, stone and especially ivory were already in broad use in the making and decoration of elite furniture since the Bronze Age, as suggested by the numerous ivories recovered from Egyptian and Near Eastern second millennium BCE contexts or the descriptions of stone tablet-tops, ivory and glass-paste inlaid decoration of chairs and footstools in the Linear B tablets from Pylos, c. 1200 BCE. However, in the Roman and Late Antique periods these materials are even more systematically employed. Trade routes for exotic materials are better established within the Empire; iron enters furniture manufacture to strengthen wood, whereas high quality furniture is used in formal public services. This is verified by archaeological finds, literary descriptions and artistic representations in murals or miniatures. Well-made furniture has also been found in domestic contexts, associated with the high quality of living in urban centers.

Metal was used for the manufacture of the three-legged tables, benches, and footstools, those found in Pompeii made of bronze. Surviving metal fittings (legs, strips from bed frames, plates that decorated beds) suggest that metal ornaments were often used as composite parts of furniture. Traces of a wooden cabinet as well as iron campstool frames found in the Byzantine shops of Sardis and dated between the fifth and the seventh centuries CE served daily needs (Crawford et al. 1990: 14, 45, 61, 65, 79, 92, 94, 96, 97). Less common were tables with bronze legs or bronze fittings on wooden couches and solid bronze stools. Bronze decorations and ivory inlays were incorporated in back supports of beds and couches or in furniture handles (Harrison 1986: n. 355, 250; St. Clair Harvey 2003: 74; Ayalon 2005: 88–116).

Iron was used for folding stools or chairs as well as beds, to strengthen the wooden legs, but then often covered with more decorative elements (Croom 2007: 14, 24, 35–7, 71, 98, 102–4, 106–7, 110–11, 114). High-quality pieces were destined for luxurious private or public buildings. It is not clear if the crossed-leg chairs with curved arms in the shape of dolphins or fishes, recovered in an ensemble of prestigious furniture at Kenchreai (second third of the fourth century CE), were either of domestic nature or were destined for formal public services (Stern and Hadjilazaro Thimme 2007: 208, 209, 212, 224–5). The backrests of armchairs and thrones made of leather and the folding stools consisting of leather straps (*sella curulis*), show that the technique of leather components on furniture was fairly common (Wanscher 1980; Parani 2003: 166, 169; Ulrich 2007: 210, 280).

Bronze folding tables, bronze and iron folding chairs, fittings of boxes, and chests were found in the Roman Terrace House 2, in Ephesos (Jilek 2003: 89–91). The production of metal and wooden furniture followed common stylistic conventions. The furniture attachments in bronze and bone, excavated in Antioch, would certainly not be equal in quantity and artistry to that of a medium city such as Anemourion in south Turkey (Russell 2000: 81; 2002: 223). Combining wood and bronze was, however, a quite common practice for adorning smaller objects, as the fourth-century CE large storage box from Karanis (Egypt) and a box with a copper alloy hinge found in Sagalassos (southwestern Turkey, dated to the second half of the sixth to the first half of the seventh century) attest (Dauterman Maguire, Maguire, and Duncan Flowers 1989: 94, no. 30; Putzeys et al. 2007: 224).

Furniture of silver and gold mentioned in literary texts was not constructed of solid metal but rather covered with plates and appliqués. This technique was probably used for the *sella aurea* of Julius Caesar, gilded or decorated with gold fittings. The life of Pope Silvester (314–335 CE) in the *Liber Pontificalis* (the book of individual biographies of popes) records among various offerings, silver furniture revetments that were offered to churches of Rome by Constantine I. These were thus accessible not only to the imperial court but to the upper levels of society and higher clergy as well. Silver-plated furniture such as altars, ciboria, and furnishings are often mentioned in religious contexts (Baldini Lippolis 1999: 25, Croom 2007: 24, 29, 101, 108, 168–71; Mundell Mango 2008: 447).

Bones and horns were sourced from locally available fauna, and in some cases the quality of artifacts proves that the technical processes of decorative applications were quite advanced (Marangou 1976: 26-27, 38; Goldfus and Bowes 2000: 188, 190–1). Excavated half-finished bone fragments with traces of sawing indicate that bone craftsmanship could produce small ornamental parts fitted to furniture in the fourth and fifth centuries CE (De Cupere, Van Neer, and Lentacker 1993: 269–78). Second-century CE bone furniture fittings from Transylvania (Roman Dacia) have also been identified (Vass 2010: 64), although much more evidence exists from the late Roman bone workshops in Carthage (Bir Massuda, site 2, in the Circular Harbour and in the Circus). Significant evidence of well-worked items comes from Alexandria and offers a complete picture of large-scale bone processing in urban centers of North Africa and Egypt from the Roman to the Early Byzantine period (Docter 2002–3: 120; Rodziewicz 2009: 87). The production of working materials, like the specific glues or pigments, was also well developed. The technique of attaching bone and ivory decoration on furniture was primarily introduced from Egypt. During the late Roman period, however, the technical know-how was spread in large urban centers outside Egypt (such as Constantinople, see Čerškov, Jeremić and Vitezović 2016, 108–9).

Artifacts of carpentry and ivory carving were sent to members of Constantinople's royal court by the patriarch Cyril of Alexandria around 432/3 CE (Rodziewicz 2009: 86–7). Ivory exported from Aksum (northern Ethiopia), according to the first-century CE text known as the *Periplus Maris Erythraei*, was accessible in the Eastern Mediterranean, and from there diffused to the Western cities of the Late Antique period (Phillipson 2009: 356–9). Constantinople gradually became the sole production center of high artistic level objects and furniture. The ivory plaques of excellent craftsmanship and iconographic perfection found in a workshop in Eleutherna (Crete), operating at the end of the third century until 365 CE, were probably destined for Constantinople or Thessaloniki (Phillipson 2009: 357–60; Vasileiadou 2011: 66–76). The combination of ivory, bone, and wood in the fourth-century CE *armarium* and chairs excavated at Kenchreai, as well as the ivory veneers of the throne-like Cathedra of Maximianus, the Archbishop of Ravenna, represent the evolution of mere technical procedures within the transitional timeframe of late antiquity (Stern and Hadjilazaro Thimme 2007: 1–7, 277–313; Rizzardi 2009: 229–43).

Furniture made of marble was of equally high cost and was sometimes of special artistic value because it demanded talent and the technical skills of a sculptor. Sculptured table legs (*monopodia*) were invariably used for household decoration of private homes (in the dining rooms or *peristyles*) and of various public spaces and places of worship (such as altars or offering tables) (Plate 4). In domestic contexts they served as stands for the statues of Lares, as, for instance, in Pompeii and Herculaneum. *Monopodia* in wall paintings were depicted with dinner sets. The *mensa delphica*, a table with three legs and one of the most renowned pieces of luxury furniture from antiquity, could also be made of marble.

A large number of different kinds of marble and a smaller amount of copper have been identified throughout the Mediterranean in Spain (Mérida and Sevilla), France (Lyon), Italy, and Sicily, as well as in Cyprus, Lebanon (Beirut), Israel, Libya (Cyrene), Egypt, the Balkan Peninsula (Slit, Stara Zagora, Sofia), the Black Sea (Crimea), and in the major cities of Asia Minor and Greece (Stephanidou-Tiveriou 1993: 28–76; Ajootian 2000: 487–507). A table leg from Dokimeion (Afyon, Phrygia) made from the local white Dokimeian marble confirms that materials were selected on the basis of availability at each site (Herrmann and Tykot 2009: 62–3).

Pieces of marble furniture, mostly table legs and counters or benches, discovered in Sardis, Corinth, and Ephesos, highlight the wide variety of household furnishings and the range of materials in the Eastern Mediterranean (Crawford et al. 1990: 14, 38, 44, 100–1; Wiseman 1969: 96–7; Bookidis and Fisher 1972: 313; Uytterhoeven 2007: 64; Quatember 2014: 711; Varner

2015: 123–38). A number of tabletops in the shape of the Greek letter *sigma* with raised borders supported by wooden or possibly metal stands known for their use in secular contexts also served the needs of the Christian ritual (Roux 1973: 133–96; Chalkia 1991: 61–131; Parani 2003: 174; Uytterhoeven 2007: 53; Vroom 2007: 323, 325, 330, 354–5). Also common in residences was built-in furniture such as beds or benches (see Chapter 4). Liturgical cupboards of different dimensions identified across the range of annex rooms in churches were also usually constructed from cut stone but in some cases were made of wood (Veyne 1987: 315–16; Caseau 2007a: 560–2; Lavan 2007b: 185, 200; Michel 2007: 590–5). Remains of wood and stone furniture have been found in the humble homes, while parts of luxurious furniture with fittings of precious metals or other materials, such as bones, ivory, marble, and bronze came to light in household contexts in the large cities of western Asia Minor and Palestine of the Late Roman Period; the production of the later apparently required the collaboration of specialists (Goldfus and Bowes 2000: 187; St. Clair Harvey 2003: 10–11, 15–16, 31, 35–6, 44; Türcoğlu 2004: 100; Baldini and Cosentino 2021: 83). At the end of antiquity, as well as in the early medieval period, the manufacture of furniture and furnishings covered both daily needs and extravagant living while the relevant textual evidence and the excavated material remains are now connected with urban everyday life and activities in capital cities or civil centres.

CHAPTER THREE

Types and Uses

GEOFFREY KILLEN, ELIZABETH SIMPSON,

AND STEPHAN T.A.M. MOLS

EGYPT

Furniture was used in ancient Egypt as a status symbol and in a ceremonial context by members of the ruling class and in a domestic setting by those of the elite, middle, and artisan classes. The survival and our detailed knowledge of the types of furniture used by ancient Egyptians are a fortunate consequence of their religious beliefs. A wide range of furniture types was placed in a funerary context with the deceased in the protective environment of their tombs.

Simple bed frames were used in everyday life as early as the Predynastic Period (c. 5500–3100 BCE), being finally placed with the deceased in their graves. The side rails were made from four carefully selected tree branches, each having a natural right-angled elbow at one end. Into each elbow a hole was bored to accept the straight end of an adjoining branch. These natural elbows formed short supporting legs and, when all four branches were assembled, constituted the corners of the rectangular frame; the corner joints were lashed together with plant fiber.[1]

With the introduction of copper woodworking tools at the beginning of the Early Dynastic Period (c. 3100 BCE), new furniture types emerged to satisfy the cultural needs of an increasingly hierarchical society. Walter Bryan Emery (1903–71) excavated an extensive collection of copper woodworking tools, including saws, adze blades, chisels, and awls, from a tomb at Saqqara (S 3471) dated to the First Dynasty (c. 3100–2890 BCE) (Emery 1949: 30–7, 42–8, figs. 18–19, 22–4). Copper tools allowed Egyptian carpenters to cut and shape wood very precisely. This, in turn, led to the development of the frame stool and bed frame using accurately converted timber elements.

Bed legs of this period are beautifully modeled on a bovine form and, with the introduction of the mortise-and-tenon joint, the bed frames display a thorough understanding of anthropometric principles and constructional technologies.[2] Slots are now cut through the side- and cross-rails of bed frames, allowing the bed deck to be strung with either rawhide or plaited plant fiber webbing.[3]

The Fourth Dynasty (*c.* 2613–2494 BCE) furniture discovered in the tomb at Giza of Queen Hetepheres I (*c.* 2600 BCE), the wife of the pharaoh Sneferu, illustrates the wide range of furniture types being used by the nobility of the Old Kingdom (Reisner and Smith 1955). Although the queen's body had not been placed in the tomb, her furniture had and was excavated by the American Egyptologist George Reisner (1867–1942), who discovered a mass of decayed wood together with glass and faience inlays and gold fittings. Reisner and his team methodically recorded and removed this fragmentary material—a major undertaking because, as the structural integrity of each piece of furniture failed, a general collapse occurred, resulting in layers of mainly nonorganic materials being dispersed among different contexts. After years of detailed analysis the queen's furniture was skillfully reconstructed using the original inlays and gold fittings on new wooden elements. Reisner's research showed that the queen's tomb had contained two armchairs, a sedan chair, a bed frame with a footboard, boxes designed to hold curtains and bracelets, and a remarkable portable canopy made from wooden beams and poles covered in gold sheet. The canopy could be easily assembled and provided the queen with privacy when the curtains were drawn. The original furniture is now preserved in the Egyptian Museum and the National Museum of Egyptian Civilisation in Cairo, with a set of full-size copies in the Museum of Fine Arts, Boston.

At present only one of the queen's armchairs has been reconstructed. This chair was covered with thin gold sheet, which was beaten around the wooden cores. The legs were fashioned as lion's legs, and each of the armrests was supported from below by a spray of three papyrus flowers tied at the center. The seat and back panels were made from wooden boards, each enclosed within a frame (Reisner and Smith 1955: 28–9, fig. 31, plates 15–16). A cushion would have been placed on the seat. Extant examples suggest that these were made from sewn linen bags filled with goose feathers.

Hetepheres also possessed a sedan chair, which was made to be carried by four attendants. It consisted of a box-type seat with arm panels and a vertical back support, allowing the queen to sit on a cushion with either her legs extended or knees drawn up to her chest. The carcase of the seat box was attached to a pair of carrying poles that terminated at each end in a palm-shaped finial covered with thick gold sheet. The sedan chair's back support was inlaid with solid gold hieroglyphs that comprise four inscriptions bearing the names and titles of Hetepheres and showing that the sedan chair was made for the queen by her son Khufu (Reisner and Smith 1955: 33–4, fig. 34, plates 27–8).

The queen's bed frame proved less complicated to reconstruct as two of the gold-encased legs still retained their original timber cores, providing evidence that the bed frame sloped from its head down to its foot. The legs were of a lion form, attached to the side rails of the bed frame with mortise-and-tenon joints that were once fastened with rawhide thongs. The ends of the side rails had terminals in the form of papyrus flowers. The footboard was designed as a separate piece that attached to the bed frame's foot rail with a pair of tapered tenons along its bottom edge; these tenons fitted into a pair of copper-lined sockets in the upper surface of the foot rail. The footboard panel was decorated with an inlaid rosette-and-feather pattern of black and blue faience set into a gold background (Reisner and Smith 1955: 32–3, fig. 33, plates 17, 25–6, 31).

To store the queen's jewelry a customized rectangular box was manufactured from wooden boards that were mitered together; these were covered with gold foil that was burnished onto a textured pattern carved on the wooden carcase. A flat lid was similarly treated and had an ivory handle; to either side of the handle was a raised band of hieroglyphs and ink inscription indicating that the box had held the queen's "rings." Examples of ring bracelets made of silver and inlaid with turquoise, lapis lazuli, and carnelian in a butterfly design were also discovered and are now displayed within the reconstructed jewelry box (Reisner and Smith 1955: 43–5, fig. 44, plates 36–8).

A second longer box and bed canopy were presented to Hetepheres by her husband Sneferu. The surfaces of the long box were decorated in a similar fashion to the footboard of the bed frame. The box had once held the curtains that were hung around the queen's bed canopy (Reisner and Smith 1955: 25–7, figs. 28–9, plates 11–12). The canopy was manufactured from wooden floor beams, roof beams, jambs, and pillars, and the entire intricate framework was covered with gold sheet. At the assembly joints, the wood was protected with copper fittings to prevent wear, indicating that the canopy was designed to be portable (Reisner and Smith 1955: 23–5, figs. 23–6, plates 5b, 7–10).

During the Middle Kingdom (c. 2055–1650 BCE), further developments (or modifications) in chair construction appear with the introduction of the curved back designed to accommodate (or support) the human frame, as illustrated on a large number of stelae from this period. These chair backs were manufactured from an arrangement of vertical and angled stiles that sprung from the chair's back seat rail and were joined to the horizontal top rail of the chair's back. The space enclosed by this framework was fitted with an arrangement of wooden slats. Chair legs are seen to be modeled on lion or gazelle forms and, in some depictions, appear to have been painted to simulate the skin of the chosen animal. This type of quality chair continued to be produced throughout the remainder of the Dynastic Period.[4]

The stool (backless chair) developed into a variety of types during the Eighteenth Dynasty (*c.* 1550–1295 BCE), each being used by a different group of people. The three-legged stool was used by artisans as it sat firmly on the uneven workshop floor, the lattice stool (constructed of vertical and horizontal elements with angled braces) by middle-class men, and the round-legged stool by middle-class men and women. However, during the Nineteenth Dynasty (*c.* 1295–1186 BCE), a change of emphasis was seen in the gendered use of round-legged stools. Women continued to utilize this type of seat, but its use by men declined as it became the seat of choice for the king. Rameses II, for example, is shown in wall reliefs on the first pylon at the Luxor Temple, in the Great Temple of Rameses II at Abu Simbel, and in the Ramesseum sitting on an elegant round-legged stool with tall slender legs that have a narrow waist, while his feet rest on a footstool (Killen 2017c: 87, plates 70–2).

Egyptians did not eat from tables, using them instead to display offerings of food and bouquets of flowers or to support various shaped pots. During the Early Dynastic Period (*c.* 3100–2686 BCE) archaeological evidence indicates the use of low tables that were cut from solid blocks of wood.[5] By the New Kingdom (*c.* 1550–1069 BCE), the quality of carpentry allowed for the manufacture of rectangular framework tables with vertical legs braced by horizontal rails, such as two notable examples discovered in the tomb of Kha and Meryt at Deir el-Medîna.[6] Better quality four-legged tables are also found with slightly splayed legs and a tabletop edged with a torus molding and cavetto cornice, a type of concave cornice seen in stone architecture.[7] The three-legged table also appears in the canon of Egyptian furniture design, and there is evidence that such tables were used not only as a means to present offerings but also in the slaughter of animals (Plate 5).[8] Tables were manufactured in reed and rush as well as wood.[9]

Slender stands used to hold single pots were made from thin timber elements, their tops often customized with a molded cup to hold the round bottoms of the vessels they supported. The framework of these stands was reinforced with a triangulated arrangement with vertical and angled braces; the entire structure was covered with a layer of gesso and then painted to replicate stone and glass inlay.

The furniture of Tutankhamun (*c.* 1336–1327 BCE) illustrates the wide range of furniture types available to the rulers of the New Kingdom. These comprised elaborately decorated bed frames, including an example that could be folded; thrones; chairs; footstools; lattice-, round-, and three-legged stools; together with various kinds of boxes designed with flat, barrel, pent (angled), and shrine-shaped lids, the last having a rounded front connected to a top board that slopes toward the back.

A folding bed frame from Tutankhamun's tomb illustrates the use of a portable type of furniture that precedes the concept of the modern "Z bed." Constructed of three frames that are supported by eight lion legs, this bed frame uses an intricate system of folding hinges that allows the bed's center frame to fold within the head and foot frames, reducing the length of the bed to one-third of its original length. One pair of hinges provides a unique solution in allowing not only the center frame to fold but also its attached pair of legs to swing inward to a position where they are stored conveniently within the bed's stringing.[10]

Numerous customized boxes, cabinets, and chests were deposited in Tutankhamun's tomb, indicating that different types of boxes were manufactured to store a wide variety of products. The king had his own razor box, its interior designed with slots that safely held a range of razors.[11] He also owned a number of jewelry boxes and cabinets as well as clothes chests. One large box with a pent-shaped lid was portable, with retractable handles that could be slid in under the box when not being carried by a pair of porters.[12] The king was also provided with a games box, *senet* being a popular board game of the period; this box was placed on a stand designed in a sled form with lion legs and made of African Blackwood (*Dalbergia melanoxylon*).[13] A further box with a barrel-shaped lid was painted with scenes of the king in his chariot hunting game or confronting his Syrian and Nubian enemies, who are shown prostrate and dying before the king and his army.[14]

One of the most spectacular pieces of furniture from the tomb was an ornate throne, manufactured in wood and encased in gold sheet. The legs were modeled as lions' legs, and above each of the front pair of legs was placed a lion's head. Each arm panel was designed with a winged uraeus (royal cobra) wearing the double crown of Upper and Lower Egypt. The backrest of the throne was embellished with a scene showing the young pharaoh's wife, Ankhesenamun, anointing him. Their faces and the exposed parts of their bodies have been molded from red glass, their wigs are of blue faience, and they wear clothes that are made from silver sheet.[15] The quality of this throne, with its elaborate footstool, indicates the wonderful craftsmanship that a range of artisans working in the royal and temple workshops could achieve. Its purpose was to project the authority of kingship in both a state and religious context. Indeed, the political value of Egyptian furniture was recognized by the Egyptian state, in that it provided those rulers of neighboring countries with gifts of furniture in exchange for tribute made to the pharaoh. Examples of ebony furniture were sent by Amenhotep III (*c.* 1390–1352 BCE) to the kings of Babylon and Arzawa.

During the Twentieth Dynasty (*c.* 1186–1069 BCE) illustrations show that Rameses III (*c.* 1184–1153 BCE) continued to use elaborate chairs and thrones. One throne seen in a wall painting in his tomb (KV 11) is designed with round legs that were incised with a scale pattern and encased in gold sheet; its seat and backrest are shown to be upholstered.[16]

The middle class strove to use similar elaborate furniture types to elevate their status. This created a thriving furniture industry based at the workmen's village at Deir el-Medîna. These workmen, who officially worked in the preparation of the royal tombs in the Theban necropolis, privately formed cooperatives to service the needs of the New Kingdom middle class. They manufactured bespoke furniture to order and rendered these pieces with painted designs replicating the quality materials they had seen in furniture being deposited in the royal tombs.[17] The carpenters and painters living at Deir el-Medîna provided a service to the middle class that gave them the opportunity to own furniture and use it to promote their own position in Egyptian society, as seen in the furniture discovered in the tombs of Kha and Sennedjem. Indeed, the workmen from Deir el-Medîna themselves recognized the importance of owning furniture, and manufactured several utilitarian types of chairs, stools, boxes, and beds for their own use.

THE ANCIENT NEAR EAST

Furniture in the ancient Near East was much like that of Egypt, used by the elite as a measure of wealth and status as well as for practical purposes, and also by ordinary people who could afford this amenity. However, the evidence for furniture in western Asia is considerably more restricted. In Egypt, the dry climate has helped to inhibit decay, such that wood and other organic materials have often survived in burial contexts—but elsewhere such items are rarely recovered. Most of what is known about the furniture of western Asia has been gleaned from depictions in art and references in ancient texts, along with numerous furniture fittings (mainly metal and ivory), and a few important collections of furniture finds that have survived intact. The situation is further complicated by geography: the ancient Near East involved a vast area comprising a multitude of cultures, yielding numerous types and styles. Nonetheless, the basic furniture forms are like those of Egypt: stools, chairs, footstools, tables, stands, beds, and chests, although their use was sometimes different.

The earliest evidence for furniture in the Near East comes from the Neolithic East Mound of Çatalhöyük in Turkey (c. 7100–5900 BCE). This was largely built-in furniture: plastered platforms that extended out from the walls of houses and into the interior of the rooms, evidently serving as benches, tables, and beds. Niches in the walls provided space for storage, along with clay bins, baskets, and wooden boxes. Mats and textiles were also in use, as attested by fragments found at the site. In addition, several statuettes show figures seated on various types of stools (Mellaart 1967: 215, 218–19, plates IX, 84–5, 105, 116–19).[18]

By the third millennium BCE, stools occur in many Near Eastern contexts, along with beds, chairs, stands, and storage furniture, to judge from numerous representations. Depictions occur on Sumerian cylinder seals of the Late Uruk/Jemdet Nasr periods (c. 3500–2900 BCE), with the simple backless stool being the earliest and most common type (Simpson 1995: 1648). Such seals show female figures seated on low stools or platforms with their legs tucked up or beneath them, engaged in cultic or practical activities, often connected with weaving. During the third millennium, elegant backless stools were used by dignitaries and deities alike: a statue of Ibikhil, superintendent of the Temple of Ishtar at Mari, shows him seated on a cylindrical stool of woven reeds or wicker, and a god is depicted on the stele of Ur-Nammu (*c.* 2112–2095 BCE), enthroned on a stool decorated with recessed paneling reminiscent of the façades of Mesopotamian temples (Simpson 1995: figs. 3–4). On a neo-Sumerian cylinder seal in the British Museum, Ur-Nammu, king of Ur, sits on a chair with a low back and bull's legs at the rear.[19]

Tables were used in this period, but these were more like trays or bowls on pedestal bases and were apparently used for offerings. One such tray table in silver was found in the richly appointed tomb of Queen Puabi (PG 800) from the Royal Cemetery at Ur in Iraq (*c.* 2600 BCE). Cylinder seals from the same tomb show men and women seated on stools, eating and drinking, alongside serving stands with food and drink on top. Puabi was buried with a wooden "wardrobe," decorated with shell and lapis lazuli, and also a wooden sledge, or chariot, adorned with gold and silver animal heads. In both cases, the wood had completely deteriorated (Woolley 1934: 78–80, plates 122–6). Puabi had lain on a wooden bed that has not survived, but terracotta bed models from the early second millennium BCE indicate the form of Mesopotamian beds (Simpson 1995: 1651). These resembled Egyptian beds, with four legs supporting a wooden frame strung with webbing, but without footboards or headrests.

Three-legged tables survive from the third-millennium BCE sites of Horoztepe in Anatolia and Ebla (Tell Mardikh) in Syria; also found at Ebla were the remains of a wooden chair with shell inlay as well as evidence for wood shelving. By the second millennium BCE, relatively well-preserved wooden furniture is known from the tombs at Jericho (Palestine) and Baghouz (Syria). Fifty or more pieces of wooden furniture were excavated from Middle Bronze Age tombs at Jericho (*c.* seventeenth–sixteenth century BCE), including three- and four-legged tables, stools, and beds, along with wooden bowls and boxes. Tombs at the site of Baghouz produced portable tables with removable legs, stools, and beds, dating to the early second millennium BCE (Parr 1996). The tops of many of the tables from these sites had rims or were concave, so that they could function as trays.

Some of the most luxurious Near Eastern furniture was fitted with ivory attachments, with spectacular examples dating to the second millennium BCE. The remains of an ornate ivory chair or throne were found at the site of Acemhöyük in central Turkey—unfortunately by looters instead of archaeologists. The valuable ivories were removed from the soil with no record of their original placement, purchased by a collector, and given to the Metropolitan Museum of Art, New York, in the 1930s. After seventy years of misattribution, one ivory plaque excavated at Acemhöyük was connected with the museum's collection, and the origin and date of the ivories could be determined (nineteenth–eighteenth

FIGURE 3.1 Ivory chair or throne from Acemhöyük, Turkey, front and side views, reconstructed. Nineteenth-eighteenth century BCE. Drawings © Elizabeth Simpson, 2013.

century BCE). The chair was finally reconstructed on paper, showing an unusual arrangement of the pieces (Simpson 2013). The legs were in the form of lion legs sitting atop finely carved sphinxes, with the lion legs facing front but the sphinxes facing to the front and sides; ivory plaques were arranged on the chair back and elsewhere (Figure 3.1).[20] The lion legs and sphinxes were clearly inspired by Egyptian models, but the combination of the two for the legs of a chair is not seen in Egypt.

Hundreds of ivory attachments have been excavated at Late Bronze Age sites, including Alalakh (Tell Atchana, Turkey), Ugarit (Ras Shamra, Syria), Pahel (Pella, Jordan), Tell al-Farah (Palestine), and Lachish (Tell al-Duwayr) and Megiddo in Israel—representing parts of a table and bed (Ugarit) and other furniture and luxury objects (Baker 1966: figs. 347–52). Found at Megiddo were 382 ivories, many displaying Egyptianizing motifs, along with the remains of furniture and other items that were disassembled and stored in the "Treasury" of the Canaanite palace. Perhaps the most famous piece of Late Bronze Age furniture from the region is the Ark of the Covenant, the chest that contained the tablets inscribed with the Ten Commandments, according to the Old Testament (Exodus 25:10–22). The chest was portable, with four gold rings at the base through which gold-plated poles were slid for transport, recalling the portable box from the tomb of Tutankhamun (Killen 2017b: plate 43). The Ark was made of wood, overlaid with gold, with a seat of gold at the top, flanked by gold cherubim; it was on this seat that the Lord was said to have been invisibly enthroned (1 Samuel 4:4). Parallels between Egyptian and Near Eastern furniture at this time are surely the result of the close association between Egypt and its vassal states, documented in the Amarna letters, an archive of clay tablets from the site of Amarna in Egypt. Diplomatic gifts of fine furniture and other prestige items were exchanged between Eighteenth Dynasty pharaohs and the kings of western Asia, including beds, chairs, and footstools made of precious woods and adorned with gold, silver, and ivory.

The end of the Bronze Age saw the demise of several powerful Near Eastern kingdoms, making way for the Assyrians, who realized a vast empire during the early part of the first millennium BCE. The kings commanded tribute from subject peoples and acquired immense wealth—which included massive amounts of magnificent furniture, both imported into Assyria and made there by native or foreign artisans. Extensive evidence exists for various types of chairs, stools, footstools, couches, stands, and tables, from depictions on Assyrian reliefs, lists of plundered items from conquered territories, and furniture fittings of metal and ivory excavated at Assyrian sites. Much of this furniture was royal, such as the beautiful backless stool and footstool of Ashurnasirpal II (r. 883–859 BCE) shown on a relief from his palace at Nimrud in Iraq.[21] The stool has turned (or metal) feet, a carved (or metal) stretcher, and calf heads projecting from the corners of the seat. The footstool has lion feet, recalling the furniture of Egypt, but the front and back feet point in opposite directions, a non-Egyptian trait. The same type of lion feet occur on a stool and three ornate tables depicted in reliefs from the palace of Sargon II (r. 721–705 BCE) at Khorsabad, along with two thrones, one mounted on a wheeled carriage (Curtis 1996: plates 45a–b, 50b–c, 51c). One of the tables has a concave top supported by a central post and standing figures, recalling earlier tray tables or offering stands. Another is square, with a flat top supported by floral and figural struts. The legs of these pieces have bases in the form of tapering cones, a typical feature of Assyrian furniture.

Assyrian thrones could be transported to the battlefield, where the king might watch his troops besiege a city or receive supplicants after their defeat. Fortified camp scenes show food preparation and furniture in tents, featuring what may be more common types: vessel stands, a folding table with food on top, low stools and tables for workers, and couches or beds with high curving headboards (Baker 1966: figs. 333–4). The most elegant couch of this type is that of Ashurbanipal (r. 668–627 BCE) shown on a relief from Nineveh in the British Museum (Baker 1966: fig. 305).[22] The king reclines on his couch, while the queen sits on a throne with her feet on a footstool (see Plate 14). In front is a tray table displaying items of food, and to the side a square table for weapons.

The royal couple drinks from fluted bowls, celebrating the Assyrian victory over the Elamite king Teumman at the battle of Til Tuba (*c.* 653 BCE). This is an early instance of the Near Eastern reclining banquet, a custom that became popular in Greece and Italy (see below).[23]

The decoration on Ashurbanipal's couch includes panels with small figures at the top of the legs, and a long carved stretcher connecting the legs at the level of the feet. These have counterparts in some of the fine imported ivories excavated at Nimrud, suggesting that the king's couch might be Syrian or Phoenician (Simpson 1995: 1658–61).[24] Similar ivory attachments have been found at other Near Eastern sites, including Arslan Tash and Zincirli (north Syria), Hasanlu (Iran), Samaria (Israel), and Salamis (Cyprus). The ivories from Tomb 79 at Salamis are associated with a chair and a bed, found along with a wooden chair with silver plating and gilded studs. Furniture with ivory and metal fittings was also produced in the kingdom of Urartu, northwest of Assyria in the region of Lake Van. A notorious raid on the Urartian city of Musasir by Sargon II (714 BCE) yielded a huge cache of fine furniture, enumerated on an inscribed tablet in the Louvre. This included an ivory couch, ivory tables, tables of boxwood (*Buxus*), boxwood chairs inlaid with silver and gold, and the silver bed of the god Haldi, covered with gold and jewels (Simpson 1995: 1657).

Among the most remarkable of ancient furniture finds are those from the royal Phrygian tombs at Gordion in Turkey. Excavations carried out by the University of Pennsylvania Museum in the 1950s yielded the remains of more than fifty pieces of fine wooden furniture and around seventy wooden objects, many in a remarkable state of preservation. Stools, footstools, chairs, tables, serving stands, a bed, and a log coffin were recovered from three rich tumulus burials—Tumulus W, Tumulus P, and Tumulus MM—dating to the eighth century BCE (Simpson 1995: 1662–6; Gordion 2021). Most of the furniture was banquet furniture, as shown by the grave goods from Tumulus MM, thought to be the tomb of the famous Phrygian king Midas or his father Gordias (Plate 6).

The king was buried in an open log coffin made of cedar (*Cedrus*), along with numerous bronze vessels, pottery, fibulae (pins), belts, textiles, and at least fourteen pieces of fine wooden furniture: nine tables, two serving stands, two stools, and a chair (Simpson 2010). The three-legged tables had tray-shaped tops, following in a long tradition of Near Eastern tables. These were portable banquet tables, as shown by one example—an ornate boxwood table with a walnut (*Juglans*) top and carved struts inlaid with juniper (*Juniperus*) in elaborate geometric patterns. The struts at the four corners took the form of handles for carrying, suggesting that the other tables from the tomb were also portable—and that Near Eastern tray tables in general could be used to transport food. The two serving stands were of boxwood, their faces inlaid with juniper, with top pieces featuring three open rings. These rings held round-bottomed cauldrons, ten of which were found in the tomb. Also included were a chair and two four-legged stools, piled with sumptuous textiles.

The placement of the parts of the coffin in the tomb indicates that it was assembled elsewhere prior to the burial. This suggests a funeral ceremony for the king before his interment. The ceremony included a banquet, as shown by an analysis of residues from the bronze vessels and other organic remains from the tomb (Plate 6). The guests ate a spicy stew of sheep or goat and lentils, and drank a mixed fermented beverage of grape wine, barley beer, and honey mead (Simpson 2010: 127–35). After the funeral the furniture, vessels, and their contents were placed in the tomb with the deceased. The study of the Tumulus MM burial provided unprecedented evidence for Near Eastern royal furniture and its use.

Tumulus P, the tomb of a child, had contained much fine furniture, including an inlaid serving stand, carved and inlaid tables, several stools, two footstools, an inlaid bed, and a small throne, along with fifty or more wooden objects such as spoons, bowls, and a parasol. Found in Tumulus W was a carved boxwood serving stand studded with bronze tacks, along with wooden plates turned on a lathe. The presence of bronze cauldrons and other banqueting paraphernalia suggests that these burials too involved a funeral and feast. The luck of preservation, careful excavation, and the long-term effort to study and conserve the wooden furniture from Gordion have contributed to the recovery of this important group of finds, adding much to our understanding of the types and uses of furniture in antiquity.

Furniture of the Babylonians and Persians, known largely from texts and depictions, continued the Assyrian tradition. The most famous furniture from Babylon belonged to the god Marduk, as noted by the Greek historian Herodotus writing in the fifth century BCE. This included a gold throne with a gold table from the temple of Marduk, and a richly appointed couch and gold table in the shrine on top of the ziggurat, said to have been used by the god when he visited. The Achaemenid Persians consciously emulated the furniture of the Assyrians and Babylonians, as seen in reliefs from Persepolis and Naqsh-i-Rustam in Iran (Calmeyer 1996: plates 73b, 74, 75a–b). These include propagandistic depictions of gigantic stools, with legs incorporating lion feet in the Assyrian manner. Tiers of standing figures support the seat and stretchers, as on Assyrian furniture, but here representing the subject peoples of the realm. On the seats of these stools the Persian king stands or sits on an elegant throne with his feet on a footstool. While these monumental stools are artistic devices, the king's throne and footstool represent actual royal furniture, as confirmed by two reliefs from the Treasury at Persepolis showing a king enthroned (identified as Darius, r. 522–486 BCE).

The frozen tombs at Pazyryk and Ukok in Siberia show that Near Eastern furniture types were in widespread use by the fourth century BCE. Well-preserved wooden furniture survives from these tombs along with other organic materials, as the contents of the chambers were frozen soon after the burials. Four-legged tables with tray-shaped tops were evidently used for serving food—as confirmed by meat found on some of the tops (Simpson 2010: 47). Near Eastern and Egyptian furniture types are found to the west as well, used in the Bronze Age Aegean and later in Greece and Italy.

THE AEGEAN BRONZE AGE

Evidence exists for furniture in the Greek Neolithic period (c. 6500–3300 BCE), in the form of terracotta figurines shown on seats or models of stools, stands, and tables. Actual furniture of this early period, likely made of wood or other organic materials, has not survived (or has not been recognized). By the third millennium BCE stools and chairs with backs are shown in Cycladic sculpture as seats for musicians playing lyres (Baker 1966: figs. 377–83). Extensive information is available for furniture in the second millennium BCE, with numerous depictions in Minoan and Mycenaean art, furniture listed in the Linear B tablets, clay models, and furniture fragments and casts recovered from excavations (Krzyszkowska 1996).

Minoan folding stools are shown in the Campstool Fresco from the Palace of Knossos on Crete (fourteenth century BCE), and a gypsum throne is still in situ in the Throne Room, flanked by gypsum benches running along the wall. The legs of the throne are carved with striations, with a swag at the front, and the chair back has an undulating edge. Furniture in a similarly fanciful style was used at Akrotiri on the island of Thera, although the actual pieces did not survive the volcanic eruption that destroyed the site (c. 1550–1500 BCE or earlier). Excavators poured plaster into voids in the pumice, however, producing casts of several beds and two ornate tables with carved legs and swag-like moldings (see Chapter 4). Additional evidence derives from gold rings, with scenes depicting chairs with high backs and straight or crossed legs, stools, and stands in the context of cultic activity.

Many types of furniture are listed in the Linear B Ta tablets from the Mycenaean palace at Pylos in Greece (c. 1200 BCE), including tables (to-pe-za, later Greek trapeza), chairs or thrones (to-no, later Greek thronos), and footstools (ta-ra-nu, later Greek threnus) made of stone, ivory, or wood, and adorned with decorations. The descriptions of this furniture are remarkable—and subject to interpretation. Ta 715 lists "two tables of yew?, of encircled type (with rim?), with supports of boxwood, nine-footers?, decorated with running spirals, (inlaid) with pa-ra-ku (emeralds?)." Ta 707: "One chair of ku-te-so (Laburnum?) with ivory back carved with a pair of heads of se-re-mo? (sirens?) and with a man's figure and calves; one footstool of ku-te-so, inlaid with ivory au-de." Ta 714: "One chair decorated with glass?, inlaid with kuwanos and *pa-ra-ku* and gold on the back, (which is) inlaid with men's figures in gold, and with a pair of gold heads of *se-re-mo?*, and with golden palm-trees/griffins and palm-trees/griffins of *kuwanos*" (for discussion and references, see Chapters 2 and 9). To this must be added actual furniture remains, including fragments of two small wooden tray tables from Shaft Grave V at Mycenae, an ivory stool leg from Thebes, ivory fittings for footstools, and painted terracotta chests. The common types of furniture from the Aegean Bronze Age continued in use into the first millennium BCE, while the elaborate types of the Linear B tablets may find echoes in the furniture described by Homer (see below).

GREECE AND ROME

The traditional view is that the interiors of ancient Greek and Roman houses were sparsely furnished, containing only essential items of furniture that were mostly functional in design. This interpretation was formed during the nineteenth century, when aristocratic houses in the Western world were anything but scantily furnished, especially compared to what was known about Classical antiquity. The early handbooks that list the items of furniture used in antiquity are based on sources of very diverse origin, but mostly drawn from depictions of furniture in Greek and Roman art, such as vases, wall paintings, and reliefs. These illustrated types are associated with names used for furniture in ancient literary sources as well as epigraphical material. Because many items of furniture depicted in Greek and Roman art are employed as part of a mythological or official setting, it is questionable whether these are representative of the furniture used in everyday life.

In the twentieth century Gisela Richter published her seminal study, *Ancient Furniture* (1926), with a second, revised edition published in 1966 (*The Furniture of the Greeks, Etruscans and Romans*). Her work is still used as a starting point for our knowledge on this topic but has its limits, following in the abovementioned tradition. She treats furniture depicted in scenes of everyday life, for example, in much less detail. Furthermore, Richter gives only limited space to Roman furniture. Her discussion deals with ancient furniture as categorized by region and culture (Aegean, Greek, Etruscan, and Roman), presenting a typology of furniture forms for each. At the time of writing this was a widespread approach. In his monograph on the Herculaneum furniture from 1999, Stephan Mols took a different approach while focusing on the wooden furniture from this city destroyed by the eruption of Vesuvius in 79 CE. He not only considered typology but also the techniques used and the function of these items of everyday Roman furniture. More recent studies have categorized furniture according to function rather than regions or cultures. Dimitra Andrianou, for example, has used this approach in her work on ancient Greek furniture from domestic and funerary contexts. New in respect to Richter and many other authors who have written on ancient furniture up until the 1980s is the treatment of simple items of furniture used in everyday life. Any discussion of Greek and Roman furniture must include wooden furniture found in everyday contexts.

Greek furniture

From the Greek Geometric period (*c.* 900–700 BCE), the evidence from actual furniture is scarce, but fortunately there are many extant depictions, especially on geometric vases, found almost exclusively in funerary contexts. Because most of these vases were made for tombs, they were often decorated with scenes showing the deceased person lying on a bed accompanied by mourners. Items depicted on the vases include beds, chairs, footstools, and stools, but details are not easily recognizable because the furniture is painted using simple geometric forms. Additional information is provided by the *Iliad* and *Odyssey* of Homer, which mention items of furniture that may reflect existing forms from the Geometric period. Occasionally, these epics include more elaborate descriptions, such as the well-known passage on the bed Odysseus made for himself and Penelope:

> Thereupon I cut away the leafy branches of the long-leafed olive, and, trimming the trunk from the root up, I smoothed it round about with the adze well and cunningly, and trued it to the line, thus fashioning the bedpost; and I bored it all with the auger. Beginning with this, I made smooth the timbers of my bed, until I had it done, inlaying it with gold and silver and ivory, and I stretched on it a thong of oxhide, bright with purple.
>
> (*Odyssey* 23, 195–201; Homer 1919: 398–9)

It is obvious that Odysseus' bed is to be considered a costly piece of elite furniture and not an everyday object. As it is still unclear whether the *realia* described in Homer's epics reflect contemporary or historical objects at the time the epics were composed, the description of the bed of Odysseus cannot, unfortunately, be used to support our knowledge of furniture used during the Geometric period.

From the seventh century onward, what are now considered the canonical forms of Greek furniture appear. These are known mostly from depictions, but occasionally actual items have been preserved. Although the types of furniture remained more or less the same throughout the Greek period, from Archaic until Hellenistic times (*c.* 700–100 BCE), many variations were possible. One can assume that Greek houses contained only the functional furniture required. Although this is not to deny that these could be richly adorned, really ornate furniture was not produced until the start of the Hellenistic period. Greek furniture types included stools (*diphroi*) and benches, as well as chairs with backs and curved legs but without armrests, the so-called *klismoi* depicted on vase paintings and grave reliefs. Thrones (*thronoi*), with both backs and armrests, are very often shown being used by gods, kings, or priests, and must therefore reflect costly honorary seats. The legs of all these seats could be plain, but more often they were decorated. They could be turned on the lathe, or shaped in the form of animal legs as previously found in Egyptian furniture, from which this type of leg design probably originated.

Chests used to store various materials were also in use, although many household items were hung on the wall with nails or pegs or stored on shelves, as is shown in vase paintings. Although not many actual chests have been preserved, there is ample evidence for their existence in the survival of bronze attachments, such as those discovered at Delos (Siebert 1973: 561–9). Terms used to describe these chests include *kiste* and *theke* (for a fuller discussion of furniture terminology, see Chapter 9). Because of the frequency of chests depicted in scenes with women, they are often seen as utilitarian objects associated with women in particular.

From the Classical period (*c.* 480–323 BCE) onward there is evidence for the existence of open cupboards (*kylikeia*) from Olynthos, Hellenistic Delos, and Toumba Thessalonikis (Andrianou 2009: 92). A depiction of a piece of storage furniture in a tomb in Agios Athanasios, near Thessaloniki, shows a sort of sideboard with three stepped shelves with a display of costly drinking vessels (Plate 7) (Tsimbidou-Avloniti 2005: 120–2). Such sideboards must have been prestigious items used primarily for the display of valuable possessions. Closed cupboards for the storage of dishes, other tableware, and household items, however, have not been found in a Greek context. The name of a cupboard that could be closed by doors, *kibotos thyridotos*, is known from inscriptions, but its exact function is still unclear. The item is included in a list on one of the so-called *Attic Stelai*, inscribed in stone and found in the Athenian agora. The *stelai* list the furniture of Alcibiades and his cronies that was confiscated after their trial in 415 BCE.[25]

Homeric heroes ate and drank while seated on stools and benches at tables, but this custom changed in the course of the seventh century BCE, when the reclining banquet came into fashion. This change from sitting to reclining probably occurred under Near Eastern influence, perhaps that of Assyria or Phoenicia, and was likely initiated by male aristocrats who wanted to distinguish themselves from non-elite male citizens by organizing drinking parties among their class. From then onward we have ample evidence for the existence of a specific room for male gatherings, especially in aristocratic houses, the so-called *andron* (male room). From the beginning of the Classical period onward *andrones* became more widespread, being also found in non-elite houses. In the city of Olynthos in northern Greece, rebuilt in 432 BCE, all houses contained such a room, showing that by then it had become a common feature. The new banqueting practices called for new types of furniture: *andrones* were usually furnished with an odd number of couches (*klinai*) placed along the walls on which one or two persons could recline during *symposia*. The only space left along the walls was for entryways. Small *andrones* included only three couches, to be used by a maximum of six persons, with each couch accommodating one or two men. There were, however, examples with space for eleven or even fifteen couches, the latter accommodating a maximum of thirty men. Normally, however, there was space for only seven couches in the *andron*, facilitating conversation between all members of the group. In depictions these couches are amply furnished with mattresses, animal skins, and probably sheets or blankets, rendering the frames mostly invisible, but often with the legs and headboards shown. Couch legs could be turned or rectangular, carved or incised, or could have the shape of animal legs. Fragments of actual couches, mainly made of metal, allow the various types to be visualized in some detail. As symposiasts reclined, the "head" boards were mainly used to support their arms. This explains why couches typically had two such boards, on both short sides, providing support for two persons reclining on opposite ends of the couch. Apart from these couches there were also beds for sleeping, but depictions of these are rare. Sometimes footstools were used with couches and chairs, as can be seen in many depictions, but actual examples have also been found. These provided status and comfort to those using them.

In late Archaic and Classical depictions of *symposia*, a three-legged rectangular table (*trapeza*), with one leg on one of the short sides and two legs on the other, was placed before each couch. All three legs terminated in the form of an animal paw. This was the traditional type of symposium table, in use until at least the beginning of the third century BCE when it was gradually replaced by a three-legged table with curved animal legs and a round top. The previously mentioned wall paintings from the Agios Athanasios tomb show a symposium scene with both table types.

William Kendrick Pritchett, who studied the terminology for furniture used on the *Attic Stelai* mentioned above, concludes that furniture with costly ornamentation was not intended for private use in the Classical Greek period, not even among the rich. The remarkably low sums given for the furniture listed are taken to be a reflection of the modest demand for furniture at the time. Hellenistic furniture shows an increase in ornamentation and radiates an almost baroque charm. Hellenistic dining couches could include bronze fittings, and the headboards could be decorated with, for example, satyrs or maenads (both followers of the god Dionysus) or other Dionysiac figures or animals, such as mules with bunches of grapes on their heads. These, however, were real luxury items. In most houses only simple and functional furniture must have been in use.

Roman furniture

Until the late twentieth century, Roman furniture forms were considered to be adaptations and developments of Greek ones. As with many art forms, the Romans were indeed eclectic in terms of furniture types and decorations, but apart from forms borrowed from Greece, the furniture of the Italian peninsula developed in pre-Roman times was also of influence (Steingräber 1979). An example is a type of cylindrical wooden chair with a high back, of which Villanovan predecessors from the seventh century BCE have been found in Verucchio near Rimini in northern Italy, and which developed into a type of wickerwork or basketry chair that was popular in the Roman west. New, hitherto unknown furniture items were also introduced, of which the most remarkable is the cupboard for storing utensils of daily use. In Herculaneum, where many items of wooden furniture have been recovered due to the miraculous preservation of wood resulting from the eruption of Vesuvius in 79 CE, an advanced form of cupboard has been found, the top part of it containing a small house chapel (*aedicula*) (Plate 29).[26]

With the colonization of parts of the Italian peninsula by Greeks in the eighth century BCE, Greek culture had a profound influence on the native peoples and, later, the Romans as well. Only a few decades after the Greeks began to recline during *symposia*, this new fashion was also introduced in native Italian aristocratic circles. The most famous evidence, of a slightly later date, consists of painted depictions of reclining banqueters from Etruscan tombs, dating from the sixth through fourth centuries BCE. But from the start there were differences between the Italian representations and their Greek predecessors, for the Etruscan parties were not only about drinking but also eating, and they included women as well as men. In addition, the Etruscans incorporated their own furniture forms, which were arranged in a different setting from that of the Greeks. Roman furniture items are known from the fourth century onward, and these show many similarities to their Greek and Etruscan predecessors.

From the second century BCE onward, Roman literary sources mention the so-called *triclinia* or dining rooms, in which the furniture was also indicated with the term *triclinium* ("three couches"). In these rooms three rather large couches, each accommodating three persons, were placed. Those using these couches included the wife of the host and other freeborn women, who reclined obliquely with cushions under their left arms, having their right hands free for dinner and drinks. The form used was that of the Hellenistic couch, sometimes with rich adornments, but the Roman couches were much larger than their Hellenistic forerunners. The three couches were usually placed in an asymmetric arrangement along three walls at the back of a room, often around a figural floor mosaic or decorated square (*emblema*), leaving an open space at the center that could be used for entertainment (see Chapter 7). The outer two couches had curved armrests on their short sides, which prevented the mattresses from slipping off the ends when people were reclining on them. These so-called *fulcra* sometimes had decorative bronze fittings. The legs of these couches were often turned on the lathe or rendered in bronze in imitation of turning. In Pompeii, many houses had one or more dining rooms—if more, the additional rooms were used seasonally. Typically, a house had only one set of dining furniture, which was moved from one room to another when required. This type of dining couch was in use until at least the second century CE.

Later this form of dining couch disappeared, to be replaced by a new type, which was introduced initially in the first century CE, as shown by depictions in early Pompeian wall paintings, but gained in popularity from the second century onward. This couch, called the *stibadium* or *sigma*, was a semicircular piece of furniture that accommodated seven or eight reclining persons. The reason for replacing the traditional *triclinium* was probably the desire for more comfort: the new type of couch provided more room for the people reclining. At the center of both a *triclinium* and a *stibadium* or *sigma* stood only one table, adopted from the Hellenistic Greek type with a round top, but with typically Roman decoration on the upper parts of the legs—such as the heads of gods or real and mythical animals (panthers, lions, or griffins), or the bodies of dogs growing out of acanthus calyces and seemingly running upward with their front legs. Such a table could be used by all those present and was replaced between courses, allowing diners the opportunity to leave and enter the room, giving rise to the use of the same word for table and course in Latin: *mensa*. It seems, however, that not everyone always reclined during dinner, for some painted scenes of inns, found at Pompeii, and also reliefs indicate that one could eat seated on a bench or a stool. In late antiquity the old custom of sitting during meals was reintroduced. In certain areas of the ancient world, however, the custom of seated banqueters apparently never went away, as evidenced by the exceptional wall painting in the tomb of Kazanluk (modern-day Bulgaria), dated to the third century BCE (Plate 8).

Apart from couches for reclining during dinner, there were beds used for sleeping. The most important finds in this respect are the wooden examples found in Herculaneum and a number of depictions of persons sleeping on beds. These often show bed frames with turned legs and high boards attached to two or three sides, probably designed to provide protection against cold and damp and to keep mattresses in place. The wooden Herculaneum material also includes a cradle, supported on curved rockers. Apart from the items mentioned, the wooden furniture from Herculaneum contains several dining tables with round tops and animal legs, a stool and benches, and for storage, cupboards, a chest, and racks (Mols 1999). The latter were found mostly in shops and contained goods such as *amphorae*.

The Herculaneum material shows that in the furnishing of Roman houses there was a differentiation between public and private space, the first being only sparsely furnished with more luxurious show pieces, the latter with more and simpler items for daily use. The wood species most frequently used for the production of the Herculaneum furniture was silver fir, probably locally sourced, but for specific purposes other species were utilized. These include walnut (*Juglans*), which was used in a tabletop, and boxwood (*Buxus*) for a table leg. The Herculaneum cradle was made of oak (*Quercus*). Wooden couch legs made of beechwood (*Fagus*) have been found elsewhere. This is an indication that Roman woodworkers used mostly local timber, provided it was available in sufficient quantity; woods other than local species would have been chosen for particular applications. It also indicates that Roman cabinetmakers undoubtedly understood the specific properties of the wood species with which they worked.

A remarkable feature is the uniformity of furniture found in widely diverse regions of the Roman Empire. The reliefs on the famous sarcophagus of Simpelveld (near Maastricht in the Netherlands) show various items of furniture that had a distribution throughout the Empire, as other depictions and actual finds show (Plate 9). There are, however, regional exceptions, probably based on the use of locally available materials, such as the tables found in the area around Dorchester in Great Britain that were made of the locally sourced Kimmeridge shale or blackstone, an oil shale containing bitumen. In parts of northern Gallia and Germania, furthermore, many depictions of wickerwork chairs have been found on tombstones, indicating a local use of this type of seating furniture made of wickerwork over a wooden frame.

Recurring elements in Roman furniture are the use of framing with loose panels for couches, beds, and storage furniture, exemplified by many furniture items found in Herculaneum and in the couch and the cupboard depicted in the Simpelveld sarcophagus. As seen with ancient furniture as a whole, furniture forms and individual elements may be adopted from elsewhere and modified to suit the needs and aesthetics at hand—as for instance furniture legs in the shape of animal legs, a motif having its origin in Egypt and the Near East, but altered to become typically Greek and eventually Roman, later to be an early manifestation of neoclassicism in furniture.

CHAPTER FOUR

The Domestic Setting

VASSILIS PETRAKIS, BARBARA TSAKIRGIS,
DIMITRA ANDRIANOU, AND PLATON PETRIDIS

THE NEOLITHIC AND BRONZE AGES

Comfort and status

One might assume that "furniture" began to be produced as soon as permanent human settlements appeared around 10000 BCE (the Neolithic period). The relationship between the two, however, appears to be less than straightforward. Neolithic terracotta models and seated figurines imply the early use of furniture (Simpson 1995: 1647). Yet the extant archaeological record suggests a long time span between the beginning of the Neolithic and the date of the earliest known furniture items (3500–2500 BCE). The oldest extant pieces of furniture, however, betray remarkable sophistication, hardly representative of a craft in its formative stage. We may wonder, therefore, whether this lacuna reflects the accidental nature of archaeological recovery or whether the first furniture was invented and developed for elite use. We must also take into account inherent biases in our extant sources, which tend to show less interest in the lifestyle of common people, as well as in our research agendas, which tend to focus on large centers rather than peripheral settlements. Nonetheless, considering the universal human need for comfort, and despite the fact that it seemingly originates in cultural responses to this need, early furniture is hardly as ubiquitous as anticipated. Instead, it makes its first appearance in our record as a category of artifact embedded in strategies of power display (see Chapters 5, 6, 8, and 9).

Differing levels of comfort may themselves be indicators of social differentiation. If so, it becomes quite difficult to comprehend how furniture production could be restricted to the elite, if its use was so obviously advantageous to all levels of society. We may enhance our understanding of this seeming inconsistency if we consider that, while one's comfort is arguably in one's best interest, the definition of such optimum comfort is almost always culturally conditioned. The very existence of furniture as a distinct category of cultural artifacts, the types and styles of furniture preferred, or the values embedded in it may vary considerably across space and time. Is using furniture an objective, rational response to a universal and homogeneous need for comfort? Anatomical and ergonomic analyses that attempt to define "comfort" in the use of seats do not correspond to stylistic or cultural preferences about these types of furniture. To quote a well-known study, "people seem to respond more to their *ideas* about comfort than to their actual physical experience of it" (Cranz 1998: 113). Chair-making does not actually aim at whatever an anatomist or physician would consider as "comfortable"; rather, "the importance of social standing has distracted chair designers and users alike from the issue of designing for the welfare of the body" (Cranz 2000: 98).

The furniture used in each particular social and cultural context relates to a specific *habitus*: the way we have gotten used to specific postures, actions, attitudes, or behaviors with little or no "objective" or "rational" consideration. How and why the gradual popularization of furniture took place may still be imperfectly understood due to the paucity of evidence, but one may conjecture that elite lifestyle emulation by aspiring social groups played a significant part in the process, shaping one's concept of comfort.

Scarcely furnished?

The integration of certain furnishings into the built domestic space itself is a common feature in the early Neolithic throughout the Mediterranean and the Near East. The absence of actual wooden furniture at the Neolithic East Mound of Çatalhöyük in Central Anatolia (7100–5900 BCE), may suggest that plastered benches or wall niches fulfilled the function of tables, beds, or seats, although it remains impossible to conjecture whether these might have been substitutes for unavailable furniture or precursors of (movable) types that had not yet been developed (for the site of Çatalhöyük see Hodder 2020). Certain anthropomorphic terracotta figurines from the site give the impression of being seated on rudimentary stools, but the rendering of these is quite abstract. The corpulent appearance of some of them and their seemingly seated posture might suggest aged individuals (Nakamura and Meskell 2009), so plausibly suggestive of some relative status within contemporary cosmology. Individuals of high rank or ancestors are two theoretical possibilities.

Scarce finds of terracotta miniature models, such as the backed chairs and tables from Ovcharovo (northeastern Bulgaria; late fifth millennium

BCE; Bailey 2005: 26–7, fig. 2.1), have a very restricted distribution and are very controversial sources for the reconstruction of typical contemporary domestic furnishings. On the other hand, the late fourth-millennium BCE settlement of Skara Brae on Orkney, Scotland (Clarke and Sharples 1990) shows remarkable stone built (fixed) furniture (cupboards, shelves, storage facilities, beds) around central hearth installations. The uncommonly good preservation there is due to the durability of the material employed and can be indicative of what has perished beyond recognition in other cases. The problem of the elusive Neolithic furniture is unlikely to be resolved without extensive excavation in sites where preservation of organic remains would be very extensive. It is nonetheless interesting that waterlogged sites, such as the sixth- to fifth-millennium BCE lakeside settlement at Dispilio in northwestern Greece, have still yielded no certain evidence suggestive of the broad use of (at least movable) furniture, although misidentification of plain furniture parts for posts or beams should not be underestimated.

In general, ancient households were very sparsely furnished by modern standards (Figure 4.1). Especially in those areas where accessibility to raw materials and skill was limited (see Chapter 2), furniture was probably difficult or even impossible to obtain, as far as the largest part of the population was

FIGURE 4.1 Examples of ancient Egyptian domestic furniture, displaying the overall simplicity of these furnishings. Top left: wooden bed frame with zoomorphic (bovid) legs (Early Dynastic Period). Bottom left: tray table cut from a single piece of wood (Early Dynastic Period). Top right: simple stool with shaped legs and rush seat preserved more or less intact (New Kingdom, Eighteenth Dynasty). Bottom right: simple chair with straight legs (New Kingdom, Eighteenth Dynasty). Drawn by Vassilis Petrakis, after Baker 1966: figs. 7, 11, 216, 185. Courtesy of Vassilis Petrakis.

concerned. During the Bronze Age, the average Egyptian or Mesopotamian household contained a minimal number of items that we could perhaps classify as "furniture" and we may reasonably assume that most domestic needs in production, maintenance, or repair were satisfied by members of the family (presumably not full-time or specialized woodworkers, whose skills and expertise must have varied considerably).

Scarce chronologically and geographically literary references may be typical of the "minimal furnishing" attitude that was prevalent diachronically in the ancient world. The small room built for the prophet Elisha by the Shunnamite couple, for example, included a bed, a chair, a table, and a lamp (2 Kings 4:10). It might be considered typical of a fully furnished interior with all the comforts a rich non-elite household could reasonably hope to attain. A similar viewpoint is conveyed through the Athenian historian and political philosopher Xenophon's observation that the greed for silver is quite unlike his contemporary (first half of fourth century BCE) Athenian attitude toward furniture, "καὶ γὰρ δὴ ἔπιπλα μέν, ἐπειδὰν ἱκανά τις κτήσηται τῇ οἰκίᾳ, οὐ μάλα ἔτι προσωνοῦνται" (of which one never owns more once he has got enough for his house) (Xen., Vect. 4.7).

Even when a desire for display can be detected this is seldom expressed through interior furnishings. The Papyrus Lansing (Twentieth Dynasty, early eleventh century BCE), an ancient Egyptian anthology of texts outlining the advantages of being a professional scribe, is a good example. It describes a beautiful dwelling with reference mostly to its exterior, rather than its interior. In Akhenaten's capital at Tell El Amarna, ancient Akhetaten (Eighteenth Dynasty, mid-fourteenth century BCE), many wealthy residences are copiously adorned with gardens and granaries that effectively recreated aspects of rural life within an urban setting (Shaw 1992), with little or no interest in furniture.

When studying the structure and function of ancient domestic space, it is also important to bear in mind that the fixed, exclusive function of certain rooms within a residential building is a relatively recent phenomenon. The portability of most furniture and furnishings suggests that shifting the function of a room was feasible (and even fixed features, such as benches, could readily change function), while limited space meant that several indoor activities would have to be accommodated within the same areas, as is the norm in many recent traditional households. Modern ethnography has suggested that "multi-functional" areas or even continuous "rotation" of functions (and pertinent artifacts) within the building were the norm in many preindustrial households (cf. Dittemore 1983 on the village of Zemzemiye in northwest Turkey; Andrianou 2009: 8–10).

Finally, we should keep in mind that iconographic evidence, with its preference to represent rulers, heroes, or deities seated on thrones, stools, or couches, cannot be properly used to construct an understanding of average contemporary household furnishings. This visual material is strongly biased toward exceptionally embellished items fit for elite, royal, or even divine comfort in settings that are removed from what we might consider as residential or domestic. As such, imagery should be examined in its social context and function within any given society. We must be prepared to consider the representation of certain types and practices as suggestive of their existence; but we cannot readily proceed to make quantitative assessments about their relative popularity or scarcity on the basis of iconographic evidence alone (see also Chapter 8).

Furniture in early households

Egyptian evidence dominates most discussions of early furniture, not least because actual organic materials (mostly perishable elsewhere) have survived alongside ample documentation regarding the production and use of these items. We therefore know that private acquisition of furniture from expert woodworkers was subject to strict control, apparently a reflection of the paucity of raw material. Carpenter workshops worked to commissioned orders, which were agreed with each workshop's overseer and then passed on to the head of the workshop. As far as Middle and New Kingdom evidence suggests, the entire enterprise (as indeed most industrial production) functioned under the ultimate patronage of the *nomarch* (the governor of a district or nome). We should not overlook the fact that our reconstruction of Egyptian domestic furniture is dominated by images in wall paintings and actual finds from middle-class or elite tombs (see Chapters 6 and 8). Ordinary furniture is usually found in a highly fragmentary state in excavated Egyptian settlements, such as the worker's settlement at Deir el-Medîna, Medinet el-Ghurab (or Gurob), or the short-lived capital of Tell El Amarna (ancient Akhetaten, *c.* 1350–1335 BCE) (David 1997: 67, 92). At the Twelfth Dynasty workers' town at Kahun, evidence has been better preserved: seats (chairs or stools) prevailed, and were mostly very plain, such as stools made of single blocks of limestone or wood (Killen 1980: 37, plates 45–6; David 1997: 151, 166, fig. 13). Of course, as suggested by some *ostraca* (inscribed pottery sherds) from Deir el-Medîna marked with sketches of various furniture types (Killen and Weiss 2009), it must have been somehow possible to own furniture of independent production, suggesting direct private transactions between makers and customers without any discernible intervention of state authorities or control (Janssen 2009).

Provided that furniture was affordable, differences in the furniture associated with groups of various standings or ranks would be most obvious in the choice of materials and the skill employed. Beds were a relative luxury alternative to the much more widely employed reed mats or animal hides, often spread directly on the floor. Wooden bed frames must have been a feature of the middle and upper classes throughout ancient Egyptian history (Killen 1994b: 28). The proper elevation of the head was achieved through bed frames that either sloped toward the feet (where footboards were necessary) or were concave; a separate curved piece known as a "headrest" was used instead of a pillow, whose practical and symbolic function is still debated. Such refinements show that comfort (or at least contemporary ideas of it, see Cranz 1998; 2000) were a prime objective in furniture design. A bed from the artisan's village of Deir el-Medîna with plain undecorated legs (Killen 1980: plate 38) and the unique folding bedstead from Tutankhamun's tomb (undoubtedly a type used for the living ruler as well) with its ingenious folding mechanism exemplify well the two ends of a wide range of elaboration and expertise in New Kingdom furniture making. Stools (usually three- or four-legged) must have been one of the most popular items in all Egyptian households. Like chairs (which must have been difficult for the lower classes to afford), they were often used with cushions placed on their reed, leather, or planked seats. The table (usually rectangular and three-legged) is perhaps the one item that never became a significant component in ancient Egyptian non-elite households. It is interesting that the *theriomorphic* (mostly bovine and feline) legs of chairs or stools are not attested in tables (Killen 1980: 33), which were mostly small and intended for individual use. Indeed, we must imagine the average Egyptian squatted on the floor when dining; indeed, some of our earliest extant examples of tables (Tarkhan cemetery, First Dynasty, *c.* 3100–2890 BCE) are low to the ground, with projecting pads or supports rather than proper legs (Killen 1994b: 26, fig. 30). Certain possessions, such as clothes or food, could be kept in wooden boxes, chests, reed baskets, or ceramic containers. Household furniture is often mentioned among "woman's things" (*nkt.w n s.ḥm.t*): property items that the wife brought when the marital household was formed (Pestman 1961: 91–102).

Most ancient Mesopotamian households may have been similarly organized, although any projection of the Egyptian pattern onto the far less plentiful evidence from this region should be undertaken with caution. Archaeological finds suggest a more widespread use of reed-work and the existence of permanent mud-brick structures that replaced portable wooden furniture in Mesopotamia. The employment of reeds (almost never preserved) should not be underestimated as a mere cheap substitute: the statue of Ebikhil, a mid-third-millennium BCE official of the Temple of Ishtar at Mari, shows him seated on a cylindrical rush stool. Scarcity of timber, especially in southern Mesopotamia, must have led to alternative solutions, such as built-in benches and platforms substituting for beds, seats, or tables and niches in walls serving as cupboards, at least in most ordinary households. The little available space in most dwellings surely necessitated the use of even more perishable furnishings, such as rugs, mats, or cushions, continuing a practice prevalent as early as the Neolithic period. These features are still to be found in traditional households around the Mediterranean and in the Near East (Al-Gailani 1996; Crawford 1996), although stools or low tables are often also used.

Furniture becomes progressively more common in non-elite (but still wealthy) Mesopotamian households from the Late Ur III period (reign of Šulgi, *c.* 2030–1982 BCE) onward (e.g., the wooden bed frame in Woolley and Mallowan 1976: 25), as stools, beds, and tables from property inventories of middle-ranking officials of that date indicate (Crawford 1996: 38–9). In those wealthy Mesopotamian households that could acquire it, furniture was valued property. As such, it features consistently in Old Babylonian (early second millennium BCE) inventories of *šeriktum* "dowries" (usually fractions of the property of the bride's father) or as personal gifts from the husbands (*nudunnum*; cf. Assyrian *nundunû* "dowry"), and were also subject to the division of inherited property. Hittite dowries (*iwaru* gifts), in contrast, were thereafter part of the husband's household. These practices are in fact broadly attested in the Ancient Near East, whenever good-quality furniture was affordable. As an example, the dowry of Princess Šimātum, daughter of Zimri-Lim of Mari (mid-eighteenth century BCE) in present-day Syria included two beds, fifteen chairs, three stools, one table, and four service trays (Küpper 1983: no. 322). This gives a good idea of what "fully furnished" meant by the standards of a royal apartment of the time. As movable items, furniture pieces were also widely used as pledges (cf. Assyrian terms *errubātum* and *šapartum*), items that creditors usually kept in their possession until the debt was paid.

While the Hittite world has yielded no precise glimpses into domestic furniture, we are a bit better served by the depictions on an Urartian bronze belt (ninth to seventh century BCE) whose figural decoration illustrates a few main types of banquet furniture that one could perhaps find in a wealthy household: tables, couches, stools, and armchairs (Seidl 1996: 181–2, plate 54). This furniture shows clear Assyrian stylistic influences, and although its precise social setting is unknown, it can be presumed to represent one of the ideal modes of Urartian domestic behavior. As in Assyria (Curtis 1996: 180), we may have reason to suspect that furniture would have been limited outside elite or other display contexts, but we should be constantly reminded that we are dealing with evidence (both archaeological and iconographic) limited to such elite contexts.

Actual wooden furniture from second-millennium BCE Aegean households has not survived, but this lacuna is partly compensated for by imagery and administrative inventories, as well as by imitations of wooden furniture into stone (see Chapters 8 and 9). However, there are exceptions from the town excavated at Akrotiri on Thera (Cyclades). The site had been abandoned before a devastating volcanic eruption that covered it under layers of pumice and ash (the absolute chronology is debated: 1550–1500 or 1650–1600 BCE; see Doumas 1983 for an overview of Akrotiri). These exceptional taphonomic conditions mean that although organic matter has largely perished, imprints of artifacts such as wooden furniture have been left in a pumice "matrix." Their forms have been retrieved with remarkable accuracy by the skilled production of plaster casts, created by pouring liquid plaster-of-Paris (strengthened by stainless steel rods) into the hole left by the disintegrated wooden artifact, using the negative imprint as a mold (Gerontas 2004).

In particular, the building complex in sector Delta of Akrotiri alone has yielded more information on actual furniture than any other Aegean Bronze Age site. Along the south wall of Room Delta 2 (well known for its so-called "Spring Fresco," found almost entirely in situ and depicting swooping swallows, alone or in pairs, above blossomed lilies springing amidst a rocky volcanic landscape) a bed or couch and a fragment of a four-legged stool were found (Marinatos 1971: 41–2, plates 34–6, 102–5); an elaborate small, round, three-legged table was similarly retrieved from the floor of Room Delta 1 (Doumas 1983: 116, fig. 18, plate 84) (Figure 4.2). From the area to the west of Rooms Delta 15 and 16, the appropriately dubbed "Terrace of the Beds," three more beds or couches were found in an open area, almost piled over the debris of the earthquake destruction that preceded the eruption (Doumas 1993: 178–80, fig. 6, plates 104β-106), probably as a measure to rescue them, an attempt that apparently was in vain (Figure 4.3). The preservation of the rope netting of one of the beds, which was salvaged from obscurity through skillful field conservation, is quite remarkable (Doumas 1993: 178, plate 105β; Gerontas 2004: figs. 12–16). A similar incidence of two beds piled on a terrace has been recovered near the southeast corner of Sector Alpha (Doumas 1999: 195, plate 137β; 2000: 172, plates 122β, 124). Perhaps the most impressive finds of all are the two three-legged tables found upside down on what appears to be a bench in Room Delta 18, with sculpted decoration and (presumably) ivory fittings whose arrangement was unfortunately not preserved intact (Doumas 1993: 182–3, plates 111–12α; Polychronakou-Sgouritsa 2001: 136–7, figs. 2–3). The elegant, probably carved, legs of these tables have "crockets" or swag-like decoration, recalling the legs of the Knossos "throne" (see Chapters 2 and 5). Other furniture recovered from this small room at various depths included two four-legged stools and part of an elaborate chair back (Doumas 1993: 182, plate 112β; 1994: 162, plates 90α, 92α; Polychronakou-Sgouritsa 2001: 137–8, fig. 4). The overall picture suggests that assorted household furnishings had been stored in this room and, after the eruption, ended up floating in the pumice-mud that filled Delta 18 (like other areas in the same complex) following the rainfalls that created the stream crossing the site ever since (Doumas 1994: 162). The architectural elaboration, exotica (ostrich eggs fashioned into *rhyta*, vessels with a second small opening used primarily for libations), and evidence for administrative activities (fragments of clay tablets and sealings, the former inscribed in the Minoan Linear A script from room Delta 18) from complex Delta all indicate

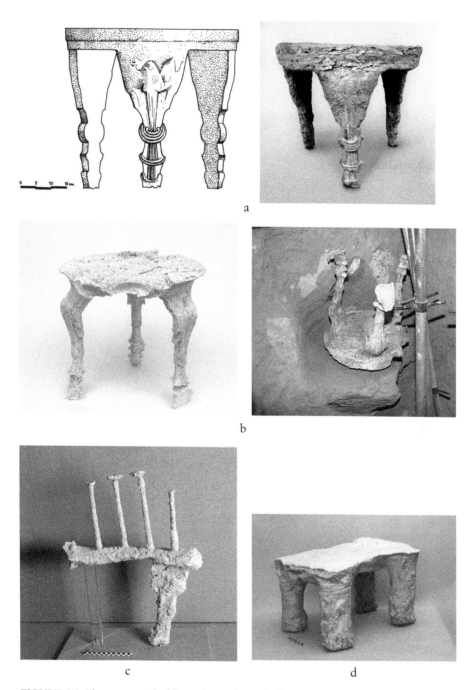

FIGURE 4.2 Plaster casts of tables and seats from the Bronze Age Aegean town at Akrotiri on Thera (Cyclades, Greece). (a) Tripod table from Room Delta 1. *Source:* Doumas 1983: fig. 18, plate 84). (b) Tripod table from Room Delta 18α. (c) Backrest of chair from Room Delta 18α. (d) Four-legged stool from Room Delta 18α. Photographs courtesy of Professor Christos Doumas and the Thera excavations of the Athens Archaeological Society.

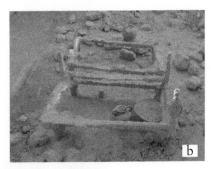

FIGURE 4.3 Plaster casts of beds from the Bronze Age Aegean town at Akrotiri on Thera (Cyclades, Greece). (a-b) Beds recovered "piled" in the open area to the west of Rooms Delta 15 and 16 in the Bronze Age settlement of Akrotiri on Thera (Santorini). (c) Finds recovered during the 1999–2000 excavations for the new shelter. Photographs courtesy of Professor Christos Doumas and the Thera excavations of the Athens Archaeological Society.

the elite functions of this building (cf. Polychronakou-Sgouritsa 2008: 163–4). Its preserved furniture, therefore, provides a good idea of at least the upper echelon of Late Bronze Age Aegean standards of furnishing.

Nevertheless, the state of preservation at Akrotiri is exceptional. Throughout the Bronze and Early Iron Ages Aegean domestic furniture is mostly known through imagery. The Greek Dark Ages are quite aptly named when it comes to household furniture. Most of our conjectures on this topic are based on the silhouettes of stools or beds in scenes of aristocratic funerals on Attic eighth-century BCE painted pottery, terracotta models of furniture or seated figures, and exceptional recent finds, such as the terracotta model from Nikoleika (Ancient Helike, Achaea) (see Chapters 6 and 8). The few and sporadic actual finds, such as the stools from the Heraion on Samos, are associated with what we would call "elite" contexts, many intended for display (see Chapters 5 and 6).

FROM THE ARCHAIC TO THE HELLENISTIC PERIOD

The Greek house from the Archaic to the Hellenistic periods was informed by social interactions and furniture as an essential element of social accommodation (Nordblah 2013: 426). While it is a truism that there was not much furniture in a Greek house (Richter 1966: 3), an examination of the evidence reveals a variety of furnishings, many utilitarian but also some items of luxury. Despite the paucity of surviving ancient material, sources suggest that furniture was used in certain Classical and Hellenistic houses not simply for functional accommodation but also as expressions of wealth and taste.

Because the written evidence stems primarily from Athens, the focus on the Archaic and Classical periods is largely on Athenian domestic material in the following section. Wherever possible, household furniture elsewhere in Greece is also presented. While representations of furniture are fewer in later periods, greater material evidence survives from Hellenistic houses.

Sources

Two important sources of information are applicable in our discussion of the Greek house and its furniture. First are inscriptions that provide valuable information about Classical Greek houses and their domestic economy. Of particular relevance are the *Attic Stelai* (*IG* I³ 421–430), ten inscribed slabs erected in the Athenian City Eleusinion, a temple to Demeter, to recognize the mutilation of the door guardians (the Herms) in 415 BCE (Pritchett 1953, 1956; Lewis 1966; Andrianou 2009: 12–13). As punishment for the crime, all of the real and movable property of the convicted men was confiscated and sold at auction. The stelai thus record valuable information (vocabulary of furniture types and prices) about the furniture owned by those wealthy Athenians. About twenty names (owners) are mentioned in the texts, but it has been suggested that the property might have belonged to as many as fifty people.

The second type of source consists of scenes painted on vases and sculpted on grave markers, which frequently depict domestic furniture (Boardman 1990: 127). Interpreting these scenes comes with its own cautionary note: never did the representations on the vessels include all elements of the setting in which an activity took place. Thus, we are left to interpret the few and sometimes enigmatic elements, including furniture, chosen for depiction by the artists.

Domestic architecture and furniture

A brief exploration of the Greek house is in order before examining its furniture. Houses of the Archaic and Classical periods were fairly small (e.g., at Olynthos

296 square meters; Cahill 2002: 75). From the sixth century BCE, many houses were organized around a central unroofed courtyard, which provided illumination, ventilation, and access to the surrounding rooms. The courtyard accounted for a significant percentage of the overall plan (Cahill 2002: 78), thus there was not much room for the accumulation of furniture. Seasonal rains would also have made the courtyard unsuitable for wooden furniture. In the Late Classical period, the courtyard was often enhanced with covered porticoes, thus providing protected spaces for any furnishings.

The Greek domestic environment was characterized by the flexible use of space as few rooms were given permanent fixtures that determined use (Jameson 1990). This flexibility also applies to several items of furniture, especially the *kline* (κλίνη), which could be used as a dining couch, a bed for sleeping, or a bier for the deceased. Flexibility was probably a factor for understanding the covered porticoes. During the day these well-ventilated spaces could be used for many different activities and during the hot summer months they may even have served as sleeping areas. Most interior doorways of houses were around one meter wide, sufficient for the easy removal of furniture from a room to the portico.

The grandest room in both scale and decoration in most Classical houses was usually the *andron* where the householder entertained male guests, although not all Classical houses had such a room (Parakenings 1989). While a *heptaklinos andron* (with seven couches, Phrynichos, frag. 66, line 1; Dunbabin 1998: 83) was the norm, *androness* of differing sizes have been recognized, from the small three-couch to the large eleven-couch *andron*. In the Classical period the couches stood on a low (3-cm high) platform whose width, 0.85 meter to 1 meter at Olynthos (Cahill 2002: 180), provides a limit for determining the dimensions of the dining couches. Its height ensured that the expensive furniture would not become wet, either by spilled wine or by water used to clean the floor. The couches were placed at the periphery of the room so that the guests could appreciate the interior decoration, especially the mosaics regularly laid in the center of the floor. The *andron* was usually the most elaborate room in the house, with permanent pavements and painted walls; the furniture and textiles would have been part of a larger decorative ensemble (Andrianou 2021).

In the Hellenistic period the platforms are absent from reception rooms, perhaps because varied arrangements of couches were preferred; the continued use of the platforms would have limited flexibility in arranging the *klinai*. Other cues in the decoration of rooms, however, indicate where couches were placed, probably to be used as beds. Mosaic panels, laid as rugs, decorate some floors and colonnettes designate the location of *klinai* in Hellenistic bedrooms (e.g., room 2, Pappalardo House, Morgantina; Tsakirgis forthcoming). To allow this architectural accommodation of furniture, there must have been some standardization in sizing, with beds regularly no more than 1 meter in width and 1.80 to 1.90 meters in length (Dunbabin 1998: 83).

Niches and built platforms served as shelves and work tables in many houses (e.g., Delos; Trümper 1998: 68–76). The preservation of niches is limited to houses built with stone walls. These installations were space efficient and were not made of the costly materials used in furniture construction. By leaving voids in a wall, builders could provide a place for storage or display. Low platforms have been recognized in workrooms (e.g., room 3, House of the Palmento, Morgantina; Tsakirgis forthcoming) and probably served as places for domestic tasks.

Domestic furniture and social activity in the house

There are many variables in the discussion of Greek domestic furniture, including the period under examination, the parts of Greece from which evidence survives, and especially the socioeconomic standing of the householder. It goes without saying that neither would every house have every piece of furniture nor would all of the pieces of furniture discussed here be used in every period. The general evolution of domestic furnishing was an increase in the number of pieces from the Archaic to the Hellenistic periods, to equip the ever-expanding size of the house (Westgate 2015). Not everyone could afford numerous pieces of furniture or houses large enough to accommodate many items. Thus, this examination covers all the furniture available to a Greek householder from the Early Archaic through Late Hellenistic periods.

Symposium   The finest pieces of furniture were crafted for the symposium, the male drinking party (Lynch 2015). *Symposia* did not take place every day and some householders probably did not have the means to conduct the symposium very often, if at all. The host of a symposium needed not only wine but also the furnishings to make the drinkers comfortable. While some houses contained an *andron*, many did not. This lack of a dedicated architectural setting was no impediment to holding the symposium, as the host needed simply guests and wine to serve them. In simpler households, the drinkers might have reclined on the ground (Lynch 2007).

The symposium ensemble of furniture included a couch and table for each guest or pair of guests (Boardman 1990: 124), as shown on the late fourth-century BCE symposium scene from the wall painting of the Macedonian tomb of Agios Athanasios at Thessaloniki (Plate 10). Plato (*Resp.* 373a) seems to say that couches and tables were the primary equipment needed for a civilized life, thus signaling how important the symposium was for Greek culture (Burnyeat 1999: 231). Vase painters agreed and the couch appears most often in Athenian art as symposium furniture. Symposiasts reclined on their left side on their *klinai* to hold their cups or food with their right hand. The couches were often laid with elaborate cushions that both adorned the *andron* and made the wooden furniture and thin mattresses more comfortable. Since textiles rarely survive in the archaeological record, we do not have physical evidence to compare their painted versions with the rest of the domestic decorative ensemble in the dining rooms.

Because many vases painted with scenes of drinking were apparently used at the symposium, the couch is the type of domestic furnishing most often depicted in Greek art (Ransom 1905; Richter 1966: 52–62). The word κλίνη derives from the verb for what one does on a couch, to recline. While another type of couch, the *chameuna*, was low in height, it was not lowly in form. The example noted on the *Attic Stelai* (*IG* I³ 421, 231, see above) was modified by the adjective *parakollos* (inlaid) and fetched a high price, so was probably a luxury item (for the ancient vocabulary on beds, see Andrianou 2009: 31–4). "Milesian" and "Chian" beds mentioned on the inscriptions were also sold at a high price in the auction and were likely purchased to impress guests (Andrianou 2009: 32–4). It is, however, impossible to say with any degree of certainty whether these 'brand-names' refer to the location of the beds' production, to their style, or to the origin of their artists (from Miletos and Chios, respectively).

In symposium scenes *klinai* appear as two different types with the fashioning of the legs distinguishing between them (Kyrieleis 1969; Baughan 2013: 44–58). The legs on Type A couches are round in section and appear to have been turned on a lathe. The legs of Type B couches have a square section, sometimes unadorned, but often represented with volute capitals and cut-out palmettes, forms borrowed from the repertoire of architectural decoration. In Classical vase painting, the *klinai* usually appear to have no head- or footboard, although the piles of cushions supporting the drinkers in many scenes may be obscuring a low headboard. Aristophanes (*Ecclesiazusae* line 907) writes of a couch with an elbow rest (ἐπίκλιντρον) and just such a couch was amongst the furnishings recorded on the *Attic Stelai* (*IG* I³ 422, 235–6; *IG* I³ 425, 14). Another couch sold at the auction had "two heads," perhaps an item with both a head- and footboard, or one double in width and thus able to accommodate pillows side by side.

Surviving examples of wooden couches are rare. While Homer (*Od.* 23. 190–2) recounts that Odysseus crafted his bed from an olive tree, this wood does not lend itself to furniture construction. Wood was very expensive in Classical Athens as proven by the *Attic Stelai*, inscriptions that record the sale or lease of houses (ὠναί), and certain texts (Lys. 19.30–1). Fragments of a wooden couch (W 23), including two legs and parts of the crossbars, were found in a well (Deposit R 21:3) located near the Athenian Agora (Shear 1940: 270).

The well was probably domestic and its contents date the fragments to the late sixth century BCE. A dendrochronological analysis determined that the wood is juniper, possibly originating in Asia Minor (Kuniholm and Striker 1983: 417), thus giving evidence of imported domestic furniture. Although the legs are incomplete, they preserve traces of turning and some of the sockets that were once part of the system of fastening. On a few vases, painters rendered wood grain on the symposiasts' couches (Apulian dinos, NY MET 14.130.13), although the depiction is too impressionistic for the species of wood to be recognizable (Baughan 2013: 27). By comparison, several woods (ash, chestnut, and walnut) were used in the *fulcra* of couches in the Antikythera wreck (the famous Roman shipwreck with the portable astronomical calculator dated to the first century BCE; Palaiokrassa 2012: 118). Traces of wood have also been recovered in furniture fragments from houses of Delos (Siebert 1976: 813; Andrianou 2010: 595) and in fragments now in museums (such as the Hellenistic bronze bed now in the Antikenmuseum of Basel, Switzerland; Seiterle and Mutz 1982: 62).

Elements of bronze *klinai* recovered from across the Mediterranean world are evidence of the Hellenistic domestic luxury that included mosaic floors, painted wall plaster, and sculpture (Kreeb 1988; Walter-Karydi 1994). The beds usually have a backrest (*fulcrum*) that ends in a protome representing an animal head (Faust 1989; Andrianou 2006: 35–8). The attachment of the elegantly curved piece to the main frame is masked by a relief medallion, commonly depicting a mythological character (Barr-Sharrar 1987, 1988). At Pella in Macedonia, two bronze *fulcra* were recovered from houses and bear a Dionysiac head medallion and an animal protome, a horse, and a mule (Oikonomos 1926; Makaronas 1961–2: 209; Andrianou 2009: 38) (Plate 11). At Priene, fragments of bronze couches were found in at least three houses (houses 8, 14, 17; Wiegand and Schräder 1904: 378–83). The legs are fashioned to imitate the turned wooden legs of earlier couches and the high tensile strength of the bronze allowed for a delicate profile. Sections of the bronze legs of *klinai* as well as a *fulcrum* were discovered in the Late Hellenistic houses on Delos (Déonna 1938: 2; Siebert 1973: 568–75; Andrianou 2010: 595). Pliny's testimony for Delos as a place of manufacture is thus far not supported by large numbers of *klinai* finds on the island (Andrianou 2009: 33). On the other hand, the island was devastated and looted twice (in 88 BCE by Mithridates King of Pontos, who was at war with the Romans, and again in 69 BCE by the pirates of Athenodoros, an ally of Mithridates). This unfortunate situation is also probably responsible for the paucity of evidence. Shipwrecks at Antikythera (between Kythera and Crete) and Mahdia (off the coast of Tunisia) included numerous examples of bronze *klinai* (Fuchs 1963: 28–34; Barr-Sharrar 1985, 1994; Faust 1994; Palaiokrassa 2012) that accord well with the examples found in houses, possibly destined for wealthy villas around the Mediterranean.

The subjects chosen for the decoration of the *klinai* (busts, protomes, and inlay on the *fulcra*) were highly appropriate for the male drinking party, with much of the imagery evoking the world of Dionysos (Lilimbaki-Akamati 1979). Thus an ivory inlay depicting a Silen head (BI 762) was recovered from a domestic cistern (Deposit O 17:5) in Athens and assumed to have belonged to the fulcrum of a couch (Hill 1963). The busts and inlays of satyrs and Dionysos himself are overt evocations of the god's realm, regularly appearing in the mosaics that adorn the late Classical and Hellenistic *andron*. The protomes of horses represent the usual mounts for the drinkers; the mules and donkeys represent the mounts for the entourage of Dionysos. Dogs depicted on protomes were companions for the men who found amusement in hunting; Artemis' appearance in this setting might also be a reference to the hunt. Thus the overall effect of furniture and pavements would have been that of a decorative ensemble.

The three-legged table that held cups and food also belonged to the equipment for the symposium (Alkman, frag. 19). For example, the so-called Pan Painter (*c.* 480 BCE) decorated a red-figured *pelike* (jar) with a couch and table being carried on the back of a nude youth, during either the preparations for or the clean-up after a drinking party (*ARV*² 555, no. 87). Tabletops were lower than the bottom of the mattress, as Kathleen Lynch (2015: 236) has recognized, to allow the drinker to set down his stemmed *kylix* (wine-drinking cup) easily on the table. Some of these tables may have been wooden, but the delicate forms often terminating in animal feet might have been rendered in metal, just as the miniature tables from the Sindos tombs were (Σίνδος 1985; Despoini 2016: vol. 3:252–9). The light, small tables would have been easily moved after a party so that the *andron* could be cleaned of dropped food and spilled wine.

Footstools appear below the dining couches less frequently in scenes of the symposium (e.g., BM 1843. 1103.99). Footstools more commonly accompany a seated figure. In life they may have enabled symposiasts to mount the couches or to dismount easily after the drinking was concluded. Footstools for *symposia* are low and unlike those represented in scenes of everyday life. Often the footstools are rendered with graceful legs that curve outward on their lower end, a decorative effect that would also have provided stability.

Bedrooms   In wealthy households, the same *klinai* used during the symposium probably served for sleeping and as the setting for sexual intercourse. Marital beds are sometimes glimpsed in wedding scenes and appear to be no different from those in the symposium (Oakley and Sinos 1993: 35–6). Like the *klinai* of the symposium, the marital beds are strewn with linens with elaborately woven patterns (for further evidence on bedclothes, see Andrianou 2009: 96–8; 2021 and Chapter 6 in this volume).

Many beds were, however, probably mere pallets on the floor, fashioned of straw rather than the more expensive wood. An easily folded mattress allowed for free passage during the day in spaces designated for sleeping at night. Rooms intended to serve only as bedrooms are not easily recognizable in Classical houses and the flexibility in the use of space seen elsewhere in the household might pertain to these rooms as well. In larger Hellenistic houses, rooms dedicated solely as bedrooms become more common. In the houses at Morgantina, Sicily, for example, there were at least two such rooms containing half columns to frame the bed (Pappalardo House room 3; House of the Tuscan Capitals room 6; Tsakirgis forthcoming). Room 4, a third small room of the House of the Doric Capital, was provided in its late Hellenistic phase with a light wall of brick to screen the bed from the doorway. Gouges on the wall plaster are probably ancient and reveal where the bed scraped the wall.

Relaxation and everyday life   Daily life in the Greek house is not detailed in any text. Most of the furniture that served regular household activities was less expensive than that used for entertaining guests. Greek women spent much of their lives in the house, separate from men unrelated to them (Nevett 1999: 15–17). Scenes of women seated in the presence of their infant children and slaves might be some of the more reliable pictures of family life. In many such representations, the mother sits on the *klismos*, a chair with a curved backrest and gently flaring legs (see, for instance, the red-figured hydria, BM 1873.0820.350, and the red-figured hydria, circle of Polygnotos Painter, Harvard 1960.342). Both women and men use this chair in many settings. Its supportive back promised comfort to the sitter and was thus desirable for those engaged in household tasks.

Two types of stools appear as seats in paintings of domestic scenes, those with straight, fixed legs; and folding stools with hinged legs. The former is usually referred to by the term *diphros*. The legs of this stool often have a convex curve at the top, suggesting that they were crafted of turned wood. The folding stools were eminently suited to the restricted spaces within the Greek house; they could be folded and stored when not in use, to free floor space for other activities. Folding stools appear frequently in scenes of domestic life on black-figure vases, painted in the Late Archaic period when houses were smaller. Women often sit on folding stools in scenes of spinning and weaving. Looms could be dismantled and stored when not in use, perhaps along with the stools. Women using the *epinetron* (a vessel placed over the woman's thigh for protection during the preparation of wool for weaving) to create rovings of wool are sometimes shown resting an outstretched leg on an unusual low support shaped like the Greek letter Λ or with a toe rest. Jenifer Neils (in a personal communication) has suggested that this stool was the *onos,* a word sometimes confused with the *epinetron.*

Another special seat particular to women was the birthing stool. Soranus of Ephesus in his *Gynecology* (2.3.20), a treatise on women's health, called this a *diphros* but specified that it should be constructed with solid walls on either side, rather than legs, and an open front or back. The stool was also fashioned with a semicircular cut-out so that the newborn child could descend unimpeded from the mother crouching on the stool. Iconography of the birthing stool was not established in Greek art, but a Roman relief (Tomb 100 at the Isola Sacra, Ostia) has been recognized as the closest depiction of Soranus' specifications (French 1987: 74–6).

Marble furniture was increasingly favored in late Hellenistic houses. The stone was chosen for its lavishness and attractiveness, marble furnishings being an expression of domestic luxury. Stone furniture often sat outdoors in the courtyard where wood would have been vulnerable to the elements. Tables in particular were crafted of marble and many of the elaborately carved ones have an almost sculptural quality, demonstrating their additional role as decorative objects. Numerous examples were recovered in the Hellenistic houses on Delos (Déonna 1938: 24–60; Andrianou 2009: 51–3). The legs of many of these tables terminate in animal paws, perhaps the model for the less expensive terracotta examples found in other Hellenistic houses, for example, Morgantina, Sicily (Tsakirgis forthcoming). These animal paws echo the feet of earlier wooden furnishings (Kopcke 1967: 127–9; Kratinos, *ap.* Athenaeus, *Deipn.* 2.49a) and those seen on the painted stelai from Pagasai (Arvanitopoulos 1928).

In paintings and on votive plaques, chests and boxes appear almost exclusively with women who open them perhaps to place linens within or to indicate generic household activities (Richter 1965; Oakley 2004: 33–57; Andrianou 2009: 65–7). In funerary scenes, smaller boxes are held by a servant. These appear to have been jewelry boxes, like that offered to Hegeso on her grave stele (National Archaeological Museum of Athens, no. 3624). The containers are rendered with horizontal lines, indicating that they were made from planks of wood. Wooden chests have not survived in the archaeological record, but the bone revetments consisting of three figures, possibly from a symposion scene, were recovered from a house in Kallipolis (Themelis 1979: 263; Andrianou 2009: 67, no. 60). Small metal boxes, like that held out to Hegeso, have been found at a few sites, including a bronze example from Eretria (Reber 1998: 84; Andrianou 2009: 67, no. 61). The size of the Eretrian box suggests that it was used for storing small valuables such as jewelry or coins.

Although the word *kylikeion* exists for a cabinet to hold pottery (see Chapter 9), there has been discussion as to whether the Greeks actually possessed such an item of furniture (Richter 1957). No definite archaeological example has been preserved, but the architectural feature of a large niche with or without stucco is usually termed as the area of a cupboard. For example, in cases such as the House of the Seals on Delos (Plate 12) and room 5 in the area of Toumba Thessalonikis, a large number of everyday vessels and carbonized wood were found in situ, something that may suggest the existence of an open cupboard (Andrianou 2009: 82–3). Portable *kylikeia* are known through the Hellenistic funerary banquet reliefs from the northeastern Aegean (especially Samos) and Asia Minor (Fabricius 1999). Many Classical vase paintings depict vessels hanging on the wall behind drinkers, a space-efficient way to store pottery (Rotroff 1999). It is unclear, though, whether this is an attempt to render the architecture of the room or to identify the activity in the scene. The decoration painted on the exterior of vessels would have been effectively displayed if thus hung on a wall; however, the deeper and stouter vessels were more suited to resting on a shelf. In his analysis of the distribution of finds in several Olynthian houses, Nicholas Cahill (2002) posits disintegrated wooden shelving. In the archaeological record shelves are usually inferred by either the nails that once secured them on the walls or the heap of objects fallen on the ground, originally stored on shelves (Andrianou 2009: 84). In Herculaneum four racks have survived in shops attached to the walls and more examples have been unearthed at Pompeii (Mols 1999: 62).

Storing textiles with citrus wood inside boxes (κιβωτοί) is also attested in Aristophanes in a nice metaphor: "Make their ideas your own, keep them in your boxes like sweet-scented fruit. If you do, your clothing will emit an odour of wisdom the whole year through" (*Vesp.* 1056; O'Neil's translation).

Death and prothesis   At the end of life, the *klinai* again supported the human body, this time as the funeral bier. The preparation of the body and the mourning of the deceased were conducted at home and from as early as the eighth century BCE, scenes of the wake (*prothesis*) abound on funerary vessels. The body is laid on a couch, very like those in the representations of the symposium and the marital chamber. While John Boardman (1990) suggested that the funeral couch was a different piece of furniture from the symposium couch or bed for sleeping, in fact it was very likely the same piece. The expense of the wood and the limited area in a house make it unlikely that there was space to store a funeral couch for very occasional use.

ROMAN AND EARLY BYZANTINE PERIODS

The evidence for the furniture of late Imperial Roman and early Byzantine houses (between the third and seventh centuries CE) is very scarce, as is to be expected considering the perishability of materials and the systematic recycling of the most valuable ones. However, the artistic production of the period and especially the numerous texts that have come down to us help to fill this gap.

The Romans adopted the more ornate forms current in Hellenistic furniture. Furniture had been transformed early on and especially from the Hellenistic period onward from a simple utilitarian object into a means of display of the social and financial status of the owner. Due to the new and safer roads built during the Roman period, the ease of acquisition of rare materials, regardless of their cost, contributed on the one hand to the homogenization of taste and on the other to increasing pretentiousness. Uniformity of form and decoration is typical of the furniture one would find in wealthy Roman and Byzantine houses, regardless of the region, revealing the standardization in several sectors of private life across the Empire. This need for display and luxury was inherited by the early Byzantines from the Romans, and was obvious in the choice of materials, the elaborate manufacture of the furniture, and the rich ornamentation of the upholstery.

The remains of secular and especially of domestic architecture are minimal compared with those of ecclesiastical architecture. In addition, when referring to domestic architecture we are dealing mainly with examples of rich houses with a clear distinction between their spaces, a fact that demanded different kinds of furniture depending on the use of a particular room or chamber. Spaces were distinguished between those used for socializing, including the reception of guests and hosting of banquets, to the more private ones, such as the bedrooms or the rooms where the women and the children of the household dwelled. The former contributed to the creation of a prestigious image of the owners and for this reason special care was given to their decoration and furniture. However, the concept of "privacy" should not be perceived in the same way as it is today, as the presence of servants was constant in all rooms and also the upper classes made intense social use of their private abodes (Bonini 2006: 67). Although the distinction between private and public rooms as well as specifically gendered spaces have been disputed by modern research (Allison 2006: 347, 348), we can nevertheless usually assume that the front or central part of a late Roman or early Byzantine house was dedicated to the reception of guests and socializing, while (in the absence of a second floor) the back or flanking sides were used for household purposes and family life. A good example is illustrated by the fifth- to sixth-century CE southeastern Villa at Delphi, where two of the reception rooms are in the front of the house, at the ground floor (A 2/3 and C 31/32), and another one at the center of the first floor (C 4 in Déroche, Pétridis, and Badie 2014: plates 8, 9). On the island of Thasos, the main apsidal reception room (PCE 13) of the contemporary urban villa (DOM 5) is situated in front of a possible central courtyard, while another reception room paved with mosaics (PCE 21) was close to the west façade (Blondé et al. 2014: fig. 1). Household activities could vary greatly, depending on the form and size of the house. According to the sources and in the case of houses with more than one floor, the bedrooms were situated on the upper floor or floors, while the guests' reception and dining rooms were almost always on the ground floor.

In the wealthy late Roman and early Byzantine houses, the main reception areas were called *triclinia* and their origins can be traced back to the Hellenistic *androns*. A rich house would have more than one *triclinia* for use by individuals of different sexes (*triclinium matronalis* for women) or in different seasons of the year depending on their orientation (*triclinium hiemale* for winter) (Petridis 2008: 250). With the exception of the *triclinium matronalis*, where loom-weights and objects related to spinning, weaving, or embroidery are expected to be found in excavations, all the other kinds of *triclinia* shared the same type of furniture, as explained below. The *triclinia* were distinguished from the other rooms by their size and the wealth of their decoration (Koukoulès 1951: 296–307). Their floors were laid with tiles or mosaics and the walls were either covered with marble slabs on their lower parts or, very often, an imitation of marble made by colored mortars or figurative mural paintings. The flat ceilings, made of cypress or cedar wood, were decorated with caissons (series of sunken panels set into a flat ceiling) or covered with ceiling paintings, sculptured and inlaid decoration made of ivory or even gold plated (Koukoulès 1951: 298–9). Rectangular in plan, the *triclinia* very often formed a semicircular apse at the narrow side situated in front of the entrance into which niches were often built (Déroche, Pétridis, and Badie 1995: 650, fig. 5; Bonini 2006: figs. 48–54 and 173).

In the center of the often slightly elevated apse stood the banquet table (*mensa*, τράπεζα) for the owner of the house and the most distinguished of the guests; the table (mensa, τράπεζα), usually of a C-shape (a "sigma table"), had a marble surface bearing very often carving to facilitate the installation of dishes and plates (Frantz 1988: fig. 72a). The banquet table could also be circular or rectangular. A circular table provided the possibility for all persons to be seated as equals in status (Koukoulès 1952: 141, 190). As far as materials were concerned, apart from its marble surface this table could be made of wood, marble, or metal (gold, bronze, or more often, silver) (Asterius of Amasea, *PG* 40, 209, 276; John Chrysostom, *PG* 57, 289; Gregory of Nyssa, *PG* 46, 468). The metal table could have relief decoration or engravings.

The most popular woods used for furniture were pine, elm, olive, ash, ilex (holly), oak, beech, maple, and the most expensive, citron. The furniture of wealthy Romans and Byzantines incorporated veneers, plating, and inlays (Richter 1966: 97, 122–3). Not only could veneers offer a much richer and more decorative effect than solid timber, but some types of timber, such as ebony and terebinth, were so expensive that they could only be employed as veneers. For inlay work, metals, precious stones, and organic materials such as ivory, bone, tortoiseshell, and mother-of-pearl were utilized. Ivory was used not only for inlaid decoration but sometimes for the creation of compact table feet. In addition, more common and cheaper types of wood could be painted to imitate the veins and grain of more precious varieties.

For more formal occasions wooden tables were covered with expensive tablecloths (μενσάλια or μινσάλια) with golden embroidery (John Chrysostom, *PG* 58, 509) or even embellished with precious stones, cabochons, and large pieces of chased metal. Around the C-shaped table wooden, portable, and possibly folding reclining seats or couches (κλιντῆρες) were arranged radially. This arrangement enabled diners to eat leaning their elbow on a long cylindrical cushion, the *stibadium* (see, for instance, the manuscript of Virgil's *Aeneid*, *Vat. lat.* 3867, f. 100v). The couches could be made of precious metals (e.g., silver) or gold and silver plated. There are cases where the set-up of the couches around a C-shaped table is reflected with precision on the mosaic floor underneath (see, for instance, Åkerström-Hougen 1974: 18, fig. 5; 117, fig. 74).

Couches were arranged not only in the apse but also along the long sides of the *triclinia* where the guests reclined to eat on circular or rectangular, stable or folding, wooden, metal, or marble tables, set-up in front of them. Those tables were rectangular with three or four legs or round with three, generally animal-shaped legs. The legs of the marble or metal tables were often richly ornamented with figures. Monopode tables of marble or metal (or both) resting on an animal or human figure, were also in use (Richter 1966: 110–13). Masonry couches could be built along the walls as well, although these are found mainly in outdoor *triclinia* of the Roman period (De Carolis 2007: 63, 66). Wooden movable benches were also in use but the habit of reclining during meals survived approximately until the tenth century CE. After the tenth century tables became rectangular and diners did not lie down during meals, with the exception of certain official occasions, for instance, the receptions held at the *Triclinos of the Nineteen Couches* in the Imperial Palace of Constantinople (Koukoulès 1952: 168).

To save space, folding furniture was preferred and was probably stored in the rooms surrounding the *triclinia*. The niches occurring in the walls of the apses (semicircular or, more rarely, polygonal) had alcoves for wooden shelves where decorative items such as statuettes but also lamps for the lighting of the room were placed. However, niches in the straight walls of side rooms of a *triclinium* must have been used simply as permanent storage installations (τοιχερμάρια), where dining sets and utensils for food and drink were kept. (Koukoulès 1951: 295; Déroche, Pétridis, and Badie 2014: 22 fig. 33). These wall cabinets had wooden shelves and were closed with wooden doors. Apart from these niches, low masonry structures with holes on the surrounding walls found in excavations can be interpreted as a form of built-in cupboard with shelves (Cova 2013: 377). The masonry is interpreted as an elevated base for the cupboard, necessary for protection from the ground's heat or humidity. The base and the side walls were covered by wooden planks or remained uncovered.

The holes in the walls have been interpreted as either holes for anchoring the cupboard or, more likely because of their regular alignment, for shelving. The whole structure was open, protected by curtains or, more often, closed by wooden doors similar to those of the aforementioned niches or those used in movable cupboards. Depending on the room where they were located, the doors of these cupboards were either plain or decorated with panels, latticework or metal fittings. Bronze rings or rectangular drop handles and locks facilitated the opening and secured the cupboard.

The need for storage was great, as a large number of activities (domestic and social as well as administrative, industrial, and even commercial) took place within a Roman or early Byzantine villa. There were certainly freestanding movable wooden cupboards and chests in all the rooms of the house where it was necessary to store more or less valuable items that had to be protected from dust, moths, or aspiring burglars. The finding of small metal locks or padlocks in addition to small keys bears out the existence of such items. From the iconography of stone bas-reliefs found mainly in Italy, we know that the form of a movable cupboard (*armarium*) was rectangular, mounted on feet, and with a flat or gabled top. Sometimes the presence of movable furniture is suggested on the basis of the design of the floor decoration, or to be more precise, on the absence of special decoration on the floors or the walls, at places destined to be occupied by movable furniture (Cova 2013: 385).

According to Vitruvius, bedrooms (*cubicula*) were oriented to the east or southeast (*De Arch*. VI. 4). Various masonry structures discovered along the sides of some rooms were probably used as benches where people sat during the day and lay down at night. In the case of bedrooms too, the arrangement of the mosaic decoration corresponds to and at the same time provides evidence for the furniture, as we have seen in the *triclinia* and in storage areas. A movable wooden bed (*lectus*, κλίνη) would have been placed along the walls over the sides of the mosaic that were decorated with geometrical or floral patterns leaving the central space free for the presentation of the main subject (Bonini 2006: 89). The beds/couches were usually wooden, with or without a back that would extend along three sides. They could be covered with bronze fittings or inlaid work. They could also be of solid bronze but the most expensive specimens, described by Roman authors (Pliny, *Natural History* XXXIII, 144) were silver-plated, silvered and gilded, or even entirely made from silver and gold (see, for instance, Österreichische Nationalbibliothek Vienna, *Cod. theol. gr.* 31, f. 16r). Higher couches necessitated a footstool (*scamnum*, σουππέδιον, or ὑποπόδιον) or even a ladder for mounting. We have such an example in Vergilius Vaticanus manuscript (*Vat. lat.* 3225, ff. XLr and XLIr) where in the first miniature Dido holding a sword lies on an elevated bed on which a ladder leans, whereas in the other miniature she lies dead. Footstools for beds or thrones were made of wood or metal and decorated with inlay work corresponding to the luxury of the furniture they accompanied. The most popular form of couches was that with turned legs, while rectangular couch legs were rare. Three-sided beds had head- and footboards (*fulcra*) and the mattresses were placed on interlaced leather or metal cords. Elements made of bronze, ivory, or silver decorated the boards with animal or human figures. Railings of the bed frame were also decorated with relief or inlay work (Richter 1966: 105–10).

Clothing apparel was kept inside the bedrooms or in *vestiaria* (wardrobe rooms) within cupboards (*armaria*) and chests (*arca, scrinia*). Wooden chests with straight, not curved, lids were also used as seats with or without cushions. Their use was restricted since the introduction of *armaria* in the Hellenistic period (Richter 1966: 114, 115). As one can deduce from the iconography of wall paintings or illuminated manuscripts, wooden chests were often richly ornamented with metal, mother-of-pearl, or stones, or entirely covered by gold or silver. Chests were also used as strongboxes for the safe-keeping of valuable items. They were of wood (mainly cypress, a tough wood) sheathed with iron and with bronze fittings. They were secured by locks. Archaeological evidence offers some direct or indirect evidence regarding these locks: a terracotta mold for the production of bronze lock bolts has been found, for example, at Delphi and dated to the Early Byzantine period (Pétridis 2010: 100, fig. 170).

Aristocratic houses also often contained libraries. They were ideally orientated toward the east to take advantage of the morning light and to avoid humidity (Vitruvius, *De Arch*. VI. 4). Niches of a rectangular rather than semicircular section along the walls of excavated wealthy houses were useful for inserting shelves to hold codices and scrolls. The latter were also kept in round boxes (*scrinia*) as seen in religious iconography representing the Evangelists. A portrait of Saint Lucas in the Basilica of San Vitale in Ravenna, for instance, shows the Evangelist in front of a circular box (*scrinium*) with a lock containing tightly wound and vertically stacked rolls (Bovini 1970: 237–8). Books had to be protected from humidity, thus insulated from any contact with the walls and floor. Library furniture also served this purpose. For example, wooden bookcases in the form of scaffolding could stand on the floor or, to avoid humidity, rest on a built bench (Bonini 2006: 91). For greater protection closed wooden cupboards were also used as bookcases. Their shape was that of an ordinary cabinet with legs, doors, and shelves on which the scrolls and codices were placed (Plate 13). One or more seats would complement the furniture. The use of desks was not common since the representations show teachers, students, and authors seated in front of open bookcases and lecterns with open scrolls, books, or tablets on their laps. Nevertheless, two scribes transcribing the speech of an orator on wax tablets lying on low desks are depicted on a stone relief from Ostia (Houston 2014: 199, 201, fig. 12). If a copying procedure took part in a private library's space small tables might have been used for writing. In the Basilica of San Vitale, Evangelist Matthew is shown seated in front of a small table with writing utensils holding an open book on his knees (Bovini 1970: 237–8).

Spacious and central rooms used as libraries could also be utilized for oratorical expression and display preceding a dinner and not only as a room for isolated reflection and study. In this case, stools and other portable furniture as well as built benches were needed.

Kitchens were closed or partly open rooms where the principal wooden pieces of furniture available were most likely open racks with shelves where the kitchen utensils and everyday tableware were kept. However, to protect and preserve the fresh and cooked food there must also have been closed wall cabinets that were most likely movable and in some cases hanging. In the different kind of storerooms for perishable materials (*cella penaria* for food storage in general, *cella olearia* for oil and *cella vinaria* for wine) there was no need for movable storage furniture as large containers lying on the floor were mainly used. Nevertheless, amphora racks of a special form (Cova 2013: 382–3, fig. 9) with a curved front panel to support reclining amphoras are also attested in Pompeian houses.

Other types of movable furniture, predominantly of wood, completed the household items. The use of *klismos*-type chairs is very rare after the Hellenistic period even though it was a very comfortable type of chair. The *klismoi* carved on marble in Dionysus' theater in Athens date back to the first century CE, but had probably replaced older, Hellenistic prototypes (Richter 1966: 101–2). *Klismoi* or *cathedrae* had curved backs resting on vertical stiles and plain curved legs.

The more common forms of seats were benches (θρᾶνος) and stools (*scamnum*/σκᾰμνος, *sella*/σελλίον, δίφρος). The former were made of marble or more frequently of wood, while the latter were made of wood with turned legs usually covered with animal skins, cushions, or even carpets. Although stools were considered a very common and less expensive kind of seat, knowing the preference of the Romans and Byzantines for luxury we cannot exclude the existence of more expensive stools made from rare woods or metal, mainly silver. Folding stools (δίφροι ὀκλαδίαι) were also used in a variety of forms (Pollux, *Onomasticon*, XI. 47): stools with curving, crossed legs, often bearing the form of animal feet; stools with straight crossed legs; finally stools with curving but not crossed legs (Richter 1966: 103–4). The folding stool in the form of a *sella curulis* was an official seat represented on coins. Stools used for special purposes are also known, such as the μαιευτικὸς δίφρος (the obstetric stool) and signify the level of specialization of furniture industry by the Roman and Early Byzantine period.

All these kinds of furniture and especially those intended for sitting or lying were used with the necessary addition of soft furnishings, to provide comfort and warmth. Covers and draperies, pillows, mattresses, bed linen, carpets, curtains, and valances were made from wool, linen, leather, animal skin, and, later, silk. Beautifully colored and lavishly ornamented with gold, silver, and precious stones, woven, embroidered, or painted, they provided splendor to the houses and a high-standard luxurious living to their owners. Such items are depicted in secular or religious illuminated manuscripts, frescoes, and wall mosaics. Some good examples come, for instance, from sixth-century CE Italy: in the churches of San Apollinario Nuovo and San Vitale in Ravenna, and the Great Palace in Constantinople richly decorated curtains are shown hanging in front of doors and arcades. In the illuminated manuscript of the first half of the sixth century CE, Vienna Genesis, beds and couches for dining with turned legs are covered by decorated covers and draperies (for example, ff. 13v, 16v, and 17v). Although strongly criticized by philosophers and Church Fathers, luxury remained through Roman and Byzantine times a main source of individual self-esteem and social recognition.

The picture we gather from this diachronic overview of average domestic contexts is one of sparsely furnished interiors by modern standards. The lack of privacy, as we understand it in modern societies, dictated multifunctional rooms and portability was a key feature. With time furniture was used not simply for functional accommodation but also as an expression of wealth and taste. It goes without saying that neither would every house have every piece of furniture nor would all of the pieces of furniture discussed here be used in every period. The general evolution of domestic furnishings was an increase in the number of pieces from the Archaic to the Hellenistic and Roman periods, to equip the ever-expanding size of the house. "Wealthy" are termed interiors characterized by more expensive items of furniture, or even items of display. More ornate forms current in Hellenistic furniture were further exploited in the Roman period. Uniformity of form and decoration is typical of the furniture one would find in wealthy Roman and early Byzantine houses, regardless of the region, revealing the standardization in several sectors of private life across the Empire and the ever-expanding trade of furniture for those who could afford expensive materials and imported pieces.

CHAPTER FIVE

The Public Setting

VASSILIS PETRAKIS AND PLATON PETRIDIS

THIRD MILLENNIUM TO FIFTH CENTURY BCE

The designation "public setting" implies that its counterpart, the domestic setting, is one of privacy. However, defining a "public" setting in antiquity can be problematic because in this period we are dealing with cultural contexts for which "privacy" (currently understood as the ability to seclude oneself) may be an anachronistic modern concept. In this chapter, "public" will be used to refer to settings that involve behaviors, attitudes, and practices pertaining to social entities larger than the single household. As will be clear from the examples discussed below, the "public" category is especially heterogeneous; in this definition, it is the "public" rather than the "domestic" setting where power display and formal appearances of important figures take place. These elements of the public setting in antiquity have been crucial in the development of its furniture.

The extant record, albeit heavily biased, supports the view that the employment of furniture was originally and broadly restricted to elite use (see Chapter 4), at least as suggested by Egyptian and Mesopotamian evidence. In quoting Moorey that ancient furniture had generally been "a luxury, not a necessity, an indicator of *elite*, not of popular cultural values" (Moorey 1996: 256; original emphasis) and with so little evidence of furniture used by common people, one admittedly runs the risk of phrasing an argument from silence, a silence that has so far been close to deafening. Such restriction of furniture to elite contexts may have been due to the paucity of raw material in the areas where primary state formation took place (Egypt, southern Mesopotamia) and the specialization required in furniture production (see Chapter 2), which both contributed to the centralization of the industry and the association of such items with elite groups (however broadly defined). As far as our record of actual pieces of furniture is concerned, there is currently no certain evidence for its wide use in non-elite contexts before the late third millennium BCE (see Chapter 4). The employment of furniture in various "public" occasions is, therefore, a fundamental diachronic use of such artifacts.

In what follows we shall explore representative examples of the uses of furniture by the elite (including royalty) as well as evidence for its employment in religious rituals and practices.

Beds and "sacred marriage"

An important group of Mesopotamian second-millennium BCE terracotta models of beds (mostly dated to the Isin–Larsa [2004–1596 BCE] and Old Babylonian [2000–1600 BCE] periods) includes attached figures of couples or nude females, often lying in explicitly erotic positions (Cholidis 1992: 123–85, plates 21–37). These have been plausibly assigned to a popular (or unofficial) level of magical/religious belief and activity, with the erotic element serving to disarm malign forces (Assante 2002 with references). Such a talismanic function is not at odds with their scholarly interpretation as popular representations of a "sacred marriage" rite.

"Sacred marriage" (or its Greek rendering as *hieros gamos*) is used somewhat technically to denote the ritual union between two deities or a deity and a human being (the deity impersonated by royal or priestly figures). The concept has been widely popularized through Frazer's interpretation of the rite as sympathetic magic to stimulate nature's fertility cycles. It is uncertain whether the rite (at least as known through Sumerian and later Mesopotamian sources) involved actual sexual intercourse between the king and a priestess as an avatar of the goddess, or whether it was purely symbolic or even fictional (Lapinkivi 2004). Nonetheless, the overall association between the ritual enactment of the "sacred marriage" and invocation of fertility remains strong.

Hittite "sacred marriage" rituals appear to have been related to the Luwian goddess Huwassannas as has been deduced by analogy with a similar ritual known from Emar (a Hittite dependency in north Syria) of a "sacred marriage" between the Storm-God and the Entu priestess (Pringle 1993: 363–8; Symington 1996: 126). Also of interest is the Mycenaean Greek festival *lekhestrōtēria* mentioned on two Linear B tablets from Pylos (*c.* 1200 BCE; gen. pl. *re-ke-to-ro-te-ri–jo*) translated as "the spreading of the bed/couch." Such an etymology may suggest the preparation of the bed for a ritual of "sacred marriage" type. In the later Greek world, although mythical accounts are well known (e.g., the union of Zeus and Hera, or of Iasion with Demeter, see Hesiod, *Theogony* 969–74), evidence for the actual performance of such rituals is scarce.[1] Given the overall absence of such erotic imagery in the Bronze Age Aegean (an exception is an ivory seal from Viannos, Crete, *c.* 2000 BCE), **lekhestrōtēria* might signify the preparation of a **lekhos* or "couch" for the periodical visit of a deity (see also Chapter 9) although it is by no means necessary that the extant iconographic *corpus* reflects the actual rituals performed.

Seat and dominance: the concept of the throne

The idea of the "throne" as a special kind of seat that was fit only for an individual occupying the top position in the social hierarchy (a "king" or "sovereign"),[2] which later came to signify the office in question, may perhaps be traceable to the Neolithic period.

Although no actual Neolithic furniture has yet been known, there is evidence that suggests a symbolic significance of the seated posture, even if the seat itself is usually rendered in a manner too abstract to be informative. A famous clay figurine of a "Goddess"—a naked, corpulent female seated on a stool with her arms resting on two felines—was found in the grain bin of a supposed "shrine" in Çatalhöyük (East Mound, Level II, *c.* 6300–6000 BCE; Mellaart 1967: 183–4, plates 67–8, IX) (Figure 5.1). It is uncertain whether the felines are living animals or intended as parts of her seat decoration, but whatever the case, the significance of the metaphor is clear: the female figure dominates over fierce wild animals or enlists their power, in a way strongly reminiscent of the "mistress of animals" (*potnia thērōn*) motifs of later periods in the Near East and the Mediterranean.[3] This cannot be dissociated from the domestication of the wild as a defining feature of Neolithic life. The Çatalhöyük "goddess" figurine appears to represent one of the earliest attestations of a fundamental symbolic metaphor in human thought: that seating reflects dominance, and that figures sit on (or with) that which they dominate or employ. This may signal the beginning of the idea that individuals of power sit on special, elaborate seats, whose form, materials, and decoration aim at conveying the message of stability, security, and power.

Extrapolations regarding the supposedly "matriarchal" structure of the Çatalhöyük community, however, are not well supported (Hodder and Meskell 2010). If the seated posture expressed any kind of social status, it should be noted that the "goddess" is not unique in this regard: a limestone figure seated on a stool from Level VI (*c.* 6700–6500 BCE) at Çatalhöyük is probably male, and dominance over wild animals is not restricted to female figures, since male figurines are apparently also shown seated on leopards and bulls (Mellaart 1967: plates 84, 86, 88).

Seats associated with important figures that may be termed "thrones" were an important part of prestige expression throughout the ancient Near East, also attested (with less straightforward evidence) in the palatial phases of the Late Bronze Age Aegean and the idea was maintained (or reintroduced) in the first

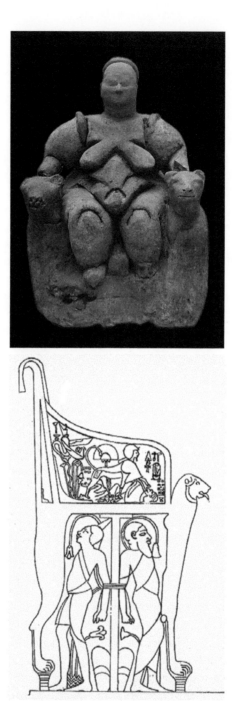

FIGURE 5.1 Examples of ancient Near Eastern thrones. (a) The enthroned "Goddess" from Çatalhöyük (Central Anatolia), Neolithic period, late seventh millennium BCE. Photograph courtesy of Wikimedia Commons. (b) Egyptian New Kingdom "lion" throne. *Source:* Kuhlmann 1977: plate II, fig. 4b. Redrawn by Vassilis Petrakis.

millennium BCE as well. Understandably, the throne of the ruler came to signify the royal office itself and the institution of kingship in general.

This metaphoric significance of the throne is particularly apparent in Hittite religious texts, where ᵈḪalmaššuit (a deity of Hattian origin adapted to the Hittite pantheon) was the personification of the deified throne itself. An Old Hittite ritual referring to the foundation of a new palace mentions the bestowment of royal insignia by ᵈḪalmaššuit to the new king. Furniture items (especially those indicated by Hurrian loanwords) may occur with the determinative sign ᴰᴵᴺᴳᴵᴿ, which indicates that they had acquired divine status (Popko 1978: 59–62).

Thrones could take a variety of forms. Although cross-cultural influences can be occasionally inferred, the details of such influence or borrowing are almost always obscure. A neo-Sumerian cylinder seal dating to the reign of Ur-Nammu, father of Šulgi and founder of the Third Dynasty of Ur (end of third millennium BCE), depicts a ruler (Ur-Nammu himself?) sitting on a throne with bovine-shaped rear legs (also depicted on the earlier "Standard of Ur") and a scrolled back. This is one of the earliest representations of this specific feature of the back of a throne, which has a long history and well-known Egyptian parallels (cf. Simpson 1995: 1649–50, fig. 6), as well as later manifestations, such as the neo-Hittite (c. 950–900 BCE) representation from Carchemish showing Queen Watis enthroned (Symington 1996: 132–3, fig. 17a). Similar high-backed chairs occur in instances lacking textual confirmation, such as the composite red polished bowl with attached figures from Vounous in Cyprus (early second millennium BCE), which includes a throne with an elaborate back that clearly highlighted the status of the oversized male figure seated on it (cf. Steel 2013).

The association between throne and footstool is strong, and seems to be linked to royal or divine status. At the opening of a letter from Biryawaza, ruler of Damascus to the Egyptian king preserved in a copy found at Akhetaten, capital of Akhenaten and present-day Tell el–Amarna (c. 1350–1335 BCE; Amarna letter EA 195), we read: "Say to the king, my lord: Message of Biryawaza, your servant, the dirt at your feet and the ground you tread on, the chair you sit on and the footstool at your feet" (after Moran 1992: 273). Biryawaza's self-derogatory description indicates the association between the king's footstool and his own vassal status. The decoration of Tutankhamun's footstools (Eaton-Krauss 2008) with figures of Africans and Asians supports this notion: in a symbolic interaction between the object's user and its imagery, the king tramples his enemies while seated on his throne. Other more literal iconography shows the pharaoh overtly performing this task, fully on view in establishing order over the chaos that the enemies represent (Jansen 2013: 47–118). In the Old Testament, similes liken various things such as the king's enemies (Ps. 110:1), Israel (Lam. 2:1), or the entire Earth (Isa. 66:1) to God's footstool.

The throne, as an immovable seat and locus of the ruler's formal appearance, might be embedded in the architecture of the "palace." Evidence from Mesopotamia is intriguing in this regard. In mid-eighteenth-century BCE Mari (Syria), the reception suite of Zimri-Lim (1775–1762 BCE), had a plastered podium at the wall facing the entrance from Court 106, taken to be the base of a statue or a throne platform. The entrance to this suite was flanked by elaborate wall paintings advertising key aspects of royal ideology, most importantly the "Investiture Scene" where the king receives the royal insignia from Ishtar herself, perhaps in a location that might be Court 106 itself (Winter 1993: 30). In these contexts, the throne is never an isolated artifact, but part of the pictorial program that shapes the experience of the viewer/ visitor. The difference between the straightforward, straight-axis sightline of the throne from the neighboring court (Mari; Nebuchadnezzar II's Southern Palace at Babylon) and the bent-axis course that one had to follow to face the throne (e.g., Ashurnasirpal II's NW Palace at Nimrud) represent two alternative traditions that are not merely aesthetic, but correspond to different ideas about the ideal relationship between the king and the outside world, including his place in the world order (Oppenheim 1977: 328; Winter 1993: 33).

Aegean Bronze Age "thrones" are scarce, but nonetheless interesting. Besides the well-known gypsum and limestone seats found at Knossos (Throne Room) or its environs (Archanes, Katsambas), as well as sunken *loci* where Mycenaean thrones would have been placed at Mycenae (Rooms 52 and 55) and Pylos (Room 6 or "Megaron"[4]), and the elaborate carved stone podium from the Great Megaron at Tiryns, we have a rich collection of imagery of chairs, folding chairs, and stools (Younger 1995: 188–93, with references). In this collection we may also include an "empty" elaborate stool on a painted *larnax* from Mesara (Rethemiotakis 1995). An interesting new addition is the charred remains of a chair found with pottery suggestive of libation or communal drinking in a sanctuary at Miletos, dating from phase IVa (*c.* 1700–1550 BCE) (Niemeier 2005: 7, fig. 18), an era characterized by strong Minoan influence manifested in the presence of locally made Cretan domestic pottery, potter's marks, and inscriptions in the Linear A script.

Furniture for the gods

Already in the late third millennium BCE, the making of elaborate furniture and the act of its offering to the deities were acts of royal piety. One of our earliest extant examples of Mesopotamian cult furniture comes from the "Riemchengebäude," a memorial monument from the Eanna sacred precinct in Uruk IV (late fourth millennium BCE), built upon the ruins of a previous "temple" building (the "Stone-Cone Building" at Uruk), where cult furnishings were apparently ritually destroyed by fire (Heinrich 1982: fig. 109).

We have ample Egyptian, Mesopotamian, and Hittite evidence for the dedication of furniture to the gods. In early Mesopotamia, in particular, such dedications were considered so important that they were used as time-defining events in naming certain years in the reigns of Mesopotamian rulers. At Isin (Iraq), for example, the king Išbi-Irra (late twentieth century BCE) established descriptive year-names such as "the year when the bed for Inanna was manufactured," "the year when a throne for Ninlil was constructed," or "when king Isbi-Irra made a throne for Ninurta," while the monarch Isme-Dagan named two successive years of his reign with reference to the making of a bed gilded with gold and silver for Ninlil (Sigrist 1988: 13–27); at Ur, the third year in Amar-Su'en's reign is "the year the king happily made the divine throne of Enlil." Such pieces were dedicated and exhibited in the cult places of the relevant deities, although it is unclear who would have been allowed to view them. The persistence of this practice is confirmed by Herodotos (1.181–3), who notes a θρόνος χρύσεος (gold throne) and a τράπεζα χρυσέη (golden table) in the shrine of Bel-Marduk (Hellenized as Ζεύς Βῆλος)—probably Ésagila—as well as a τράπεζα χρυσέη (gold table) and a κλίνη (bed or couch) in a shrine on top of the ziggurat; the god himself was supposed to visit the shrine and rest on the κλίνη, a visitation that Herodotos dismisses as incredible (1.182).

Ritual furniture in early Greek cult places may not have been scarce, although such finds rarely survive. The small-sized wooden "stools" (or footstools?) from the Heraion on Samos (perhaps as early as late eighth century BCE but found in a seventh-century BCE deposit) are an exception (Kyrieleis 1980). Horse figures were used as stool supports (many bronze horse trappings were also found in the deposit), suggesting that these might have served as stands for wooden or terracotta cult images. Although no wood analyses have been carried out, a recent stylistic analysis (Pautasso 2004) suggests that these "stools" are Cretan products, possibly imported as dedications to the sanctuary.

Although the Heraion "stools" are unique in terms of preservation, we have evidence that points to luxury furniture deposited in major Greek sanctuaries. Bronze figures possibly used as supports of throne armrests with Assyrian parallels were also found in the Samian Heraion (Jantzen 1972: plates 69–71). Ivory plaques from the sanctuary of Artemis Orthia in Sparta (late eighth century BCE) formed part of the furniture decoration as well (Kopanias 2009).

This matches the abundant epigraphic evidence for the dedication of furniture in Greek sanctuaries in Classical and Hellenistic times (Andrianou 2006; 2009: 107–22, 131–52, with references), generating the intriguing question of whether Greeks reserved their most lavish furnishings for such religious dedications. Repairs and production of new pieces commissioned by the priests themselves are also attested (Andrianou 2009: 107, 121–2).

Iconographically, distinguishing thrones intended for either "human" or "divine" rulers can be extremely difficult. Using the degree of the elevation of the throne (with "high thrones" suggesting divinity while less elevated ones are associated with mortal figures) as a way to differentiate between them is an appealing working hypothesis (Otto 2011), although hardly applicable unless entire pictorial programs can be reconstructed.

The idea of the "empty throne" (a religious concept defined as "sacred emptiness" by Mettinger [1995: 19]) is essentially based on Yahweh's place of invisible contact with Moses on the lid of the Ark of the Covenant between two gilded *cherubim* (Exod. 25:22; 1 Sam. 4:4; see also Chapter 9 in this volume). It may also gain support from a second-century CE reference to the "empty throne" of the Sun God in Hierapolis Bambyce (north Syria) (θρόνος Ἡελίου, αὐτοῦ δὲ ἕδος οὐκ ἔνι: *De Dea Syria* 34). It is unclear whether this idea reflects a more extended religious attitude in the ancient Near East. Parallels to Israelite aniconism are rather controversial, although Phoenician "empty thrones" in the area of Sidon (e.g., "the throne of Astarte" at the Eshmun sanctuary; first century CE), as well as Nabataean "thrones" (actually elevated 'platforms' or podium-like structures, *mwtb* (in Aramaic)) can be cited as evidence of such "sacred emptiness" (Mettinger 1995: 100–6). It should be noted that "sacred emptiness" is explicitly anti-anthropomorphic and obscures the widely held Mesopotamian (and Egyptian) idea of a conceptual proximity between political and divine rulership (cf. Hendel 1997). In the Aegean, Porphyry (third century CE) reports that Pythagoras, upon his visit to the Idaean Cave, birth-place of Cretagenes (Cretan-born) Zeus as a young god who died annually, saw "τὸν στορνύμενον αὐτῷ [referring to Zeus] κατ' ἔτος θρόνον" (the throne that was spread every year for him [Zeus]) (Porphyry, *Life of Pythagoras* 17). Despite its late date, Porphyry's testimony has been interpreted as evidence for an "empty throne" cult at the Idaean Cave. The excavator sought to confirm the cult in the remains of ivory inlays of ninth- to seventh-century BCE Near Eastern manufacture from the cave, some of which might possibly have belonged to an elaborate throne (Sakellarakis 2006).

Ivory furniture and the political significance of "koine" styles

Ivory was a highly valued material throughout antiquity and was often used on prestige and display items that can be considered "public" in a general sense. Egyptian evidence for the production of ivory decoration or the production of ivory furniture parts (especially Early Dynastic bull-shaped ivory legs) is well attested (see Chapters 1 and 3). Outside Egypt, our earliest secure evidence for its application on wooden furniture is the group of fittings known as the Pratt Ivories, which are now assigned a nineteenth- to eighteenth-century BCE Anatolian provenance, most likely from the Acemhöyük palace (Simpson 2013, with references) (Figure 3.1). Simpson was able to plausibly reconstruct most of this hitherto disparate group into an elaborate chair with ivory fittings, including lion legs ending in sphinxes, and a back adorned with ivory figures of a falcon and gazelles. The chair legs incorporating sphinxes are of special interest, as they form the earliest attestation of a remarkable fashion that persisted into Hellenistic times: the designated κλῖναι σφιγγόποδες (bed-couches with sphinx-legs) from Delos, paralleled in Etruscan urns of the second century BCE (Andrianou 2010; Chapter 9 in this volume).

Ivory furniture fittings from many sites throughout the Levant dating to the second half of the second millennium BCE have been found. The sixteenth- to fifteenth-century BCE palace from Pella (Pahel, Jordan) yielded some interesting wooden ivory-decorated boxes, among which the "Lion Box" is remarkable for its mixture of Egyptian(izing) and Levantine motifs and styles (cf. McGovern 2004: 292–3). Stylistic mixtures are also found in the ivory decorations of a bed and table from Court III in the palace of Ugarit (modern Ras Shamra, 1400–1200 BCE), and the large ivory "hoard" from the so-called Treasury of the Canaanite palace of Megiddo (deposited at Level VIIA; *c.* 1200–1100 BCE) (see also Chapters 1 and 3 in this volume). Besides those from Egypt and the Levant, ivory plaques and panels, often with drill holes or grooves that indicate their function as inlays, are also widely distributed throughout the Aegean (e.g., Mycenae in the Argolid; Thebes in Boeotia; Archanes near Knossos on Crete; Spata and Athens in Attica; Artemision on the island of Delos) and Cyprus (Enkomi; Kition) *c.* 1500–1200 BCE (cf. Feldman 2006: 129–44).

Although these items appear in diverse geographic and cultural contexts (the Megiddo ivory "hoard," for instance, has been interpreted as part of a "termination ritual" [Feldman 2009], whereas the Late Bronze Age ivories from Artemision on Delos [Cyclades, Greece] as part of a later, Iron Age "foundation deposit"), we must consider the political significance of such shared stylistic trends and the emergence of stylistic "hybrids." Why and at what initiative were they produced? Because several regional workshops were involved, the mixture of different styles is never the same; however, the similarities are sufficient to indicate the existence of a *koine* or "International Style," which appears to be largely restricted to luxury objects, including furniture. The so-called Amarna letters (mid-fourteenth century BCE) containing fragments of the royal diplomatic correspondence dated to the reigns of Amenhotep III, Amenhotep IV (later Akhenaten), and perhaps his successors Semenkhare and Tutankhamun (Moran 1992), as well as contemporary Hittite sources, are our primary evidence for a circuit of diplomatic exchange among royal elites of the time, chiefly from Egypt, Hatti, Mittani, Babylonia, and Assyria (in which one Aegean polity, mentioned in the Hittite sources as *Aḫḫiyawa*, might have been briefly included). Furniture features prominently in many of these texts (see also Chapter 9).

These rulers address each other as "brothers," a metaphor of parity and alliance. One of the Amarna letters (EA 5), for instance, refers to a furniture collection sent by the Egyptian pharaoh to Kadašman-Enlil for his palace at

Babylon (Moran 1992: 10–11). Such an example is by no means isolated (see Chapter 9 in this volume). Feldman (2006) has contended that such an ideological structure of "elite brotherhood" was supported through the production of luxury artifacts employed as diplomatic gifts (Akkadian *šulmānu*) that had been designed in a way to deliberately conceal their regional cultural affinities and local provenance. Even if the justification for grouping these items of various materials, types, and contexts is debatable, it is interesting how, in their figural decoration, divine imagery is generally downplayed in favor of images emphasizing kingship and deliberately vague notions of power and dominion that each and every ruler could conveniently adapt to their own political agenda.

In the reshuffle that followed the collapse of Anatolian and Levantine polities at the end of the Late Bronze Age,[5] a considerable degree of stylistic continuity is evident in furniture production (see Chapter 3 in this volume). The so-called Nimrud ivories, recovered from three principal locations at the Assyrian center of Nimrud (the Northwest Palace, the Burnt Palace, and the Fort Shalmaneser arsenal), include numerous ivory inlays, many of which functioned as furniture decoration (Simpson 1995: 1658–61, with references). Similar ivory furniture decoration has been found at many Iron Age centers in the ancient Near East, such as Sargon's capital in Khorsabad (ancient Dur-Šarrukin in present-day north Iraq), Arslan Taş (ancient Hadatu in present-day north Syria), Zincirli in southeast Anatolia, and Samaria in north Israel. The fact that there is stylistic diversity within the Nimrud material suggests it was booty (Assyrian *šal-la-at*) or tribute from destroyed cities, as often advertised in the annals and reliefs of Assyrian rulers (ninth to seventh century BCE). In an inscription narrating the plundering of the Babylon palace of Marduk-apla-iddina II by Sennacherib (702 BCE), booty of furniture and "all of the craftsmen, as many as there were" is explicitly recorded (Grayson and Novotny 2014: 296, no. 123, lines 30–3). Sennacherib's interest in abducting craftsmen suggests his wish to maintain the production of new luxury items for the Assyrian elite.

Feasting furniture

As "public" social occasions, feasts provided the opportunity for communal consumption. The economic and political aspects are clear: as a commodity-sharing mechanism, a banquet has a redistributive leveling function; it also generates obligations between the sponsor(s) and other participants. Moreover, it provides a suitable vehicle for elite display, which makes it a very popular iconographical theme throughout the Ancient Near East and the Greek and Roman worlds.

On the "Standard of Ur" (perhaps a lyre's sound-box) and the limestone plaque of Ur-Nanshe, king of Lagash in Mesopotamia, banquet scenes lack tables and focus on seated drinking, a pattern paralleled in many third-millennium BCE cylinder seals with the same theme (see also Chapters 3 and 8 in this volume). Banquet scenes (or the far more common depiction of a husband and wife having a meal) are typical themes in the decoration of New Kingdom Egyptian middle-class and elite tombs, and most of our representations of contemporary Egyptian furniture come from them. They illustrate what was enjoyable in life and, therefore, what the owner of the tomb wished to recreate in the afterlife. Banquets became a persistent theme in ancient Near Eastern art throughout the third and second millennia BCE, where Egyptianizing and Mesopotamian motifs and ideas appear to mingle (Ziffer 2005).

Besides the royal tumuli (see Chapter 6 in this volume), evidence for Phrygian banquet furniture has also been recovered from public buildings in the destruction level of the city of Gordion (late eighth century BCE), most notably fragments of a "Mosaic Table" (paralleled in a similar table from Tumulus P) from Megaron 3, Room 3 (Simpson 1996: 207). In the Phrygian capital, feasting played an important role outside the mortuary setting as well.

The relatively low visibility of tables (as opposed to various types of stools or chairs) in our early imagery may be associated with their original function as trays for the transport of food. The carved raised border of a tabletop from Room 2601 from Palace G at Ebla (Syria) (2500–2300 BCE) facilitated its use as a tray (Simpson 1995: 1652). The development of the table out of a simple stand, as hinted by early pedestal examples, such as those found at Ur and elsewhere (see Chapter 6 in this volume), may indicate that tables were originally rather peripheral items in feasts, perhaps explaining their omission from feasting scenes. Depictions of banquets (if correctly identified as such) from the Aegean Late Bronze Age, such as the fragmentary Knossos "Campstool Fresco" (*c.* 1300 BCE), seem to focus on the seated posture and the toasting gesture (raised arm with cup), with no other furniture items shown on extant fragments of the composition (cf. the greater variety of items inventoried in the Pylos Linear B tablets of the Ta series). In Room 6 (the so-called megaron) of the Pylos palace depictions of pairs of "banqueters" seated on folding stools either side of three-legged tables are associated with an oversized lyre player (a divine figure?) and—according to one reconstruction—a bull trussed on the sacrificial slaughtering table (*c.* 1200 BCE) (McCallum 1987; cf. Otto 2011: 240, fig. 6).

Later Greek *symposion* (συμπόσιον: "communal drinking occasion"), characterized by the participants reclining on κλῖναι (couches rather than beds), is a novelty of ultimately Syro-Phoenician origin (ninth to eighth century BCE) that spread along with Phoenician trade around the Mediterranean. In a recent wide-ranging analysis, Baughan (2013: 198–224) has suggested that Greeks adopted the custom—associated with luxury and eroticism—in western Anatolia, where Lydian influence upon Ionian Greeks had been crucial. Reasonably, a key point would have been its appropriation by Assyrian rulers, most notably Ashurbanipal, who is depicted reclining beside his enthroned queen in the

"Garden Party" relief from Nineveh (*c.* 650–645 BCE) (Plate 14). Representations of reclining banquets also occur on Cypro-Phoenician bronze bowls as well as on bronzes from the Idaean Cave in Crete from the eighth century BCE (Baughan 2013: 202–7, figs. 134–8), roughly contemporary to Amos' protests against exuberant luxury attested in Samarian *marzeah* feasts, where "lying upon ivory beds" is expressly mentioned (Amos 6:4). Although we might acknowledge some influence on reclining banqueting from Homeric emblematic feasting—which, like later *symposia*, was also closed, group-defining, exclusively male, and centered upon the consumption of mixed wine—Homeric participants sit on chairs and never recline on couches. The word κλίνη does not occur in Homer, although this may be due to the deliberate archaization of the heroic world as represented by the poets themselves. The ambiguous κλιντήρ (Hom., *Od.* 18.190), as mentioned in the context of Penelope falling asleep on it, may suggest that she might have been reclining; yet κλιντῆρες are not mentioned in Homeric feasts.

Apart from the reclining position of the participants, Greek *symposia* do not resemble Assyrian royal banquets: the former originated as group banquets among peers and can be considered private affairs (unlike public festivals or other events). Representations of *symposia* on late seventh-century BCE Corinthian κρατῆρες ("kraters" or mixing bowls, chiefly for water and wine) and a verse from the contemporary lyric poet Alcman (fr. 19: κλῖναι μέν ἑπτὰ καὶ τόσαι τράπεσδαι "seven couches and as many tables") provide our earliest unambiguous testimonies for sympotic κλῖναι. Alcman also refers to the correspondence in number between couches and tables, which is reflected in Archaic and Classical iconography of *symposia*. Κλῖναι reach their apogee of elaboration during the Archaic and Classical periods (Baughan 2013: 15–86), when they were even used as the measurement unit for the size of drinking rooms (the latter being usually named ἀνδρῶνες "halls for men": besides ἑταίραι [companions, courtesans, prostitutes], women were normally excluded from *symposia*).

Trade brought the *symposion* to foreign shores: Archaic Etruscan elites became major consumers of Greek wine, fine drinking pottery and the practices accompanying these items, including the sympotic lifestyle; this was also adapted into their conception of the deceased as banqueters, a development reflecting Greek and Lydian influences upon local traditions of funerary beds (Baughan 2013: 226–32). In Greece, the rise and fall of sympotic practices largely coincided with that of a dominant aristocracy. Priorities changed in post-Ephialtes (462 BCE) Athens, where the assembly and public festivals became the focus of political life (Murray 2009, with references).

Associated with feasting and other rites of commensality are representations of seated musicians. The late fourth and third millennia BCE have yielded explicit evidence for such "public" uses of furniture. The statue of the "Great Singer" Ur-Nanše from Mari (*c.* 2500 BCE) seated on a low, cushion-like stool is interesting in its association of seat and musical performance; stools (including folding stools) are frequently shown in representations of musicians in Mesopotamia (cf. Al-Gailani Werr 1996: 30, plate 10b). This is a recurrent feature in other regions and eras too: marble figurines of harpists (or lyre-playing deities?) are shown seated on stools or even elaborate chairs coming from mid-third millennium BCE contexts on the Aegean islands of the Cyclades (Naxos, Thera, or Keros), although the authenticity of certain of these figurines is not beyond doubt (for the diversity of early Cycladic seats, see Krzyszkowska 1996: 87–8, fig. 1). In a wall painting from the Pylos megaron (*c.* 1200 BCE) an oversized (divine?) lyre player seated on a rock is associated with pairs of seated banqueters. In Homer, both Phēmios and Dēmodokos perform on the occasion of such feasts, an apparently familiar occurrence to the epic audience. Dēmodokos is seated on a silver-studded chair (θρόνος ἀργυρόηλος). The depiction of seated musicians continues to be popular in later Greek art, as shown by the bronze figurine of a lyre player from Crete (eighth century BCE) and scenes in late Archaic and Classical vase painting (cf. Baker 1966: figs. 434, 442), while such performances in *symposia* are associated with the female ἑταῖραι (companions, courtesans, also prostitutes) in Classical vase painting.

LATE ROMAN AND EARLY BYZANTINE PERIODS

In the Late Roman and Early Byzantine period (*c.* third to seventh century CE) our information on the furniture from the public setting is rather rich all over the Mediterranean world and especially from the Oriental part of the Empire. In secular public buildings, portable wooden furniture or masonry benches along the long sides of the halls were dominant. In the case of the local councils of the late Roman cities (Bouleuteria/Curiae), the benches were semicircular and had at the opposite side a rectangle of low steps for placing wooden seats (Lavan 2007a: 122). Cabinets for safe-keeping of utensils or documents were also necessary as well as any related hardware. Gradually and mainly since the sixth century CE an important role was played in the administrative and economic life of a city by the local bishop, who had replaced other local dignitaries or archons. Their buildings (ἐπισκοπεῖα or bishoprics), which resembled in structure palaces and *praetoria* (the residencies of cities' governors), were located adjacent to the most important Christian church of a city (for instance, the large edifice adjacent to the great central church in Bosra, South Syria, see Piraud-Fournet 2010) and had rooms serving administrative needs (a reception hall or audience room) as well as economic ones (storerooms).

Palaces, *praetoria*, and *episkopeia* combined residential and administrative activities: they constituted public buildings with many features of domestic architecture but on a quite different scale. Being the most luxurious type of house, their furniture likewise reflected the wealth and economic and political power of the *archon*. In addition to the presence of functional furniture in all public sector buildings, the throne (*solium, θρόνος, καθέδρα*) was also found in both secular and ecclesiastical palaces and constituted special furniture with a strong symbolic use. Palaces, *praetoria*, and *episkopeia*, that is to say the places where supreme local power was exercised, had hierarchically arranged rooms to which the public had different degrees of access. The most important of these was the "throne hall" where the emperor, local *archon*, or bishop held audiences. For this reason the hall had to serve many practical and ideological aspects of the administrative system. In the period we are interested in, these halls were usually of a round or rectangular shape with all sides equidistant from the center. This allowed the simultaneous presence of many and, most importantly, equally distributed persons around the *archon*. We can easily imagine the luxury of these halls whose primary purpose was to impress the public, particularly in the case of representatives of other countries. The dominant element was the throne, whose size and luxury would have reflected the power of the state.

Made of precious materials, most usually marble, the throne had always played the role of the leader's *cathedra*, the seat par excellence of the secular or ecclesiastical *archons*. The two types of thrones evolved by the Greeks, with turned or rectangular legs, are often illustrated on Roman frescoes but are rare on early Byzantine mosaics. Front legs often take the form of animal legs while the back legs remain rectangular. In later periods marble thrones with solid sides were more common, especially for what we could call "official" circumstances. They have a rectangular or, more often, a rounded back. The sides are decorated with various relief motifs while the front could be shaped in the form of animals or animal legs (Richter 1966: 100–1). Thrones with solid sides are very typical in religious and imperial iconography. They were also made of other materials, such as metal or ivory.

Of comparable luxury were the thrones placed in the Christian churches as a seat for the bishop during the holy liturgy, usually in the middle and at the highest point of the *synthronon*, a series of rounded low steps in the apse of the sanctuary. The most famous bishop's chair of the Early Byzantine period was made of ivory, the "Throne of Maximian," belonging to the bishop Maximianus (499–556 CE) of Ravenna, the western capital of the Empire at the time of Justinian I (527–565 CE) (Plate 15). Carved in one of the big artistic centers of the Greek East (Constantinople or Alexandria) it is made of ivory panels on a wooden frame. The figurative panels are framed by winding vines and grapevines. In the center of the front panel John the Baptist is surrounded by the four Evangelists with Maximian's monogram above Saint John. The scenes on the sides and back of the throne represent, respectively, events from the story of Joseph and the life of Christ (Shapiro 1980; Wedoff 2009).

We lack archaeological evidence for the portable furniture of the Christian churches of the Early Byzantine period (fourth to seventh century CE) with the exception of some marble items that have survived. Altars are among the most impressive examples of portable tables. The humblest of these were wooden while those of higher status were made of marble or even more precious materials like ivory or metal, such as the sheathed-in-gold and jewel–studded altar of Hagia Sophia in Constantinople (Procopius, *De Aedificiis* 1.1.22–3). Secondary tables (παρατραπέζια) on which liturgical objects were placed, along with the majority of altars, were mostly made of marble. However, a combination of materials was also possible: bronze feet with marble or wooden upper sections, or wood covered with metal plates. Reliquaries were made from marble, limestone, or metal.

Apart from the *synthronon* inside the apse reserved for the members of the clergy, benches were built in some cases into the lateral walls of the nave. Although we lack archaeological evidence for wooden benches or seats (καθέδραι ξυλίναι) their presence in inventories (Caseau 2007a: 576) and other texts confirm their existence in churches of all sizes to provide seating for worshippers during the liturgy. Seats and stools would also exist in more valuable versions for specific elite groups of worshippers.

In the sacristy (*diakonikon*) we can imagine the presence of portable wooden cupboards where utensils as well as the offerings of the congregation were kept. Cupboards were also built across the walls of annexe rooms: interstices between the stones correspond to racks or shelves made from stone or wood (Michel 2007: 590–5). These might contain religious texts, liturgical vestments, objects such as chalices and patens, relics, and probably the church's treasury.

The church setting (as a whole) was completed by cushions, curtains, and hangings (βῆλα, καταπετάσματα), which covered doors and windows, separated the various parts of the temple, and covered the altar or other movable tables. All of these, including the numerous liturgical vessels and lighting devices, were visual displays of wealth and their value was proportional to the importance and wealth of the church.

Christian healing shrines (holy places where people went in the hope to be miraculously cured by a saint) were equipped with a different kind of furniture than ordinary churches: pilgrims intending to stay for a short or a long period of time would bring with them bedding and other movable furniture necessary for their comfort and according to their lifestyle and social status (Caseau 2007b: 626).

Temples of other religions that were in use until the fifth century CE continued to be equipped with the portable furniture of previous periods, mainly altars and portable chairs but also thrones, chests and other containers, stools, and tables (Andrianou 2006: 567). In the case of pagan healing sanctuaries, for instance the Athenian Asklepieion, still in use during the fifth century CE, bed-couches and pillows were also inventoried. The construction of built benches along the walls is noticed in Christian as well as pagan temples.

Christian charitable institutions (hospices and inns, hospitals, orphanages, homes for elderly people, leper-houses) provided lodging for travelers and destitute people as well as medical care for the sick. One of the most representative examples was the sixth-century CE *xenon* (hospice) of Sampson in Constantinople, founded during the reign of Justinian by a distinguished doctor. It was a complex of philanthropic institutions including a hospital and spaces for the accommodation of destitutes. The furniture of such buildings can be traced through analogies with domestic accommodation of a poor and unpretentious style: it consisted mainly of beds, mattresses and pillows, and many utensils like basins or chamber pots related to the cure of sick or hosting of strangers, poor, elderly, and orphans.

Public audiences and paying homage to the emperor or local authority were not the only chances to receive guests in the palaces, *praetoria*, and episcopal mansions. The official or state dinners held on the occasion of public anniversaries, secular ceremonies, or visits of official and important guests constituted another opportunity to display wealth and power. In the Great Palace of Constantinople they were taking place mostly in three halls: (a) the *Triclinos of the Nineteen Couches*, a great hall used for receptions during the twelve feast days of Christmas and Epiphany, whose foundation is attributed to Constantine the Great (306–337 CE); (b) the *Chrysotriklinos* (Golden Triclinium), which was built by Justin II (565–578 CE) and decorated by his successor Tiberius II (578–582 CE); and (c) the *Triclinium of Justinian*, which was constructed by Justinian II (668–711 CE) at the end of the seventh century (Koukoulès 1952: 195). The guests would have dinner reclined exactly as described above, although here the luxury of the furniture and the tableware was incomparable to that of the Greco-Roman period. Of equal luxury were the mattresses and cloths covering the *stibadia* on which the guests reclined, the cushions, the tablecloths (*mensalia*), and the napkins with which the guests would clean their hands before and after dinner.

The table destined for the emperor and the most eminent of his guests was placed at a higher level reached by ascending three steps. The other tables were placed on the level of the *triclinium* floor and near the walls leaving free space in the middle for the chanters praising the emperor, or for games, dances, and performances with mimes and dancing. The central and secondary tables were metal-plated, mainly in silver, or they were entirely made of compact metal such as silver or even gold. Their decoration with precious materials varied. The fact that the use of round tables is mentioned as extraordinary should lead us to the conclusion that the C-shaped (sigmoid) or rectangular tables were the rule in these official dinners (Koukoulès 1952: 142–3). Those who were not reclining for dinner were seated in cathedrae or rather on folding stools made of wood with inlay decoration, possibly using precious metals, and covered with cushions or tapestries. Sitting on a stool rather than reclining was also a sign of humility or independence vis-à-vis the emperor (Malmberg 2007: 84).

In the local *praetoria* or *episkopeia* official dinners were held in *triclinia*, some of which had relative autonomy from the rest of the building.[6] Due to the fact that these *triclinia* served other functions as well, such as judicial procedures and public audiences, we can conclude that their furniture must have been portable and indeed foldable. The luxury of the materials and craftsmanship of the furniture and fabrics would have depended on the political and economic power of the local secular or ecclesiastical archon. The total lack of wall cabinets in the *triclinia* (with the exception of the niches opened in the apses that, however, were of a decorative nature, as we have already seen [in Chapter 4]) leads to the conclusion that the foldable furniture, soft furnishings, tableware, and utensils would have been kept in the side rooms of the *triclinium*, the number and the size of which varies (Petridis 2008: 251). In these rooms, the tableware and the furniture were kept in wall or portable cabinets, on wooden shelves or in chests. The presence of niches in many of those rooms, as in the case of some side rooms of the Southeastern Villa at Delphi (Déroche, Pétridis, and Badie 2014: dépl. 1, C19) proves their use as wall cabinets or simply as alcoves for shelves.

Libraries constituted an important institution in the *metropoleis* of the Roman and early Byzantine world. Introduced by Romans, this new type of monumental public building was specifically designed to combine storage rooms, reading areas, lecture halls, and open meeting spaces, all decorated with works of art and providing an impressive backdrop for cultural activities of various kinds, like public lectures, recitations, or philosophy lessons. The use of libraries was open to all cultivated citizens searching for knowledge and spiritual elevation. In the course of three or four centuries we pass from the first private Roman collections consisting mainly of manuscripts seized as war booty from their Greek owners to the prestigious foundations made by the emperors. Philosophical, literary, and historical works in Greek and Latin abounded, but natural sciences, engineering, and medical treatises were also present. The most important of all libraries established in Rome was Ulpia, founded by Emperor Trajan (113 CE) inside its Forum; it rivaled the most famous libraries of the ancient world, those of Pergamum and Alexandria. During the reign of Trajan, Ephesos was embellished by the famous library of Celsus, one of the richest of the Roman world. In Constantinople, the new capital of the Empire, the most important library was the imperial one, founded in the fourth century CE, but other important libraries also existed in the patriarchate, the university, and especially in monasteries during the entire Byzantine era.

One could find different kinds of facilities for the organization and storage of codices and book rolls used in both important and minor libraries (Houston 2014: 180–8). Small groups of manuscripts for instance could be vertically stored in portable wooden cases (*cista, scrinium, κιβωτὸς*), sometimes of beech, that were round, cylindrical, or rectangular, making them easily portable (Pliny, *Natural History* XVI, 229). Horizontal storage, on the other hand, consisted of shelves (*pegmata*) lining the walls or inside niches. To protect the books from humidity, wooden bookcases rest on a built bench. Indeed, the archaeological evidence for shelves consists mainly of holes in the walls of rooms or regular interstices between bricks or stones and sometimes low masonry isolating the wooden structure from the floor. Wooden cupboards or cabinets (*armaria*), as the one shown in Plate 13, were safer for the books. Armaria were freestanding, rectangular, mounted on feet, with a flat or gabled top, had shelves in the interior, maybe drawers in the lower part, and were closed by doors. The value of the manuscripts made the use of locks necessary as for all the valuable items kept in a cupboard.

If private bookcases in the form of closed cupboards were not very tall, those in the libraries used by a large public should have been taller and larger. They could also have been fit to rectangular niches in the walls to house a large number of rolls securely. That was the image of all the important libraries of the Roman and early Byzantine world: rows of high wooden cabinets made perhaps of precious woods and inlaid with ivory embedded in the walls of large reading rooms. In that way, the bookshelves became one of the most imposing decorative elements of the library and the storage and reading rooms ceased to be two separate spaces (Petrain 2013: 336–7). The large halls with fitted *armaria* were probably equipped with chairs and stools and perhaps benches but no big tables for reading, just small tables for scribal equipment or the temporary layout of rolls. In fact, no tables used as desks appear in the visual evidence of the period with the exception of the small tables depicted on a stone relief from Ostia representing two scribes (see above Chapter 4). On the contrary, all the figures engaged in reading and writing are shown seated and holding the roll or the tablets on their laps (Houston 2014: 199–202). Stepladders would have been indispensable for reaching the books on the top shelves of the *armaria*.

Lectures were also held in rooms of the libraries where stone benches lined the walls, as in the case of other lecture halls, not necessarily related with libraries, for example, the fifth- and sixth-century CE *auditoria* at Kom el-Dikka in Alexandria. Portable wooden furniture (benches or, more likely, stools) was used in case of large audiences.

In the baths, few pieces of furniture were necessary in the cold and hot bathing or sweating sections (*frigidaria, caldaria*, and *tepidaria*, respectively) as built benches would cover their needs. Perhaps small wooden, portable pieces of furniture, especially stools, were scattered where the bathers would sit to be rubbed or to get some rest between the various stages of the bath. In the sections or rooms we identify as vestiaries (*ἀποδυτήρια*) where the bathers would undress and hand over their clothes to the attendants of the bath, no traces have been found on the walls and floors that could allow for the possibility of wall cabinets similar to the ones we have described in Chapter 4. The clothes therefore were most likely kept in light, open, wooden constructions with shelves. In portable wooden cabinets they would probably have kept clay or glass vessels (*unguentaria*), which contained the scented oils for rubbing or smearing, as well as the medicines or other toiletries used for depilating or grooming (Koukoulès 1951: 450).

Finally the existence of rooms for rest in the public baths and the relevant evidence of the historical and literary sources (Koukoulès 1951: 435, 455) premise a series of furniture items such as beds, benches, chairs, and small tables where the bathers would lie or sit after the bath to enjoy a stimulating drink and meal, to talk or even sleep. This furniture, as well as the coverings that would accompany it, did not necessarily belong to the permanent furniture of the public baths but they could be brought in together with their bath toiletries by the bathers or the slaves escorting them (John Chrysostom, *PG* 62, 259). All these constituted a means of showing off and their luxuriousness depended on the economic status of the bather.

In the big central streets of the cities (ἔμβολοι), shops and artisan workshops were located behind the porticoes but they could also be found scattered in other points within the city walls. Dye- or tannery workshops could be found outside the city walls too, by the side of highways and at the same time near water sources. The kind of shop or workshop would also determine the kind of furniture used in it. For example, there must have been a different kind of furniture in perfume shops and, in general, in luxury products shops, and another in a shop selling clay vessels. It is probable, judging from the size of the vessels and their price, that luxurious items would have been stored in closed cupboards and on narrow shelves. Built-in high and narrow benches that ran along interior walls were used for displaying goods. Wooden portable cabinets with compact wooden doors or perforated doors to allow merchandise to be seen, covered the walls mainly of shops selling luxury products (Plate 16). The cabinets could be separated into two parts: a taller upper one and a lower one underneath. Their use was dictated by the need of protection from the conditions (heat, humidity) prevailing in the shop. Their doors bore locks for the protection of the merchandise. Valuable fabrics or other luxurious items would also be kept in locked chests. On the other hand, in most shops and workshops of a city, open shelves or racks lining all the walls, wooden counters set on tripods, and hanging items would be the most usual images one could see. In food-selling shops, for instance, wooden counters set on tripods exhibited fresh products for sale, as in the case of a stone relief depicting a flower and vegetable seller (Plate 17). The wooden shelves were not only used in the interior of the shop but also on its front or even outside. Shops with a colonnaded area in front of them could have taken advantage of that space expanding their area of activity outside the shop or workshop. Many items were hanging from light constructions set in the walls or the ceiling so that no space of the shop or workshop remained unexploited, as in the case of the belt and cushion seller depicted on a second-century CE stone relief (Plate 18). Other necessary objects were the stools for the sitting of craftsmen, as well as the wooden cabinets where their tools would be kept. In cloth workshops, looms were present as well as tables for cutting and sewing garments in tailors' shops. In butchers' shops a necessary item was a cylindrical wooden counter, a butcher block on which the meat would be cut. In inns (*cauponae*) and taverns (*popinae*) the furniture was of course different from other shops: a built counter sometimes with a barrel-vaulted basin at the bottom, masonry benches or wooden tables and stools or more usually adjoining wooden benches for the customers to sit would be complemented by shelves or cabinets for the keeping of the tableware, which would be made of clay or wood.

Retailing of a wide range of products took place in open-air markets where the products were displayed in stalls probably protected by tents. Small portable and folding furniture was used by a large number of professionals such as scribes, money changers, barbers, and so on.

A furniture item often seen in public places in the Roman and Early Byzantine period was the *lectica* or *sella*, a portable form of litter (or sedan chair), usually wooden, with both valuable and inexpensive decoration, depending on the economic status of the owner, and carried by four slaves. Four turned poles in the corners held the roof, flat or curved. Mattresses, cushions, and sheets covered the litter, while curtains were hung from the roof to screen the passenger from onlookers.

Finally, wooden beds, a common kind of furniture, were used to lay the dead upon (Koukoulès 1951: 163). These beds, which were carried on the shoulders for the funeral, must not have been different from the ones used at home as shown in representations, as, for instance, in the oldest, well-preserved illustrated biblical codex (the sixth-century illuminated manuscript of the Vienna Genesis) and the scene with Joseph leaving the bed of Potiphar's wife (Plate 19). In accordance with the luxury that accompanied their lives, wealthy people would be carried on hired golden or silver beds after death while the emperors were laid on golden beds embellished with pearls and precious stones (Gregory of Nyssa, *PG* 46, 868).

Palaces for ecclesiastical or secular dignitaries, gathering places for cultured citizens (such as libraries), or gathering places for the general public (such as shops and baths, churches and other religious buildings), all public spaces at the end of the Roman and at the beginning of the Byzantine era, offer a rich picture of furnishings. Although wooden furniture has been preserved in our area of investigation almost only through representations (miniature manuscripts or stone reliefs), their presence is indisputable. Built benches that line the walls as bases for wooden libraries, or more commonly as benches to sit, were also very common.

CHAPTER SIX

Exhibition and Display

VASSILIS PETRAKIS, JEAN MACINTOSH TURFA,

AND DIMITRA ANDRIANOU

Although in private life wealthy individuals presumably exhibited their power and status through their possessions, we have neither *direct* literary sources nor enough extant objects from domestic settings pertaining to furniture to fully substantiate this. Only occasionally literary evidence, such as in Aristophane's *Wasps* (1214–15), praises metal vessels, the decoration of the ceiling, and the woven hangings in a private banquet as a proper way to start a discussion during the party. On the other hand, surviving temple inventories make it clear that temples were built to house precious dedications of gold and silver, along with gemstones, ivory, fine woods, and luxurious textiles. Precious materials added to their appeal and manifested the wealth and power of their donors.

In Greek thought the possession and appreciation of extravagant accoutrements not only demonstrated wealth and refinement, but also were associated with the excesses of kingship and tyranny. The word *tryphe* (softness) had largely negative connotations. It was potentially disruptive, led to softness, effeminacy, and corruption (Andrianou 2009: 123–9). Luxury goods derived mainly from the East became unfashionable around the time of the Persian Wars in the early fifth century BCE and were especially suspect in democratic Athens, yet *tryphe* was not an entirely negative concept (Lapatin 2015: 2). Literary evidence for deliberate, clear display in conjunction with furniture only becomes available at a later date, associated with the life and the public processions of Hellenistic kings and the royal elite.

On the other hand, closed and better preserved funerary contexts, though tainted by beliefs about the afterlife, enable us to follow many aspects of exhibition and display in pre-historic and early historic societies much more easily. Funerary deposition of costly artifacts was also embedded in the concept of "sacrifice": the destruction of something valued to provoke regeneration, ensure supernatural protection and overall prosperity. In particular, elite burials (where furniture is predominantly found) are above all statements of power addressed to the funeral attendees and the community of the living; the elite dead acquire a "mortuary persona," which is nonetheless generated, enacted, maintained, and controlled by the living. The funerary setting, therefore, is a special kind of public setting.

In all periods, tombs and grave goods (consisting of the deceased's belongings, furniture, and objects given to them in the funeral ritual—we detect details of the burial ritual and anniversary or other observations from the archaeological study of tombs and offerings) were assembled/constructed for the purpose of display. First, they were intended to demonstrate the importance of the deceased and their family/clan to their fellow citizens or subjects, and also they served to remind the gods of the individuals' worthiness in the afterlife.

The use of furniture in funerary contexts occurs cross-culturally, and can be associated with aspects of the funerary ritual (e.g., mortuary meals or exposition and transport of the deceased on a bier or bed) or beliefs about after-life sustenance (as Egyptian evidence suggests). Besides actual furniture, reduced-scale models (usually of terracotta or metal) were also deposited for various economic or ideological reasons, especially when actual furniture might have been unaffordable. Such depositions presuppose elaborate mortuary rites often employed as an area of social and political competition or negotiation of identities. The mortuary record reflects beliefs and practices that are enacted by the living; these may or may not reflect the actual properties of the deceased: a chief who has never fought a single battle could still be buried with elaborate weapons or items that reflect the ideal of a ruler. Yet, idealization of the dead is only one category of options. The diverse ways in which the living chose to represent the deceased are cultural statements embedded in a milieu that not only reflects but also shapes the social landscape. In a way parallel to (yet different from) iconography (see Chapter 8 in this volume), the funerary record participates in the active production—rather than the passive reproduction—of ideas about the world order.

An often-vexing question with regard to furniture found in tombs is whether these pieces were especially made for funerary "consumption" or whether they consisted of items that had already been used in life. More often than not, the latter idea seems to have been assumed rather than actually investigated. The critical evidence would typically be the identification of "wear-marks" (cf. Snape 2011: 235) and non-practical construction methods or materials, rather than the type or degree of elaboration of the items found.

BRONZE AND EARLY IRON AGES

Both Egypt and Mesopotamia have yielded evidence for the deposition of furniture as part of elite mortuary ostentation. From the Royal Cemetery of Ur, for example, we have a wooden chest with traces of red painted decoration and shell and lapis lazuli inlays from the burial of "Lady Puabi" (*puabi nin* on a cylinder seal accompanying her), probably a royal or highly esteemed priestly figure who was deposited on a wooden bed/bier inside her tomb (PG 800; mid-third millennium BCE, see Woolley 1934: 80–4). Hers was one of the most lavishly ornamented burials in the entire cemetery accompanied by extravagant items such as a "cape" of beads and remarkable gold jewelry. A rather modest table or large stool made of reeds set in a wooden frame also accompanied another burial placed in tomb PG 1847 of the Ur Royal Cemetery (Woolley 1934: 194, plate 84b).

Similar use of furniture occurs elsewhere in the ancient Near East. A burial from Horoztepe (Pontic region, Anatolia; late third millennium BCE) yielded two bronze tables with anthropomorphic bronze sheathings riveted over the decayed wooden cores of the legs and one remarkable pedestal table or stand. Further bronze fittings suggest additional furniture items that had deteriorated in the soil (Özgüç and Akok 1958). There is evidence for intentional (possibly ritual) destruction of the larger table, matched in other finds from this tomb. The intentional destruction of valuable grave goods occurs cross-culturally and may be interpreted as a "killing" of the artifacts themselves, so that they would follow the death and decay of the deceased.

The Egyptian attitude was somewhat different. Within the concept of the tomb as "the dwelling-place of the Afterlife" (already attested in First Dynasty cemeteries of Abydos or Saqqara, *c.* 3100–2890 BCE), furniture and storage vessels aimed to provide quasi-eternal supplies. However, it must be emphasized that conspicuous consumption of items associated with the world of the living, including furniture, is not a consistent feature of Egyptian mortuary practice.

The burial of Queen Hetepheres I, mother of the Fourth Dynasty pharaoh Khufu (the well-known Hellenized form of her son's name being Kheōps or Cheops; r. *c.* 2589–2566 BCE), offers our best glimpse into the achievements of Old Kingdom furniture design and manufacture. Such deposition seems to have been a royal prerogative: furniture is not found, for example, in the slightly later tomb of Impy, a court official under Pepi II (Sixth Dynasty; r. *c.* 2278–2184 BCE), where copper models of offering tables are present rather than actual furniture items. The simplicity of the gilded furniture in Hetepheres' burial stands in contrast to the flamboyant embellishments of New Kingdom royal furniture, as exemplified by Tutankhamun's grave goods (Eighteenth Dynasty; r. *c.* 1332–1323 BCE) (Eaton-Krauss 2008).

The Eastern Cemetery at Deir el-Medîna yielded evidence suggesting emulation by the middle class of contemporary elite practices, such as those of the rich tombs of the Theban necropolis. These include the deposition of large quantities of furniture, albeit without the marks of ownership seen in elite burials (Snape 2011: 234–5). Although comparisons of funerary investment are hampered by the large number of robbed tombs, large pieces of furniture (i.e., besides chests and boxes) were scarcely deposited even with the burials of important individuals at the cemeteries of Ghurab or Sidmant (Wada 2007: 360–1, 372), whereas chairs or beds are standard even in wealthy middle-class assemblages at Thebes (Smith 1992: esp. 219, table 18). It is clear that local socioeconomic conditions influenced the scale of mortuary expenditure, at the top of which furniture deposition stood.

Wooden furniture was found in Middle Bronze Age (seventeenth to sixteenth century BCE) extramural shaft tombs (some of them reused from the late third millennium BCE) near the tell of ancient Jericho in Palestine. Three-legged tables and stools of plain design are dominant (funerary beds were found in only three burials out of almost sixty-nine tombs, each used for multiple burials) in the material preserved through unusual conditions of desiccation (Ricketts 1960; Parr 1996). Those burials containing furniture must have belonged to individuals of some status, such as a young disabled woman from tomb P19 who was accompanied by what appear to be two wooden staves/walking sticks although other burials in the cemetery seem to be quite poorly furnished.

Funerary furniture is also mentioned in the detailed descriptions of Hittite royal funerary rites: after cremation (which seems to be the norm for Hittite royalty), the royal charred remains are cleaned and placed on a chair/throne (for a king) or a footstool/stool (for a queen), taking part in the funerary banquet as its honored guests; the bones are carried to the *ḫekur* (dwelling-place of stone), the final resting place of the Hittite king, where they are placed on a couch in the burial chamber (Bryce 2002: 176–7). Unlike contemporary Egypt, however, and despite textual references to the *ḫekur* as elaborate structures, there has so far been no monument that has been identified with certainty as a Hittite royal tomb (for the possible locations of such monuments, including Chamber B at the Yazilikaya sanctuary, see Balza and Mora 2011: 220–2, with references).

Furniture has also been found in a number of elite Late Bronze Age Aegean burials. Two small three-legged tables from the exceptionally rich Shaft Grave V from Grave Circle A at Mycenae (sixteenth century BCE; Muhly 1996: 197–202) (Figure 6.1), for example, may be paralleled in the scant remains of wooden tables supporting bronze grave goods from Grave H from Mycenae Grave Circle B (sixteenth century BCE; Mylonas 1972–3: 92). One may also mention the elaborate table with ivory fittings from the "Tomb of the Bronzes" (Tomb III) at the Areopagus Hill in Athens (Immerwahr 1971: 171), ivory-inlaid footstools from Dendra Tomb 8, Mycenae Tomb 518, Prosymna Tomb 2,

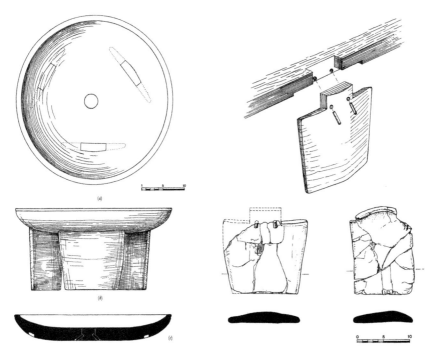

FIGURE 6.1 Reconstruction and drawing of extant fragments of a three-legged table found in Shaft Grave V of Grave Circle A, Mycenae (Argolid), late seventeenth or sixteenth century BCE. *Source:* Muhly 1996: 199–201, figs. 2–5. Courtesy of Polymnia Muhly and the National Archaeological Museum (Department of the Collections of Prehistoric, Egyptian, Cypriot and Near Eastern Antiquities), Athens.

Phylaki Apokoronou, and Archanes Tholos Tomb A (Sakellarakis 1996). It is interesting that, while Mycenaean footstools can be reconstructed from their ivory fittings, we have no certain evidence for the seats (chairs or thrones) that they might have accompanied.

Remains of wooden funerary biers, beds, or coffins have been widely discussed in the scholarship (Muhly 1996: 207–11, with references). It is certain that the Cretan terracotta chest-shaped burial *larnax* ("chest"; plural *larnakes*) copied a wooden prototype (coffin or storage-chest?), at least as early as c. 1800 BCE, when the first example of such a *larnax* dates (Platon 2012). Their role in ritual mourning and elaborate funerary processions to the grave (cf. later *prothesis* and *ekphora*) was surely important. Besides the sporadic occurrence of evidence on the Greek mainland (as in Mycenae Circle A, Dendra Tomb 8, Chamber Tomb XL at Athens and Prosymna Chamber Tombs X, XXIX, and XLII), most examples come from Crete, including the "Warrior Graves" or "Burials with Bronzes" found around the palace of Knossos (New Hospital site, Ayios Ioannis, Sellopoulo, Upper Gypsades).[1] Pieces of ivory and gold-foil decoration have suggested a reconstruction of a wooden coffin from the

Prehistoric Cemetery area at Mycenae that probably dates to the late fifteenth century BCE (Papazoglou-Manioudaki 2012). These burials are clustered around important centers, such as Knossos and Mycenae, during a period critical for the consolidation of Mycenaean palatial power (late fifteenth to fourteenth century BCE): the deposition of furniture in them must be viewed as an expression of mortuary expenditure intended to impress the local communities and therefore meet the urgent need of these emerging elite groups to establish themselves.

Excursus: The funerary interpretation of the Pylos Ta tablets

British linguist and classicist Leonard Palmer (1957) suggested that the furniture, vessels, and other utensils recorded on the Pylos Linear B tablets of the Ta set (see Chapter 9 in this volume) constituted a tomb inventory. This is based on his interpretation of the verb *thēke* (spelled *te-ke*) in the heading line of the entire set as "[he] buried," producing a translation of the line as "when the king buried *Augewās* [personal name], the *dāmokoros* [a term now understood to be a title]" (PY Ta 711.1). Even if the Pylos inventory compares roughly well with the contents of intact tombs, it must be remembered that grave goods found in well-furnished Mycenaean tombs have typically been deposited over the course of many burials (with previous remains pushed aside to make room for new ones). Items, such as seats, however, have not been identified in Mycenean tombs. If the inventory is indeed that of a *single* Mycenaean interment, as Palmer's translation of the heading suggests, the quantity of artifacts would have no par in the extant archaeological record. An added difficulty with this "mortuary" interpretation of the inventory is the certain interpretation of *da-mo-ko-ro* as the title of an official (Olivier 1967; this was not known with certainty when Palmer's theory was published). Given our current understanding of the context of these records, the likeliest translation of *thēke* is "[he] appointed."

FIRST HALF OF FIRST MILLENNIUM BCE

Arguably the most remarkable case of well-preserved furniture of this period is that found in the eighth-century BCE Gordion Tumuli K-III, P, W, and most notably Tumulus MM (for "Midas Mound," although the occupant of the mound has not been identified with certainty). The Gordion wooden furniture is now fully published in exemplary fashion and detail (Simpson 2010). The Tumulus MM burial consisted of a wooden chamber without an entrance covered by a huge clay mound, which was responsible for the remarkable preservation of the wooden remains. As many as one inlaid and eight plain traytop banquet tables, two serving stands, two stools, and a probable chair accompanied the deceased who was placed in a large uncovered coffin (originally interpreted as a funerary "bed") and who certainly enjoyed royal status. Given the fact that the burial

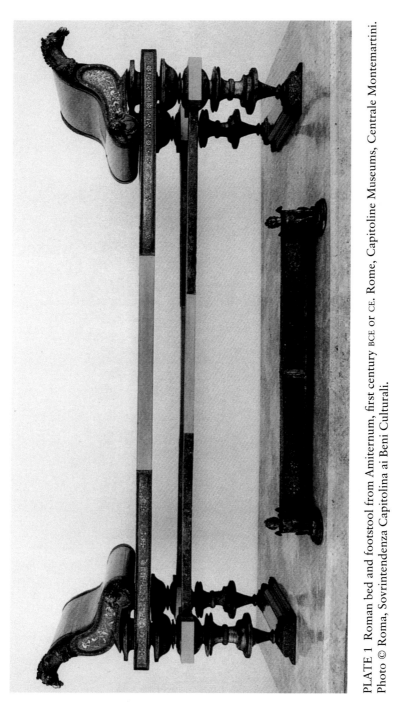

PLATE 1 Roman bed and footstool from Amiternum, first century BCE or CE. Rome, Capitoline Museums, Centrale Montemartini. Photo © Roma, Sovrintendenza Capitolina ai Beni Culturali.

PLATE 2 Marble table holder depicting Orpheus, fourth century CE, Byzantine and Christian Museum of Athens, inv. no. BXM 1. Photograph © Hellenic Ministry of Culture and Sports/Archaeological Receipts Fund.

PLATE 3 Model of a carpenter's workshop, from the tomb of Meket-Rē, Eleventh Dynasty Egypt. Cairo Museum JE 46722. Photograph courtesy of Jürgen Liepe. © Cairo Museum, Egypt.

PLATE 4 Marble leg from a monopode table depicting the Good Shepherd, fourth century CE. Museum of Byzantine Culture, Thessaloniki, inv. no. ΑΓ 2491. Photograph © Hellenic Ministry of Culture and Sports/Archaeological Receipts Fund, Museum of Byzantine Culture, Thessaloniki.

PLATE 5 Round-legged stool, three-legged table, and chair. New Kingdom (*c.* 1550–1069 BCE). Photograph © The Trustees of the British Museum, London.

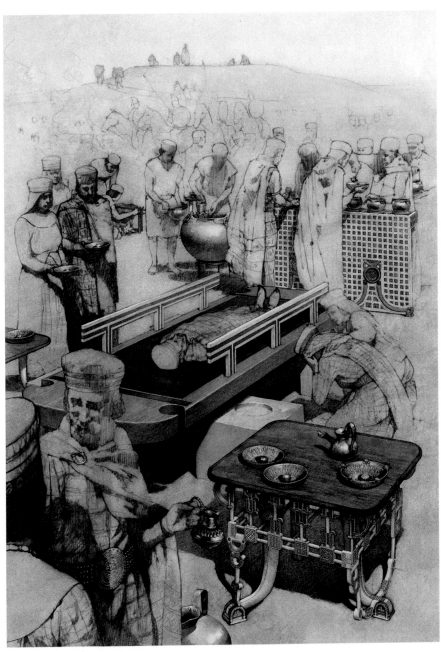

PLATE 6 Reconstruction of the king's funeral outside Tumulus MM at Gordion, Turkey, eighth century BCE. Painting by Greg Harlin. © Greg Harlin and Elizabeth Simpson, 2001.

PLATE 7 Wall painting depicting a symposion scene with a *kylikeion* from the Tomb of Agios Athanasios, Thessaloniki. Last quarter of the fourth century BCE. Photograph © Hellenic Ministry of Culture and Sports/Archaeological Receipts Fund, Ephorate of Antiquities of Thessaloniki Region.

PLATE 8 Wall painting depicting a banquet (?) on the tholos of the Hellenistic Tomb at Kazanluk, Bulgaria. Third century BCE. Photograph courtesy of Wikimedia Commons.

PLATE 9 Sarcophagus found in Simpelveld, the Netherlands, *c.* 200 CE. Rijksmuseum van Oudheden (National Museum of Antiquities), Leiden, inv. nr. I 1930/12.1. Photo courtesy of the National Museum of Antiquities, Leiden, The Netherlands.

PLATE 10 Symposion scene from the wall painting of the Tomb of Agios Athanasios, Thessaloniki. Last quarter of the fourth century BCE. Photograph © Hellenic Ministry of Culture and Sports/Archaeological Receipts Fund, Ephorate of Antiquities of Thessaloniki Region.

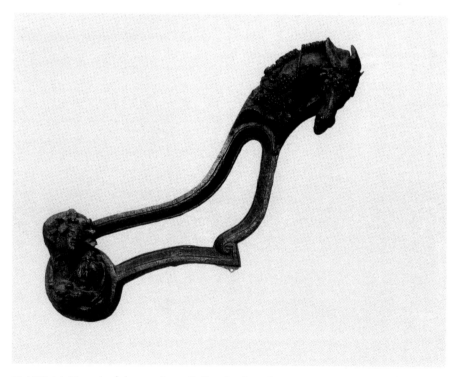

PLATE 11 Bronze *fulcrum* from Pella. Archaeological Museum of Pella, inv. no. Δ311A. Second-first century BCE. Photograph © Hellenic Ministry of Culture and Sports/Archaeological Receipts Fund, Ephorate of Antiquities of Pella.

PLATE 12 *Kylikeion* in the House of Seals, Delos. Second century BCE. Photograph courtesy of Dimitra Andrianou.

PLATE 13 Doctor reading next to an open cupboard containing a stack of book rolls on its top shelf. A kit of medical instruments is seen at the top of the cupboard. Marble relief, detail of a sarcophagus found near Ostia, fourth century CE. The Metropolitan Museum of Art, New York, 48.76.1. Gift of Mrs. Joseph Brummer and Ernest Brummer, in memory of Joseph Brummer, 1948. Photograph courtesy of the Metropolitan Museum of Art.

PLATE 14 The "Garden Party" relief from the North Palace of Ashurbanipal, Nineveh (modern Iraq), *c.* 645 BCE. Photograph © The Trustees of the British Museum.

PLATE 15 Throne of Bishop Maximian. Sixth century CE. Museo Arcivescovile, Ravenna, Italy. Photo: Leemage/The Universal Images Group/Getty Images.

PLATE 16 Funerary relief depicting a wooden cupboard in a cutlery shop, second century CE. Museo della Civilta Romana, Rome, Italy. Photo: DEA/A.DAGLI ORTI/De Agostini/Getty Images.

PLATE 17 Funerary relief depicting a flower and vegetable seller, third century CE.
Museo Ostiense, Ostia, Italy. Photo: DEA/A.DAGLI ORTI/De Agostini/Getty Images.

PLATE 18 Stone relief showing a belt and cushion shop, second century CE. Museo della Civilta Romana, Rome, Italy. Photograph courtesy of DEA/A.DAGLI ORTI/De Agostini Picture Library/Getty Images.

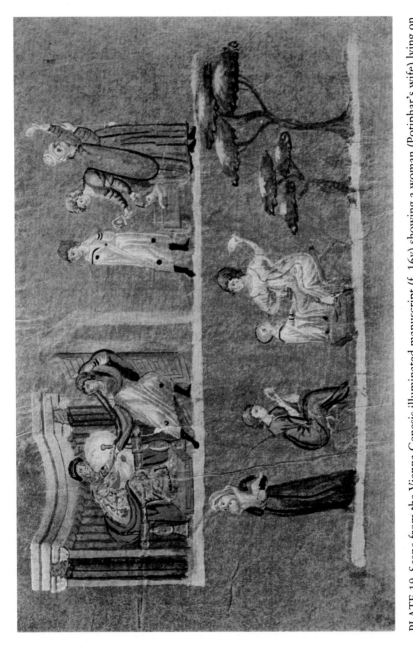

PLATE 19 Scene from the Vienna Genesis illuminated manuscript (f. 16v) showing a woman (Potiphar's wife) lying on her bed, sixth century CE. Österreichische Nationalbibliothek, Vienna, Austria. Photograph courtesy of Österreichische Nationalbibliothek/Wikimedia Commons.

PLATE 20 Interior of the Tomb of the Reliefs, Cerveteri. Third quarter of the fourth century BCE. Photograph courtesy of Wikimedia Commons.

PLATE 21 Tomb of the Shields and Chairs, Cerveteri. Second half of the sixth century BCE. © Photo Scala, Florence. Courtesy of the Ministero Beni e Attività Culturali e del Turismo.

PLATE 22 Marble throne of "Eurydice's tomb," Vergina (Aigai), 344–340 BCE. The Museum of the Royal Tombs at Aigai. Photograph © Hellenic Ministry of Culture and Sports/Archaeological Receipts Fund, Ephorate of Antiquities of Hemathia.

PLATE 23 Silver *diphros* from Stavroupolis, Thessaloniki. Fourth century BCE. Archaeological Museum of Thessaloniki, inv. no. MΘ 7440. Photograph © Hellenic Ministry of Culture and Sports/Archaeological Receipts Fund, Ephorate of Antiquities of Thessaloniki City.

PLATE 24 Textile from the "Tomb of Philip," Vergina (Aigai), 336 BCE. The Museum of the Royal Tombs at Aigai. Photograph © Hellenic Ministry of Culture and Sports/ Archaeological Receipts Fund, Ephorate of Antiquities of Hemathia.

PLATE 25 François vase. Early sixth century BCE. Ministero dei Beni e Attività Culturali e del Turismo, Polo Museale della Toscana, Florence. Photograph courtesy of Ancient History Encyclopedia/Wikimedia Commons.

PLATE 26 Marble throne from the theater of Dionysos, Athens. Fifth–fourth century BCE. Photo: DEA/A. VERGANI/ De Agostini/Getty Images.

PLATE 27 Table with silver appliqués and silverware from the Tomb of Vestorius Priscus, Pompeii, *c*. 70 BCE. Photograph courtesy of Stephan Mols.

PLATE 28 Roman atrium with cartibulum, Pompeii. First century BCE- first century CE. Photograph courtesy of Wikimedia Commons.

PLATE 29 Wooden cupboard with an *aedicula* (house shrine), Herculaneum. First century CE. Photograph courtesy of Elizabeth Simpson.

PLATE 30 *Andron* with pebble floor depicting Bellerophon mounted on Pegasos fighting the Chimaira, House VI 3, Olynthos. Fifth-fourth century BCE. Photograph courtesy of Christaras A/Wikimedia Commons.

PLATE 31 Representation of two men seated on backless stools flanking a tripod within a probable athletic competition from a *naiskos* terracotta model of an apsidal building at Nikoleika (ancient Helike) in Achaia, northwestern Peloponesse. Eighth century BCE. Photograph courtesy of Anastasia Gadolou, Ephorate of Antiquities of Achaia.

PLATE 32 Red-figure cup by Douris, Berlin. 490–480 BCE. Berlin, Antikensammlung F2285. Source: courtesy of bpk Berlin/Antikensammlung, SMB/Johannes Laurentius for the image bpk 00006794.

PLATE 33 Black-figure amphora, 520–510 BCE. Photograph © Museum of Fine Arts, Boston.

PLATE 34 Basel relief of a healer. Antikenmuseum Basel, Sammlung Ludwig, inv. no. BS 236, 480 BCE. Photo: © Antikenmuseum Basel und Sammlung Ludwig, inv. no. BS 236.

PLATE 35 Butcher cutting meat on an *epixenon*, red-figure *pelike*. Inv. no. 486, 480 BCE. Photograph courtesy of Georg Pöhlein. © Antikensammlung Erlangen, Friedrich-Alexander-Universität Erlangen-Nürnberg.

PLATE 36 Red-figure lekythos depicting an open chest, Gela, Sicily, *c.* 460 BCE.
Photograph courtesy of Yale University Art Gallery.

PLATE 37 (a) Variants (in relative scale) of "ideogram" *220 "footstool" named *thrānus* in Mycenaean Greek. (b) Representation of a footstool from the great ring from the Tiryns treasure (enclosed in red rectangular frame in the drawing of the impression of the ring). (c) Variants of "ideogram" *169. (d) Stylized renderings (not in relative scale) of beds and seats on Late Geometric pictorial pottery. (e) Linear B tablet from Pylos recording single *thrānuwes* "footstools" (PY Ta 721). *Sources*: (a) and (c): Permissions granted by the late Jean-Pierre Olivier and Louis Godart. (b): Diamantis Panagiotopoulos (CMS, Heidelberg). (d): redrawn and rearranged by Vassilis Petrakis based on Laser (1968: figs. 1 and 7). (e): Thomas G. Palaima (Director, PASP, University of Texas at Austin).

PLATE 38 Wooden core and bronze fitting from a sphinx-leg of a *kline* (?) from the Styra shipwreck, South Euboea. Inv. no. BE 2010/4–7, Late Hellenistic. Photographs © Hellenic Ministry of Culture and Sports/Archaeological Receipts Fund, Ephorate of Underwater Antiquities.

chamber had no entrance, all grave goods must have been lowered from above, before the construction of the roof and the erection of the mound. The massive scale of the enterprise clearly indicates that the royal funeral of the king buried in Tumulus MM must have been a most memorable public event for Gordion. A similarly rich (if not richer) assemblage of at least twenty-two pieces of furniture has been recovered from Tumulus P, which contained the burial of a child, including an inlaid serving stand of boxwood and a remarkable inlaid stool. The male burial in Tumulus W was, by comparison, modestly accompanied by a probable serving stand (Simpson 1996: 196–207, figs. 7, 9).

Although no textual sources survive to help us in reconstructing the mortuary rites in the Gordion tumuli, analyses of organic remains from bronze and pottery vessels have enabled us to recover much information about the pertinent funerary banquet, for which most of the furniture may have originally been intended: sheep or goat stew served with lentils and other vegetables or spices was accompanied by an intriguing mixed beverage of wine, barley beer, and honey mead (McGovern cited in Simpson 2010: 177–87).[2]

Pictorial representations on Attic Geometric pottery of the mid-eighth century BCE inform us of the employment of chairs, stools, and beds/biers in contemporary aristocratic funerals. The ritual stages of mourning accompanying *prothesis* (laying out the deceased on a bier or bed) and *ekphora* (the processional transport to the grave; occasionally the funerary *kline* itself is put on a wheeled horse-drawn carriage), which took place prior to the funeral feast and burial, are especially well represented (Ahlberg 1971). Mourning and *prothesis* also occur in Mycenaean representations, such as those on terracotta chest-shaped containers or *larnakes* from the chamber tomb cemeteries at Tanagra in Boeotia (Cavanagh and Mee 1995: figs. 4, 7) or on a twelfth-century BCE pictorial krater from Ayia Triada near Elis. During the mid-eighth century BCE, such imagery is almost exclusively Attic (the region of Greece including Athens), although this does not necessarily indicate that the custom was exclusively Attic, even if the aristocratic ideals conveyed through these representations must have been particularly popular in Athenian upper classes of the time. The eventual deposition of the *kline* and stools remains problematic (the *klinai* could have been consumed in the cremation). Some of the amphorae depicting such furniture were large and conspicuous grave markers (again, an almost exclusively Athenian trait).

Evidence for the elaborate mortuary consumption of furniture has also been found in Early Iron Age Cyprus. In the fill of the *dromos* (passageway) of Tomb 79 of the necropolis of Salamis (late eighth century BCE), the remains of actual pieces of elaborate furniture were found, including three chairs (thrones), two stools, two footstools, one bed, and two fragmentary tables (Karageorghis 1973–4). The wooden frames had decayed, but the elaborate ivory and metal fittings (inlays, plates, and sheathing) allowed restorations (in some cases tentative) of the entire assemblage. The bed and one chair (Throne Gamma) were decorated in the same Egyptianizing style seen in some of the contemporary Nimrud ivories (see also Chapter 5 in this volume). Although these restorations are somewhat conjectural, this remarkable assemblage clearly suggests an elaborate mortuary ritual that recalls the Homeric description of the funeral of Patroklos, Achilles' companion, in the *Iliad* (Hom., *Il.* 23.108–261). The significance of this correspondence, however, is not certain; it may suggest an imitation of the Homeric description, or, as Karageorghis (2006: 668) recently argued, the possibility that the epic narrative described the customs of contemporary elites. Although the Homeric associations of the Salamis (and Gordion) assemblages are interesting, we may observe that the deposition of furniture is not explicitly noted in the description of Patroklos' funeral, with the exception of a funerary λέχος (bed) (Hom., *Il.* 23.171).

Beyond the Aegean, the kingdom of Urartu (ninth to seventh century BCE), centered in the region of Lake Van in the Armenian highlands, has also yielded remarkably well-preserved examples of furniture deposited in elite burials placed in rock-cut chamber tombs. Most important are the eighth-century BCE assemblages from Adilcevaz (Chamber Tomb I in Slope H) and Altintepe (Tombs 1 and 3).

The sixth century BCE was a monumental time for Athenian burials. Rich tombs were adorned with commemorative *kouroi* (the statues of standing young men), *stelai* with sphinxes, or covered by/set in large mounds. In this setting, furniture was seldom deposited, with a few notable exceptions from the Kerameikos, an area of Athens to the northwest of the Acropolis both inside and outside the ancient city walls. The *kline* from Grave 3 (HW 37) in the South Mound (*c.* 540 BCE; Knigge 1976: 60–83, figs. 21–38, plates 101–11) is a remarkable find, whose reconstruction has been inferred from the ivory and amber decoration found in situ (Figure 6.2). Its elaborate decoration is paralleled in contemporary vase painting, as in the elaborate couch on the red-figure side of the Attic bilingual amphora in Munich (inv. no. 2301) attributed to the Andokides Painter, but most likely the work of two different painters due to structural details rendered in paint.[3] Grave 3 contained east Greek and Lydian pottery, and it has been well argued from a stylistic analysis of its decoration that this *kline* is an Ionian import, even if the identification of the deceased male as Ionian remains conjectural (Knigge 1976: 82–3). Μιλησιουργεῖς κλῖναι (beds/couches of Milesian craftsmanship) are mentioned in the *Attic Stelai* among confiscated possessions from rich Athenian households (Pritchett 1956: 228–9; cf. Chapter 4 in this volume), and this suggests that imported furniture from Asia Minor (or, at least, made after Milesian fashion) was still much sought after during the fifth century BCE. Similar ivory and amber inlays have been recovered from at least three other graves (1, 2, and 5) in Kerameikos Mound G (*c.* 560 BCE) and, despite lacking the ivory veneer of the Grave 3 example, they have similarly been attributed to elaborate *klinai* (Kübler 1976: 5–6, 17–18, 21, plates 4:2–3, 8.3).

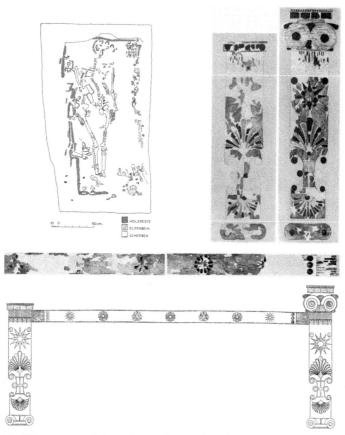

FIGURE 6.2 *Kline* recovered from the south tumulus of Kerameikos, *c.* 540 BCE. The plan (top left) shows the distribution of the remains of the *kline* within the grave. *Source:* Knigge 1976: figs. 21–2, plates 103, 109; arrangement following the reproduction in Baughan 2013: 62, fig. 43. Courtesy of the German Archaeological Institute.

THE ETRUSCAN WORLD

The Etruscans were known in antiquity for their *luxuria*, a high standard of living based on rich natural resources as well as highly developed international contacts (Diodorus Siculus 5.40.5). The social aspects of their furnishings were of great importance to them, the symbolism of these were intelligible to their Greek and Italian neighbors as well. Etruscan design, homes, and furnishings ultimately lie behind many aspects of modern interiors, via the development of Roman material culture and architecture, which were heavily influenced by Etruscan material culture (de Grummond 1986: 18–46; 1996: 149–89). The loss of Etruscan literature (in contrast to that of Greece and Rome) and the scarcity of evidence for Etruscan domestic or civic structures cause us to rely on funerary contexts of the first millennium BCE for our understanding of Etruscan furniture. While the tombs sometimes resemble scaled-down houses or *palazzi*, they never held the full contents of a real home. Some burials, however, do contain items (chariots, chairs, stools, banquet or cultic equipment) that had been used in life. The inclusion of items used in life, such as folding stools, thrones, or chariots in the tomb was symbolic of special status and functions in life, when only a magistrate sat in court or a ruler or priestess was driven to public gatherings. A survey of tombs and funerary offerings shows several distinctive Etruscan or Italic furniture types as well as a strong interest in foreign furnishings from the Near East and Aegean. Valuable materials such as bronze and ivory coverings and fittings are also evident in the furnishings of Etruscan family tombs. Grave goods were never random selections. What has been preserved was all chosen to be emblematic of the family life and social symbolism of Etruria, from its Iron Age origins (*c.* 1000 BCE) to the late first-millennium melding with the cultures of the Hellenistic East and Rome. In other words, objects selected for display in the funeral ritual and burial as grave gifts were carefully selected for their expression of the identity and importance of the deceased, for instance the deposition of a chariot indicated the noble's participation in civic ceremonies (processions) and his/her control of wide lands on which to breed horses. Foreign connections, too, were displayed, in the form of fine textiles, wood-carved and ivory-clad furniture, vases and/or luxury goods in ivory, amber, gold, glass, and so on from other parts of Italy, Sardinia, Europe, Greece, the Levant, and beyond; the practice continued in general through the first millennium BCE.

The development of underground chamber tombs in Etruria at the end of the eighth century BCE (continuing through the fourth century BCE) created the opportunity for display of funerary furniture, preserving actual furniture or replicas carved in the living rock, while the few surviving, excavated Etruscan houses or public buildings did not have furniture in place. A major assumption is that the tombs of Cerveteri (ancient Caere) replicate, in telescopic scale made necessary by the need to carve interiors out of the bedrock, the appearance of real homes. The earliest houses in proto-historical Italy are the elliptical thatched huts of the Villanovan (i.e., Iron Age, proto-Etruscan) and Italic cultures at sites such as Veii, Tarquinia, Sorgenti della Nova (near Vulci), or the village containing the "Hut of Romulus" on the Palatine Hill of Rome. They were sparsely furnished; a low raised bench of rubble covered in clay sufficed to hold storage jars/baskets, the family's bedrolls and belongings. One of the earliest monumental tombs at Cerveteri, the "Tomb of the Hut," is believed to replicate such huts: carved into the living rock, it has a ridgepole, sloping ceiling, and raised bench along the interior walls (Haynes 2000: 111, fig. 92).

When terracotta roof-tiles began to be installed around the middle of the seventh century, houses acquired a rectilinear plan, with small interior courtyards (as at Acquarossa) developing into the atrium essential to Roman (and Pompeian) urban plans. Early examples (*c.* 510 BCE) were excavated at Marzabotto near Bologna, and on the Roman Palatine. The Etruscan term *athre* (room, house, building) is the source of the Latin *atrium* (see Haynes 2000: 138–41, 188–90).

The sixth-century tombs in Cerveteri's Banditaccia necropolis seem to preserve tokens of the atrium in some plans: while they could not be open to the sky with an *impluvium*, some, such as the "Tomb of the Tablinum" (Steingräber 2013: 665; Prayon 1975: plate 45) have a central space surrounded by smaller chambers resembling bedrooms or *cubicula*. The Caeretan *Tombe Campana I, dei Leoni dipinti, degli Scudi e delle Sedie, della Sedia Torlonia,* and *della Cornice* of the end of the seventh to the sixth century, contain beds/couches, large storage baskets, cylindrical chairs or thrones, and features such as paneling and cornice/plate rails carved out of the bedrock, and must have imitated the woodwork and furniture of aristocratic townhouses (Prayon 1975: 107–15, plates 42–7, 59–65; Steingräber 1979 *passim*). In general, rock-cut couches held male depositions, and rectangular, bed-like "sarcophagi" with gabled head and concave pillows held women's remains; a few tombs have a smaller bed beside the mother's to hold a child's body (*Tomba della Quercia*, Haynes 2000: 90, figs. 73–4). Carved stone headrests on some beds/couches reflect a type employed in the burial chambers of eighth- to sixth-century Judaea and probably attest to the influence of elite Levantine immigrants (Magness 2001: 85–90).

The funerary Montescudaio urn, a large biconical ceramic jar intended for burial of cremated human remains, has small clay figures on the lid depicting a banquet: a man sits on a four-legged rectangular stool at a round, three-legged table being served from a cauldron on a high stand; a scar to his right may be the remains of a cylindrical chair for his (missing) consort (Camporeale 2011: 179, plate 5; Haynes 2000: 111–12, fig. 92). Cylindrical thrones with footrests carved in the anterooms of some Caeretan tombs may have represented the Etruscan *materfamilias* (Steingräber 2013: 665). The *Tomb of the Five Chairs* held statuettes of ancestors seated at banquet on low, straight-backed chairs with footrests facing two rectangular tables; two cylindrical chairs and a large basket stand on one side, an altar opposite (Haynes 2000: 92–4, figs. 76–8). The seated banquet with rulers attended by servants was an integral feature of early Etruscan society (Tuck 1994); it would morph into the reclining banquet as, during the seventh century BCE, visitors from the Levant/Near East and Greece came to deal for the metals of Italy. The addition of furniture, allowing rulers to sit comfortably in public, to make them special by reclining at a banquet, and by traveling in speed and comfort with wheeled vehicles, set the "princes" apart from the commons and aided in maintaining order in the growing cities. All the accoutrements of civilized urban life may be found in the tombs of these generations, especially the "princely tombs" of the early and mid-seventh century. Their permanent display (for the gods of the Underworld?) in the tomb must have reflected the display of such emblems of power (jewels, scepters, thrones, footstools, etc.) in the homes/palaces of rulers, visually setting them apart from their subjects.

A necropolis excavated in the twentieth century at Adriatic Verucchio, near Ravenna, has yielded amazing examples of furnishings made in organic materials, including a wealth of textiles and wooden furniture deposited around 680 BCE in several rectangular wooden tombs preserved by waterlogging (von Eles 2002). Tomb 85-Lippi held a woman's cylindrical throne with flaring back carved from a tree trunk and three small, round tripod tables with complex curved legs (von Eles 2000). The wooden finds from tomb 89-Lippi must have been used in a princely home before deposition with a man's remains in the wood-lined chamber: a cylindrical throne and footstool, box and fan-handle, all intricately carved in intaglio (Bentini and Moretto 2002). A cart and chariot were also displayed. The throne was decorated with bronze studs set into carved scenes of life in the Etruscan town. Such thrones usually appear in female burials, but this, from a man's tomb, has been interpreted by some scholars as indicating his status as a priest, or perhaps the son of a priestess; his unusual helmet is said to have symbolized his warrior father (cf. Bonfante 2005). Textiles played an important part in burial rituals, as in the civic and religious ceremonies of the ruling classes; most of the Verucchio textiles are clothing, however. Images of the coverings, bedding, tents, and draperies displayed in festivals, funerals, and feasts appeared later in Tarquinian tomb frescoes.

One of the best documented furnished tombs is the Regolini-Galassi Tomb excavated in 1836. It was built around 675–650 BCE perhaps for a "Larthia, wife of Velthur" (according to inscriptions) and held her burial and others of the family (Sannibale 2013). The tomb built of stone slabs was decorated with bronze parade shields hung along the walls; vases and other items were also hung on pegs probably simulating normal household storage. Furnishings of bronze and wood include a chariot, a cart, two simple stools, and a bronze-clad, wooden object with a wing-back originally restored as a throne (Pareti 1947: 239–44, plate 23, no. 217). It has now, on analogy to rock-cut versions in other Caeretan tombs, been restored as an altar with step or stool and a top punctuated by three cup-like depressions for offerings (see Prayon 1975: 112–13, plates 39, 62). The funerary bed was constructed of a bronze sheet with six tubular legs, a raised headrest, and interwoven strips for the "mattress." Bronze conical stands and gilded silver vessels formed a wine service for at least fifteen (for vehicles, see Emiliozzi 2013).

A tomb at Poggio alla Sala (Montepulciano) to the north held a young man's cremated bones in an urn draped in a cloak and placed on a straight-backed chair constructed of sheet bronze. Before it stood a small, low table constructed of sheet bronze, made for the tomb and intended to simulate a seated banquet (end of seventh century; Rastrelli 2000). Other examples of fine furniture of the mid-seventh century have been found in two tombs at Palestrina (Praeneste) in the region of Latium, south and east of Rome, which was the territory of the Latin-speaking tribes; these are the arbitrarily named Barberini and Bernardini Tombs (Canciani and von Hase 1979). In addition to bronze floor stands holding deep mixing bowls for wine, there was a cylindrical throne of wood covered in repoussé-decorated sheet bronze (MacIntosh 1974: 22, plate 13.3; Steingräber 1979: no. 28). Ornamental bronze fittings perhaps came from a rectangular seat or dais, with railings ornamented with humans in feather crowns and monstrous animals eating human victims. A conical stand is an Assyrian-style import while others, with rod-like legs ending in hooves and human figures peeking into the cauldron, are of native Italic style (Canciani and von Hase 1979: plates 46–9).

Fragmentary ivory inlays related to North Syrian and Phoenician furniture found in Assyrian palaces (e.g., Nimrud) attest to lost wooden chairs, beds, and chests imported from the Near East (Canciani and von Hase 1979: 65–72, with references).

By the end of the seventh century, tombs had become more elaborate, with each city-region characterized by its own unique style. In the north of Etruria, Populonia, a coastal city involved in the metal trade with the eastern Mediterranean, had a necropolis with round tumuli covering masonry chambers. Some rooms had carved stone beds or high-legged couches imitating heavy, turned wooden legs with large convex moldings (cf. Steingräber 1979: 65–8), presumably alluding to the reclining banquet introduced from the Near East as a symbol of privilege (Prayon 1975: plate 67).

By 575–550 BCE, additional foreign models for banquet/burial couches were introduced from Greece, though their earliest appearance, on the Murlo frieze plaques, places them on a large monumental building rather than a tomb. These were long slabs of terracotta used to sheath the exterior beams of the roof, and decorated in low relief with scenes from courtly life and myth (an assembly of gods, an aristocratic wedding procession, a banquet, and a horse race). In a relief of men and women banqueting, the couches have cut-out legs made of flat boards decorated in a style set by Corinthian painting. The other Murlo frieze series furnish additional fine evidence of real-life furniture, including folding stools, cylindrical thrones, and a two-wheeled lady's cart—all of which also appeared in southern Etruscan tombs (MacIntosh 1974). Numerous reliefs, ritual and decorative objects across Italy depict people, often matrons, sitting in these cylindrical chairs (Steingräber 1979: plates 15.2, 18.2–3, 19.1).

With time, the interiors of rock-cut, underground tombs became simpler, but the furnishings—depicted on sarcophagi and urns in stone or terracotta—continued to reflect high banquet couches with headboards and intricately sawn legs in the form of volute-and-palmette ornaments, as on the two famous

Sarcophagi of the Couples from Cerveteri (*c.* 530–510 BCE, now in Villa Giulia, Rome, and Louvre, Paris) (Gaultier 2013). These depict the married couple at banquet, on couches with plump pillows and fine coverlets. The frescoed walls of chamber tombs in Tarquinia's Monterozzi necropolis, an extramural site of small rectangular chamber tombs overlooking the sea, with rare interiors painted with funerals, games, banquets, and religious ceremonies (*Tombs of the Leopards, of the Funeral Bed, of the Ship, of the Black Sow, of the Shields*) depict the same couches with brightly colored, even plaid, blankets and pillows in red, blue, green, and yellow, along with tents (the funeral caterer's tent?) in black-and-white checkerboard (Steingräber 1986: plates 105, 110–11, 118, 140–4, 146–7). Care is taken in some murals to depict the *kylikeia*—sideboards, shelves, or tables on which wine service (like wedding gifts) ranging from Attic black- or red-figure ware to gold is displayed at the funeral (*Tomb of the Ship, Tomba del Orco*: van der Meer 1984; Steingräber 1986: plates 119, 132). The scenes include servants waiting upon the family at a funeral banquet and may also have suggested the display of gifts such as at an aristocratic wedding. The tall, painted terracotta wall panels known as the *Boccanera* and *Campana plaques* of the second half of the sixth century once hung on the walls of tombs at Cerveteri and are now displayed in the British Museum and Louvre. They attest to monumental scenes of myth such as the Judgment of Paris and religious rituals displayed in Caeretan tombs, implying that some houses were so decorated (Roncalli 2013).

The sixth to the fifth century have yielded a small number of actual pieces of furniture, surely laden with symbolic civic meaning, in the form of magistrates' folding stools. Many that survive in museum collections are made of wood with cast bronze fittings (bovine feet, hinges, etc.) (Turfa 2005: 29, 150, no. 112). In the *Tomba degli Auguri*, Tarquinia (530–510 BCE; Steingräber 1979: no. 58, plate 10.1) a boy carries a folded stool for one of the referees in traditional funeral games of wrestling, boxing, etc. celebrated near the tomb in honor of the deceased painted. Men sit in a meeting on such stools on a funerary *cippus* from Chiusi (fifth century; Steingräber 1979: plate 13.1 no. 164). The fourth-century *Boston Sarcophagus* of Ramtha Viśnai from Vulci shows a noble husband and wife attended by servants carrying her parasol(?), fan, jewelry chest, and kithara and his *fasces* and folding stool (prototype of the Roman senator's *sella curulis*), symbols of his civic authority (Schäfer 1989; Haynes 2000: 289, fig. 232b; Steingräber 2002: 141–3) (Figure 6.3). A special find from the *Tomba dello Sgabello* in the Giardini Margherita necropolis at Bologna is a folding stool with legs made from ivory tusks (Steingräber 1979: 193, no. 2, plate 5.2). The delicate, bronze, palmette-ornamented hooves of wooden folding stools have been found in numerous Etruscan and Italic tombs, and have been recognized in votive deposits at international sanctuaries such as Delphi (Naso 2012: 327, 332, fig. 10), evoking reference to the "Throne of Arimnestos" dedicated by the

FIGURE 6.3 Sarcophagus of a married couple. *c.* 530–520 BCE. Photograph: Museum purchase with funds donated by Mrs. Gardner Brewer and by contribution and the Benjamin Pierce Cheney Donation, Boston Museum of Fine Arts.

legendary Etruscan king, the first foreigner to dedicate at Olympia (Pausanias 5.12.5). It may have been a bronze-clad cylindrical chair like many that held cinerary urns in Chiusine tombs (Steingräber 1979: 22–34), designed, like a modern "photo-op," to be an ongoing visual reminder of its royal dedicant and his importance.

The *Tomb of the Reliefs* (of the Matuna family) at Cerveteri is a unique, single chamber carved in bedrock reminiscent of the atrium, dining room, and/ or bedrooms of a noble house condensed into a rectangular room supported by two pillars (Blanck and Proietti 1986; Steingräber 1986: no. 9) (Plate 20). Niches cut into the walls are articulated as if they were banquet couches or beds, with a simpler, tile-lined bench running in front of the inscribed niches to hold additional burials. Carved and finished in plaster on all surfaces of the pillars and walls are relief representations of furniture and household goods. Beneath the central "bed" is a low stool with a girl's red sandals on it, as if she had just climbed into bed; beside it are a low chest with lock and key and a cloth "linen book" depicted in relief. The chest, like a low cradle on wheels that "hangs" on one pillar, is painted in several colors (red, brown, tan, yellow) to indicate different woods or leather finishes. Walls are decorated with sculpted busts, shields, helmets, greaves, and swords; knives (in wooden holders), tools, vessels, a knapsack, and a game board all appear as if hung on pegs on the walls and pillars (Plate 21). This probably reflects actual housekeeping, where few cupboards or chests existed.

Later sarcophagi of the fourth to the third century, especially at Tarquinia, seem to portray the deceased reclining or sleeping on a bed with gabled head- and footboards (Steingräber 1979: plate 21, nos. 440, 447). At Chiusi to the north, however, some late Hellenistic (second to first century BCE) urns in terracotta depict banquet couches with heavy turned legs and low stools with stretchers, designs that would continue in Roman furniture (Steingräber 1979: plates 23–6; Briguet and Briquel 2002: 105–8). Certainly banqueting continued, but funerary iconography took a different course (see Rathje 2013). At Vulci, the painted *Tomba François*, and the Tomb of the Volumnii at Perugia show late fourth-century and Hellenistic house plans with symmetrical rooms stretching from an atrium, but few furnishings are preserved (Haynes 2000: 380, fig. 296; Moretti Sgubini 2004: 29–34).

In summary, the furnishings of Etruscan tombs comprised objects of symbolic use, indicators of status such as folding stools or banquet couches, as well as carved or painted representations of household furniture including chairs, beds, stools, or tables. The tomb and funeral afforded a final (in the human sphere) and eternal (as regards the gods and the cosmos) opportunity to assert the individual's significance in city and society, and her/his family's worthiness to rule that society. Some early tomb furniture such as heavy couches with turned legs betrays Near Eastern influence; couches with cut-out legs owe their inspiration to Greek art (see Steingräber 1979: 79–135). The useful folding stool (*diphros okladias*) of military men and civil servants is also seen in Greece, while cylindrical thrones and the lavish use of bronze are native Etruscan and Italic traits. Rome produced less extravagant tombs, but noble homes and imperial palaces would include forms descended from Etruscan designs such as the cylindrical throne and curule chair. The throne continued as the medieval "bishop's throne" (see MacIntosh 1974: 23, nn. 48–50).

THE HELLENISTIC WORLD

In the Hellenistic Greek world, and specifically in Macedonia, we encounter the political background against which royal public processions clearly exhibited secular luxuries, wealth, extravagance, and ostentation. The Hellenistic king displayed his wealth and power in the furnishings and size of his banquet and the extravagance of his entertainment. The Ptolemies who ruled Egypt employed displays of magnificence, beneficence, and delicacy as a major component of their political strategy. The literary sources offer some information regarding the display of wealth and status by the king, especially when dealing with descriptions of royal parades and banquet halls. We read, for instance, of legendary processions, such as Ptolemy II Philadelphus' and Antiochos IV Epiphanes', the most famous formal *ekphrases* of banquet halls (Rice 1983; Thompson 2000; Athenaeus, *Deipn.* 5.194–5 and 10.439). During the latter and among the furniture three hundred sacrificial tables, eighty women seated on φορείοις (portable seats) with gold supports and another five hundred with silver supports, one thousand *triclinia* and fifteen hundred more with extravagant furnishings complete the parading luxury that took place at Daphne, a suburb of Antioch. The *pompe* was so large that the source admits τὴν πομπὴν λέγειν ἐστί δυσέφικτον (it is impossible to describe it)! In this instance Antiochus presented a pageant to exhibit the power and wealth of his kingdom; projection and propaganda were his goals, a powerful message to the Hellenic world of the east and the west for even greater ventures (Gruen 2016: 356–7).

The luxurious life of King Alexander the Great is known through various, often dubious sources, and is restricted to his life in Asia. He is reported as having slept upon a golden couch and having sat on a golden *diphros* while holding court (Athenaeus, *Deipn.* 12.539). His tent is legendary in literature, his court at Babylon is described with a royal throne and silver-footed couches on either side, reserved for the king's companions (Arrian, *Anabasis* VII.24.1–3; Athenaeus, *Deipn.* 12.537d). His pavilion is embellished with fifty golden posts and extravagant embroideries (Athenaeus, *Deipn.* 12.539 d–e). In addition, the Roman writer Aelian (*Varia Historia* IX.3.14–17) refers to its golden ceiling and the Greek historian Heracleides of Kyme (Athenaeus, *Deipn.* 12.514c) to the four posts with jewels and an embroidered porphyry cloth stretched on them. Even the less well-known son of King Philip II of Macedonia, Philip III Arrhidaios, received two opposing Athenian embassies under a golden canopy (Plutarch, *Life of Phocion* 33.8; Paspalas 2005: 81–2).

Macedonian luxurious lifestyle within Macedonian boundaries is evident only in the sources that deal with *symposia*. Fictitious or not, certain narratives remain legendary, such as the passage in Athenaeus that deals with Karanos' sumptuous wedding banquet (*Deipn.* 4.128c–130d), placed in the first quarter of the third century BCE. Silver cups, gold tiaras, and bronze, silver, or crystal platters were presented before the guests. Here only the number of pieces of furniture is noted and not as part of the excessive decoration. Outside Macedonia, however, Ptolemy II arranged a pavilion in Alexandria with Phoenician hangings, one hundred gold couches spread with purple rugs, and two hundred gold tripod tables (Athenaeus, *Deipn.* 5.196–7). Here a couch (instead of a *kylikeion*) was used for the display of the vessels appropriate for the occasion. As a reminiscence of this banqueting tent was interpreted the elaborately decorated ceiling of Anfushy Tomb II (room 2) in Alexandria by Richard Tomlinson (1984: 263; Nowicka 1984).

Other than the literary sources mentioned above, luxury is exhibited in Hellenistic tombs of Macedonia. Beds, thrones, stools, chests, tables, and benches used for offering tables or altars are often found in Macedonian tombs.[4] The significance of these pieces of furniture (to what degree they served practical functions, how much they reflect symbolic values, and how literally should we interpret the many hints provided by the extant funerary furnishings) is a matter of ongoing discussion (Miller 1993: 17–20). It is in any case possible that some objects were made specifically for the grave, others were ordinary useful items but placed new and unused in the grave, while others belonged to the deceased in real life and accompanied her/him in the afterlife.

Although the identity of the tombs' owners is also a matter of discussion, one should bear in mind that other than the king and his immediate family, the king's companions and other wealthy individuals, not necessarily of royal descent or directly related to the king (such as the competent administrators, the high officers, advisors, or diplomatic envoys, the so-called civic elite), competed with each other. The functional elements and the eschatological meaning of the Macedonian tombs has led to the conclusion that iconography, architecture, and design were intricately connected to (or, better, expressed) the belief in the heroization of the deceased, very popular in Hellenistic Macedonia and a common background for every expression related to the afterlife. Against this heroic background the comparison between royal and non-royal tombs points to differences in wealth (display) and not status (Guimier-Sorbets 2002; Guimier-Sorbets and Morizot 2006).

Thus, marble thrones are, for example, part of the funerary furniture of three Macedonian tombs at Vergina (the royal cemetery of ancient Aigai) but also in one (non-royal) tomb at Eretria (Huguenot 2008; Andrianou 2009: 27, 30–1). More specifically, the marble throne from tomb VIII at Vergina (the so-called Eurydice's tomb) was set on a rectangular podium, has four legs with relief decorations, and its high back is decorated with a painting of Pluto and Persephone in the chariot (Plate 22). The armrests are constructed in two tiers, each divided alternatively by pillars and sphinxes (the upper tier) and Caryatids (the lower tier). The base of the seat is decorated with griffins attacking a deer. A marble footstool bearing relief and painted decoration was placed in front. The marble throne found in tomb VI (Bella Tumulus) at Vergina is dated to the beginning of the third century BCE and its unique characteristic is that it has no back but instead a painted version of a backrest on the wall. The artist painted the sections of the "back" of the throne in white (possibly imitating marble) and the space between them in red. A footstool was placed in front of the throne with impressions of feet on its upper surface. The third throne at Vergina was found in the so-called Rhomaios' Tomb and is dated to the beginning of the third century BCE. The back of the throne is sculpted and divided into nine rectangular parts, the arms rest on sphinxes and the left side of the throne is decorated with a painted scene of two griffins attacking a deer. A marble footstool accompanied the throne. All the thrones from Vergina apparently played a symbolic role, something underlined by their luxurious decoration as well.

At Eretria, however, two marble thrones were found in the Macedonian Tomb of the Erotes, dated to the second quarter of the third century BCE

(Huguenot 2008: 87–90 [A] and 91–5 [B]; see also Huguenot 2006) (Figure 6.7). Throne A has four flat feet and no indication of a backrest. It is probably a type of throne without back and armrest, as depicted in vase painting (see, for instance, Richter 1966, figs. 76, 78, 88, 94, 96). It is decorated with double volutes, palmettes, and acanthus leaves. The names of two women are inscribed on the lower tainia of the thone. Throne B, of the same type but less elaborate in execution than throne A, bears painted decoration of a female figure, which stands between two animals, a panther to her right and a griffin to her left. Under the painted decoration an inscription with a female name is preserved. Here the thrones acquire a practical role: a cavity on the seat of the thrones served as a receptacle for the remains of the deceased after cremation and in the first case (Throne A) for two persons.

The notion that the interior of a furnished Macedonian tomb echoes a banquet scene has been a recurrent theme in scholarship (most recently, Despoini 2016: vol. 1:118–19). It has been suggested, but not widely accepted, that funerary thrones were part of a female burial custom, based on the evidence of the inscriptions with female names carved on the thrones from Eretria and the custom of seated (rather than reclining) women in the iconography of banquet reliefs. However, this interpretation runs into problems when we deal with the rest of the excavated material from the Vergina tombs that points toward male burials as well (Huguenot 2006: 44–6). Honor or display of status may have been the underlying principal for the use of thrones in these tombs, a piece of furniture that functioned as a symbol of solemnity and underlined the political or social grandeur of the deceased. As with other types of evidence from Macedonia, furniture in tombs should be viewed against the particular context of the tomb in a case-by-case study.

Other than thrones, which allude to royal or elite status, remains of *diphroi*, *klinai* (beds), presumably tables, and containers are also attested in Macedonian tombs. Seats, beds, and tables have been related by modern scholars to the funerary banquet and the heroic cult, the belief that the dead were treated as heroes and their chamber as the setting of their eternal *prothesis*. Beds normally receive the body of the deceased, or in the case of cremation burials, the *larnakes* (funerary boxes) contained the cremated ashes. Beds and bed-shaped structures have been found in the principal chambers of Macedonian tombs (Sismanidis 1997; Andrianou 2009: 39–50) and coexisted with inhumation and cremation burials. Appliqué decoration, usually of bone or ivory but also of gold and glass, presumably once attached to a (lost) wooden bed frame, have been found in a number of Macedonian tombs. The bed in the thalamus of tomb III at Vergina (the so-called Tomb of Philip) is unique not only because of its exquisite multi-figured ivory decoration on its wooden frame, but also because it received the weapons and not the ashes of the deceased.

Contrary to Macedonia, where real, wooden *klinai* were also placed in tombs, in Hellenistic Alexandria *klinai* are cut in the rock and project from the

a)

b)

FIGURE 6.4 (a) Marble throne B from the Tomb of the Erotes, Eretria. Second quarter of the third century BCE. (b) Furniture from the interior of the tomb. Photographs © Hellenic Ministry of Culture and Sports/ Archaeological Receipts Fund and the Swiss School of Archaeology in Greece.

wall as would a real couch (Venit 2002: 19–20; Guimier-Sorbets and Nenna 2003: 550–64). The Alexandrian *klinai* are conceived as full-scale beds with flat legs sculpted in relief and painted (or carved) with intricate ornaments, such as a richly decorated mattress and a bier cloth that hangs down between the legs, and painted cushions carved in the round, usually set at both ends. The *kline* in the Sidi Gaber tomb, dated to the end of the third or the first half of the second century BCE, is exceptional since it is one of the few in Alexandria to preserve figured decoration, possibly of a complex narrative, on the rail inset between the cross-bars of the *kline*. Hermann Thiersch identified an Amazonomachy or a battle between Greeks and Persians (Thiersch 1904: 4). A late third-century BCE (?) tomb at Moustapha Pasha (Tomb 2) preserves a *kline* that provides some of the best evidence for the opulence of the decoration of Alexandrian tombs. The bed is painted to replicate a real *kline*, but one with sumptuous materials. Stylized floral motifs painted red on an ivory background ornament its legs; Macedonian-type stars, rosettes, and vertical lines, painted light brown on ivory. On the red rail between the two raised crossbars, small ivory-colored Erotes and Psyches driving *bigas* drawn by stags race toward the left. A richly fringed cloth, painted as if hanging from the lower crosspiece, is framed by six bands of varying thicknesses in light blue, red, and white (Adriani 1936: 51). Everything indicates that this is not an ordinary *kline*. Its ornament and paint propose exotic woods inlaid into ivory and ivory figures inlaid in exotic wood; the tapestry bed-cloth simulates fine weaving or embroidery wrought with golden thread.

Rock-cut *klinai* in tombs are known from other areas of the ancient Greek world, as for instance, the island of Rhodes, where along the walls of the so-called Kerameas-Tsikkis tomb in the Agia Triada district three rock-cut *klinai* provided with cushions and footstools and adorned with relief friezes were excavated (Dietz and Papachristodoulou 1988: 205–6). The domed ceiling is reportedly coated with sky-blue stucco and supported by four youthful female figures.

Furniture evidenced in the principal chambers of Macedonian tombs indicates both ritual and a display of wealth. A silver-coated *diphros* has been excavated in the fourth-century tomb at Stavroupolis in Thessaloniki (Rhomiopoulou 1989: 215, no. 22) (Plate 23) and a wooden *diphros* is surmised from the fourth-century Macedonian tomb at Agios Athanasios (Tsimbidou-Avloniti 2005: 105). The best preserved and fully published example of a funerary table is found in the fourth-century chamber tomb of Tekirdağ in southeastern Thrace (modern-day Turkey), an area annexed by Philip in 341 BCE (Delemen 2006: 257–8). The uprights of the table have a fluted face tapering downward to a lion's paw. The tabletop is laden with plates and bowls in relief, a unique decoration in the Greek world.

Funerary containers used to house the remains of the deceased are another common furnishing in Macedonian tombs. The two gold *larnakes* of the "Tomb of Philip" at Vergina stand out. The larnax of the chamber was found inside a marble sarcophagus, it is rectangular, its corners are formed by vertical posts that extend below the floor of the box to form the feet, and its body consists of two sheets bent at right angles to form the four vertical sides. A fourth sheet bent at right angles on three sides formed the lid. The top of the lid opposite the hinge is supplied with two bosses or knobs to facilitate opening. These knobs are matched on the front side of the box with another pair of knobs, possibly to secure the lid with a string sealed with wax, clay, or other material. The excavator, Manolis Andronikos, believed that this method of closure might have been important for the sealing of the box in the deceased's lifetime, something that was not necessary in the tomb, but that might indicate the *use* of the box in real life (Andronikos 1984: 170). The top of the lid is decorated with a starburst of sixteen rays. The center of the star is decorated with a double palmette of gold petals. Five blue rosettes across the front and back, and four on each side complete the decoration. Four lion paws decorate the corners of the larnax.

The second larnax of the tomb, found in the antechamber, is similar in design to the larger larnax, mentioned above, with less complicated rivet work. Rosettes decorate the sides and the corners. The top of the lid is decorated by a starburst of twelve rays.

Ivory and bone decoration from wooden boxes is known from various tombs (Andrianou 2009: 71–81). Among them, the fourth-century cist grave Γ at Vergina (Kyriakou 2005: 200–3) and the third-century tomb of Philimina at Elis in the Peloponnese (Themelis 1994: 156–7). Remains of paint are preserved on the wooden larnax at Aineia, in Macedonia (Vokotopoulou 1990: 24, 32); a silver-sheathed wooden box was used as a larnax in a monumental chamber tomb at Agios Athanasios in Thessaloniki (Tsimbidou-Avloniti 2000: 547–50; 2005: 92); a bronze box was found in a fourth- or third-century BCE tomb at Derveni (Themelis and Touratsoglou 1997: 90). It is clear from the excavated objects that the best containers were buried along with the dead in their tombs, tightly connected to the beliefs for the afterlife.

Expensive textiles were used to wrap the bones of the deceased before being placed in the funerary container (*larnax*) but also as decorative hangings from the walls and ceiling of the tomb (Andrianou 2012; 2021). These funerary furnishings are noted already at the end of the fifth or the fourth century BCE at Koropi in Attica and the Kerameikos in Athens, the fourth-century tomb at Vergina (the "Tomb of Philip") (Plate 24), the chamber tomb at Agios Athanasios in Thessaloniki, the early second-century BCE Macedonian Tomb B at Pella in Macedonia (Andrianou 2009: 92–6; 2012; Drougou 2018; Andrianou 2021). In one example a multicolored textile in the late fourth-century BCE tomb Γ at Sedes in Thessaloniki covered the wooden roof of the tomb (Kotzias 1937: 866–95; Andrianou 2009: 93). A similar example to that at Sedes may be the textile in a Thracian tomb at Golemata Mogila (modern-day Bulgaria) (Filow 1934: 103–4). According to Guimier-Sorbets the funerary chamber may be envisioned as the setting of an eternal prothesis for the heroized dead and the painted textiles on the ceiling of the chamber over the *kline* as an imitation of the hanging of a "baldachino" (Guimier-Sorbets 2001, 2002). Many small gold discs bearing the Macedonian star were evidently found scattered over the disintegrated organic material of the antechamber, in the "Tomb of Eurydice" at Vergina. They have been interpreted by the excavator as decoration to a large piece of cloth that was hung high up (Andronikos 1984: 179). A simple canopy with a deep-yellow central area surrounded by a border is painted in the tomb of Malathria at Dion in Macedonia (Makaronas 1956: 135–6; for further examples, see Miller 1993: 45–6). Current research underlines the various uses of textiles in funerary interiors and seeks to differentiate between remains of textiles worn by the deceased (i.e. garments, diadems), remains of furniture textiles placed on the funerary kline (i.e. mattresses, bedding), and remains of decorative textiles hang on nails on the side walls or the ceiling of the burial chamber (i.e. canopies, ribbons) (Andrianou, forthcoming).

Decoration imitating a woven textile stretching over the whole funerary chamber is also evidenced in Hellenistic Cyprus: Rock-cut Tombs 1 and 2 at the locality of Ammoi (north of the ancient walls of Nea Paphos) preserved such decoration (Michaelides 2004: 90–1; Guimier-Sorbets and Michaelides 2009: 226–9). In tomb 1 the "knots" of the tassels at its two short sides, hanging down onto the vertical part of the walls, make it look even more realistic. These tombs are thought to belong to well-to-do Cypriots who tried to emulate the style and trends of Alexandria and thus display their wealth. This comes as no surprise, as Cyprus formed part of the Ptolemaic Kingdom in the Hellenistic period.

In Gabbari (the western necropolis of Alexandria) Fort Saleh Tomb I interweaves Greek and Egyptian motifs by positioning a Greek *kline* between Egyptian decorative elements. Dated to the Late Ptolemaic period, the sarcophagus imitates the type of bed with finely turned legs, carved cushions at both the head and the foot of the bed, a *fulcrum* to hold the mattress in place and a painted bed-cloth with richly varicolored bands descending almost to the ground (Venit 2002: 93). The ceiling of the niche had been decorated to imitate rich drapery, creating a baldachin, possibly an imitation of the Persian ceremonial canopies over the throne (Guimier-Sorbets 2001: 220–1).

In summary, expensive pieces of furniture are common in funerary contexts in the Greek world. This does not mean that such pieces were reserved for the afterlife, but rather that the conditions inside funerary settings are most friendly for the preservation of such evidence. To what degree these funerary interiors mimic real-life, everyday interiors may only be surmised. It is, however, certain that the choice of furniture types found inside Macedonian tombs is tightly connected to the, still very summarily known, beliefs for the afterlife. The tomb interior, either transformed to a banquet room or to a baldachin that housed the eternal *prothesis* of the deceased, contains the best furniture the owners could afford and is thus understood as evidence of display.

CHAPTER SEVEN

Furniture and Architecture

Greece and Rome

STEPHAN T.A.M. MOLS

The relation between furniture and architecture in antiquity is rather vague and far from the medieval notion that saw furniture as "micro-architecture," as explained by Ethan Matt Kaveler in Chapter 7 in the Middle Ages and Renaissance volume in this series. A great handicap in our discussion is the limited pieces of ancient furniture that have come down to us and the even limited literary sources that speak about furniture and its makers. The finite evidence forces us to deal with this duality free from later (medieval, Renaissance) perceptions that are based on more substantial evidence and cautions us not to extrapolate them to Greek and Roman antiquity.

First, our observations are necessarily based on architecture and furniture other than wood, which has not been preserved, and second, on the depictions of furniture on various media (reliefs, vases, wall paintings, coins). We should, for instance, bear in mind that wooden structures used for dining close to ancient sanctuaries have left no traces. Our only evidence in such instances is the occasional remains of nonperishable pieces of furniture (i.e., of bronze), as in the case north of the Sanctuary of the Mother of Gods and Aphrodite at Pella, where the dining area was identified by the bronze *fulcrum* of a *kline* and the remains of bronze vessels used during the banquets, dated to the middle of the second century BCE (Andrianou 2009: 38, no. 18, with earlier bibliography; Lilimbaki-Akamati and Akamatis 2015: 33).

In antiquity similar forms naturally led people to the same types of decoration in architecture and furniture, but we cannot overestimate this observation by relating the importance of architecture over furniture or vice versa. We know of famous architects that built monumental buildings but not of furniture craftsmen that constructed, for instance, the luxurious funerary furniture at Vergina (see Chapter 6 in this volume). Furniture was certainly inspired by architecture, in the sense that certain architectural motifs were borrowed to decorate parts of furniture pieces. On the other hand, the function of certain rooms (*andro:nes*) dictated the arrangement of furniture (*klinai*) and thus the architecture of interior spaces. Fixed furniture was also related to specific types of rooms (as the *cartibulum* in the atrium, discussed below). Thus, the few remains or traces of furniture in architectural spaces and the decoration of extant furniture will lead us through the juxtaposition of ancient furniture and architecture.

FURNITURE MOTIFS BORROWED FROM ARCHITECTURE

From the sixth century BCE onward we cannot detect many similarities between furniture and architecture regarding motifs in the Greek world, other than the thrones.[1] The legs of thrones depicted in mythological scenes in vase paintings and reliefs, and in visual representations or statues of gods and rulers, form an exception. These throne legs often bear decorations or carvings derived from architectural orders or adopt ornaments such as volutes and palmettes, commonly seen in the Ionic order of Greek temple architecture. As statues with enthroned gods were often placed in Greek temples, these thrones must have complemented the austerity and majestic look of the temples themselves.

We similarly encounter grand thrones and depictions of them, for example, in wall paintings, in elite tombs. The legs, and often also the backs of these thrones, bear architectural ornamentation such as volutes and palmettes (Richter 1966: 23–8). As far as we know, the oldest thrones of this type appear in the painting of the so-called François Vase (a crater for mixing wine and water; Florence Archaeological Museum inv. 4209) as seats for Zeus and Hera, datable to the early sixth century BCE (Plate 25). From this moment on we encounter many depictions of this type of throne, especially on vase paintings, reliefs, and even on freestanding sculptures of seated gods in the course of the fifth and fourth centuries BCE. That this type of throne was still popular even in the fourth century is shown by a marble statuette of an enthroned woman from the Delos island in the Cyclades (Richter 1966: 28, fig. 119; Delos no. 16237). The armrests of the throne with a solid and often rounded back also ended in volutes, showing similarities with architectural motifs that, as mentioned above, mostly derived from the Ionic, but sometimes also from the Corinthian order, having smaller volutes and stylized acanthus leaves as decoration. Well-known examples of this type are the thrones used by priests and other high-ranking people attending spectacles in Greek theaters, such as the theater of Dionysos in Athens (Plate 26).

The exquisite marble throne from the "Tomb of Eurydice" at Vergina, dated by the excavators to 340 BCE, has armrests constructed in two tiers, each divided alternatively by pillars and sphinxes (the upper tier) and Caryatids (the lower tier), possibly influenced by architecture (Andrianou 2009: 30, no. 9, with earlier bibliography). Sphinxes and Caryatids in this example possibly acted as bearers of the entablature, in this case the armrest. Throne A inside the Macedonian tomb of Eretria, dated to the second quarter of the third century BCE, is decorated with double volutes, palmettes, and acanthus leaves, all motifs known through architecture (Andrianou 2009: 31, no. 12, with earlier bibliography).

The decoration of table legs sometimes derived from architectural decoration as well. We encounter tables with almost straight legs and fluted fronts, designed almost like miniature columns, crowned with a volute, apart from the lion paws at the bottom, which only appear in the furniture items, and not in the architecture. An example is, for instance, a pair of bronze table legs from Palermo (Richter 1966: 65, figs. 350–1; Palermo Archaeological Museum no. 1449). But apart from this striking example many marble Hellenistic table legs from all over the Mediterranean had a similar form, such as the marble table legs found in the house of Hermes on Delos, dated to the second century BCE (Andrianou 2009: cat. no. 48, fig. 14b) (Figure 7.1). Legs of this originally

FIGURE 7.1 Marble table from the House of Hermes, Delos, EFA 19142. Second-first century BCE. Photograph © Hellenic Ministry of Culture and Sports/Archaeological Receipts Fund, Ephorate of Antiquities of Cyclades and the French School at Athens.

Greek type were also in use in Etruscan and Roman contexts, in both thrones and tables. Most of the preserved examples are made of marble, but bronze specimens have also been found. Side tables are mentioned in Roman literature as related to dining rooms and used for the display of food or drinking cups and other drinking utensils. A depiction of such a side table is the famous table with straight legs and a display of silver drinking vessels on top in the tomb of Vestorius Priscus in Pompeii (Plate 27).

The legs of Greek *klinai* often had similar motifs (volutes or palmettes), and these were also imitated in the Italian peninsula. However, while Etruscan couches follow the Greek decoration sketched above, Roman couches do not. Two very fine and well-known Etruscan examples are the terracotta funerary coffins in the shape of couches with a reclining couple on them, both from Cerveteri, one of which is nowadays in the Museo di Villa Giulia in Rome and the other in the Musée du Louvre. Most Roman couches had legs turned on the lathe, sometimes following Hellenistic examples, but more often newly created forms, like the legs of the couch depicted on the Simpelveld Sarcophagus (Plate 9).

Although Roman cupboards and sideboards will not be discussed extensively, it is obvious that their storage function demanded a practical form, which often had much in common with interior architecture, such as small storerooms and architecturally fixed cupboards. Their paneled sides and, importantly, paneled doors were designed like real doors in architecture (Ulrich 2007: 178–201). Wooden examples of cupboards with their doors still preserved, although mostly in fragments, have been found in Herculaneum, and show many similarities to actual doors found in the same city.

FURNITURE FIXED TO ARCHITECTURE

Fixed, specifically, not portable, furniture is clearly taken into consideration in an architectural space and in this sense dictates shapes (Roaf 1996: 21). Built-in benches in public spaces, like Greek and Roman porticoed buildings (*stoa* and *porticus*), can be presented as important examples of furniture fixed to the architectural environment. For example, the *cavea* (seating facilities) for the audience in Greek and Roman theaters, or in *stadia* for athletic games and the Roman *circus* (hippodrome). These were often made of stone or masonry and were arranged as rows of steps. The same counts for provisions for reclining during dinner in front of tombs, a phenomenon we encounter from the first century CE onward, as can be seen, for example, in the well-preserved dining couches in the Isola Sacra necropolis between Ostia and Portus, the harbor cities of ancient Rome (see, for example, tomb 80: Ostia-Antica 2020).

In private buildings built-in benches have been found along the façades of many houses in Pompeii and Herculaneum, and sometimes also indoors, such as the long masonry benches in the corridors of the famous Villa A at Oplontis near Pompeii, or beds for slaves in the Villa of the Mysteries in Pompeii. Furthermore, excavations in Pompeii and Herculaneum have yielded stone or masonry dining facilities in Roman gardens that acted both as furniture and architecture (discussed below).

FURNITURE ITEMS FOR SPECIFIC ARCHITECTURAL CONTEXTS

With the exception of one specific architectural context, that will be dealt with later, the relationship between furniture and architecture is rather elusive, as noted above. There are cases, however, where particular types of furniture were designated for particular types of rooms in Roman houses.

In several texts, for example, *Digesta* 19.2.19.5 (Ulpianus), a strongbox with iron or bronze fittings is connected with the *atrium* or another central reception room in the Roman house, where it could be admired by visitors after having entered the house through the main door. It seems that these strongboxes were made for this specific architectural context and to impress the guests, stressing the very important function of the *atrium* of Roman houses. In some Pompeian houses such strongboxes are still present, as in the House of Marcus Obellius Firmus (IX 14, 4). In the written sources these chests are referred to as *arcae aeratae* or *arcae ferratae*, meaning chests with bronze or iron fittings (Juvenal, *Satyres* 11.23–7 and 14.259; Mols 1999: 104).

Another furniture item that was tightly connected to the *atrium* of many Roman elite and sub-elite houses is the *cartibulum*, or rectangular table, originally made of stone. In his *De Lingua Latina* 5.125, the first-century BCE author Marcus Terentius Varro states that this was a table with only one support, originally made for placing buckets on it that carried water for daily use. This *cartibulum* stood next to the *impluvium*, a water basin corresponding with an opening in the roof of the *atrium* for the collection of rain water. After being collected, the rain water was led to a cistern underneath the *atrium* and could be pitted using a bucket that could be placed on the original *cartibulum*. This was probably the simple prototype of the more elaborate marble tables that have been found in many *atria* of Roman houses (Plate 28). These were mostly made of marble and their plain rectangular tops were almost always carried by two supports at the sides, decorated with reliefs. These decorations very often contained griffins, sometimes single and sometimes in pairs. Examples of this type of table have been found in Pompeii and Herculaneum and are dated to the first centuries BCE and CE (Mols 1999: 139–40). Together with the already mentioned strongboxes these were real showpieces, as their size and often rich decoration gave visitors an idea of the wealth of the patron of the house.

Furthermore, in ancient as well as modern literature on Roman furniture, a special type of cupboard of unknown form is mentioned as a typical type of furniture to be placed in an atrium. It served as a cupboard for storage of wax models of the heads or faces of the family ancestors. In addition, but not exclusively related to the atrium, was the Roman private devotional altar (*aedicula*), often erroneously called *lararium* (a term correctly used for a room where sacred objects were stored). In the preserved wooden examples from Herculaneum, as well as in depictions, *aediculae* often seem to have the form of a temple front, with two columns at the front side, bearing an entablature and often also a pediment. One of the few actual examples of these wooden *aediculae* from Herculaneum is shown in Plate 29 (Mols 1999: 58–62, 132–4, and 138). This example shows a true architectural form on a furniture piece.

We have so far discussed examples of furniture motifs derived from ancient architecture (be it the architectural orders or architectural ornamentation) and examples of furniture related to architecture (used in specific rooms or architectural spaces). In the following furniture used in the Greek *andron* or the Roman *triclinium* (the rooms used specifically for drinking and dining) will be presented.

ANDRONES AND *TRICLINIA*

Greece

Andrones and *triclinia* were important rooms in Greek and Roman elite and sub-elite houses. They served for private Greek *symposia* or Roman *convivia*, and were important reception rooms in ancient houses, in which furniture and architecture often seem to have been designed as a single whole or at least the one seems to have been adapted to the other.

In Archaic and Classical Greek houses there was mostly only one *andron*, a room where the patron of the house received his male guests for conversation, entertainment, and drinking. We encounter the earliest examples in the mid-seventh century BCE (Hoepfner 1999: 139 ff). The room often had a small vestibule, and the combination of these two rooms was called the *andronitis*. The *symposion* was taking place in the *andron*, commonly a square or rectangular room (Hoepfner 1999: 145–8; Wecowski 2014). Along the walls an uneven number of couches was placed, one against the other along the walls. The number of couches in one room was usually five or seven; less frequently three, eleven, or fifteen. The couches were very often placed on a slightly raised podium, thus indicating how the couches should be distributed according to the architecture of the room. This raised feature makes the rooms directly recognizable and allows archaeologists to identify their function even when no furniture has been found, as is usually the case. Small *androns* only contained three couches, medium sized five or seven, and large ones nine or more. Each couch was around 1.7 meters long, allowing a maximum of two persons to recline on it. However, in the Archaic and Classical periods only one person most usually used it, as depictions on, for example, Attic vases show. Next to each couch a rectangular table was placed. These tables had three legs, two at one short side and only one at the other, ending in animal paws. *Androns* often had a strategic place in the house, mostly not very far from the entrance of the house, and they could be reached by visitors without coming in contact with the other members of the family (Hoepfner 1999: 268–79; Cahill 2002; Nevett 2010: ch. 3). During *symposia*, the open space in the center of the *andron* was used for the placement of a *crater*, a large vase for mixing wine and water, and of course, also for entertainment. The division between space for the couches and the *central* space could be designated in the decoration of the floor of the *andron*, with, for example, a figural mosaic covering the central space (Plate 30). In the luxurious house of Dionysos at Pella (Macedonia), dated to the post-Alexander era, the famous mosaics of Dionysos riding the panther (hence the name) and the lion hunt are centered in two such *androns* on the south side of the complex and the *klinai* were arranged around them so that art was visible to every banqueter (Akamatis 2011: 398). In the luxurious house of Helen, also at Pella (Macedonia), banqueting halls are arranged north and east of a large Doric peristyle with central mosaic floors depicting a deer hunt (signed by its creator, Gnosis), the abduction of Helen by Theseus, and an Amazonomachy. In all these examples the function of the room as an *andron* dictated the arrangement of both furniture and decoration.

Few public buildings in Greek cities had *androns* as well. Some of these most probably served a cultic function, as, for instance, the nine rooms that are placed along two sides of the central courtyard of the sanctuary of Artemis Brauronia in Attica. The rooms could be entered from a *stoa* that ran along the courtyard (Travlos 1988: 55–80, esp. plates 58 and 70). The rooms all measured about 5.5 × 5.5 meters. Another example is the sanctuary of Asklepios on the south slope of the Athenian Acropolis, which was also equipped with rooms for *symposia* (Hurwitt 1999: 219–21, esp. fig. 193). Public dining areas (*hestiatoria*) also had provisions for *klinai* (Andrianou 2009: 35). For example, in the late fourth century BCE *abaton* of the Asklepieion at Corinth, fragments of beds and tables cut from a single large poros block are preserved, whereas two rooms with stucco sills for the placement of *klinai* were unearthed in a *hestiatorion* at Pella (Kanali area) dated to the third century BCE, and thus have been interpreted as a dining area. The latter building is associated with gatherings of worshippers of Darron, whose healing sanctuary was located nearby (Lilimbaki-Akamati and Akamatis 2015: 31).

The *androns* in the so-called South Stoa on the Athenian Agora, built in the last quarter of the fifth century BCE, were also part of a public building, but probably did not serve a cultic function (Camp 1990: 166–72). This building had fifteen rooms of 4.8 × 4.86 meters, each with enough space for seven couches. The building may have been a place where city officials could organize their *symposia* or where rooms could be hired by private individuals who did not have such rooms in their own houses.

Multiple dining rooms were also part of Macedonian and Hellenistic palaces. Sometimes these were much like their Classical predecessors, but some of these were very large and therefore cannot have been used for the intimate gatherings the *andron* was initially designed for. An important example is the palace of Aigai built by Philip II, the father of Alexander the Great. It started being built a little after the middle of the fourth century BCE and had been constructed by 336 BCE (Kottaridi 2011: 304). The palace had three large tripartite complexes (E–G, N1–N3, M1–M3 on the plan of the palace; Kottaridi 2011: fig. 32b) with side *androns* of approximately 10 × 10 meters. Three *androns* (M1–M3) were even larger, more than 15 × 15 meters, all directly recognizable by their slightly raised borders along the walls to put the couches on, as in Classical *androns*. Covering a space of around 267 square meters each, these three spaces are perhaps the largest roofed rooms without internal supports in Classical architecture. In each of these two *androns* (M1, M3), at least thirty couches would fit, holding up to sixty banqueters, and in the antechamber (M2) five hundred men could sit (Kottaridi 2011: 325). At the palace of Aigai a total number of 230 couches has been estimated in the rooms that functioned as *androns*, whereas at the palace of Pella, a total of 278 (Building I; Chrysostomou 2011: 60–1). Three of these even gave room to a total of thirty couches each (Hoepfner 1999: 327–9). None of the parts of the Pella palace complex appears to predate the second half of the fourth century BCE (Akamatis 2011: 399–401).

One of the tripartite complexes at Aigai (A, A1, A2) gave access to an isolated area, space B, which was, according to the excavator, an archive. The three remaining supports were probably connected with four identical niches with shelves, similar to those that existed in libraries of later periods (Kottaridi 2011: 327). It is worth noting here that based on the most recent archaeological evidence and the study of its ground plan, the palace at Aegae had, according to its excavator, no space for family life, beside the public life and the exercise of power that were the core of its existence.

Rome

In Roman houses of the elite and middle classes provisions for the so-called *triclinium* are often found. These were common from the second century BCE onward until at least the end of the first or the beginning of the second century CE and probably well into the third century CE. Although the name *triclinium* is of Greek origin, meaning "three couches," the provision greatly differs from its Greek counterpart, the *andron*, as I will explain hereafter. The name is used both for the furniture and its architectural environment, showing their close relation even in this respect. The rooms are usually long and narrow, and divided in two parts, an antechamber, through which the diners entered the room, and a main chamber, where the three couches were placed. In well-preserved examples, mainly in houses in Pompeii and Herculaneum, the division is also made visible through the decoration on the walls, the floor, and the ceiling. The antechamber could be empty or it could be used for side tables for dining and drinking service, utensils for keeping food and wine warm or for entertainment of the guests. Very often the entrance at the short side was made of wooden doors that could be opened when the weather allowed it. Side doors in the entrance could be used by servants during banquets.

A combination of finds, primarily from Pompeii and Herculaneum, both destroyed in 79 CE by the eruption of Vesuvius, gives us the possibility to reconstruct *triclinia* and their furniture. In the few extant examples of whole, fixed *triclinia* built in masonry and plastered with mortar in open rooms overlooking gardens, we gather a lot of important information regarding the arrangement of couches. In these rooms we see an asymmetrical arrangement in the form of the Greek letter *pi*. Mattresses were laid on these "couches" on which normally a maximum of nine people could recline. The mattresses were held in place by two decorated elevations, or side supports at the head and foot of the pi-formed device, called *fulcra*. These garden *triclinia*, however, were exceptions. Most couches used in *triclinia* were single, freestanding, and therefore movable items of furniture, made of wood of which not much has been preserved nowadays. But, fortunately, we can identify many *triclinia* in the houses from both cities and the villas in the Vesuvian area. Although, as has been said before, the furniture is almost always lost, the architecture of the room gives many clues regarding their function for *convivia*, the Roman counterpart of the *symposion*, in which eating was combined with drinking. Many of these rooms show recesses or niches in walls to give room to couches in the inner part of the *triclinium*. As the rooms with these niches gave place to three couches of around 1.20 × 2.40 meters, it is clear that the couches had standard measurements and that their measurements determined the architecture of the rooms they were made for. In the center of the three couches there was room for a table, mostly a small one, placed there after the people attending the *convivium* had taken their places. From depictions and a few preserved examples from Herculaneum we know that these tables had three legs and round tops. The table was probably replaced by a new one every time a new course was served. The word *mensa* is used in Latin for the table and the course as well. A reconstruction of a *triclinium* arrangement is shown in Figure 7.2. To complete the room, wall paintings with figural scenes or still lifes could decorate the center of each wall and a figural mosaic, visible for the guests while entering the room, could decorate the floor.

In houses with ample space for the layout of rooms, larger *triclinia* were built with walking space along the outside of the couches. This made reaching and leaving the couches much more comfortable for the diners, because they did not have to wait until the table was removed.

Wealthy Roman houses often had more than one dining room, as we can deduce from Pompeii and Herculaneum, as well as from Roman literature. Pliny the Younger, for example, had three *triclinia* in both his Tuscan villa (Letters 5.6) as well as his Laurentine villa (Letters 2.17), mentioned in two letters in which the famous author enters into the delights of two of his country villas in Roman Italy. The first also had an open-air provision for *convivia* in the garden, the so-called *stibadium*, probably in masonry, comparable to the ones in Pompeian gardens mentioned above, but probably covered by a pergola. In elite houses it is possible that these rooms were all furnished with a reclining arrangement of three loose couches, but finds from Pompeian houses also indicate that a set of reclining furniture was moved from one room to another, so that one could choose a certain *triclinium* according to the season in which the *convivium* took place: a *triclinium* absorbing sun from the southwest could be best used in winter, while another oriented to the north was in use during late afternoons in the summertime, to avoid the sun's heat (Dunbabin 2003: esp. 36–63; Mols 1999: 126–7).

A very important aspect of *triclinia* was the view when the main doors at the entrance were open. In some cases the view from a *triclinium* was even decisive for the layout of the adjacent garden. In a few instances even the architecture of the whole house was in service of the *triclinium*. This was, amongst others, the case in the House of the Stags in Herculaneum (Jashemski 1993: 264–6). Here the main *triclinium* 5 looked upon both the garden and the sea at the horizon. Catering was practically invisible as the kitchen was located behind the *triclinium*. Servants could enter the room through doorways on the sides of the room and did not have to use the main entrance.

Depictions on wall paintings found in Pompeii made just before 79 CE point to another type of reclining arrangement, in the shape of a moon sickle, named *sigma* because of its resemblance to the Greek letter-character with the same name (see Chapter 4 in this volume). These early depictions show only provisions for outdoor reclining, but later also indoor *sigmata* became popular in elite houses and villas. A *sigma* gave place to circa eight people reclining, and was more comfortable than the traditional rectangular disposition of three couches, as the people reclining on it had more room for their bodies and legs than in the traditional arrangements. The new fashion was also responsible for a new architectural form of *triclinia*, stressing

FIGURE 7.2 Reconstruction drawing of a *triclinium*. Drawing © Theo Mols.

again the close relation between furniture and the architectural design of dining rooms in antiquity. Thereafter, the name of the room was no longer compatible with the furniture placed in it, as it was still called a *triclinium* but no longer contained the traditional three rectangular couches. For this very reason Servius in his fourth- or fifth-century commentary on Virgil's *Aeneid* (1.698) had to explain to his readers what a *triclinium* meant. During that period the room had one or up to three semicircular apses for the placement of one or more *sigmata*.

The described phenomenon of creating recesses or niches for couches in *triclinia* can also be detected in the case of Roman rooms used for resting or sleeping, in Latin literature mostly indicated as *cubicula*. In these rooms there was apparently not enough space for a bed or beds to be placed, and the rooms were therefore slightly enlarged. Here, as was also the case with *triclinia*, the recesses indicate the use of a standard measurement for beds placed in this sort of room (Anguissola 2010).

Marble tables in gardens had purely formal and decorative functions. They are often found in Pompeii and Herculaneum, but were surely more widespread in the Roman world. As these were also specifically designed for these architectural spaces, we may detect a strong relationship between furniture and architectural space here. There is evidence, especially from the cities and villas around Vesuvius, that house owners appreciated formal gardens, in which not only trees, shrubs, and flowers were carefully arranged, but also garden sculptures and garden furniture were part of a planned design (Jashemski 1993: 25–59).

In this chapter we first explored why furniture and architecture are sometimes difficult to divide in Classical antiquity because much of the furniture that has survived and of which we are certain of its shape and size was fixed to the surrounding architecture. Motifs used in furniture could derive from the Greek architectural orders and from temple architecture. The relation between furniture and architecture was strongest in rooms with specific functions where furniture and architecture were both decisive for creating an agreeable environment. This was very clear in rooms used for dining and entertainment by the Greek and Roman elite, but could also be encountered in Roman bedrooms and gardens.

CHAPTER EIGHT

Visual Representations

VASSILIS PETRAKIS, ATHINA CHATZIDIMITRIOU,

AND STEFAN FEUSER

THIRD MILLENNIUM TO SEVENTH CENTURY BCE

Two- or three-dimensional imagery in a variety of artistic media can be an important source of information about ancient furniture. However, exactly like textual evidence, this material needs to be used with caution because it is imbued with its own *emic* agendas and biases as well as an overall tendency to reproduce ideal modes of behavior, rather than statically to reflect ancient realities. Moreover, it is important to remember that the ability to sustain the specialist skilled craftsmen that actually produced such images has been the prerogative of elite groups that often exercised strict control over the final product and its ideological connotations. Iconography is therefore rarely objective, but consistently representative of the specific sociopolitical conditions of its production and consumption.

Such limitations should be kept firmly in mind, especially since in many areas where actual furniture has not been sufficiently preserved such visual representations constitute our main (or exclusive) source of information. Instead of viewing imagery as objective indications of real life, we may appreciate it as a visual statement about the significance of what is depicted.

Besides the miniature terracotta models of seats and tables produced and "consumed" in often poorly understood Neolithic contexts (see Chapters 4 and 5 in this volume), our earliest representations of furniture include the seated "goddess" from Çatalhöyük (late seventh millennium BCE) (see Figure 5.1 top). With her arms supported by two felines (or resting on two feline-shaped sides of a throne?) the "goddess" as represented conveys a message of dominance over wild nature (which the felines presumably represent), and this is our earliest explicit manifestation for the association of seats with aggressive animals (see below). This is also perhaps our earliest clear indication of the special power implications of the seated posture (see Chapter 5 in this volume). Variations of this motif recur throughout antiquity, from Old Akkadian images of the goddess Ishtar with her reclining lion under her throne up to the imagery of Cybele (and other female deities syncretized with her) during the first millennium BCE (Roller 1999). Seating on wild predatory animals—as a visual metaphor for enlisting or exercising dominance over the forces of nature—forms the conceptual basis for seats and other furniture with bovine or feline legs, already attested in Early Dynastic Mesopotamia and Archaic Egypt. This zoomorphic tendency (often focusing on feline paws) persisted throughout antiquity and well into recent times.

By the time of the early Egyptian and Near Eastern states (roughly the late fourth or early third millennium BCE), furniture imagery takes a more comprehensive form, being now more eloquently (at least from our perspective) embedded in elite strategies and political ideologies.

In Mesopotamia, furniture is shown on a variety of media. Already from the late Uruk and the following Jemdet Nasr period (*c.* 3300–2900 BCE), various types are represented on seals, even if their exact forms are difficult to interpret. The common occurrence of the stool in Ancient Near Eastern glyptic may be associated with its simple conception and production, which made it an ubiquitous item in most households (however minimally furnished these might have been; see Chapter 4 in this volume). Finely carved stools are shown as seats of rulers or other powerful figures, as in the diorite statues of Gudea (king of Lagash in south Mesopotamia in present-day south Iraq, r. *c.* 2144–2124 BCE), the stele of Ur-Nammu (king of Ur, r. *c.* 2047–2030 BCE, well known for the earliest preserved legal code, the Code of Ur-Nammu, associated with his reign), and the enigmatic decorated box known as the "Standard of Ur" (probably an elaborate lyre's sound box) (Simpson 1995: 1648–50, figs. 4–5). In the latter, an oversized figure in the banquet scene on the so-called Peace panel (Woolley 1934: 268, plate 93) represents a person of high status. Chairs (differentiated from stools by the addition of backs) are shown from the Ur III period (*c.* 2100–2000 BCE) onward. An Ur III cylinder seal now also in the British Museum has yielded one of the earliest attestations of a special (perhaps Egyptianizing) throne (the seated king may be Ur–Nammu) with a backrest that curves out toward the rear at the top (Simpson 1995: 1650, fig. 6). This type of throne recurs in Levantine and Anatolian art, as the depiction from Face A of an ivory box from Acemhöyük (eighteenth century BCE) shows (Ziffer 2005: figs. 15–15a; see also Metzger 1985b: plates 109–10). Strong Egyptian influence in Levantine and later Phoenician furniture must be acknowledged, with feline-legged thrones occurring on north Syrian seals already in the early second millennium BCE (Gubel 1996: 140–2, fig. 2).

In the Near East during the second millennium BCE, important groups of furniture representations are the terracotta models of beds, as well as banquet-scenes (mostly on seals) representing seated individuals who are often on either side of food-laden tray tables (see Chapters 3 and 5 in this volume). Already on late third-millennium BCE seals with the "Royal Presentation Scene" (Ur III period), the ruler is commonly represented seated, usually with a cup in his hand (Winter 1986). The seats of these "enthroned" figures vary considerably: depictions on seals from Ebla (Syria), for instance, illustrate the king and queen on chairs made of wicker as well as on backless stools (cf. Ziffer 2005: 146–7, with references). The relatively low "visibility" of tables in iconography from this period (cf. also Gubel 1996: 149–50) may reflect their actual paucity in the third millennium BCE (see Chapters 3, 4, and 5 in this volume), because their most important use seems to have been as offering stands or portable trays (Simpson 1995: 1649, 1651).

The association of thrones with fantastic creatures is also significant and widespread, although regional variations may be recognized. These can be considered variations on the general theme of zoomorphic or beast-associated seats (cf. the Neolithic "goddess" figurine from Çatalhöyük, see above). The "sphinx-throne"[1] is considered typically Canaanite (Ziffer 2005: 158; Types Ia–Ib in Gubel 1996: 142–6). Famous examples of depictions of such sphinx-thrones from the late second millennium BCE occur on the sarcophagus of Ahiram, a Phoenician king of Byblos in present-day Lebanon, and ivories from Megiddo in present-day north Israel (Loud 1939: nos. 2b, 3a). The idea may be Egyptian in origin, and early representations of sphinxes (on the "Pratt Ivories" from Acemhöyük, see also Chapters 1, 3, and 5 in this volume) may be Anatolian adaptations of Egyptian, or Egyptianizing prototypes (Teissier 1996: 80). Sphinx-thrones are also commonly (although not exclusively) associated with footstools (Gubel 1996: 149), and it is perhaps revealing that the Semitic term for "footstool" is Egyptian in origin (see also Chapters 5 and 9, esp. Table 9.1, in this volume). The association of thrones with griffins[2] occurs in the Aegean (see below). Within an international *koine* formed during the late second millennium BCE (see Chapter 5 in this volume) such composite feline creatures (including the horned, winged lion, a monster characteristic of the Ugaritic iconography) were almost interchangeable as embodiments of aggressiveness and divine support (Figure 8.1).

Various types of seats, ranging from backless stools to chairs with elaborate backs, are known from marble figurines of the Early Cycladic period (mid-third millennium BCE) in the Aegean (Krzyszkowska 1996: 88, fig. 1). This material, consisting of a number of items without provenance or even suspected forgeries, needs, nonetheless, to be treated with caution. Although certain features, such as the arched back and curved side-struts of the chair of the famous "harpist" marble figurine from Keros, might be convenient artistic devices rather than

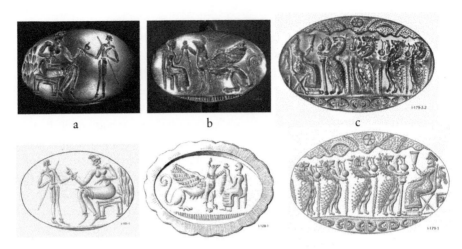

FIGURE 8.1 Representations of "enthroned" figures in Aegean Late Bronze Age art (photos and drawings). (a) golden ring with "Sacred Conversation" scene from chamber tomb 66, Mycenae (Argolid); (b) golden ring from chamber tomb 91, Mycenae (Argolid); (c) great gold ring from the Tiryns treasure (Argolid). All rings were probably manufactured during the fifteenth century BCE, but were found in later (fourteenth- to twelfth-century BCE) contexts. Photographs courtesy of the Heidelberg Corpus of Minoan and Mycenaean seals.

faithful reproductions of (steam-bent?) parts (Krzyszkowska 1996: 89), these representations remain our most important sources for Aegean Early Bronze Age furniture.

We have more evidence from the palatial cultures that developed in Crete and the Greek Mainland around 1450 to 1200 BCE. It is interesting how actual furniture, such as the Knossos gypsum throne, or the missing throne of Pylos (whose place is suggested by a rim on the stucco floor), were combined with wall paintings of griffins and lions flanking them in true "multimedia" pictorial programs aimed to convey the image of the powerful sovereign (for Pylos, cf. McCallum 1987). An object similar to the unique scalloped back of the gypsum throne of Knossos (c. 1500–1400 BCE; see also Chapters 1, 2, and 5 in this volume) and possibly interpreted as a baetyl[3] appears flanked by wild goats on a stone relief libation vessel (rhyton) from the Minoan palace of Zakros in east Crete (c. 1450 BCE).

The painted side of a terracotta chest or larnax (dated c. 1350–1250 BCE) from Klima in the Mesara region (south Crete) is dominated by the image of an empty stool (Rethemiotakis 1995), while a number of stone "stools" have been recovered from Knossos and adjacent sites (Archanes, Katsambas, Prinias). Such finds and representations may serve to show that stools (presumably elaborate) could also, like elaborate chairs or "thrones," enjoy considerable status.

Late Bronze Age Aegean imagery places great importance on seats with folding legs. A well-illustrated example is the probably divine figure seated on a chair with folding legs facing a procession of "Genii" (theriomorphic demons) on the famous gold signet ring from the Tiryns treasure, dated stylistically to around 1500 to 1400 BCE (Baker 1966: figs. 398a–b; cf. the high-backed folding chair depicted on an ivory box from Tel el-Far'ah (Israel) in Gubel 1996: 148, fig. 6). Similar stools are also featured in the eponymous "Campstool Fresco" from Knossos (c. 1400 BCE), as well as the "Two Men at Table" wall-painting fragments from the *megaron* (hall) of the palace of Pylos (c. 1200 BCE). In both compositions banqueters facing each other raise kylikes (high-stemmed cups) in what seems to be a toasting gesture (McCallum 1987: 90–1). Tables are, however, omitted in the "Campstool Fresco," while three-legged ones (perhaps with circular tops?) are shown on the Pylos wall painting. Depictions on seals and their impressions on clay sealings also occur, but are too schematic to be of help.

Besides the "offering tables," often three-legged or pedestalled (actual examples made of stone or plaster, or models made of terracotta), most of our extant representations of tables can be considered as representing "sacrificial" or "slaughtering" tables (Sakellarakis 1970: 166–82, fig. 9; Platon and Pararas 1991; Krzyszkowska 1996: 94–6, fig. 4). Representations of beds are almost nonexistent (the scarce representations of funerary beds on pictorial *larnakes* and pottery being an exception, see Chapter 6 in this volume), but a few interesting terracotta models exist. An early bed model from Phaistos in south Crete (eighteenth century BCE) features six legs and a slightly raised head-rest(?) (Kopaka 1987). The latter feature, which might suggest a couch for reclining, is, however, absent from the few actual examples of beds recovered from Akrotiri on Thera (see Chapter 4 in this volume).

Mycenaean terracotta models of furniture, especially three-legged chairs, tripod tables, and beds, deserve special mention. These are usually found with burials or in contexts identified as religious (caution is needed, however, when the occurrence of figurines is used as a criterion for such an identification) (Polychronakou-Sgouritsa 2003). Three-legged chair models, in particular, also included among the Mycenaean figurines found at Delphi, have been ingeniously associated with the Delphic "tripod" on which Pythia stood by Amandry (1986). Similar contextual associations of furniture models can also be observed in the Levant, such as chair and bed models found in Iron Age Israel, which should be distinguished from the "Ashdoda" figurines (as twelfth- to eleventh-century BCE Philistine schematic terracotta representations of seated females are customarily known) (Albertz and Schmitt 2012: 68, with references). Unfortunately, the significance of furniture models is often obscure. Their plain appearance leaves little doubt that they imitated contemporary perishable items; in cases of modestly furnished burials these could be substitutes for actual furniture, which was unaffordable for this kind of consumption; it may also be conjectured that models of seats (thrones?) could also be *pars pro toto* representations of enthroned deities, although this would suggest a tradition of aniconicity that finds little support elsewhere (see the discussion of "sacred emptiness" in Chapter 5 in this volume).

Imagery is our chief source for Aegean furniture in the Early Iron Age as well. Besides isolated finds of actual furniture, such as the "footstools" from the Samian Heraion (see Chapter 5 in this volume), funerary scenes of *prothesis* and *ekphora*[4] on Attic late Geometric pottery (e.g., the well-known "Dipylon Master," *c.* 760–750 BCE) have given us numerous glimpses of contemporary furniture—albeit rendered in silhouette technique: funerary beds or biers, chairs, and stools (Laser 1968: figs. 1 [beds] and 7 [stools and chairs]). The rendering of these objects in silhouette makes it difficult to assess the possibility of typological continuity from the Bronze Age. We should be reminded that these images show furniture intended for a specifically funerary use; it is to be assumed that the same types of furniture would have been in use in everyday life (see also Chapter 6 in this volume).

Additional evidence about Greek Geometric furniture comes from the painted decoration on a votive terracotta model of the gabled roof of a *naiskos* (small cult building) found in an apsidal building at Nikoleika (Ancient Helike in Achaea, northwestern Peloponnese), perhaps associated with the local cult of Poseidon Helikonios (Gadolou 2011) (Plate 31). The representation of two men seated on backless stools (Greek δίφροι) flanking a tripod (a typical prize in games) on one side of the roof must be associated with the fragments of a chariot race scene on the other, which have been plausibly interpreted in the context of athletic competition. It would thus seem that these male seated figures were members of the local elite (*basileis?*) responsible for the tripod prize itself (Gadolou 2011: 264–6). It is notable, as Gadolou observed, that the legs of these stools are similar to those of the bier on a twelfth-century BCE *prothesis* scene from Ayia Triada near Elis (west Peloponnese) (see Chapter 6 in this volume).

A remarkable bronze model of a chair from a pit under the debris of an eleventh-century BCE house at Enkomi (Cyprus) provides us with a remarkably detailed picture of its plaited seat (Figure 2.6 right).[5] This unique miniature masterpiece is probably Cypriot (Laser 1968: plates 3a–b; Theodossiadou 1996: 77, fig. 5). Cypriot Late Bronze Age glyptic, especially on cylinder seals, has also yielded a wealth of information on types of stools and chairs used, as well as footstools or tables (Theodossiadou 1995, 1996: 77–9, figs. 6–7). Cypriot visual arts flourished toward the middle of the eighth century BCE. From this period come three remarkable representations of elaborate chairs with backs: on the well-known Hubbard amphora, on the side-panels of an amphora from Ormidhia, and on a jug from Chrysochou (Karageorghis 1968: 101, figs. 17e–g; Theodossiadou 1996: 81, figs. 8a–b). The "Hubbard amphora" bears a banqueting scene focusing on an enthroned figure with feet resting on a footstool, attended by a female figure carrying jugs for pouring wine. The "enthroned" figure drinks from a long straw, a motif already known from cylinder seals from Ur.[6] A Syrian-style sphinx sniffing a lotus flower appears on the panel to the right, while a bull protome appears to the left. Such images may be associated with the popular concept of hospitality and commensality being under divine protection, an idea also made explicit throughout Homer's *Odyssey*; there, the punishment of the suitors is justified by their disgraceful and inappropriate behavior as guests in Odysseus' home.

Hittite evidence is exemplified by the representations on the four registers of the elaborate Inandiktepe relief vase, which probably, like the similar relief vase from Bitiktepe, represents the preparation of a "Sacred Marriage" rite (Özgüç 1988: 84–106, plates F–L, 36–59). Following the collapse of the Hittite state (*c.* 1200 BCE), new principalities arose to fill the power vacuum in southeast Anatolia and north Syria. Such neo-Hittite (twelfth- to ninth-century BCE) evidence is richer, but limited in genre, consisting of representations of furniture in reliefs on funerary stelae and orthostates from Maraş, Carchemish, Zincirli, Malatya, Karatepe, and Kızıldağ (Symington 1996: 128–38, figs. 16–21). Reliefs of seated rulers from Zincirli, Karatepe, and Kızıldağ show contemporary Assyrian and Phoenician influence rather than continuity of Anatolian themes (Hittite kings and gods are rarely shown on seats). Those from Malatya and Carchemish, by contrast, display the strong preservation of thematic and stylistic elements associated with the Hittite glyptic tradition. In this context, Urartian representations of thrones (Merhav 1991: 246–8, fig. 1) are interesting in combining a vague Assyrian influence (see below) with indigenous iconographic preferences, such as the representations of rulers or deities standing or seated on thrones on the backs of felines or bulls.

Late Assyrian reliefs have yielded a great number of furniture representations, although depicted furniture appears almost exclusively in royal or other elite contexts, including booty. Variants of an elevated seat with curved armrests and a high back (a "throne") are shown on many reliefs during the reign of Tiglath-Pileser III (744–727 BCE), where typical Assyrian features, such as tapering pine-cone feet already appear (Curtis 1996: 168–9, fig. 1d). Wall paintings (eighth century BCE) at the provincial town of Til-Barsib (in present-day north Syria) also depict an elaborate throne with footstool and purple textile covers (Thureau-Dangin and Dunand 1936: plate 49; reproduced in Curtis 1996: 169, fig. 2). A feasting scene depicted in Sargon's palace at Khorsabad (ancient Dur-Šarrukin in present-day north Iraq) shows two people each sitting on a stool, an apparent artistic convention for two stools placed side by side (Kyrieleis 1969: 8, n. 12). There is also ample evidence for stool-like, backless thrones in Assyrian art (e.g., the reliefs from the SW Palace at Nineveh, second half of the seventh century BCE) (overview by Curtis 1996: 171–3). Footstools follow closely the stylistic elaborations of the seats they accompany: zoomorphic and pine-cone feet both occur in relief representations (Curtis 1996: 173–4, fig. 6).

Of great historical significance is one of the earliest representations of a couch for reclining during a feast, a plausible ancestor for this use of the Archaic Greek *kline* (κλίνη) (see Chapter 5 in this volume). This occurs on the well-known "Garden Party" relief from the North Palace of Ashurbanipal at Nineveh (*c.* 650–645 BCE): the king is depicted reclining on an elaborate couch with pine-cone feet, with an enthroned queen and a table beside him (Plate 14). The occasion for this royal celebration is the Assyrian victory over Elam (present-day west and southwest Iran) (*c.* 653 BCE).

ARCHAIC AND CLASSICAL PERIODS

The richest visual source of ancient furniture is undoubtedly the Attic iconography of Archaic and Classical times (sixth to fourth centuries BCE). Vases and other works of art were decorated with themes deriving from mythology and the worship of gods. Gradually there was an increase in depiction of genre scenes such as *symposia*, festive and wedding ceremonies, as well as scenes from the women's quarters. Among the scenes of everyday life a small number depict various workshops where artisans are represented working with clay, metal, leather, and wood for the manufacture of corresponding products. In the following section we will visit the furniture depicted in some of the pictorial representations mentioned above.

The most usual types of furniture depicted mainly on Attic vase painting are seats, tables, couches, chests, selves, and various stands, which forms present great typology.

SEATS

The *throne* was a stately seat used by gods and goddesses, the heroic dead as well as respectable elders, both male and female (Athenaeus, *Deipn.* 5.192e). According to vase iconography we can distinguish four types of thrones that differ in the form of their back and feet (Richter 1966: 13–33). The most popular type of throne during the sixth and the first half of the fifth century BCE is that with animal feet, deriving from an Egyptian prototype (Kyrieleis 1969: 186–92). Some thrones also possess a back ending in a swan head and animal feet (Richter 1966: 15–18, figs. 42–3, 51; Prückner 1968: plate 22; Salapata 2014: 122). This type of throne also occurs on the votive *pinakes* of the fifth century BCE from Epizephyrioi Locroi in Southern Italy (Prückner 1968: plates 4.4, 7.6).

The *klismos* is an elegant chair, less formal than the throne and more luxurious than the *diphros* (Robsjohn-Gibbings and Pullin 1963: 43–65; Baker 1966: 277–83; Richter 1966: 33–7). This kind of comfortable seat occurs mostly in scenes of women's quarters, as well as in scenes with divine and respectable senile figures (Richter 1966: 33–7, figs. 166–93) (Plate 32). In Homeric poems the *klismos* is mentioned as a seat for the gods and heroes; especially Hera and Athena sat down upon their golden *klismoi* (*Iliad* 8.436: "αὐταὶ δὲ χρυσέοισιν ἐπὶ κλισμοῖσι καθῖζον"). The same literary source gives evidence for the "ποικίλον," inlaid or painted klismos (Homer, *Odyssey* 1.132).

The feet of the *klismos* are shown curved or perpendicular and sometimes terminating in animal feet. The end of its back takes several forms, one of them has the form of a swan head. The seat of the *klismos* was made of leather thongs fixed outside or inside the frame, and in some cases it was covered by an embroidered cushion (Robsjohn-Gibbings and Pullin 1963: 32; Andrianou 2021: 97).

The *diphros*, a backless stool, is depicted with perpendicular legs, and leather thongs both outside and inside the frame (Robsjohn-Gibbings and Pullin 1963: 72–93; Richter 1966: 38–43; Athenaeus, *Deipn.* 5.192f). Richter (1966: 38–43) distinguishes five types of *diphroi* according to the shape of their legs. In the first type a rounded part connects the frame with each tall and thin leg. This type occurs in vase paintings of the sixth and fifth century BCE, as well as in sculpture (Richter 1966: 39–40, figs. 200–8). The most representative example of this type is the *diphroi* on which gods and goddesses are seated in the Parthenon east frieze (Richter 1966: 39, fig. 204). On the same frieze two maidens carry stools probably for the guests at the religious festival of the Great Panathenaia. They were easily movable and ready-made for provisional purposes (Jeppesen 2007: 123–4, fig. 18, 127–9, figs. 23–4, 164–5). *Diphroi* are also listed among the treasures of the Parthenon (see Chapter 9 in this volume).

Diphoi are also known from various funerary stelai and the famous votive relief of a potter from the Acropolis (510–500 BCE, Athens, Akropolis Museum, inv. no. 1332; cf. Raubitschek 1949: 75, no. 70; Trianti 1998: 215, figs. 227–8; Chatzidimitriou 2005: 179, 225, no. St2, plate 59). In vase painting, the parts connecting the stool with wooden joints and metal nails are depicted in white color on the black-figure representations and in black color on the red-figure representations. Another example on a black-figure amphora from Boston (Museum of Fine Arts, inv. no. 01.8035) shows a shoemaker seated on a *diphros* of this type (Plate 33) (Beazley Archive Pottery Database [hereafter *BAPD*] 2188; *Corpus Vasorum Antiquorum* [hereafter *CVA*] Boston 1, plate 37; Chatzidimitriou 2005: 216, no. S1, plate 36).

In the second type the legs of the *diphros* consist of two superimposed concave parts connected with a protrusive wooden hinge standing on a low narrowing mount. The *diphroi* of this type are more popular in the Athenian votive stelai of the fifth and fourth century BCE than in Athenian vase painting (Richter 1966: 40–1, figs. 214, 219–20). The *diphros* of the statuette of a seated scribe (500 BCE) from the Acropolis (Akropolis Museum, inv. no. 629) belongs to this type (Furtwängler 1881: 174–80, plates VI.1–2; Trianti 1998: 199–201, figs. 211–13).

In the third type, which is not as popular as the aforementioned, the legs consist of an elongated and rounded member, which tapers downward supported by a low mount with perpendicular sides (Richter 1966: 41–2, figs. 222–7). In the Late Archaic period the shape of the legs changes and the upper part becomes thinner. During the second half of the fifth century BCE a knob appears at the end of the upper part and the mount's sides appear flaring.

In the fourth type a short, four-sided, sometimes rectangular, or rounded member connects the seat frame with each leg of the stool (Richter 1966: 42, figs. 228–31). This type became very popular because of its simple design in the red-figure vase painting of the fifth century BCE (Plate 32).

Finally, in the fifth type the legs of the stool are plain, straight, four-sided, and connected directly with the seat of the stool (Richter 1966: 42–3, figs. 233–5).

Diphros okladias (ὀκλαδίας δίφρος) is a folding stool with a leather top and crossed curving legs, usually ending in animal feet (Robsjohn-Gibbings and Pullin 1963: 67–71; Baker 1966: 275–7; Richter 1966: 43–6, figs. 237–49). It was an easily portable stool for Athenian citizens and, according to Athenaeus (*Deipn.* 12.512b–c), "slaves carried folding stools for them so that they should not sit as chance might have it." Because of their particular structural characteristics, the stools were often used outdoors, as for instance, in scenes of retail selling and workshops (Chatzidimitriou 2005: plate 36, no. S2; plate 47, no. E12; plate 48, no. E14; plate 51, no. E19). On a white-ground pyxis, dated to 460–450 BCE (Boston, Museum of Fine Arts, inv. no. 98.887) a lyre player, identified with the poet Archilochos, is shown holding a lyre (*BAPD* 209554; *ARV*² 774, 1). He is seated on an elaborate ὀκλαδίας δίφρος with black and white decoration on its legs, perhaps made of ivory or ebony (Richter 1966: 39, fig. 205). This type of seat is also evidenced in sculpture: on the Basel relief, dated to 480 BCE, a person (interpreted as a healer) is seated on an elaborate stool with twisted legs (Basel, Antikenmuseum und Sammlung Ludwig, inv. no. BS 236; Stampolidis and Tassoulas 2014: 333–6 [Vlachogianni]) (Plate 34).

In vase painting we also find a type of an informal box-like seat. These are used mostly by young people and manual laborers, but also gods and heroic figures (see, for instance, youths [Kavvadias 2000: plate 48.41], retailers [Chatzidimitriou 2005: plate 50, no. E16], and potters [Chatzidimitriou 2005: plate 16, no. K46]). The box-like seat on which the goddess Athena is depicted on a fragmented red-figure cup from the Acropolis (Museum of Acropolis, inv. no. 166) is quite characteristic (*BAPD* 200761; *LIMC* s.v. *Athena* no. 49, plate 707). Especially in the uncommon scenes of workshops and markets, the seats are square or rectangular with concave or upright sidewalls, made of wood and clay (Chatzidimitriou 2005: plate 18, no. K49; plate 21, no. K53; plate 22, no. X2; plate 50, no. E16).

In vase paintings, benches used for more than one person are rare. The use of benches (βάθρα) by students is specifically attested by Plato (*Protagoras* 325e) and found as such in iconography (Chatzidimitriou 2012: 279, n. 18, drawing 2, fig. 4).

Tables

Tables can be divided into two types: the three-legged and the four-legged (Robsjohn-Gibbings and Pullin 1963: 96–111; Baker 1966: 272–4; Richter 1966: 6–372). Most of the three- and four-legged tables are small and appear in symposion scenes for meals and offerings (Richter 1966: 63–72; Bruit 1990: 171; Simpson 2002: 315–16). Small three-legged tables occur widely in scenes of choes (a special form of oinochoe) related to the festivals of Anthesteria in honor of Dionysos (Lezzi-Hafter 1988: 200–1, no. 215, plates 137, 138d; 201–2, no. 214, plate 136; on the connection of the cult of Dionysos with benches, see Goudineau 1967: 97–103). The horizontal part of the three-legged table is formed by two superimposed slabs, while its three legs are depicted from the side, ending in lion paws. Where the two horizontal slabs connect with the legs, there appear three nails at each connection, demarcated in black.

During manual work craftsmen used tables and workbenches (Chatzidimitriou 2005: 162–3). On a few representations of shoemakers at work, which describe the process of shoemaking, a recurring motif—the cutting of the leather on the benches—is depicted. In these shoemaking scenes luxurious four- and three-legged tables are depicted (Chatzidimitriou 2005: 162–3, plate 36, nos. S1–S3), also evidenced on the Boston Museum amphora (520–510 BCE) where a rectangular four-legged table is supported on vertical legs, ending in lion feet (Plate 33). Where the horizontal surface connects with the legs, decorated volutes on a horizontal beam parallel to the table's surface are added. On a *pelike* (a jar with two handles used for liquids) in Oxford (Ashmolean Museum, inv. no. 563) the central leg of the three-legged table is decorated with volutes in front, imitating an Ionian column (*BAPD* 302990; *ABV* 396.21, 696). A *kylix* at the British Museum (inv. no. 86) portrays a simple undecorated three-legged table; under the table surface there appears to be a shelf, possibly for storage (*BAPD* 209681; *ARV²* 786, 4; Chatzidimitriou 2005: 216–17, plate 37, no. S3).

Another type of table can be found in a shoemaking scene depicted on a relief stele now at the Museum of the Agora of Athens, dated to the first half of the fourth century BCE (inv. no. I 7396; Camp 1986: 147, fig. 126; Chatzidimitriou 2005: 226, no. St4, plate 60). Here, four men seated on *klismoi* with curved supports and high backs are making shoes. On the right, there is a long and low table with vertical supports.

In livestock market representations, *mageiroi* (butchers) and fishmongers are shown chopping or slicing meat or large fish (Chatzidimitriou 2005: 121–7). Here, the surface for chopping is a small table with three legs, the ἐπίξηνον (*epixenon*) (Plate 35) (Sparkes 1975: 132; Van Straten 1995: 151), a pillar-like bench or table also used for hanging slices of meat (Chatzidimitriou 2005: 121–7, nos. E25–E27, plate 52–3; E33, plate 55).

Klinai *(Bed/Couches)*

The *kline*, used as a couch or bed, is the principal item of furniture for resting during meals and banquets or *symposia*, for sleeping as well as for the *prothesis* of the dead (Richter 1966: 52–63; Boardman 1990: 122–31). The word first appears in the work of the seventh-century BCE lyric poet Alcman (*Lyrica Graeca Selecta* 15; frag. 19). *Klinai* were made fairly consistently of wood and metal, but there was variation in the form of their legs. Couches with animal legs appear rarely in archaic vase painting; more often we come across depictions of couches with turned legs. This type of couch is of Eastern origin and its use extends from the Geometric to the Late Classical period (eighth to fourth century BCE) (Kyrieleis 1969: 118–29, figs. 22d, 23, plate 17; Tzachou-Alexandri 1989: 86, plate 18). In this type the couch legs consist of two superimposed parts: a wide upper and a lower thinner member with concave sides. These legs are supported by a small base.

Klinai used during banquets were mostly accompanied by side tables. These beds/couches had straight legs with curves that form a characteristic cut-out motif, decorated with palmettes above and below and a raised headboard. Sixth-century BCE Corinthian vase paintings, however, depict banquet couches without raised headboards, but with a cushion for support (Richter 1966: 59, fig. 311; Arvanitaki 2006: 179–88, figs. 128a–b, 129a–b). The legs at the head of the *klinai* are customarily taller than those at the foot and are crowned by an Aeolic capital, with two vertically springing volutes (Simpson 2002: 310–11, plates 79a–b). The top of the bed is covered with a mattress and sometimes with rich blankets (see, for instance, the bed on the red-figure crater of the Triptolemos painter in Saint Petersburg, inv. no. 1602 [637]; *BAPD* 203792; *ARV*² 360, 1, 1648; Andrianou 2021). This *kline*, which has been considered a Greek invention, became the most common type in Attic vase painting as well as in sculpture, both in the round and in relief (Simpson 2002: 311–12).

Finally, in fifth- and fourth-century BCE votive reliefs from the Asklepeion of Piraeus, we encounter a simple type of bed/couch, which is made of a horizontal surface on four simple undecorated legs (see, for instance, Kaltsas 2001: 136, no. 261; Stampolidis and Tassoulas 2014: 181–2, no. 63 [Chryssoulaki]).

Kibotos *(Chest)*

Chests were used for storing clothes, jewelry, and other items, and they appear mainly in women's scenes, where the chest is rectangular with a horizontal lid and stands on four legs ending in lion paws (Richter 1966: 73–7; Brümmer

1985: 41–55, figs. 9a–c, e; 11a–b, 12a, c, 14a, c, e, 15a). The frontal or one of the narrow sides of the chest is usually depicted, frequently decorated with painted or inlaid palmettes or stylized star motifs. Scenes of the Danae myth include the iconographic episode of the construction of the chest for her journey with Perseus.[7] Between 490 and 480 BCE the emblematic depiction of the myth of Danae includes a carpenter with a finished chest.

One of the most characteristic depictions of chests is found on a terracotta relief *pinax* (a votive plaque), from the sanctuary at Epizephyrioi Locroi in southern Italy (Tarent, National Museum, inv. no. *IG* 8332) where Persephone and other deities were worshipped (Prückner 1968: 39–40, type 14, plate 4.4; Humphreys 1995: 107, fig. 7). The *pinax*, dating from the first half of the fifth century BCE (500–450 BCE), depicts the narrow side of the chest, decorated with a meander motif and pictorial compositions. It depicts the moment when a young woman lifts the chest's cover to place the folded woven textiles inside. In other reliefs from the same sanctuary, chests are intended for ritual paraphernalia (Prückner 1968: 49, type 31, plate 7.6; 85–6, type 132, plates 31.1, 31.5). A similar scene is depicted on a red-figure lekythos at Yale (inv. no. 1913.146), dated to around 460 BCE (Plate 36). An open chest and a woman standing over it with a bundle of clothes are shown in a domestic context (*BAPD* 207688; *ARV*[2] 658.30).

Kylikeia

Wooden constructions, mostly with shelves, used for displaying vessels for sale or simply storing vessels and other domestic objects in houses, have been identified as *kylikeia* (*Suidae Lexicon*, s.v. Κυλικεῖον: "ἡ θήκη τῶν ποτηρίων"). Shelves also appear in scenes of pottery workshops on Corinthian and Attic vase paintings (Chatzidimitriou 2005: 48, 206, K13, plates 3 and 51–2, 211, no. K46, plate 16b, respectively). On a *kylix* at the British Museum (inv. no. B 432) one shelf is shown storing vessels (*BAPD* 4357; Chatzidimitriou 2005: 51, 209–10, no. K40, plate 11).

In Etruscan tomb paintings of Tarquinia (520–330 BCE), *kylikeia* are depicted in symposion scenes as sideboards bearing vases and other utensils, a variation not found in similar representations of Attic black- and red-figure vase paintings (van der Meer 1984: 298–304).

Stands

Stands (like modern coat racks) were apparently used for hanging various domestic objects during *symposia*. On a red-figured skyphos in Malibu (J. Paul Getty Museum, inv. no. 86.AE.265) such a stand with a base ending in lion paws and hooks hanging from its top is used for hanging symposion utensils (ladle, strainer, and jug), such as those seen in relevant scenes (*BAPD* 10146; Lissarrague 1995: 94, figs. 3–4).

A red-figure *pelike* dated to 470 BCE, now in Munich (Staatliche Antikensammlungen und Glyptothek, inv. no. 2347), shows among the butcher's equipment a peculiar wooden stand (Chatzidimitriou 2005: 122–3, 224, no. E32, plate 55). On its upper part there is a flat shelf on which pieces of meat are hanging, while in the middle of the main stem a vertical protrusion was used either as a second shelf or as a carrying handle. This construction was used for placing and storing meat, similar to the long bench seen on other depictions.

Carpentry tools

Iconographic evidence of carpentry or masonry during the Classical era is scarce. On a red-figure cup (510–500 BCE) a young carpenter holds a long-handled *adze* (σκέπαρνον) in his right hand and is working on a thick beam with a square projection below apparently cut to receive a tenon joint (London, British Museum, inv. no. GR 1836–24.231; *BAPD* 201642; Chatzidimitriou 2005: 102, 217, no. X1, plate 38). We could assume that the piece of furniture under construction here was a couch and the carpenter was a *klinopoios*.

On a Campanian bell-crater dated to the fourth century BCE, the craftsman uses a jagged saw with a curved handle for cutting a triangular piece of wood (Paris, Museum of Louvre, inv. no. K 259; Trendall 1960: 24, no. 34, figs. 20a–b; Schauenburg 1976–7: 23, fig. 15). In the scenes of the mythological episode of Danae, where a carpenter is depicted manufacturing the chest, he uses a drill-bow for the opening of holes (*LIMC* s.v. *Danae* 331, nos. 42, 48, plate 247; Chatzidimitriou 2005: 217, nos. X2, X4, plate 38).

Generally, the depicted furniture items of the Archaic and Classical periods are plain or with simple decoration. Everyday furniture items (such as *klismos*, *diphros*, *kline*, etc.) are found in a variety of types. This variety of types reflects the technological development of furniture making, and the gradual tendency to construct more comfortable and luxurious furniture. For example, a *klismos* could be made more comfortable and elegant by varying the swing of the legs and by changing the position of the back.

In certain worship scenes or scenes with divinities and heroic figures, luxurious furniture is also used as a means to highlight significant figures. In an Attic vase, for instance, Zeus, the father of gods, is depicted seated on a luxurious throne, decorated with palmettes and other ornaments (*ARV*² 639.62). On another example, the story of Croesus' punishment by Cyrus is depicted: Croesus, the king of Lydia, dared to raise an army against the Persian Empire. He was defeated by Cyrus in 547 BCE, who ordered him to be burnt alive along with fourteen noble Lydian youths. It is this particular moment that is depicted on the vase: Croesus is placed in the pyre seated on a luxurious throne decorated with Ionic capitals and his feet are resting on a footstool (*ARV*² 237, 238, 238.1, 1638). The king is shown in all his majesty even in a scene that narrates his punishment.

On the other hand, the small number of shoemaking scenes in vase painting is most probably indicative of the condemnation with which the Athenian citizens looked upon professional tanners and shoemakers (Aristophanes, *Knights* 44, 893; *Wasps* 38). The depiction of elaborate furniture in these workshops or the depiction of shoemakers being crowned in the presence of figures identified as their clients, may be interpreted as an attempt of these workers (or the vase painters) to idealize their condemned craft.

HELLENISTIC AND ROMAN PERIODS

In Hellenistic and Roman times (*c.* 300 BCE–300 CE) various kinds of furniture were depicted on different objects such as sarcophagi and grave reliefs, wall paintings of private dwellings, cultic or votive reliefs as well as on coins and public monuments. In modern times, these images were used as an important source for reconstructing the appearance and usage of furniture and furnishing in ancient times (Richter 1966; Croom 2007). However, it is important to keep in mind that only on a few occasions is it possible to apply the terms used for furniture in ancient texts to the objects depicted in visual representations. In the following section we will focus on three questions concerning the visual representations of Hellenistic and Roman times on the basis of selected examples: (a) What kind of furniture was depicted? (b) In which contexts is it shown? (c) Why was furniture depicted and what might have been its meaning in the representations?

Mainly three different kinds of luxurious furniture were depicted in grave reliefs and sarcophagi from Italy, the Eastern Mediterranean, and the northwestern provinces (modern-day France, Germany, and Great Britain) in images of Hellenistic and Roman times (Fabricius 1999: 86–9; Croom 2007: 51–2): couches for lying down during a banquet, thrones and chairs for sitting, and different kinds of tables for serving food and displaying vessels. Banquet scenes—beyond the veil or among the living—were depicted on grave reliefs from the Eastern Mediterranean in a highly stylized fashion such as on a relief from Byzantium (modern-day Istanbul) in the Archaeological Museum of Istanbul (inv. no. 16) dated to the first century BCE (Pfuhl and Möbius 1979: 489–90, no. 2035) (Figure 8.2). A man is lying on a lavishly decorated couch upon which a mattress and two cushions are placed. Both cushions have an ornamental seam. A blanket or cloth is hanging in front of the couch. A woman is sitting on its lower end putting her feet on a footstool decorated with winged figures at each corner. A table with a molded top and three swan's legs is placed in front of the couch. While both figures are rendered prominently due to their size, the furniture and furnishing also play a major role within the image as both are larger than the servants next to the table. For the beholder their decorated elements are prominently visible: the ornamentally turned leg and headrest of

FIGURE 8.2 Grave relief with banquet scene, first century BCE. Archaeological Museum of Istanbul no. 16 (DAI Istanbul neg. 64/78 [P. Steyer]). Photo courtesy of the İstanbul Arkeoloji Müzeleri and the Deutsches Archäologisches Institut.

the couch, the winged figures on the footstool, the swans on the table as well as the colorful painting of the blanket hanging from the couch. Like the man's and woman's fine clothes and their servants, the furniture is an element of the grave owner's self-representation as a wealthy member of the elite.

Similar scenes are depicted on Roman sarcophagi, for instance the one in the Museo Gregoriano Profano/Vatican (inv. no. 9538) dated to around 270 CE (Amedick 1991: 167–8, no. 286; plate 16, 1). A man is lying on a couch with turned legs, a frame decorated with two figural reliefs, and a curved board on three sides ornamented with a dolphin at the front. The man's arm rests on a small cushion. A three-legged table with supports in the shape of lion paws ending in a lion head is placed half under and half in front of the couch. A woman playing a string instrument is sitting on an elaborate wicker chair next to it. As on the grave relief the human figures are the main components of the image. The furniture—the three-legged table underneath the main figure and the couch with its curved board and turned legs—is centered within the image.

In most of the visual representations of the Late Hellenistic and Roman periods, furniture and furnishings simply serve as background details in banquet scenes. In these images, the decorated couches and tables were status symbols depicted as a representation of the relief owner's wealth.

In a few rare occasions furniture is shown as an object of value in its own right as, for instance, in a wall painting from the tomb of Vestorius Priscus in Pompeii dated to the first century CE (Croom 2007: 70; color plate 13). It shows a table on which nineteen different silver vessels are displayed. The luxury of the setting is not only suggested by the silver vessels but also by the design of the rectangular table with its four legs: the table is not of plain workmanship, but the front of the tabletop is decorated with a brown intarsia; the table supports are topped with elaborate capitals and end in lion paws.

The reliefs of a sarcophagus from Simpelveld in the Rijksmuseum van Oudheden in Leiden (inv. no. I 1930/12.1), dated to the second half of the second century CE, depict several different kinds of household furniture not to scale (Galestin 2001: 63–76; Croom 2007: 38, 131, 138, 182, fig. 3.6). The sarcophagus was the grave of a wealthy Roman lady. It is unique because the images are carved on the inside and not the outside, thus, once sealed the images were not visible anymore. The reason for this must lie in the buried woman's beliefs in the afterlife where she wanted to take with her all the necessities for a pleasant life. On one of its longer sides the figure of a woman—presumably the deceased—is lying on a couch with a board on three sides decorated with geometric designs. The legs of the couch are turned. An empty wicker chair is placed on the shorter side next to the couch. The other longer side is decorated with several different kinds of furniture: a cupboard with three large vessels on top, a table with three legs in the shape of lion paws and heads, and a second cupboard with three storeys for different kinds of storage vessels. It is followed by a closet without feet and a flat top, which has two doors with elaborate moldings, a batten covering the joint between the doors and two horizontal handles on each door. All of this furniture was part of the interior of a wealthy Roman household.

Although these examples come from different chronological, geographic, and functional backgrounds, all of them display furniture from a wealthy household. The furniture was part of images depicting the social status and wealth of the respective owners. However, although the images do not aim at representing everyday life, the depictions of furniture and furnishings seem to be highly accurate if compared to preserved wooden and marble furniture. Although they are not the images' main elements, the elaborately decorated furniture is placed centrally within the visual representations revealing the high value of furniture and furnishings as status symbols within Hellenistic and Roman societies.

The idea of displaying a luxurious lifestyle in visual representations through elaborate furniture and furnishings was found throughout the Hellenistic and Roman world not only among the members of the wealthy elite in the Mediterranean region but also at the northwestern and eastern edges of the ancient world: several fragments of reliefs depicting furniture, for example, are known from sites in the Rhine valley. A small relief from the so-called Igel monument—a grave monument in the vicinity of Trier from the middle of the third century CE—displays a banquet scene in the middle and servants preparing drinks and cleaning plates to the right and left (Ritter 2003; Croom 2007: 80–1; Feuser 2013: 23). In the central banquet scene, two men are reclining on a couch lavishly decorated with a cloth. Two women are sitting in wicker chairs next to the couch; a rectangular table with a tablecloth is placed in front of it. On the left side of the banquet scene two servants prepare drinks with vessels placed on a tall table with a single leg decorated with a lion head. On the right side two servants clean the plates for serving the food and put them on display on a chest. The wealth and status of the grave owner is emphasized by the servants, the furniture and furnishing, the plates and drinking vessels. This same kind of wealth and status display can be found in a relief fragment of unknown function from Palmyra (Archaeological Museum Palmyra, inv. no. 2906/9422/b) located on the eastern edge of the Roman Empire. From right to fractured left it displays a monumental krater (vessel for mixing wine with water), a local nobleman in traditional dress with a sword, a monumental one-legged table with a figural support representing a satyr engaging a maenad (a female follower of Bacchus), a second local nobleman, and a table leg with a lion paw and head that must have originally been part of a three-legged table. The larger-than-life size of both the tables and the krater reveal that they (rather than the two noblemen) are the most important elements in the image. Thus, in both reliefs furniture plays a major role in representing the owner of an elite household on the edges of the Roman Empire (Feuser 2013: 24–5; plates 1, 4).

Compared to the luxurious furniture of the upper classes depicted in visual representations in late Hellenistic and Roman times, the plain furniture of craftsmen and merchants appears only rarely in images. In a scene on a Sarcophagus in the Museo Gregoriano Profano/Vatican (inv. no. 3262) dated to the last quarter of the third century CE two carpenters working on a wooden table support sit at a table with a plain top and two trestles with A-frames underneath (Richter 1966: table 614; Amedick 1991: 167, n. 283; plate 112, 2). A similar plain table with two trestles used for exhibiting bread can be found on a sarcophagus fragment in the Museo del Palazzo dei Conservatori/Rome (inv. no. 2685/S) dated to the end of the third century CE (Zimmer 1982: 222, no. 183; Amedick 1991: 153, no. 193; plate 110, 2). It also appears on a relief from Ostia depicting a shop-owner presenting vegetables (Croom 2007: 91–3, fig. 39). Nevertheless, even in these representations of artisans and merchants the furniture can be elaborate. A sarcophagus in the Museo Nazionale in Rome (inv. no. 184) from Ostia dated to the beginning of the second century CE, for example, displays a closet with carved moldings (Amedick 1991: 149–50. no. 173; plate 117, 2). Thus, the plain furniture of these images cannot be interpreted as symbolizing the low social status and poverty of artisans and merchants. With these everyday scenes on reliefs of sarcophagi and grave monuments the owners proudly figure their professions and their social esteem—and plain furniture is an important abbreviation of their working environment.

Within late Hellenistic and Roman visual representations the use of certain furniture was restricted to particular groups of people. Lavishly embellished thrones, for instance, can only be found in representations of gods, goddesses, and mythological figures. This can be seen in a wall painting from the House of the Punished Cupid from Pompeii (Naples, Archaeological Museum no. 9249) dated to the first quarter of the first century CE, in which the courtship of Mars and Venus is depicted (Richter 1966: plate 655; Ling 1991: 139, fig. 144). The goddess is sitting on a throne with a high back, turned legs, and arm-rails with figural decoration. In a wall painting from Pompeii dated to the first century CE (Naples, Archaeological Museum no. 9456) the god Dionysus is seated on a throne with rectangular legs, cut-out incisions, and a high back covered with a heavy cloth (Richter 1966: plate 484). The feet of the god rest on a footstool. A bronze statuette in the Archaeological Museum of Naples (no. 1550) depicts the goddess Fortuna sitting on a similar kind of throne with a high back (Richter 1966: plate 487). The design of these thrones derives from Greek prototypes (see above).

Whereas throne-like seating was used for gods/goddesses and mythological figures, two types of stools were restricted in use to Roman emperors and magistrates. Both were depicted prominently in official representations. One of these two types, the *sella curulis* or ceremonial seat of office, is shown on coins, grave monuments, and bronze vessels; it has the form of a folding stool with curved legs, cross-pieces at the back and front, a thick cushion on the top and no back or arms (Wanscher 1980; Schäfer 1989; Croom 2007: 97–101). It became a symbol of its owner's power and status and was thus depicted without a person sitting on it as a *pars pro toto* (a part taken for the whole). A relief from a grave monument in Rome, now in the collection of Hever Castle in England dated to the late first century CE, shows a lavishly decorated *sella curulis* in lateral view (Schäfer 1989: 243–8). As a symbol of the owner's power military scenes are depicted several times on the seat: the center of the cross-piece shows a depiction of a cavalry battle between three barbarians and two fully armed Roman horsemen in a profiled frame. The area above and under the frame as well as the ends of the cross-piece are adorned with representations of weapons, shields, and armor. The S-shaped curved legs are adorned with winged genies at the top, which have raised *tropaea* (trophies) in their arms.

Another seat of honor given to officials was the *bisellium* (double seat) (Richter 1966: 104; Croom 2007: 101). Like the *sella curulis* it was depicted on grave monuments as *pars pro toto* of the owner's power and status. This can be seen on a tombstone in Pompeii dated to the first century CE (Croom 2007: 101–2, fig. 46). The connection between the *bisellium* and imperial power is emphasized on the so-called Gemma Augustaea dated to *c.* 10 CE (Galinsky 1996: 120–1, fig. 57). Augustus is sitting on a *bisellium* next to the goddess Roma and is crowned by the goddess Oikoumene both symbolizing his supernatural power. The bench is of a rather plain workmanship with turned legs but without ornamental or figural decorations. Thus, the value of these pieces of furniture—both *sella curulis* and *bisellium*—is not exhibited by an elaborate style and decor but mainly by the people who were allowed to use and sit on it.

To summarize, furniture and furnishing in the visual representations of late Hellenistic and Roman times can be found in a wide array of genres within ancient art. These images were displayed in funerary contexts, private dwellings, and cultic settings as well as in public representations. The images depicting different kinds of furniture were not restricted to the Mediterranean, but can also be found on the northwestern and eastern edges of the ancient world, thus, demonstrating the impact of Hellenistic-Roman culture. Whereas some of these images date to the Hellenistic period the main body of evidence derives from Roman times.

Three types of furniture are mainly displayed: couches, tables, and thrones/chairs in various forms. With their lavish decoration they are an essential part within the images for displaying the luxurious world of the upper classes. The furniture and furnishing within these visual representations were used for representing the owner's social status. However, we also find images showing the plain furniture of craftsmen and shop-owners. This furniture is an abbreviation of their working environment, which is not to be understood as a sign of their low social status and poverty, but rather as a representation of their professions and their social esteem.

The use of certain furniture was restricted to particular groups of people: gods, goddesses, and mythological figures were seated on thrones, whereas only Roman emperors and magistrates were allowed to use the *sella curulis* and the *bisellium*. Thus, on coins or on the reliefs of grave monuments their depictions without a seated person were used as a symbol for the owner's power.

CHAPTER NINE

Verbal Representations

VASSILIS PETRAKIS, DIMITRA ANDRIANOU,
AND ILIAS ANAGNOSTAKIS

THIRD MILLENNIUM TO SIXTH CENTURY BCE

Our earliest verbal documentation of furniture comes from the early states developed in Egypt and the Near East (including Hittite Anatolia in the second millennium BCE). However, furniture documented in records of transactions or inventories throughout its history is seldom descriptive. Except for the materials used, we mostly find simply the terms for different types of furniture. Uncertainties surround details in their form and means of construction. These problems notwithstanding, this chapter will focus on the terms used for furniture in written documents. A primary selection of such terms from Egypt and the Near East has been gathered in Table 9.1 with suggestions for further reading.

Some of our earliest evidence is interesting in the way it reveals aspects of the ancient conceptualization of objects that we categorize as "furniture." One Sumerian word for "throne," for instance, is the compound g̃išgal "great wooden" (g̃iš "wood"/"wooden thing" + gal "great"), the only Sumerian type of furniture to explicitly indicate its high elite function through such a transparent formation. Besides the terms included in Table 9.1, furniture vocabulary is greatly enriched by periphrases formed by the modification of terms used generically, as is frequently the case with Sumerian ᵍⁱšgu–za "seat," ná "bed," and banšur "table" (Akkadian kussû, eršu, and paššūru, respectively) (Salonen 1963: 34–75, 110–37, 176–92).

As a conceptual category, furniture is often explicitly associated with portability and mobility, a property most explicitly shown by the frequent examples (in both imagery and actual finds) of folding legs, collapsible parts,

TABLE 9.1 Table of the selected Egyptian, Near Eastern (including Hittite), Mycenaean Greek and Homeric terms regarding main furniture types. Terms for parts of furniture and references to specific documents or passages have been omitted. Further reading: Janssen (2009) and Kuhlmann (1977) (Egyptian); Salonen (1963) and Röllig et al. (1993) (Sumerian and Akkadian); Mitchell (1996) (Semitic, focusing on Hebrew); Symington (1996) (Hittite); Varias García (2008) (Mycenaean Greek); Laser (1968) (Homer).

Category	Egyptian	Semitic	Akkadian	Sumerian	Hittite	Mycenaean Greek	Homer
Beds or couches	ḥꜥti (bed); krkr (type of bed or couch); ytit (funerary couch); ḥnkit; nmit; mnK (wicker bed); mn (funeral bed or bier); ꜣtt (bier); mrt (bed frame); irꜣ; kr (type of bed or couch)	mškb [H, Ph, U]; mṭb [H]; mṭt [U]; ʿrś [H]; ʿrš [H, U]; ʿarsā [Ar]	eršu(m) (bed [generic also]); ḫāmū (leaves and reeds used as bed); gišnû [< S]; ḫuralbu/ ḫurallu [< ?]; izzidarû/ zidarû; munû/ manû; muruš; namallu; teniḫu/ tenû; zigarrû (bed with sidepieces); taknītu (luxury bed); ummultu; dargiš (couch; diwan); dinnû/ dunnu (bed or couch); kitbarattu; madnanu; majjālu; mar(a)šu; nēmedu (cf. fem. nēmettu 'backrest of a chair') [= Ass. nēmadu/ nēmattu]	ĝišnàd/ ĝišná/ ĝišnu/ ĝišú (bed [generic also]); ĝiš-ḫur-ĝišná (bed-model); ĝišná-zi-ga/ ĝišná-tuš-a (bed); ĝišná-aš-ná (bedstead; couch); zag-ša (bed or couch); ĝišma-(a-)al-tum (couch)	ĜIŠNÁ* = (ĜIŠ)šast(a)-ĜIŠGU.ZA.GÌD.DA* = ĜIŠḫaputi-ĜIŠnatḫit- [L]; ĜIŠnamulli- [Hu]	*re-ko /lékhos/ (in compound re-ke-to-ro-te-ri-jo /lekhestrōtēríon/ Gen. Pl.) 'bed'; de-mi-ni-jo /démnion/ 'bed'	εὐνή κοῖτος/ κοίτη λέχος λέκτρον δέμνιον

Seats						
ḳniw or *ḳni* (chair; also palanquin); *isbwt* (folding-stool?); *ḥˁt* (also means bedframe, bed or couch); *ꜣṯ.t* (also means bed, bier or canopy); *ḥndw*; *sṯ*; *bꜣỉ*; a throne (royal or divine seat) is *nst*; *wṯs.t*; *bhd.t*; *isbt*; stepped throne is *ḥmr* or *ḥndw*; *ḥryt* (stool?); *ḥwt* ('block-throne')	*ks'* [H] *'pryun* [H] *krs?* [Ar] *mwtb, mwtb?* [Ar]	*kussû* (seat [generic also]); *kussû arattītu/ kabittu* (chair of Aratta-type/ armchair); *kussû nēmedi* (armchair); *paltingu* (sedan-chair/ palanquin); *šadittu* (sedan-chair/ palanquin); *tallu* (stool or palanquin?); *durga(r)rû* [< S] (luxury seat/ throne); *mūšabu* (stool); *kalṣtu* (throne) [Amarna term < W.Sem.]; *gišgallu* (throne-podium) [< S]; *littu* (stool, also footstool?); *nakbasu* (stool); Ĝiš*papannu* (stool or footstool?); Ĝiš*šušubtu* (stool); *šubtu*; Ĝiš*urbatu* (reed stool)	ĝiš*gu-za/ guz-za*(seat [generic also]); ĝiš*gu-za-Aratta* (chair of Aratta-type/ armchair); ĝiš*gu-za-zag-bi-ús/* ĝiš*gu-za-zag(-gú-ús-sa)* (armchair); ĝiš*gu-za-ki-ús* (non-luxury stool); ĝiš*gu-za-ĝiš-gàr* (stool); ĝiš*gu-za-ní-ma-lá* (stool); ĝiš*gu-za-kaskal* (sedan-chair/ palanquin); ĝiš*gal/* ĝiš*kal(ag)* (chair; throne); ĝiš*dúr-ĝar* (luxury seat/ throne); *dag/ dúr/ ki/ unú* (stools or chairs); *zag-gal(-la)* (armchair);	Ĝiš*ŠÚ.A** = Ĝiš*keshi-* (chair or throne); Ĝiš*GU.ZA** (royal throne) [Hittite reading unknown] Ĝiš*DAG** = (Ĝiš) d*Ḫalmaššuit-* (throne -in religious contexts only) (Ĝiš)*sarpa-* Ĝiš*kupiš(sar)-* (stool) (Ĝiš)*zaḫurti-* Ĝiš*tarmal-* Ĝiš*taprit-* [L]; Ĝiš*tuni-* [Hu] Ĝiš*kišḫit-* [L < Hu] *ḫamāu-* (birth-stool)	*to-no/ *to-ro-no-* (the latter in compound *to-ro-no-wo-ko* */thronoworgoí/*) /thórnos/ or /thrónos/ (occurrence in compound *to-no-e-ke-te-ri-jo* doubtful) 'seat' or 'chair' (not yet 'throne') \ \ **e-do* /hédos/ (in phrase *o-pi-e-de-i* /opihedehi/) 'seat'	θο̃κος/ θόοκος ἕδος ἕδρη δίφρος θρόνος κλισίη κλιντήρ (couch??) κλισμός

	West Semitic / Egyptian	Attested forms	Akkadian	Sumerian	Hittite (cuneiform)	Mycenaean	Greek
					GIŠAB.GI.NA* (stool); KAN.TAR. TUR* (stool); GIŠŠILIG.TUR* (stool); GIŠŠILIG. ZAG.GU.ZA* (stool); KI.TUŠ.DÚR* (seat)		
Footstools	hdm.w / ḥdm g3wt ? kbś ?	hdm [U, Ph, H < Eg.] kbš [H]	girgubbu [< S] (also chariot-footboard); cf. also synonyms kilṣappu, gerṣeppu/ kerṣappu, kartappu, galtappu, gištappu, kiltappu, kilṣappu kibsu [cf. Eg. W.Sem.]; GIŠšapal šēpē	GIŠgìr(i)-gub(-ba) gìr-tab-ba (cf. podium/ platform)	(GIŠ)GÌR.GUB* = GIŠḫassalli- (also stool) GIŠkupiš(šar); GIŠkuppiš-	ta-ra-nu /thrā́nus/	θρῆνυς σφέλας (also stool?)
Tables	wṭḥw (offering table or altar); mšr (loanword of unknown origin); ṯṯ	šlḥn [H]; ṭlḥn [U]; ptwr, ptwr? [Ar]	paššūru(m) (cf. paššaru/ pašuru/ pašru; table [generic also]) būru (table); eriqā'u (table); diškû (table; cf. Greek δίσκος); gub/pru (table); kabru (table); (kaḡiš)kakarakku [< S] (type of table; dressing table?); lī'u (table);	GIŠbanšur/ GIŠbanšur/ GIŠKARA$_4$ (table [generic also]); bur (table); zag (food-table)	GIŠBANŠUR* (= GIŠpapu- ?) GIŠBANŠYR AD.KID* = GIŠḫariuzzi- GIŠGAN.KAL* = GIŠlaḫḫura- (offering table) GIŠwašša-	to-pe-za /tórpedza/	τράπεζα

Category	Egyptian	Akkadian	Sumerian	Greek
		mākalu (food-table); ᴳⁱˢMES.SANG.DU* (table); *mešdugudû/ meštugudû/ meštegudû/ meštigudû* (type of table); *meškalallû* (type of table); *meštegerrû* (type of table); *mušākilu* (food-table); *nabramu* (elaborate decorated table); *niatu* (table); *nigsiliqum* (table); *nun'u* (table); *surriḫumunû* (table); *guduttû* (offering table); *dugudû* (offering table)		
Chests or boxes	*škr/šgr* (wooden box/ chest); *mḥn* (chest); *g3wt* or *g3wt* or *g3wt* (box); *g3tі* or *gt* (type of box?); *3tp* (type of box?); *ʿfdt* or *ʿft* (small box or cupboard); *krf* (chest or shrine?); *pds*	*pisannu(m)/ pišannu(m)* [< S]; *kattaddu* (chest?); *papatum* (chest); *quppu(m)* (chest); ᴳⁱˢ*šunanu* (chest); ᴳⁱˢ*turpinnu* (earlier reading *umninu* or *umninu*)	*pisaĝ / pisán* (basket; box); ᴳᴵPISAN* (box; chest)	χηλός φοριαμός λάρναξ ὄγκιον κίστη

ᴳⁱˢGANNUM*
= ᴳⁱˢ*kistu*
(stand)

	Egyptian	Akkadian	Sumerian	Mycenaean Greek	Greek
	(chest; often for clothes); ꜥꜣy/ ꜥꜣiw (type of box); bni/ bnw (large box or chest); mḥtm.t (box/ chest; also for keeping documents); itr (šꜣbty-box); hꜣr or hr (box or foot-rest?); tbt or dbi (chest or bench?)				
Furnishings (mats, pillows etc.)	wrš (pillow); kn (mat); tmꜣ (mat); pj (reed-mat); wrś (head-rest)	ᵀᵁᴳmardatu(m)/ ᵀᵁᴳmardutu (mat/rug); arānu (cover); erimtu (leather?-cover for seats); ḫullānu (textile?-cover for beds); pitiltu (palm fibres for mattress stuffing); būru (reed-mat); zibnu (reed-mat); ᵀᵁᴳkirmu ša erši (bed-pillow); ᴳᴵˢtagabarušḫe [<Hu] (head-rest); uruššu [< Eg] (head-rest); paššūr qaqqadi ('table of the head'/ head-rest);	gi (reed or reed-mat); kid/ gi-kid (reed-mat); gi-kid-dúr (reed-mat);	te-pa cf. τάπης? ko-wo /kṓwos/ (on PY Un 718.4)	χλαῖνα τάπης ῥῆγος κῶας

Note: Ar = Aramaic; Ass = Assyrian; Eg = Egyptian; H = Hebrew; Hu = Hurrian; L = Luwian; Ph = Phoenician; S = Sumerian; U = Ugaritic; W.Sem = West Semitic; < = lexical borrowing; * = Sumerogram used also by other cuneiform cultures (Mesopotamia, Levant, Anatolia).

and metal hinges. Semantic associations between "furniture" and "mobility" are apparent in Greek ἔπιπλα (pl. "movable goods; furniture": the term occurs first in Herodotus 1.150) and modern European languages (French *meubles*; German *Möbel*; cf. also Akkadian *muttalliku* "movable [items]"). Furniture is commonly contrasted with immovable property, such as agricultural land, buildings, or other permanent installations (hearths, ovens, and wells). Another common semantic association is between furniture and household. Collective names for furniture in Sumerian (níg-gá and níg-gu-na-é-a, "household goods") and Akkadian (*gaširūtu*, "furniture; household items") are transparent in this respect (cf. Akkadian *unūtu(m)*, "household items"; Greek ἐνδουχία, "things that are held inside"; Polybius 18.35.6).

An association between seats and institutions is expressed through written language, where the association of terms for "chairs" with those indicating "branches" or "cups" came to signify kingship itself. "Branch" (apparently with a scepter-like quality: Ugaritic *ḫṭ*; Phoenician *ḫṭr*; Akkadian *ḫaṭṭu*) is combined with "chair" (Semitic *ks'*; Akkadian *kussû*; Aramaic *mwtb* 'seat; dwelling place' as in Greek ἕδος). The bestowment of royal insignia on kings by the gods is widely attested, from the "Investiture" panel, an eighteenth-century BCE wall painting from the palace of Zimri-Lim at Mari in present-day Syria, which shows the goddess Ishtar presenting the king with a ring and a staff, to the narrative regarding Agamemnon's scepter, made by Hephaistos for Zeus himself and passed on to mortal kings through Hermes (Homer, *Iliad* 2.101–8). A similar use of the term for "throne" to denote the royal office in *pars pro toto* fashion is, for instance, reflected in the Hittite use of the Sumerogram ᴳⁱˢGU.ZA "throne."

In the ancient Near East, the Mari archives provide abundant evidence of royal projects during the reign of Zimri-Lim (*c.* 1775–1762 BCE) including the manufacture of divine thrones and other elaborate furniture (Bardet et al. 1984). Dowry inventories from this period, such as that of princess Šimātum, one of Zimri-Lim's daughters, also include a fair amount of elite domestic furniture (Küpper 1983: no. 322).

Egyptian documentation on furniture is occasionally intriguing. A clear sign of the value of furniture is indicated in a copy of a legal document from the Sixth Dynasty (*c.* 2345–2181 BCE), which suggests that a payment in kind for the construction of a tomb included a bed and associated textiles and furnishings (Sethe 1903: no. 157). Documents from Deir el-Medîna (dated to the New Kingdom Ramesside period, *c.* 1295–1069 BCE) show highly variable prices for most furniture types (bed frames, chairs, folding stools, footstools, and tables) suggesting that size, materials, and quality of craftsmanship played a very important role in determining the value of these items (Janssen 2009, with references). In Year 25 of the reign of Rameses III (perhaps 1162 BCE), the inspection of a "ruined" (robbed?) tomb by an *ad hoc* committee of village notables took place at Deir el-Medîna. The resulting inventory of funerary items on an *ostracon* (potsherd with an inscription made after the vessel was broken) includes a repaired ebony folding stool, a footstool of papyrus, three headrests, two couches, and various chests and boxes (Zonhoven 1979).

The furniture vocabulary from ostraca and papyri from Deir el-Medîna has now been systematically studied by Janssen (2009). His work reveals how little we know about the differences in nuance between the terms for different types of furniture, particularly chests or boxes. Indeed, besides those most commonly used (e.g., *ḥˁtì* "bed"; *ḵnìw* "chair"; *hdm* "footstool"; or *mšr* "table"), exact typological correspondence with most of these terms is very difficult to determine. The generic Egyptian term for "furniture" *ḥtwt* means "wooden [things]" and *ḥt* (wood) was a common "classifier"-sign for many terms for furniture.

An archive of 350 tablets found at Tell el-Amarna (ancient Akhetaten) during Akhenaten's reign (*c.* 1350–1335 BCE) consists of diplomatic letters (and their attached inventories) between the pharaoh and foreign (independent or vassal) rulers (Figure 9.1). They are written in cuneiform in Babylonian-based idioms that also include Hurrian-Akkadian or West Semitic elements (Moran 1992). Furniture is primarily mentioned in international correspondence, and good examples are provided by tablets EA 5 mentioning ebony chairs, footstools, and beds decorated with ivory and gold and sent by the pharaoh to the Kassite king Kadašman-Enlil for his palace at Babylon; EA 13 containing the fragmentary dowry inventory of a Babylonian princess, perhaps a daughter of Burna-Buriaš; EA 14 presenting an inventory of gifts sent by the pharaoh or Burna–Buriaš; EA 22.III.22–3 listing an ebony chest sent by King Tušratta of Mittani as a wedding gift to the pharaoh; and EA 120 consisting of an inventory of stolen goods (Moran 1992: 10–11, 24–37, 55, 198–200). Unsurprisingly, furniture combining luxury and portability figures prominently in the context of international diplomatic gift exchange.

In Hittite texts, furniture largely appears in religious contexts where temple items including beds, tables, and chairs are inventoried. However, the limited contextual information at our disposal obscures the differences between the various terms that appear on our sources. ^{GIŠ}GU.ZA, for example, is the term for a royal throne par excellence (Sumerogram ^{GIŠ}ŠÚ.A read ^{GIŠ}*keshi-* renders "chair") but may also indicate the Hittite royal institution and office. An interesting aspect of Hittite terminology is the differentiation between "male" and "female" seats, with Sumerogram $^{(GIŠ)}$GÌR.GUB (read ^{GIŠ}*hassalli-*) "footstool" occasionally rendering the stool appropriate for women (KUB 29.8 obv. i 58–60 [a purification ritual]). This extends to the different ritual treatment of the cremated bones of the king and queen, placed on a throne or a footstool/stool, respectively (see also Chapter 6 in this volume). A similar distinction is reflected in the Hittite monumental reliefs at the Sphinx Gate of Alaca Höyük (central Anatolia), showing the Weather-God enthroned and his spouse (Hepat?) on a stool.

FIGURE 9.1 Fragment of one of the letters from the Tell el-Amarna archive (EA 5), listing furniture sent by the Egyptian pharaoh to the Kassite king of Babylon, Kadašman-Enlil. Middle of the fourteenth century BCE. Photograph © The Trustees of the British Museum.

The large number of Hurrian loanwords in Hittite furniture vocabulary is associated with the Hittite adoption of Hurrian and Hattian religious ideas. Hurrian, spoken in southeast Anatolia, Syria, and north Mesopotamia, and the Hattian, an autochthonous Anatolian language, still spoken but perhaps already fading during the second millennium BCE, survived as the languages of liturgical ritual texts used in Hittite religious practice (cf. the current use of Latin and New Testament Greek in Christian rituals). In such documents, of special importance is the frequent concurrence of the throne (^{ĜIŠ}DAG) and the ^{ĜIŠ}*kalmuš* (golden curved staff or lituus, cf. the Akkadian *gamlu*; perhaps of Hattian rather than

Mesopotamian provenance), whose formal place is at the right side of the throne (cf. KBo 4.9 iii 27, 29–31; KBo 27.42 i 4, 8–10). The pairing of these two royal insignia is reflected in what may be a "deified personified *kalmuš*" (rendered in Hittite as *ᵈḪalmutili* or *ᵈḪalputili*) that appears as the male consort of the goddess of the "deified personified throne" *ᵈḪalmaššuit* (KBo 37.9; see Chapter 5 in this volume). Description of the Hittite royal funerary rite also involves funerary furniture (see Chapter 6 in this volume). Texts from Emar (modern-day Tell Meskene in Syria) describe an elaborate ritual involving the enthronement and marriage of the Storm-God to the Entu priestess impersonating his spouse Hebat (Pringle 1993: 366–7; Symington 1996: 126).

In second-millennium BCE Aegean, as in the Ancient Near East, our extant (and accessible) written sources are mostly inventories or records of transactions related to the function of central "palatial" administrations, written in syllabographic scripts (i.e., using signs standing for entire syllables and not separate vowel or consonant sounds like an alphabet does), such as the "Cretan Hieroglyphic," the Linear A and the Mycenaean Linear B writing systems. Furniture is recorded with certainty only in Linear B records, which is the only fully deciphered Aegean Bronze Age script, rendering in a syllabographic manner a form of early Greek used by the Mycenaean palace administrators around 1400 to 1200 BCE.

A set of thirteen elongated clay tablets from the "Palace of Nestor" at Pylos (*c.* 1200 BCE), all written by the same hand and classified as the Ta series, records an inventory of furniture and other utensils that were apparently used during a palace banquet (Killen 1998). The opening line of the inventory includes a temporal clause that defines the occasion and purpose of this celebration: *hote wanaks thēken Augewān dāmokoron* (when the king [*wanaks*; cf. Homeric ἄναξ "ruler; lord"] appointed *Augewās* as *dāmokoros*) (PY Ta 711.1). It is reasonable to assume that the *wanaks* himself participated in the event. An inventory of five chairs (sing. *thornos*;[1] cf. θρόνος; spelled *to-no*), seventeen footstools (sing. *thrānus*; cf. Homeric (Ionian) θρῆνυς; spelled *ta-ra-nu*), and eleven tables (PY Ta 642; 713; 715; sing. *torpedza*; cf. Ion.-Att. τράπεζα; spelled *to-pe-za*)[2] is mentioned alongside other sacrificial and banquet paraphernalia, such as tripods, metal vessels, sacrificial swords, and stunning axes. The descriptive adjectives and phrases that accompany these items aim to provide precise information about materials, decoration techniques, or even designs (Shelmerdine 2012, with references; see Chapters 2, 3, and 8 in this volume). The Ta set is carefully organized: tables (Speciale 2000) are listed in separate records, while chairs are listed alongside their footstools, perhaps intended as "sets," on PY Ta 707, 708, and 714 (Plate 37). This is not reflected in the mortuary record, where footstools have been identified in certain rich burials (Sakellarakis 1996), but not their corresponding chairs. *Thornos/thronos* and *thrānus* are derived from the IE root **dher-* 'to hold/support', while *torpedza* is etymologized as **tʷr̥-ped-ya*

< *k^wtur-ped-ih$_2$- "four-legged." It is therefore an interesting inconsistency that most of our earliest Aegean tables are in fact *three*-legged (actual examples from Mycenae or Thera and tripod offering tables from many Late Bronze Age Aegean sites; see Chapters 3, 4, and 8 in this volume). It is possible that etymology reflects a four-legged archetypal table.

Our understanding of the technical vocabulary in the Ta records is fraught with problems (see the sample discussed in Chapter 3 in this volume). Besides gold, ivory, or glass-paste, some decorative materials or motifs are not identified with certainty, such as *pa-ra-ku* ("emerald" or "turquoise"; perhaps related to Akkadian *barrāqtu*, Hellenized as σμάραγδος?) or *ku-te-so* (perhaps *Laburnum* wood, if the same as later Greek κύτισος); references to "heads of *se-re-mo* (Sirens?)," "Phoenixes" (palm-trees or griffins?), or the still unidentifiable *au-de* remain obscure, while *a-pi-qo-to* (understood as *amphigwōtos*) may indicate a circular tabletop with a raised border; adjectives in *-e-jo* modifying objects generally denote the structural material, but this may not apply to *we-a$_2$-re-jo* "decorated with [rather than 'made of'] glass/rock crystal(?)" Tables of six or nine feet (spelled *we-pe-za* and *e-ne-wo-pe-za*, respectively) have also been interpreted as referring to length and not the actual number of legs. There is still much to clarify, while we need to contextualize the Ta tablets and associate them with the remains of burnt animal bones (remains of burnt sacrifice?) found with the tablets themselves (Stocker and Davis 2004) or the fragments of a circular marble tabletop from a nearby court (Blegen and Rawson 1966: 229–30, fig. 271:4).

Tables are also associated with religious festivals or feasting at late fourteenth- or early thirteenth-century BCE Knossos, probably during the month *Wordewiōn*. Bedsteads (*demnia*) may be mentioned on records from Pylos, while Linear B sign *169 may also indicate "bedsteads" on some tablets from the same palace (*c*. 1200 BCE).[3]

Two Pylian festival names can be etymologically associated with furniture items: *lekhestrōtēriōn*, "on the occasion of spreading of the couch/bed" (spelled *re-ke-(e-)to-ro-te-ri-jo*, PY Fr 343; 1217.3), and *thornohektēriōn* or *thornohelktēriōn*, initially interpreted as "holding/dragging of the *thornos*" (spelled *to-no-e-ke-te-ri-jo*, PY Fr 1222). Reasonably, *lekhestrōtēriōn* is interpreted as some ritual of the "sacred marriage" type where *lekhos* (bed) is a key element, but other interpretations are possible: the spreading of the *lekhos* might concern an empty couch/bed in a sanctuary, which the deity was expected to be visiting periodically (cf. Herodotos' [I.182] skeptical report of such a κλίνη in a sanctuary of Marduk at Babylon). Rituals involving the "dragging" or carrying of chairs or thrones, however, are so far unknown from the rich Bronze or Iron Age Aegean imagery. It remains therefore possible that *to-no-e-ke-te-ri-jo* may have nothing to do with *thornos* (throne/seat). Rather, understood as *thornohektēriōn*, it may instead involve the holding of **thorna* (pl.)

"flowers/herbs," an image familiar from Aegean Late Bronze Age iconography, including processional female figures from Pylos itself (Petrakis 2002–3).

Homeric furniture plays a role in certain important episodes, notably in the *Odyssey*. Seats, tables, beds, or chests are reported, even occasionally described as furnishings of the (usually domestic) settings for the actions of heroes. In the palace of Circe, Odysseus refers to her περικαλλής εὐνή (all-beautiful bed) (Hom., *Od.* 10.347), as well as a magnificent θρόνος (chair) described as ἀργυρόηλος, καλός and δαιδάλεος ("silver-studded," "beautiful," and "manufactured with great skill'), equipped with a θρῆνυς (footstool) (10.313–14). The description of this extravagant luxury is supplemented by references to feasting furniture, namely τραπέζας ἀργυρέας (silver tables) located "in front of chairs" with "beautiful purple-colored covers" placed on them (10.352–5). On Ithaca, Penelope sits on a "chair decorated *vel sim* with ivory and silver," covered with κῶας (fleece) and accompanied by a θρῆνυς (footstool), manufactured by the (presumably famous) carpenter Ikmalios (19.55–8). We should be cautious in assessing the relative significance of the different terms, which the epic does not appear to use in an exact technical sense. In a number of passages, people invariably sit (or cloaks are placed) "on chairs and thrones" (1.145; 3.389; 10.233; 15.134; 17.86; 17.179; 20.249; 24.385). Although it appears as if the epic treats κλισμοί (chairs) and θρόνοι (thrones) without true respect as to their relative status,[4] this does not necessarily signify that the two terms are interchangeable and their differences insignificant. Perhaps the epic uses a metrically suitable formula (always in the same verse location) without attention to distinctions such as those that Athenaeus later makes explicit.[5]

Only once does a piece of furniture occupy the central place in a story; such is the case of the bed of Odysseus and Penelope, whose construction included a secret known only to the married couple—namely the fact that the bed had been carved from the trunk of an olive tree still in place, and was therefore impossible to move. The epic tradition on which Homer drew employed the bed as the symbol par excellence of wedded life: only the couple could have known the σήματα εὐνῆς (signs of the bed) (*Od.* 23.225–6). Here, the firmly rooted bed that still keeps its own secrets, known only to the core of the family, is a powerful metaphor for the solidity of Odysseus' household.

The historical relevance of Homeric furniture is uncertain: are these items reflections of the splendor of Mycenaean palatial contexts (such as those inventoried in the Pylos Ta tablets) or Early Iron Age luxury furniture (reflected in contemporary finds from Cyprus or the Levant)? Descriptions of furniture are rarely detailed (the bed of Odysseus being the only exception) and the information given focuses on luxury materials that would indeed fit both contexts. It may be decisive that important aspects of Mycenaean palace life are altogether absent from Homer's account, most notably literacy and wall paintings; in any case, the epic account aims to convey the impression of extravagance and luxury rather than provide accurate descriptions of actual pieces of furniture.

Among Old Testament furniture, Solomon's ivory throne overlaid with gold is perhaps the most elaborate (1 *Kings* 10:18–20). Interesting features are the armrests adorned with lions, recalling the "master of animals" posture traceable as far back as the Çatalhöyük "goddess" (see also Chapters 5 and 8 in this volume). It seems likely that Solomon's throne was a product of tenth-century BCE Phoenician craftsmanship (cf. the artisans sent to Solomon by Hiram I of Tyre: 1 Kings 7:13–51), but Israelite ivory-working of the time is not sufficiently known so as to preclude native workmanship.

The Ark of the Covenant, the portable gilded acacia chest intended to keep and carry the tablets inscribed with the Ten Commandments, is described in Exodus 25:10–22. The Ark, lost after the Babylonian conquest of Jerusalem in 587 BCE, is of unknown date (depending on the debated historicity of the Exodus events), but may be well accommodated within Late Bronze Age or Early Iron Age furniture production. The lid of the Ark, known as the *kapporet* or "Mercy Seat," bore cherubim figures that flanked the location of God's invisible communication with Moses (Exodus 25:22; 1 Samuel 4:4), a most apt example of the concept of "sacred emptiness" (see Chapter 5 in this volume).

Certain furniture pieces perhaps dating between the ninth and the sixth centuries BCE, although now lost to us, were famous enough to be described in Greek literary sources. Herodotos (1.14) reports that Midas, the historical king of Phrygian Gordion (see Chapter 6 in this volume), had dedicated at Delphi his own "royal throne on which seated he made judgments," which Herodotos considered "well worth-seeing." In addition, in his *Description of Greece*, the Greek traveler and geographer Pausanias (second century CE) mentions a folding stool attributed to Daidalos and shown to visitors of the temple of Athena Polias on the Athenian Acropolis (1.27.1), the throne of Danaos at the sanctuary of Apollo Lykeios at Argos (2.19.5), the cedar chest (λάρναξ) dedicated by the Kypselids at Olympia, and the colossal built throne of Apollo at Amyklai (actually an elaborate podium for the Archaic statue of the god) made by Bathykles. These works were famous in antiquity, and their rich figural decoration is meticulously described by Pausanias (5.17.5–5.19.10; 3.18.9–3.19.5, respectively; cf. Snodgrass 1998: 109–16, fig. 43).

FROM THE CLASSICAL TO THE EARLY ROMAN PERIOD

Contemporary literary evidence for furniture and furnishings of the Classical and Hellenistic periods is limited. Texts occasionally mention furniture, but a greater wealth is found on inscriptions, and more specifically on sacred inscriptions that list the furniture property of the temple. Such lists, often too fragmentary, do not lend themselves for cultural history discussions but the wealth of words has its own merit since we have lost the largest body of furniture made of perishable materials (Andrianou 2009: 109–15). The rich vocabulary for containers, for example, might point to a rather specialized industry of such items, although very few have been found in the archaeological record. On the other hand, one should always bear in mind that some of the Greek words in the same context might have been synonyms (much like the great variety of furniture terminology in modern Greek). The word σορός, for example, is glossed as θήκη, μνῆμα, λάρναξ, ζύγαστρον, κιβωτός, χηλός, by later (Byzantine) lexicographers. Even if there was a difference in meaning in the fifth and fourth centuries BCE, when the inscriptions are dated, such nuances may have been lost by the time of the lexicographers, such as Hesychios (fifth or sixth century CE), Photios (ninth century CE), and Suidas (tenth century CE). Thus, bearing in mind the wealth of furniture vocabulary and its limitations at the same time, in the following we will touch upon various verbal contexts that give some information on ancient furniture.

In the fifth century BCE furniture is occasionally mentioned by philosophers in the context of luxurious living, often accompanied by derogatory remarks. Plato, through the voice of Socrates, identifies three common personal needs (χρεῖαι): food, shelter, and clothing (*Resp.* 369d). When these needs are met there is no point in wanting more, and all members of the polis should therefore be satisfied. Glaukon, a conversant with Socrates, interrupts Socrates' speech to say that this description would fit "a city of pigs" (ὑῶν πόλις) (372d). When the philosopher asks him what is missing, Glaukon replies "ἅπερ νομίζεται" (what is customary), since people "must recline on couches ... if they are not to be uncomfortable, and dine from tables and have made dishes and sweetmeats such as are now in use" (372d–e). Furniture is introduced into the discussion in the context of comfort, only to be rejected by Socrates as luxury. He continues by saying that Glaukon's reply envisions a "luxurious, fevered or inflamed polis" (πόλιν τρυφῶσαν, φλεγμαίνουσαν), and that such a polis is "neither true (ἀληθής) nor healthy (ὑγιής) and admits that some will not be contented (αὕτη ἡ δίαιτα οὐκ ἐξαρκέσει), but couches (κλῖναι) and tables (τράπεζαι) and other furniture (σκεύη) will have to be added" (373a). This interesting passage builds gradually upon Plato's understanding of the essence of luxury; overstepping the limits of necessity is the cause of all private and public evils.

Luxury is raised a number of times in the fourth century BCE. Aristotle does not analyze luxury per se but he does talk about it in passing when referring to the *technai* that contribute to luxury and *technai* that contribute to living the good life (τρυφήν ἤ τὸ καλῶς ζῆν) (*Politics* 1291a). Archestratos of Gela, in his *Hedupatheia*, or "*Life of Luxury*," deals specifically with food and dining luxuries. Two fragments of his work refer to furniture but provide limited information with statements such as "everyone should dine at a single table set for an elegant meal" (Olson and Sens 2000: 18–19, frag. 4); later in the text, he refers to "second tables" for the serving of dried fruits and sweetmeats for desert (Olson and Sens 2000: 229–30, frag. 60, l. 6; Athenaeus, *Deipn.* 14.640e-641f).

In the epigraphical record the earliest and most extensive account of furniture, a true thesaurus of terms, can be found on the so-called *Attic Stelai*, dated to the last quarter of the fifth century (415 or 414 BCE) (see also Chapter 4 in this volume). The stelai list the confiscated property of Alcibiades (a prominent Athenian statesman raised and taught under the roof of Pericles) and his followers, recording movable, domestic objects and land in Attica, Euboea, Eretria, Thasos, Abydos, and the Troad (Pritchett 1953: 225–99; 1956: 178–317; Amyx 1958: 163–310). About twenty names (owners) are mentioned in the texts but it has been suggested that the property might have belonged to as many as fifty people (Lewis 1966: 182). Apart from recording the terminology for various types of furniture, the *Attic Stelai* offer a sense of their commercial value because auction prices are recorded. However, the record of sale for the confiscated furniture listed in the *Attic Stelai* shows that there was little sense of personal luxury in Athens in the last quarter of the fifth century, even among men of wealth such as Alcibiades and his followers. Costly, elaborate pieces of furniture were most probably reserved for the gods; they were dedicated and deposited in temples and lists of these expensive pieces (often inlaid with precious metals) were recorded in sacred inventories. Furniture types mentioned in the temple inventories of the fourth and third centuries BCE are also noted in the *Attic Stelai*, something that speaks for the continuation of forms and uses in later centuries.

Additional epigraphic evidence pertaining to real estate and property is provided by inscriptions known as ὠναί (deeds of sale). During the Late Classical and Hellenistic periods, it was customary for a man who was borrowing a large sum of money to pledge property as security for the repayment of a loan. Such inscriptions record loans with surety and deeds of sale and have been found in the Chalkidike (central Macedonia) and Tinos (Cyclades) (Hennig 1987; Hatzopoulos 1988: 58–61; Giouni 1991: 25–50; Tenos: *IG* XII 5, 872, and 873, discussed in Étienne 1990: 51–84). Although houses (οἰκίαι) are explicitly mentioned in these documents, and one would expect occasional reference to furniture and furnishings, there is very little mention of specific types of furniture sold or rented separately. Two ὅροι (boundary stones), one from Naxos and the other from Amorgos (Cyclades), inform us that the furniture was legally encumbered but not fully at the disposal of the proprietor. More specifically, the Naxian stone, dated to around 300 BCE, states that the furnishings carried a value of 500 drachmas, an amount that accords with the evidence from the auction prices found on the *Attic Stelai* a century earlier (*IG* XII, suppl. 195, lines 6–8; Finley 1952: 163, no. 156). It is possible, according to legal speeches, that creditors who accepted furniture as security for debt would normally have insisted on immediate possession since its portability would have made it easy for the debtor to run off with the furniture as happened in the case of Aphobus, the legal guardian of Demosthenes' (Demosthenes, *Against Onetor* 28), and may be the reason why furniture was not often included in similar transactions. Furniture or bedding could also be bequeathed to relatives, as recorded in the case of Diodotus (Lysias, *Against Diogeiton* 6).

The general picture outlined by literary evidence from legal speeches and the epigraphical record is that furniture did not raise the selling price of a house and that its overall value in ordinary houses was insignificant. These low prices likely reflect a low demand for commodities like furniture as opposed to items such as the θύραι (doorframes) or embroidered furnishings placed over furniture, which in the epigraphical record of the *Attic Stelai*, Delos, Epidauros, and Eleusis, are recorded as having much greater value (Pritchett 1956: 211, table A; Andrianou 2021). These prices most probably also reflect the meager materials from which the furniture was made.

The fourth-century BCE comedies of Menander, New Comedy's chief playwright, preserve bits and pieces of information as well. Furniture is mentioned almost exclusively in the context of cooking and the humorous cooks who attend to dinners and set tables. Sometimes furniture is borrowed by wealthier neighbors when needed, as in the case of the Thracian slave Getas who asks peevish Knemon (the bad-tempered man) to contribute cooking pots, seven tripods, twelve tables, a bronze wine krater, nine rugs, and a woven barbarian curtain a hundred feet long to his master's banquet (*Dyskolos* 920–45). Here the various slaves and servants whom Knemon had insulted in the past take their revenge by beating at his door and shouting demands to borrow all sorts of unlikely objects.

About the end of the second and the beginning of the third century CE, the Greek rhetorician and grammarian Athenaeus, much in the same vein as the poet Archestratos, celebrates eating and drinking in his work *Deipnosophistae*, where he lists dinner paraphernalia and presents a variety of terms quoted from earlier authors. He introduces the reader to the life of luxurious living, where extravagant food is laid out on expensive furniture. Athenaeus' contemporary, the author Julius Pollux of Naucratis, supplies us with a great deal of information on Classical furniture types and pertinent quotes from lost works in his *Onomasticon*, a Greek dictionary of Attic synonyms and phrases.

Despite the wealth of information on shapes, names, and component materials of furniture and furnishings preserved in these sources, the pairing of known Greek terms with excavated pieces remains problematic. The issue of nomenclature becomes even more difficult to untangle when ancient sources quote even earlier sources or identify furniture types by a variety of names. Some types of furniture can be reconstructed from the contexts in which they appear in the text; others bear specific features that help us identify them with modern equivalents. However, the use of different names for one piece of furniture is not infrequent, as is the case with most of the names that have come down to us for "boxes." Literary and epigraphic sources enhance our understanding of most furniture types but, unfortunately, do not come with pictures. Conversely, visual representations show furniture in use but do not provide inscriptions alongside. Thus, a researcher is asked to study the thesaurus of words and based on the fragmentary textual context or the surviving archaeological evidence pair these words with actual pieces. When it comes to linguistic survival, the role of lexicographers should not be underestimated.

Another significant piece of information concluded from the examination of furniture terms found in literary texts is that *any* piece of furniture may be made of expensive materials, when thus ordered, or with the addition of a piece of furnishing or attachment it may become more comfortable or expensive. A kind of bed (χάμευνα) is humble (ταπεινή) according to Hesychius, sometimes covered with rushes or leaves (φυλλόστρωτος) but it may also be worth twice the average price of a Milesian bed in the *Attic Stelai* when decorated by expensive materials (παράκολλος).

In the following we will present examples of the rich vocabulary of beds, seats, tables, shelves, and cupboards in Greek and Latin texts.

The literary evidence for beds proves richer than the surviving physical evidence. Terms for beds range from the Homeric λέχος and δέμνια, to the Classical κλίνη or κλινίς, κλινίδιον, κλιντήρ, σκίμπους, κράββατος, χάμευνα (once φυλλόστρωτος, but also παράκολλος, veneered or tesselated), ἀσκάντης, στιβὰς (of wood, rushes, straw, or leaves), ἡμίκλινον, κλιντηρίσκος, and ἐπίκλιντρον (an elbow- or headrest for a couch that could be fitted or removed at will) (Andrianou 2009: 31–2, 113–14, with references). A unique type of bed that appears in the sacred accounts on Delos is the ὑπόσπαστον τραπέζιον, possibly beds with small and light tables that could be pulled out from underneath (*IDélos* 1403BbII, lines 29–30, 33–4). A "Milesian" bed with two risers (ἀμφικέφαλος) is mentioned once in the *Attic Stelai* (*IG* I³ 421, line 206) but is a type still unknown in the archaeological record with the possible exception of the recently published bed from the Macedonian tomb III at Agios Athanasios (Tsimbidou-Avloniti 2005: 104–5, 161–5, fig. 21). Ἀμφικνέφαλλοι, however, if not an error by Pollux (X.36), are most probably κλῖναι with pillows on either side. Repairs made on κλῖναι are frequently mentioned in the Delian accounts, something that suggests that they were too valuable to be thrown away when broken.

Textual sources often mention the terms Χιουργής (Chian) or Μιλησιουργής (Milesian) as adjectives for beds, and Θετταλικός (Thessalian) as an adjective for a *diphros* or throne (Andrianou 2009: 32–3, with references). These adjectives raise certain problems in current scholarship (Andrianou 2009: 32–3; Baughan 2013: 74–8). These were probably renowned beds and seats but there is no way to describe them with any accuracy. In other words, we cannot say with any degree of certainty whether these 'brand-names' refer to the location of the beds' production, to their form and style, or to the origin of their artists. They may be expensive pieces of furniture, but there is also an example of a Milesian bed on the *Attic Stelai* valued at only a little more than a simple bed.

Components of beds, such as τὸ ἐνήλατον (nailed bedstead), οἱ τόνοι (interlacings, cords), and οἱ πόδες (legs), have also come down to us through literary texts. Wood is the most common material for the frame and the legs. Precious decorations are also attested: ἀργυρόπους κλίνη (bed with silver feet), ἐπάργυροι πόδες (silver-coated feet), and κλῖναι χρυσαῖ σφιγγόποδες (golden beds with sphinxes) (Andrianou 2009: 32, with references). The legs of the furniture are usually recorded by material or decoration. The adjective σφιγγόπους is epigraphically attested only in the temple accounts from Delos (for instance, IDélos 1416AI, line 38; 1417BI, line 38) and most probably refers to beds with turned legs where one of the decorative elements is a small sphinx, as seen on beds depicted on funerary banquet reliefs in Asia Minor and the two remains of legs found in a late Hellenistic shipwreck in the south Euboean gulf, off the island of Styra (Koutsouflakis 2017: 34, fig. 3.8) (Plate 38). Entire furniture supports in the shape of sphinxes (not just partly decorated with sphinxes) have a long history in the Near East (Baughan 2013: 125–6) but the Greek tradition does not support such a reconstruction. On Keos, another term, a σφηνόπους *kline*, is attested in a fifth-century BCE inscription (IG XII 5, 593, line 6); it is the only known reference to a wedge-footed couch-bed. In this case, the term applied to the *kline* indicates a type of bed still unknown in the excavated record.

Finally, it is no coincidence that Plato in book X of the Republic chose the κλίνη as an *exemplum* in discussing the "ideal form" and "mimesis" to emphasize that an ideal form is not specific. It is possible that the very variety of couches in antiquity, as the textual evidence indicates, makes this piece of furniture a perfect example for Plato's discussion of forms (Baughan 2013: 86).

The *Attic Stelai* provide us with a variety of words for different types of seats, such as ἀνάκλισις, βάθρον, δίφρος, θρανίδιον, θρόνος, πρόσκλιντρον, κλιντὴρ, and ἐπίκλιντρον (Andrianou 2009: 22, with references). Specifically a βάθρον is a bench or seat but also a pedestal or low podium, as often depicted on funerary reliefs with banquet scenes from Asia Minor and neighboring areas (Andrianou 2017: 219–20, no. 37). It is glossed with words that denote "seats" because iconographically seats (probably of expensive materials) are placed on it.

Tables are known as τράπεζα and further identified as being τρίπους or τετράπους, τραπέζιον, φάτνη, and ἐλεὸς (Andrianou 2009: 50, with references). According to William Pritchett, there are no literary references to round tables before the first century BCE, when one is mentioned by Asklepiades of Myrlea (Athenaeus, *Deipn.* 11.489c; Pritchett 1956: 242). They do, however, appear in iconography much earlier than this. *Τράπεζαι* mentioned in the *Attic Stelai* and the Delian inscriptions were probably rectangular with three legs and of a size that could fit under a couch. It is generally assumed that tabletops were manufactured separately from their supports (legs), thus the separate term ἐπίθημα in Pollux (X.81).

The tables listed in the *Attic Stelai* were fairly low-priced, costing only four to six drachmas each, but in the first century CE Pliny reports that Cicero paid half a million sesterces for a table of Mauretanian citrus wood and ivory. Pliny informs us that Mauretanian citrus wood was highly esteemed (Pl., *HN* XIII.29.95), thus the high price of Cicero's table. Another table, worth a million sesterces, was in the possession of Gallus Asinius (XIII, XXIX.92–3). Apuleius, in the *Golden Ass* (the only full-length surviving Latin novel, a work of fiction, written in the second century CE), describes tables made of citrus wood and ivory and couches spread with cloth of gold in a rich lady's house (Byrrhaena II.19). Livy, writing in the first century BCE to the first century CE, describes the triumph of Gnaeus Manlius Vulso over the Gauls in Asia Minor in 189 BCE. In his famous passage about luxury being imported to Rome as war booty, he lists couches of bronze (*lectos aeratos*), valuable robes used as coverlets (*vestem stragulam pretiosam*), and what was apparently at that time considered luxurious furniture (*magnificae supellectilis*), namely, tables resting on only one leg (*monopodia*) and sideboards (*abacos*) (Livy XXXIX.VI.7).

Furniture used for storing agricultural products, jewelry, clothes, vessels, and books are often depicted on vases (Andrianou 2009: 63–4, 110–13). As mentioned above, the impressive number of literary and epigraphic references to such boxes extends from the Homeric epos and the Athenian and Delian inscriptions of the fifth through the second centuries BCE to the antiquarian dictionaries and scholiasts of ancient texts: λάρναξ, κιβωτός, κιβώτιον, χηλός, φωριαμός, κίστη, ζύγαστρον, σορός, θήκη, ἀντίπηξ, κοίτη, and καλπίς (Andrianou 2009: 65, with references). Κιβώτια of ivory or metal are attested epigraphically; literary sources record boxes used for storing clothes, jewelry, money, scrolls and documents, tools, and other articles; citrons (κιτρία) were used to perfume chests for clothes. In Lysias' house a box with valuables (money and four silver *phialae*) was stored in his bedroom (*Against Eratosthenes* 10); the tyrant Klearchos of Pontos used a κιβωτός as a bed (Plut., *Mor.* 781D–E). The dowry was symbolically depicted as a box (Brümmer 1985: 111).

Open cupboards, κυλικεῖα and ἐγγυθῆκαι, are mentioned in Athenaeus (Andrianou 2009: 82, with references). According to these literary references, the κυλικεῖον had a linen curtain in front and was used specifically to store gold or silver cups. In Kallixenos' account of the *pompe* of Ptolemy II the two silver κυλικεῖα on display were eighteen-feet long and nine-feet high; they had ornaments adorning the top and figures graced the sides and the legs, which were two- to three-feet tall (Athenaeus, *Deipn.* 5.199c). Theophrastos' account notes that κυλικεῖα could be sealed (σεσήμανται) (Theophrastos, *Characters* XVIII.4). Fragments of Euboulos and Kratinos the Younger mention a κυλικεῖον storing statuettes (Kock 1884: 185, no. 62; 197, no. 96; and 206, no. 118). The epigraphically attested κιβωτὸς θυριδωτὸς was, perhaps, a type of cupboard closed with doors decorated with columns, as is often depicted on funerary banquet reliefs of Samos (Fabricius 1999: 121).

Ρυμοί (possibly the word for shelves) frequently appeared in domestic, sacred, and funerary contexts. They are mentioned in the Attic and Delian sacred accounts[6] followed by a list of the objects stored on those very shelves.

Latin sources use an array of words denoting furniture (*supellex, supellectilis*). Trimalchio, the protagonist of Petronius' *Satyricon* (a Latin work of fiction in a combination of prose and poetry, possibly written in the first century CE), comes first to mind when considering Latin descriptions of furniture. Unlike the epigraphical texts discussed above, the *Satyricon*'s continuous narrative and wealth of furniture vocabulary allows us to visualize furniture in a luxurious house, though we must always bear in mind that Petronius exaggerates liberally throughout the text. In the description of his famous dinner party for a group of friends and hangers-on, for instance, Trimalchio is carried in on a *lectica* (a portable bed or bier), or seated on a bed with *cervicalia* (pillows; *Sat.* 32). *Culcitae* (mattresses or cushions for a bed or a couch) are highly estimated in his house, as they are stuffed with purple or scarlet stuffing (38). Painted coverlets (*toralia*) are spread over the beds (*toris*). A *lectum stratum* (bed and bedding) is even bequeathed to one of Trimalchio's slaves in his will (71). Elsewhere Trimalchio himself sits upon a *pulvinus* (cushion or pillow; 59). A variety of tables are employed in serving food to this overloaded dinner party. The first dish, a relish of eggs, salt fish, and mead, is served on a *promulsidare* (31), a sideboard often depicted in funerary banquets; additional smaller food items were served on a *repositorium* (stand; *Sat.* 35, 36, 39), while individual *mensae* (tables) were provided for each guest to avoid crowding (34). *Mensae* were also used as a surface on which to place lamps and statues of the Lares (60, 64). In one of the corners of Trimalchio's house, Petronius describes an *armarium* with silver statuettes of Lares and a golden *pyxis* (29).

Beds are given various names in Latin sources: *lectus, lectulus, sponda, torus, grabatus, grabatulus, cubile,* and *cubitus* (for specific references in Latin texts for these words, see Glare 1982). The upright board forming the back of the bed is the *pluteus*. The stuffed mattress or cushion (*culcita*) rested upon firths or strings (*restes, fasciae, institae,* or *funes*), which connected the two long bed rails. The *lectus genialis* or *adversus* was the bridal bed, which usually stood in the atrium, opposite the image of Janus, whence it derived the epithet *adversus*.

Bedding was known as *stragula vestis* and *plagula*. Small cushions or pillows were called *pulvilli*. Mattresses were originally filled with dry herbs or straw but, later on, the wealthier substituted these with wool or feathers. *Operimentum* and *toral* are understood as coverlets. *Peripetasmata Attalica* were a famous kind of embroidered coverlet seen hanging down over the sides of couches. These are possibly the furnishings depicted already in Hellenistic Asia Minor in funerary banquet scenes on reliefs. The *aulaea,* mentioned in the context of a *lectus tricliniaris,* seems to have been a cloth that prevented dust from raining down upon the people lying on the bed; it was most probably also used in earlier periods, judging from the remains of cloth in the late fourth-century BCE tomb at Sedes (Thessaloniki) that hung directly below the wooden ceiling of the tomb. It was probably mounted originally on wooden planks forming a flat, decorative ceiling alluding to a baldachin. (Kotzias 1937: 866–95; Andrianou 2009: 93, n. 92; Chapter 6 in this volume).

Tables were known by a number of names: *mensae* and *mensulae*; *abaci* and *monopodia*,[7] which might have been of smaller dimensions; and, of more obscure etymology, *cilliba*, *cartibulum*, and *urnarium*, which are mentioned in Varro (*De Lingua Latina*). *Mensae* were made of marble, maple wood, African citrus wood, or silver. They were portable and were brought in at meals, laden with food; some are noted as pricey or, even, old (Petron., *Sat.* 135). *Mensa* can also denote a course of a meal (*mensa secunda*, the dessert, for instance, Pl., *HN* 9, 104), the meal itself (Petron., *Sat.* 93), the notion of hospitality (Pl., *Mil.* 51), or even the banker's or money-changer's counter (*mensanummularia*; for references, see Glare 1982; for further discussion on *mensae*, see Chapter 3 in this volume). *Mensae lunatae*, crescent-shaped *mensae*, are attested by the first century CE (Mart. X.48; XIV.87) and are paired with a couch-bed of the same shape, the *stibadium*. Expensive hanging tables (*pendentes*) are briefly mentioned by Pliny (*HN* XIII.29.92). Large tables are mentioned, as well as tables made of two large semicircular slabs (*orbibus dimidiatis duobus*; XIII.29.93). Pliny praises the "hidden" joins in tables as an artistic mastery. In general, veins and spirals in the wood were apparently considered outstanding, whereas dull, patternless uniformity was considered a fault (XIII.30.96). The technical term used by Pliny, and possibly by furniture makers of the time, for this sort of uniformity is *lignum* (translated as "woodiness"; XIII 30.98). The highest value resided in the color of the wood, honey-color (*mulsus*) being the most favorable (XIII 30.97). Sources also tell us that tables and beds were often set side by side (Petron., *Sat.* II.16) and that tables were cleansed with wet sponges (Mart. XIV.144, something already noted in the *Odyssey* [I.111]) or fragrant herbs (Ovid, *Met.* VIII.665).

Chairs were recorded as *sedes*, *sedile*, *arcisellium* (chair with a rounded back), *sella* (stool), *sessibulum*, *solium*, *siliquastrum* (or *seliquastrum*), *subsellium* (a low seat or bench), *bisellium* (a seat for two persons and a seat of honor), and *cathedra* (an armchair or easy chair; for specific references in Latin texts for these words, see Glare 1982).

Furniture used for storage, such as boxes, is called *pyxides*; larger cupboards were known as *promptuaria*. Other terms include *arcula*, *cista*, *cistella*, *cistula* (a covered chest large enough to hide a person in Apuleius, *Golden Ass* [IX.40]), *forulus* (shelf for books), *arca* (chest for money-keeping), *armarium*, and *armariolum*. It is interesting that the words for storage furniture are usually associated with books and the same terms are used for funerary receptacles.

EARLY BYZANTINE PERIOD

In the Early Byzantine period (fourth to sixth centuries CE) special features of the furniture terminology discussed so far continued in use. This continuation of terms most possibly speaks for the unaltered types and uses of furniture. However, established trade routes within the Empire were reflected in the use of more expensive materials on furniture such as that described in the Palace of Constantinople. In the following we shall look at the problems created by lexicographers' interpretations, the contribution made by papyri to relevant research on household effects, and the role played by Egypt in the trading of ivory furniture.[8] Then we shall confine ourselves to the example of the special use of the bed (*κλίνη*), denoting changes in reclining, seating, and dining during the transitional period leading up to Byzantium. We shall close with a very brief reference to furniture in the Byzantine palace, which essentially reveals a world related to antiquity, yet very different.

One feature regarding the names of furniture during the post-Classical and Christian era is the compound words describing either material, construction, or special use (Box 9.2).

Many ancient words, such as *δίφρος, λέκτρον, στιβάς τρίπους* used in early Byzantine texts, hardly relate to current terminology and real furniture. Even in cases where the Byzantines used them to describe existing furniture, we find it hard to understand (apart from their general use as seat, bed, table) what the things they mention correspond to and what is their vernacular name. Of the various pieces of furniture used in professions, such as that of the copyist, the notary, the physician, the banker, the grocer, the hotelier, and the inn-keeper, according to the sources (even in many vernacular texts) the terms for tables, seats, various boxes, and storage vessels are, apart from only a few exceptions, often or almost the same as those used in antiquity. Exceptions include, for example, the Latinate *ἀκ(κ)ούβ(β)ιτον* for couch, *ἀρμάριον* (cf. *ἀρμαρίτης*, "bank manager") for closet, chest, place for implements or tools; *σκρίνιον* or *σκρινίον* (cf. *σκρινιάριος*, secretary) for box, chest, and office; and *κάμψα* for basket or case, all these words were probably formed already in the Hellenistic and Roman times (Box 9.1).

In the work of lexicographers we come across numerous words for utensils and furniture not found anywhere else and we are never sure, unless specific detailed explanations are given, whether they are dialectical or terms of restricted use. As an example of this, in the sixth century CE four different words are given for the bread-basket: *ἀρτοθήκη, πευδρία, πυελίς, σιπύη* (Hesychios, *Lexicon*, letter pi, entry 2077, letter pi, entry 4292, letter sigma, entry 711). We do not know whether they refer to a utensil, a piece of furniture, or to a storage place in the house. Yet the Byzantines equated *ἀρτοθήκη*, the bread-basket, with the *ἄρκλα*, which they considered a *κιβώτιον*, a box for storing money and food and specifically bread

BOX 9.1 A sample of new names or new meanings bestowed upon Byzantine furniture. Compiled by Ilias Anagnostakis.

ἀκ(κ)ούβ(β)ιτον (< *lat. accubitum*), dining room or couch and bed (*PAntin.* 3 204, 3; *PSI* 3 225, 5; *PFouad* 1 85, 4; Hesychios, *Lexicon*, letter alpha entry 7685; Photios, *Lexicon*, letter sigma entry 554; *Suda Lexicon*, letter sigma entry 1097).

ἄρκλα (< *lat. arcula*), ἀρμάριον (< *lat. armarium*), κάμψα-κασσέλα (< *lat. capsella, capsa*), πανδέκτης-παντέκτης, σενδούκι -σινδούκιον: chest, receptacle (Hesychios, *Lexicon*, letter kappa entry 620; *Basilika*, Series B, bk. 60, title 12, ch. 21, § 27, title 45, ch. 11, § 2; Kyrillos of Skythopolis, *Life of Euthymios* 69.14 and 22; Sophronios, *Miracles*, Miracle 10, lines 53–7; *Book of Ceremonies*: 468; Haldon 1990: C 208: 106–7; *Commentary on Aristophanes*, Scholia in Plutum, Argumentum v. 711; *Actes de Xéropotamou* 80.16, 84. 23; *Actes de Chilandar* 216.41).

ἀναπαύστρα, καθιστήριον, καθισμάτιον= σελ(λ)ίον: seat (*Commentary on Lucian*, work 46, § 6, line 1; Kougeas 1912–13: 250; Eusebios, *Church History* bk. 10, ch. 4, § 66, line 2; Hesychios, *Lexicon*, letter delta entry 2000; *Life of Lazaros of Mt. Galesion*: 520, col. 1; 558, col. 2.29–39; 586, col. 2.33).

θρονεῖον, θρόνιον: small chair (*Actes de Xéropotamou* 80.16, 84.24).

κρά(ε)β(β)αττος- κρα(ε)β(β)άτι(ο)ν, κραμβάτιον: couch and bed (Hesychios, *Lexicon*, letter alpha entry 7685; Photios, *Lexicon*, letter sigma entry 554; *Suda Lexicon*, letter sigma entry 1097; Grosdidier de Matons 1979a: 363–73; *Actes de Xéropotamou* 80.16, 84.23).

ποδαρούλλιον, σεμσέλλιον- συμψέλλιον- σουβσέλλιον (< *lat. subsellia*)-σουπέδιον (< *lat. suppedaneum*): footstool (*P.Grenf.* 2, 111 = *Chrest. Wilck.* 135, 37; *P.Masp.* 6 v 89; *PAntin.* 3 204, 5; *Suda Lexicon*, letter alpha entry 2160; *Basilika*, Series B, bk. 44, title 13, restitutus ch. 3, line 2; *Belthandros and Chrysantza*, v. 669).

σελ(λ)ίον (< *lat. sella*): seat (*Book of Ceremonies*: 468.8–9, 545.29, 558.5; Haldon 1990: C 214–16: 108–9; *Suda Lexicon*, letter delta entry 1294; *Actes de Xéropotamou* 80.16, 84.24).

σκάμνος, σκαμνί(ο)ν: bench (*PDura* 33, 12; *Book of Ceremonies* 465.8, 466.1, 531.5–17; Leontios of Neapolis, *The Life of Saint John Merciful* 382.22; *Basilika*, Series B, bk. 44, title 13, restitutus ch. 3, line 2; *Actes de Xéropotamou* 80.16, 84. 25).

σένζον, σέν(τ)ζος (< *lat. sessus*): throne (Theophanes, *Chronography* 125.4, 297.24, 375.8; τά σένζη, *Escorial Taktikon*, 275.3–13; *Book of Ceremonies* 506.19, 507.3 and 9; Dagron et al. 2020: 3:129–31; Haldon 1990: C 860, 864: 148–50).

σκρινίον (< *lat. scrinium*), χαρτοφυλάκιον: box, chest and office (*BGU* 40.10; Hesychios, *Lexicon*, letter alpha entry 7591; *Suda Lexicon*, letter sigma entry 697 and letter chi entry 43).

BOX 9.2 A sample of compound words used in the post-Classical period for Byzantine furniture. Compiled by Ilias Anagnostakis.

δίσκαμνον: the bench for two persons (*Metaphrasis of Alexias*, ch. 277, line 3).

κραββατοπόδιον: foot of the bed (Herodianos, *Partitiones* 170.7).

κλινοκαθέδριον: easy chair (Photios, *Lexicon*, letter kappa entry 788; *Commentary on Lucian*, work 17, § 8, line 6; Kougeas 1912–13: 250).

κανοθήκη: dish stand (*Escorial Taktikon*, 275.10; Dagron 2005: 109–17; Angar 2015).

μακρόσκαμνον, μακροσκάμνιον, μακρισκάμνιον: long bench (*Book of Ceremonies* 531. 5–11; Dagron et al. 2020: 3:41–3; *Actes de Xéropotamou* 80.17, 84.25).

ξυλοκράββατος: wooden bed (John Apokaukos, *Letters,* Epistle 7, line 5).

ξυλοσέλλιον: wooden seat (*Typikon of Pantokrator* 99.1148).

νανουδοκράββατον: baby's bed (*Callimachos and Chrysorrhoe*, v. 1099).

παρακράββατον: side-bed (*Typikon of Pantokrator* 85.917).

παρατράπεζα -παρατραπέζιον: side table (*Paschal Chronicle* 1832: 714.14; *Book of Ceremonies* 594.9 and 12; Dagron et al. 2020: 3:141; *Escorial Taktikon* 275.2; Kougeas 1912–13: 250).

πενταπύργιον: a vast imperial wardrobe made of five towers (*Escorial Taktikon* 275.9–10; *Book of Ceremonies* 582.1–10; Dagron et al. 2020: 3:121–3).

ποτηροπλύτης- ποτηροθήκη: cupboard, stand for drinking vessels (*Commentary on Lucian* 46, 7–10.10; *Escorial Taktikon* 275.10; *Alexander Romance*, bk. 3, § 28, line 60; Kougeas 1912–13).

τετραπόδιον, four-legged table in churches for placing bread, wine, and oil for blessing or for placing the gospel book (*Actes de Xéropotamou* 80.17, 84.25).

χωλοκράββατον: small couch, pallet (*Suda Lexicon*, letter sigma, entry 607).

(*Basilika*, Series B, bk. 60, title 45, ch. 11, § 2; *Commentary on Aristophanes, Scholia in Plutum Argumentum*, v. 807, line 5; *Ptochoprodromica*, poem 3, line 97). Hesychios also gives about nine different corresponding words for the bed (some only in his *Lexicon*, such as λάγρον, λαγρός, σκάνθαν=ἀσκάντης?) whilst ninth-century CE Photios in his *Lexicon* equates the ἀσκάντης with κλινίδιον, the vulgar little bed, and the σκίμπους. Photios states that the common word for bed κράββατος cannot be found in any of the ancient writers (Hesychios, *Lexicon*, letter lambda, entry 64 and 583, letter sigma, entry 847 and 994–7; Photios, *Lexicon*, vol. 1, letter alpha, entry 2958).

To provide yet another example, the chest, the basket for valuables was defined by lexicographers and text commentators in ancient words as *kibotos, kibotion*, and *kistis* (κιβωτός, κιβώτιον, κίστη, or κίστις), as well as in many other terms, including *theke* (θήκη), chest, as a second part of the word (see below). The *kibotion* for clothes, money, jewelry, and other valuable items could often be locked and the existence of a key (κλεῖς) is stressed (*Basilika*, Series B, bk. 13, title 2P, ch. 1, § 39–40). According to *Suda Lexicon* "a *kibotos* and a *kistis* are different, because the *kistis* is for storing food, but the *kibotos* for [that of] garments and money" (*Suda Lexicon*, letter kappa, entry 1578). In addition, *zygastron, sigistron* (ζύγαστρον, σίγιστρον) was considered a kind of wooden box (Hesychios, *Lexicon*, letter zeta, entry 186–7; *Suda Lexicon*, letter zeta, entry 177). Moreover, these ancient Greek words *zygastron* and *kistis* according to Eustathios of Thessalonike, were in common, popular use in Byzantium in the twelfth century CE, and *kistis* can be found in modern Greek dialects even in the present day (Eustathios of Thessalonike, *Commentary on Homer Odyssey*, vol. 1, 307.31–3; Eustathios of Thessalonike, *Commentary on Homer Iliad*, vol. 3, 541.13–15; Koukoules 1948: 83–4).

Some Byzantine words including *theke* (θήκη), "chest," as a second part are ἀλευροθήκη, "flour-basket" (Hesychios, *Lexicon*, letter pi, entry 4292), ἀρτοθήκη, "bread-basket" (Leontios of Skythopolis, *Life of Euthymios* 27.20), ἐδεσματοθήκη, "meal-case," equated with the Attic κίστη (Eustathios of Thessalonike, *Commentary on Homer Odyssey*, vol. 1, 239.17–18), ἱματιοθήκη, "wardrobe" (Hesychios, *Lexicon*, letter kappa, entry 648), κανοθήκη, "cup or dish stand" (*The Escorial Taktikon*, 275.10), μυροθήκη/ μυροθήκιον, "box of unguent" (*POxy.* 1026.21; *PMasp.* 6 ii 90), ποτηροθήκη, "cup stand" (*Alexander Romance*, bk. 3, § 28, line 60), σολιοθήκη, "shoe rack" (*P.Bodl.* I, 48; Kramer 1998: 38–41), and φαρμακοθήκη, "medicine-chest" (*P. Osl.* 54.6). These words may define either large storage vessels/pieces of furniture or small storage boxes, without ruling out in some cases their meaning as a particular storage place, such as the ancient σκευοθήκη, "dresser," and *bibliotheke* (βιβλιοθήκη), "bookcase, library" (Photios, *Lexicon*, vol. 3, letter sigma, entry 301; *Basilika*, Series A, bk. 44, title 3, restitutus ch. 52). Moreover, extensive references to *bibliotheke* (library) are never explicit, as they could describe the actual places or simply the collections of texts, although we believe that these references often imply the furniture too, *armaria* (ἀρμάρια), or any container or box for books. But regarding information on furniture from lexicographers (who often try to explain ancient terminology by giving the corresponding new term), it can ultimately be concluded that their references add few details to our knowledge on Byzantine households. Therefore since the interests of lexicographers and commentators are obviously first and foremost to provide information on the interpretation of a word to further the commentators' understanding of ancient texts, it is important to keep in mind that archaeology alone can ultimately provide us with sufficient information on Byzantine furniture (Oikonomides

1990: 205–14; Russell 2000: 79–90; Papanikola-Bakirtzis 2013: 218–22; Baldini and Cosentino 2021: 65–110).

The way in which Byzantine authors and scholiasts deal with this terminology and obviously their interpretation and understanding of households is no different from the way in which we attempt to comprehend and interpret certain ancient monuments, sculptures of kings seated on pieces of furniture. One of the best examples of interpreting an ancient monument with furniture, and of the manner of presentation (which uses the present to explain the past) can be found in a description by Kosmas Indikopleustes from a journey in around 550 CE. He describes a monument of Ptolemy III Euergetes (r. 246–222 BCE) in Adulê, the port of the Axômites and much frequented by traders who came from Alexandria:

> Here is to be seen a marble chair (δίφρος), just as you enter the town on the western side by the road which leads to Axômis. This chair appertained to one of the Ptolemies, who had subjected this country to his authority. *It is made of costly white marble such as we employ for marble tables, but not of the sort which comes from Proconnesus* (τραπέζια τὰ λευκά, οὐ μέν τοι προκοννήσιος). Its base is quadrangular and it rests at the four corners on four slender and elegant pillars, with one in the middle of greater girth and grooved in spiral form. The pillars support the seat (κάθισμα) of the chair (θρόνος) as well as its back (ἀνάκλιτον) against which one leans, and there are also sides to the right and left. The whole chair (δίφρος) with its base, five pillars, seat (κάθισμα) and back (ἀνάκλιτον) and sides to the right and left, has been sculptured from a single block of marble into this form. It measures about two cubits and a half, and is in shape *like the chair we call kathedrai* (ὡς αἱ παρ' ἡμῖν καλούμεναι καθέδραι).
>
> (Kosmas Indikopleustes, *The Christian Topography*, bk. 2, § 54;
> translation by McCrindle [1897] 2010: 54–7)

In the aforementioned description, of particular interest is the way in which ancient seats are related to Byzantine ones, as is the construction material ("white marble such as we employ for white-marble tables, but not of the sort which comes from Proconnesus," i.e., a well-known, high-quality marble from the island of Proconessus, present-day Marmara) and names ("like the chair we call *kathedrai*") used in the sixth century CE. This example enables us to move on both to another special case giving information on the trade of ivory *kathedra* in Egypt, as well as to the abundant documentation on furniture provided by Byzantine papyri from the fourth to the eighth century CE. Yet it is worth noting that sixth-century CE writers, such as the Alexandrian merchant and traveler Kosmas Indikopleustes, and the scholar in Constantinople John

Lydos referring to Roman customs and things, give their own interpretations of the Latin word for the Greek term *kathedra* (καθέδρα). John Lydos says *kathedra* is called by the Romans *sella* (σέλλα), while the king's *kathedra* or *thronos* (θρόνος) was known by the Romans as *solion* (σόλιον) (John Lydos, *On Powers* 18.9, 50.3). In fact Lydos mentions an ivory *kathedra*. Contemporary writers with Lydos speak of different wooden, stone, ivory, gold, silver *kathedrai* (καθέδραι), seats, chairs, thrones either in simple rhetorical figures of speech or refer to ancient or contemporary seats. For example, a Byzantine embassy to the Turkish khan in 568 to 571 CE is preserved by the late sixth-century CE historian, the Constantinopolitan Menandros Protector, who describes the golden *kathedra* (καθέδρα) inside the tent of the great khan of the Turks, a chair that had two wheels and could be moved around wherever needed, drawn by a horse (Menandros Protector, *De legationibus* 193.17–18). A little later, Isidore of Seville (560–636 CE) provides information in book XX of *Etymologies* (*de domo et instrumentis domesticis*) about food, tools, and furnishings in the ancient world.

Furniture production trade and destination: an example

As we have already mentioned, there is an abundance of references, unfortunately lacking detailed descriptions, to valuable as well as simple furniture in writers' texts from the Byzantine period. The copious references to furniture, beyond the rhetoric that sometimes distinguishes them, reflect to a certain degree realities of the large cities and provinces in the Empire where the writers lived and worked, namely, Constantinople, Antioch, Rome, Asia Minor, Cyprus, Syria, and Palestine. In many cases the production cities or provinces are clearly stated, as well as the regions where the furniture was exported. These accounts have already been used in various studies of late Antique and Byzantine households (Koukoulès 1948: 60–85; Russell 2000: 79–90; Parani 2003; Uytterhoeven 2007: 25–66, 51–5, 64; Andrianou 2009).

An exemplary case, which provides valuable information on the origin and destination of furniture and household effects, is the letter by Kyrillos of Alexandria (*c*. 376–444 CE). This letter lists amounts of money and gifts (in fact a great deal of furniture is in ivory) that had to be distributed to officials of the palace in Constantinople to bribe them during theological disputes in the Christological controversies in which Kyrillos, as the patriarch of Alexandria, was a leading protagonist. The gifts and the letter, which survived in Latin and thus its terminology is of particular interest, were sent to Constantinople in 432/3 CE (Kyrillos of Alexandria, *Letter*, 224–5; McEnerney 2007: 151–3). According to the commentators of the letter, who have calculated the number and value of the gifts (Batiffol 1911: 247–64; Brown 1992: 15–17; Phillipson 2009: 358; Rodziewicz 2009: 86–7), 60 *scamna* (stools, of which 8 of ivory, *eburnea*), 14 *cathedrae eburneae* (ivory high-backed thrones), 36 throne covers, *tabulae maiores* (larger tables), and 22 *mensalia* (tablecloths), along with 1,080 pounds of gold (=77,760 gold pieces), were sent from Alexandria to Constantinople. Also sent were *accubitalia* (cushions or place covers), *scamnalia* (stool covers), many other carpets, woolen tapestries, hanging carpets, silken veils, curtains and cushions. The gifts mentioned include *persoina* and *strouthiones*, it is not certain if it is furniture, a long bench with a back, a pew, and upholstery (McEnerney 2007: 152–3, n. 4). Interestingly during this period as well as in older times the most sought-after furniture, in particular *scamna,* cathedrae, and *tabulae* made of ivory, originated from the area of Alexandria. Also of interest are the preferences of a class of people who crave for them in Constantinople. In this particular case most are eunuchs with important positions in the palace, probably known to Kyrillos for their indulgences and expensive tastes and for whom gold coins and this particular furniture were the fitting gift to make them change their views and opinions. Finally, the aforementioned *cathedrae eburneae* (ivory high-backed thrones) would have resembled in shape, but probably not in carved decoration and artistic attention, the preserved ivory throne of Ravenna that was made for the archbishop Maximianus of Ravenna and dates back to the mid-sixth century CE (545–553) (Plate 15). It is generally accepted that it comes from the Greek East, in other words from Constantinople or probably from Alexandria. It is made entirely from ivory, 1.50 meters in height and 0.60 meters in width, and was initially formed from twenty-six panels of carved ivory with two different narrative cycles: scenes from the life of Christ and scenes from the life of Joseph in Genesis. It is believed to have been given as a present by Justinian to Maximianus, since they are both depicted in the mosaics of Ravenna. Although it is an episcopal throne fit for use, it is believed that it was never actually used but instead stood inside the church as a symbol of the power of God or of the emperor, or both (Baldwin Smith 1917: 22–37; Phillipson 2009: 358; Rodziewicz 2009: 83–96, here 86–7).

The testimony of the papyri

References are made to furniture in Byzantine papyri from Egypt, in fact in various documents such as petitions, contracts, buying/selling transactions, records of assets. The terms used are commonly known, although words of Latin origin that had already passed into the early Byzantine vernacular hold a significant place. We have selected typical examples from the prolific references and have discovered the following (see also the samples of Boxes 9.1 and 9.2): (a) for the various seats, throne, couch, stool, in household use, the following terms are used: δίφρος, also referred to as δίφρον, θρόνος, θρόνιον, wooden καθέδρα, σέλλα, σόλιον, one σέλλιον made of iron, and σκάμνον, an iron bench, (b) for the footstools: ὑποπόδιον and σεμσέλλιον, (c) for beds and couches for sleeping or dining: κλίνη and κλινίδιον are used frequently, ἀκκούβιτον, ἀκ(κ)ουβιτάλ(ρ)ι(ο)ν, κράβακτον, some described as light, κραβάκτιον, a big bed in the τρίκλινον in the dining room, κράββατον ἐρματικόν, a fixed, not movable, bed, (d) for the tables: τράπεζα, τραπέζιον, one made of marble referring to a church altar, or made of copper, μονόπτυχος, wooden and folding once, ὑαλίνη, glass table, ἀλαβαστρίνη, made of alabaster, (e) for large or small containers, boxes, and cabinets: γλωσσοκομεῖον, κάμπτρα, καμψί(ο)ν made from ebony, ivory, and wood, κιβώτιον, σκρίνιον made of silver, another for women made of copper, and also (f) other furniture or constructions for various household uses: σολιοθήκη, shoe cabinet, τρισκέλιν, τριπόδιον tripod or three-legged furniture used as table.[9] All these words for furniture belong to the so-called *koine* that borrowed terms from the Hellenistic Greek and Roman periods.

As can be ascertained from the aforementioned selection, although most furniture (beds, boxes, seats) is described as wooden, references mention constructions from various other materials as well. A wooden table may be described as folding once while certain beds are referred to as light, most likely made of wood. Tables made of copper, glass, and alabaster are also mentioned, along with various seats made of iron. Some boxes and chests are made of wood, ebony, and ivory, as well as copper and silver. In fact, in the petition from Antinoopolis (*P.Cair.Masp.* 1 67006), that dates back to 566–570 CE, there is one of the few references to ivory objects: mention is made apart from two *sellia* (σελλία) made of iron and a wooden *kathedra* (καθέδρα), of five *kampsia* (καμψία), chests, cases, or baskets, three of them wooden, one of ivory, and one of ebony (*P.Cair.Masp.* 1 67006, v 91–2; Drescher 1944: 91–6; Worp et al. 1990: 179–82; Russo 1998: 149–53). It should be noted that the papyri speak of an ἐλεφαντουργός, a man working on ivory, without specifying his workplace (*P.Athen.* 64; *P.Genova.* 1.2).

Finally, in third-century CE papyri an Egyptian-type bed, κράβακτος Αἰγύπτιος, is mentioned, made of heather, μαγίς ἐρικίνη (*P.Michael. Gr.* 18, 8), and also a barber's table, τράπεζα κουρική (*P.Michael. Gr.* 18, 11), and barber's chair, δίφρον κουρικόν (*Sammelb.* 4292; *POxy.* 646; *SB* 8 9834 b, r40). Also, although it is an ancient type of seat and an ancient word, the *diedros,-on* (δίεδρος, δίεδρον), a seat for two persons, frequently found in Hellenistic papyri, seems widely known later as διέδριον in late antiquity and is more often referred to in a medical context. It was considered to have been a kind of *chaise longue*, but ultimately it is translated as a double seat, a kind of carriage with seating for two (Oribasios, bk. 10, ch. 37, §§ 5, 9, 17; *Suda Lexicon*, letter delta, entry 896).

It should also be noted that in cases of furniture trade, as in the case we have just mentioned of the table made from heather, both materials as well as prices are usually given. This is significant information on the economy, the various prices in each period and furniture trading. And one last finding concerns the relatively small number of valuable and mainly ivory furniture in the papyri, which in fact covers a long period of time as opposed to the gifts given at one particular moment in time, as in Kyrillos' letter. The explanation is relatively simple. The papyri that we indexed concern agricultural *nomoi* of Egypt, provinces that despite their relative prosperity cannot be compared to wealthy Alexandria. Alexandria, a great administrative, financial, and cultural center, essentially absorbs all valuable materials and processes them, before sending the products either as marketable goods or as gifts to places throughout the Mediterranean and primarily to Constantinople and Rome (Cutler 1993; Rodziewicz 2009: 83–96). The furniture discovered in Kenchreai in the Peloponnese is probably from Egypt (Olch-Stern and Hadjilazaro-Thimme 2007: 2–29, 276–312).

Reclining, sitting, and dining: Kline and Stibas

The simple overview that we shall attempt below focuses mainly on the typical example of *kline* and *stibas* (κλίνη, στιβάς) from late antiquity and shows the gradual changes in use and names of furniture. These changes were obviously a consequence of the transformation gradually taking place in the customs of the population (catering, entertainment, relaxation) within an empire undergoing Christianization and denote changes in reclining, sitting, and dining during the transitional period leading up to Byzantium.

The ancient words *kline* and *stibas* although used through time primarily by learned Byzantine writers, can also be found as popularly used diminutives such as *klinarion, klinidion, stibadion* (κλινάριον, κλινίδιον, στιβάδιον). Although *stibas* could generally denote any couch and "bed," it was mainly used to signify, as opposed to *kline*, any conventional or makeshift mattress, couch of straw, rushes, or leaves (Verpoorten 1962: 147–60; Grosdidier de Matons 1979a: 363–73; 1979b: fasc. 438–9: 17–18; Paradiso 1991: 31–6; Smith 2003: 112–17; Poulsen 2005: 358–62). The terms *kline* or *stibas* are used throughout Byzantine literature to describe the bed and the couch that are used for banquets, for resting and sleeping, but everyday practice concerning dining was quite different. There is no continuation of the habit of eating while lying down, even though in some cases *stibadion* is mentioned for eating. For example, in *The Life of Saint Nicholas of Sion* from the seventh century CE it is mentioned that on the festival of Saint George eight oxen were slaughtered, one hundred measures of wine were provided and two hundred *stibadia* were made, namely dinner-couches, where a large number of people could eat their fill (*The Life of Saint Nicholas of Sion*, section 55.10). But there is more to it than that, the *Life* provides us with this unique testimony: two kinds of couches with different names and most certainly differing in quality, the *stibadia* for the masses and the *akkoubita* for men of the church (Grosdidier de Matons 1979a: 365). In this case the *ak(k)oubiton* (ἀκκούβιτον) from the Latin *accubitum* was not exactly a piece of furniture but a luxury or a well-prepared couch and the word was used by extension to describe the dining room and even the built-in table itself. The most famous *akkoubita* were the nineteen *akkoubita* in the Byzantine Palace, in the Hall of Nineteen Couches (Baldini and Cosentino 2021: 65–110). *Stibas* is mainly a word for scholarly use, although it gradually began to be regarded, along with *klinarion*, as an equivalent to the more popular words *krab(b)atos*, *kreb(b)atos*, and *kreb(b)ati(o)n* (κράβ(β)ατος, κρέβ(β)ατος, κρεβ(β)άτιον) that simply mean bed, makeshift, or carefully made constructions for reclining and sleeping. Yet in Byzantine texts these words and the *skimpous* are not clearly distinguished from the *kline* or *stibas* but they are rarely associated with *symposia*. There are though some exceptions, such as, for example, on a papyrus from seventh-century CE Egypt, which mentions a large *krabaktion* in a *triklinon* (POxy. 16 1925. 4; Grosdidier de Matons 1979a: 369–71). As far as Egypt is concerned, in papyri we frequently come across the very distinctive expression "to be in bed," to *kline* (εἶναι αὐτοὺς ἐπὶ κλίνης or δειπνῆσαι εἰς κλίνην), which despite appearances, is an invitation to a meal or a symposium in honor of ancient gods, obviously in non-Christian circles in the provinces of Egypt (POxy. 1 110; P.Mich. 8.511, 4 and 18; POxy. 20 2268, 16). But it has been argued that during the Early Byzantine era, particularly in monastic communities, they always ate seated and not lying down (Grosdidier de Matons 1979a: 363–4). In middle Byzantine texts the use of *kline* or *stibas* at meals and of verbs suggesting reclining and dining is merely a scholarly imitation of older expressions and it does not imply a continuation of the habit of eating while lying down. The only exception was in the Hall of the Nineteen Couches in the Byzantine Palace, where only there, according to Arethas of Caesarea, was this old custom still preserved during the tenth century CE (*Commentary on Klemes of Alexandria* 2, 326.27; Grosdidier de Maton 1979a: 363–6).

Furniture in the byzantine palace: The reality as myth

Great and possibly unique interest is generated by *The Escorial Taktikon* and the tenth-century CE treatise about court ceremony that refer to the Ceremonies and Order of the Palace, and *The Book of Ceremonies*. In these works many of the names and types of furniture mentioned continue the tradition of late antiquity, when the Roman administration influenced corresponding Hellenistic terminology creating a Greco-Roman *koine* in verbal representation for furnishing and together with familiar ancient terms they used terms of Latin origin (see Box 9.1). However, the existing splendor and luxury of the materials are textually highlighted to impress and, as a result, reality became a myth. As regards materials, shape, size, and use, relevant information is given, but specific and analytical descriptions are again rare. Thus in the palace there were apparently various majestic thrones as well as large and small gold tables and above all the emperor's gold table encrusted with precious stones and pearls (*The Escorial Taktikon* 275. 6–7). Indeed the imperial furniture along with the *automata*, those Byzantine mechanical constructions (lion, golden tree, and singing birds), always drew admiration and yet wonder, but was there truth or fantasy in their description?

In the treatise about court ceremony the emperor's throne is hardly ever referred to as *kathedra* (καθέδρα) but as *thronos* (θρόνος) and the Latin origin terms *senzon* (σένζον< *session, sessus*) and *sella* (σέλλα<*sella*) are used, a fact that testifies to the continuation of Roman imperial nomenclature and tradition in the palace (*The Book of Ceremonies* 407.3, 419.1, 431.18, 506–7, 587.1–10; Haldon 1990: C 860, 864, 148–50; Dagron et al. 2020: 2:401, 419, 441; 3:129–31; *The Escorial Taktikon*, 275.3–13). A throne, imperial or episcopal, was often equipped with a footstool (ὑποπόδιον, σουβσέλλιον < lat. *subsellia*, σουπέδιον < lat. *suppedaneum*, see Box 9.1). The old or those considered old and the newer thrones in the palace were unique symbols that were displayed and used by the emperors (Dagron 2003: 179–204). Reference is made to the early Byzantine thrones (σένζη, *The Escorial Taktikon*, 275.3–13) of the emperors Konstantinos I (324–337), Arkadios (395–408), and Maurikios (582–602). Of special interest is the so-called throne of Solomon in Magnaura palace (*The Book of Ceremonies*, 566.12–14, 567.8-9, 570.16–17, 583.19, 593.20), the description of which is recorded amidst all that was rumoured in the Middle Ages about Solomon and in between the reality and fiction legendary constructions of Byzantine mechanical automata:

> the emperor's throne was made in such a cunning manner that at one moment it was down on the ground, while at another it rose higher and was to be seen up in the air. This throne was of immense size and was, as it were, guarded by lions, made either of bronze or wood covered with gold, which struck the ground with their tails and roared with open mouth and quivering tongue.
> (Wright 1930: Antapodosis VI, 5, 8; Brett 1954: 477–87; Mango 1972: 209; Canavas 2003: 49–72; Dagron 2003: 188–9)

In the palace furniture and utensils of particular construction and use are mentioned, some with special symbolism, for instance the *Bed of Sorrow*, the *Bed of Joyce*, the mysterious *pentapyrgion* (πενταπύργιον, πυργίον), "this famous object of art," which stood in the imperial dining room, in the admirable Gold Hall, *Chrysotriklinon*, near the golden thrones and golden table of the Byzantine emperor. This unique gold *pentapyrgion* is considered by Byzantinists to be a sort of vast wardrobe—a treasure—made of five towers "une sorte de vaste armoire – un trésor composée de cinq tours" (*The Escorial Taktikon* 275.9–10; *The Book of Ceremonies* 582.1–10; Vogt 1935: 1:103–4; Dagron 2005: 109–17; Angar 2015: 181–200).

Apart from the palace furniture, the wealth of gold and luxury was also apparent in those items the emperor took with him on campaigns: "two chairs (σελλία) for the cortege, chairs (σελλία) for the chamber-pot of metal gilded with beaten gold (ὁλόκανα, διάχρυσα, κοπτὰ), with covers, and with other covers above concealing the space for the latrine; and for the distinguished refugees two other, similar, seats, bound in silver" (Haldon 1990: C 214–17, 108–9). When on campaign he also took with him some folding benches, tables (σκαμνία, τραπέζια συστελτά). The folding benches are described as being big enough to seat three men on each individual bench (C 168–70: 104–5).

Worth noting the complete lack of references of the above sources to ivory beds, tables, and seats in the palace, while other sources cite ivory tablets and doors, and abundant ivory chests and boxes have been preserved (Cutler 1993). Typical of the past wealth and grandeur is the table referred to in a provincial aristocratic house in Paphlagonia in the ninth century, an ancient, very large, circular, ivory, gold-encrusted table that could seat thirty men (*The Life of Saint Philaretos the Merciful*, line 418).

In every respect, apart from the thrones and valuable tables in the palace, the thrones and tables in the churches, particularly in Hagia Sophia, stood as iconic constructions in the collective conscience, symbols of wealth and power, both because of their location and their precious materials. And if the gold tables in the palace and especially the emperor's gold table encrusted with precious stones and pearls are considered spectacular, then another table, the holy altar table in Hagia Sophia, was outstanding and extraordinary. It is moreover the only altar table, supposedly constructed in the time of Justinian, for which we have a very detailed but probably half-legendary description (sixth to ninth century CE). The detailed enumeration of the materials used in the making of this altar table highlights precisely its uniqueness which complements the uniqueness of the church (*Story on the Construction of the Hagia Sophia* 74–108, § 17; for an English translation, see Berger 2013: 256–7).

It should also be noted that adjacent to these tables in the churches and monasteries lay the sacristies (σκευοφυλακεῖον or σκευοφυλάκιον). This was a special independent place, a kind of storehouse, where in various boxes (κιβώτια), priceless vessels and relics, and other artifacts from the past or valuable contemporary vessels in use were kept. There was even a special service with a storekeeper in charge of it, known as a sacristan (σκευοφύλαξ, *The Book of Ceremonies*, 540.16, 549.7, 550.21).

The case of this altar table of Hagia Sophia, like many other cases of built-in tables, beds, or seats, reveals furniture as architecture. According to relevant research and studies (Oikonomides 1990: 205–14; Parani 2003: 167–8; Angar 2015: 181–2; Baldini and Cosentino 2021: 65–110) the palace and monasteries, in some extent, but especially a middle-class Byzantine house contained built-in structures of beds, benches, and tables (Chapter 4 in this volume).

NOTES

Chapter 1

1 From Tarkhan, Grave 415. Petrie Museum of Egyptian Archaeology, London (UC 17173) (Petrie 1913: 11; Killen 2017a: 65, plate 68).
2 For a Middle Kingdom limestone stool from Lahun on a pair of runners, see Petrie (1890: 24, note 41).
3 In this discussion, "rounded" or "round" legs denote legs that are round in section; "square" legs are square in section. A "round" (table) top is circular.
4 The use of cubits, palms, and fingers recorded on the Palermo stone was recognized by Breasted as indicating the possible height of the Nile's inundation (Breasted 1906: §83).
5 The important work of Pieter De Bruyne established the link between linear measurement, proportion, and geometry in furniture forms, providing a remarkable data set that allows us to peer into the cognitive world of the ancient Egyptian furniture designer (Bruyne 1982: 40–3, figs. 27–8, plate 13).
6 A number of First Dynasty sites provide archaeological evidence for the use of wood and ivory bovine-form furniture legs: Tarkhan (Petrie 1913), Abydos (Petrie 1901), Saqqara (Emery 1949), and Naqada (de Morgan 1897).
7 Three-legged stool, tomb of Tutankhamun, Egyptian Museum, Cairo, JE 62043. The "running spiral" motif is also found on the cedar throne (JE 62029), ebony throne (JE 62030), and child's chair (JE 62033) from the tomb.
8 For a folding stool with lion-shaped legs, see British Museum, London, EA 37406.
9 For a folding stool with duck-head terminals from the Eighteenth-Dynasty tomb of Ani, see British Museum, London, EA 29284 (Killen 2017a: 62–3, fig. 21, plates 57–60).
10 For a fine round-legged stool with inlaid decoration, see British Museum, London, EA 2472 (Killen 2017a: 69, fig. 23; plates 82–3).
11 F. 1964/1.3 and 1964/1.4 (Raven 2014: 191–204; figs. 2–3).
12 British Museum, London, EA 2371 (Pinch 1993: 209).
13 For a complete range of woodworking joints used in Egyptian carpentry, see Killen (2000: 358–66).
14 Ashmolean Museum, Oxford, E1255 and E138 (Killen 1994b: 21–2, fig. 24).

15 Egyptian Museum, Cairo, JE 61446 (Baker 1966: 91–2, fig. 106; Killen 2017b: 75–8, fig. 67).

16 Egyptian Museum, Cairo, JE 61447 (Baker 1966: 92; fig. 107).

17 Egyptian Museum, Cairo, JE 62029 (Eaton-Krauss 2008: 57–67; figs. 7–9; plates XI–XVI).

18 Egyptian Museum, Cairo, JE 62048 (Killen 2017b: 113–15; fig. 85).

19 Two boxes from the tomb of Perpaut: Oriental Museum, University of Durham, EG4572 (Killen 2017b: 49–51, fig. 53, plates 29–34) and Museo Civico, Bologna, B 1970 (Killen 2017b: 52–3, fig. 55, plate 39).

20 "Through tenons" go all the way through the open mortises cut in the tops of the legs; "half-lap joints" consist of two board ends reduced to half their thickness and lapping over one another, providing ample surface for glued attachment.

21 This type of table surely influenced the design of the three-legged stool with curved legs from the tomb of Tutankhamun discussed above.

22 A sphinx throne is also depicted on the sarcophagus of King Ahiram of Byblos (Baker 1966: fig. 337).

23 See Baughan (2013: 201–7) for the idea that the custom began earlier, with a Syro-Phoenician bowl given as evidence, although the date of this bowl is debated.

24 In this article, the caption of figure 3 is incorrect: figure 3a (the drawing at the left) is actually "Screen B" (serving stand B), and figure 3b (the drawing at the right) is "Screen A" (serving stand A).

25 One of the table tops may be maple (*Acer*) or *Prunus*.

26 Metropolitan Museum of Art 14.130.14.

27 King Midas (r. eighth century BCE) dedicated his throne at the sanctuary of Apollo at Delphi, which was later praised by Herodotus (1.14) as "well worth seeing." See Simpson 2020 regarding this throne.

28 Staatliche Antikensammlungen und Glyptothek, Munich, 2301. The black-figure side is attributed to the Lysippides Painter.

29 Kerameikos, Grave 3, HW 37, *c*. 520 BCE.

30 A stone version of one such couch from a chamber tomb suggests that these legs were made from thick boards (Simpson 2002: plate 80b).

31 The legs of the Gordion tables were made from naturally curved or trained branches (Simpson 2010: 199–200).

32 Richter's captions refer to *fulcrum* plaques erroneously as *fulcra*; the use of the term *fulcrum/fulcra* is somewhat ambiguous in the text (Richter 1966: 105–8).

33 The brazier from the Temple of Isis (Pompeii) is misidentified as a table by Richter (1966: 112).

Chapter 2

1 However, there is evidence for the use of the barks of specific trees in carpentry, such as the decorative use of silver birch bark for chariot axles and bows in Tutankhamun's burial (Hepper 2009: 40, 44–5).

2 The term is strictly applied to elephant tusks only. However, it may also be used for tusks of hippopotamuses (or even cetaceans) (for an overview, see Krzyskowska and Morkot 2000).

3 Greek κύανος< */kuwanos/ (spelled *ku-wa-no*) is surely a loanword (possibly Hittite *kuwanna(n)*, but this was also borrowed), but its precise significance has been debated: is it an ornamental blue stone (e.g., lapis lazuli) or an artificial material of a similar hue (e.g., glass-paste colored by cobalt oxide)? Besides the broad attestation of glass-paste ornaments in Mycenaean contexts (as opposed to the extreme scarcity

of the exuberantly exotic lapis lazuli), a final solution seems to lie in the mere fact that a specific term exists in Mycenaean Greek for "workers of *ku-wa-no*" (*ku-wa-no-wo-ko*, see below), and this suggests that specific expert knowledge was required. While it does not make much sense to differentiate between workers of lapis lazuli and workers of other stones, glass-paste workers were a separate entity in ancient crafts.

Chapter 3

1 A range of bed frame types was discovered in the cemetery at Tarkhan by W.M.F. Petrie (Petrie 1913: 23–4, plate VIII:4).

2 Two types of bed frame construction show that the bed frame cross-rail was jointed either above the leg (Petrie 1913: 23–4, plate VIII:2) or in the side-rail away from the leg (Petrie 1913: 23–4, plate VIII:3).

3 A particularly fine example of a bed frame with slots in the side- and cross-rails to accept the deck webbing is now preserved in the Manchester University Museum, Manchester, 5429 (Killen 2017a: 35–6, fig. 6, plates 31–4).

4 For an analysis of Middle Kingdom chair types, see Killen (2017a: 91–4, fig. 28).

5 Examples of low tables were discovered at Tarkhan and are preserved in the Manchester University Museum, Manchester, 5456 (Petrie 1913: 25, plates XI:23–XII:7), and in the Ashmolean Museum, Oxford, 1912.603 (Killen 2017a: 117, plates 103–4).

6 Two tables from the tomb of Kha and Meryt at Deir el-Medîna, TT8, were discovered by Ernesto Schiaparelli (Schiaparelli 1927: 118, fig. 100). They are now preserved in the Egyptian Museum, Turin, 8257 and 8258.

7 Tables with splayed legs and with the tabletop edged with a cavetto cornice and torus molding are preserved in the Metropolitan Museum of Art, New York, 14.10.5 (Killen 2017a: 119, plate 108), and The Brooklyn Museum, New York, 37.41E (Killen 2017a: 119, plate 109).

8 A three-legged table is preserved in the British Museum, London, EA 2469 (Killen 2017a: 119–20, fig. 34, plates 111–13).

9 A reed and rush table from the tomb of Kha and Meryt at Deir el-Medîna, TT8, was discovered by Ernesto Schiaparelli (Schiaparelli 1927: 118, fig. 101). It is now preserved in the Egyptian Museum, Turin, 8343.

10 Egyptian Museum, Cairo, JE 62018; Carter No. 586 (Killen 2017a: 43–4, figs. 15–17, plates 42–3).

11 Egyptian Museum, Cairo, JE 61455; Carter No. 68 (Killen 2017b: 80–2, fig. 70, plate 56).

12 Egyptian Museum, Cairo, JE 61445; Carter No. 32 (Killen 2017b: 67–9, figs. 60–1, plate 43).

13 Egyptian Museum, Cairo, JE 62058 a-o; Carter No. 345 [box]; Carter No. 580 [stand] (Baker 1966: 99, fig. 126). *Senet* was a board game played by two players on a board of thirty squares, arranged in three lines of ten squares each. Each player had seven pieces distinguished by shape or color. Pieces were moved around the board through squares signifying good and bad fortune. The number of moves each player made was determined by the throwing of a type of stick.

14 Egyptian Museum, Cairo, JE 61467; Carter No. 21 (Killen 2017b: 69–70, plates 44–5).

15 Egyptian Museum, Cairo, JE 62028. Carter No. 91 (Eaton-Krauss 2008: 25–56, figs. 2–6, plates III–VIII).

16 The French traveler Frédéric Cailliaud (1787–1869) recorded a set of furniture paintings that were found in the tomb of Rameses III (KV 11). Unfortunately, these wall paintings were subsequently destroyed (Cailliaud 1831).

17 For an analyses of furniture types and the system of manufacture found at Deir el-Medîna, see Killen and Weiss (2009: 137–58).

18 For recent work at the site, see Çatalhöyük Research Project (n.d.).

19 British Museum, London, ME 89126. See British Museum (n.d.-a).

20 It has not been possible to understand where all the ivory plaques were situated on the chair; only the falcon and gazelle plaques appear in the drawing, located at the top of the chair back, based on evidence from Egypt.

21 British Museum, London, ME 124565. See British Museum (n.d.-b).

22 British Museum, London, ME 124920. See British Museum (n.d.-c).

23 For components of an Assyrian royal banquet, see the Banquet Stele from Nimrud (Mallowan 1975: 69–71).

24 Northwest Palace; Fort Shalmaneser, SW 7, SW 37, and NW 15.

25 For a publication of these inscriptions, see Pritchett (1953, 1956). For the particular cupboard, see Pritchett (1956: 225).

26 For the Herculaneum furniture, see Mols (1999). For the cupboard–*aedicula*, see Mols (1999: 192–7).

Chapter 5

1 One may cite the union of the βασιλίννα, wife of the Arkhōn Basileus (a major official in Classical Athens), and the god Dionysus (impersonated by the Arkhōn perhaps?) taking place at the Boukoleion during the festival of Anthestēria (Aristotle, *On the Athenian Constitution* 3.5).

2 It can be argued that Greek θρόνος (whence English "throne" and other European cognates are derived), although perhaps a luxury seat already in the Late Bronze Age (Mycenaean Greek *thornoi* are cited as furniture used in a celebration possibly presided by the Pylian king, see Chapter 9 in this volume), does not seem to have acquired its exclusive meaning as the "seat of a ruler" before the Classical period.

3 *Potnia Thērōn* ("Mistress of the Wild Animals") is a designation for female deities that extend their dominion over powerful wild animals, either herbivorous (e.g., deer) or predators (such as lions or other felines). The expression occurs once in Homer (*Iliad* 21.470) where it refers to Artemis, but it is used by scholars to refer to any female deity of similar properties, as well as to describe the iconographic motif of a female figure seated on or holding wild animals in a way conveying her dominance (e.g., by their necks, horns, or tails).

4 Greek *megaron* denotes, amongst other things, spacious halls in the royal residences of Homeric heroes. Its use by modern scholars to indicate the great halls with central hearths in the Mycenaean palaces is conventional, originating in an early belief in the historical authenticity of the epic narratives, especially following the discovery of the Mycenaean palace in the citadel of Tiryns in the Argolid. There is no positive clue that the contemporary (i.e., 1400–1200 BCE) Greek name of these halls was *megaron*.

5 For an accessible account of the collapse phenomena throughout the Eastern Mediterranean c. 1200 BCE, see Cline (2014). The movement of certain groups named in Egyptian sources as the "Sea Peoples" are often central in attempts at explaining these events that brought about the end of the Mycenaean palaces, the Hittite New Kingdom in Anatolia, and several principalities in the Levant (e.g., Ugarit), even if

the pharaonic Egyptian state survived intact. However, even in regions where the collapse of the Bronze Age centers truly transformed the sociopolitical landscapes, such as the palatial polities of the southern Aegean, there was a considerable degree of continuity, especially in those aspects of life less associated with the central political institutions, such as popular religion or domestic production.

6　If the "Palace of the Giants" in the Athenian Agora was used as a *praetorium*, the great central chamber of the South court (Frantz 1988: plate 54, no. 14) with a probable colonnaded front must have had such a function (see Frantz 1988: 103, plates 52–4 [H. Thompson]). The *triclinium* of the unit A (A2/A3) of the Southeastern Villa at Delphi could have a similar use (see Déroche, Pétridis, and Badie 2014: plate 6).

Chapter 6

1　These are often associated with the takeover of Knossos (*c.* 1450 BCE) by Greek-speakers that thereafter used the Linear B script and the arrival and establishment of a new militaristic mainland aristocracy.

2　This Phrygian beverage closely resembles Homeric κυκεών (mixture) prepared from of grated cheese, barley flour, honey, and wine by Hekamede for Nestor (*Il.* 11.630–1 and 638–41) and by Circe (*Od* 10.234–6, where φάρμακα λυγρά [baneful drugs] are added), as well as the κρίθινος οἶνος mentioned by Archilochus (quoted in Athenaeus, *Deipn.* 10.447a–b) and Xenophon (*Anabasis* 4.5.26–7) as drunk with straws, as on the contemporary Cypriot "Hubbard Amphora," see Chapter 8 in this volume. Similar mixed beverages are known from the Late Bronze Age Aegean, where the mention of *melitios* (honey-flavored) wine on an inscribed clay sealing from the Palace of Nestor at Pylos is matched by organic residue analyses from Gordion (McGovern in Simpson 2010: 183).

3　Simpson has observed a structural detail—that the ends of tenons extending through open mortises have been rendered with vertical strokes (apparently representing the wood grain at the cross-section of the tenon)—indicating that the red-figure painter's "unusual knowledge of wood joinery" was not matched on the black-figure side of the same vase (Simpson 2002: 313).

4　"A Macedonian tomb in its narrowest scholarly definition can be described as a built chamber tomb roofed with a barrel-vault, covered by an earth tumulus and found in Macedonia or areas where Macedonian influence may have been particularly strong" (Miller 1993: 1, n. 1).

Chapter 7

1　By Greek world we include the areas of the Greek mainland and Asia Minor, the areas colonized by Greeks along the Black Sea and Southern Italy.

Chapter 8

1　A sphinx is a creature with feline body, human head, and (optional) bird wings (Greek σφίγξ<σφίγγ-ς, often interpreted as a loan from Egyptian *šsp 'nḫ* "living image"; association with σφίγγω "to bind tightly" is probably due to folk-paretymology). For a recent hypothesis reviving the association with σφίγγω and deriving the sphinx in Oedipus' legend from Semitic 'strangler' demon *ḫnqt/ ḫnqt* see Jagiełło 2018.

2　Griffins were creatures with feline bodies, bird heads, and (optional) bird wings (Greek γρύψ<γρύπ-ς, perhaps a loan from Akkadian *karūbu* "winged creature, griffin"; cf. Hebrew *kerūb* "cherub"; European *griffin, griffon, Greif* through Latin *gryphus*).

3   Baetyl (Greek βαίτυλος, perhaps Hellenized form of Semitic Bethel "House of El")
     is a term used for single stones that are the focus of ritual. Hesychius (s.v.) glosses
     βαίτυλος as the stone swallowed by Kronos instead of Zeus. Such "sacred stones,"
     seen as embodiments or abodes of deities, are known throughout Mediterranean
     antiquity, including the *omphalos* at Delphi, or the black stone of Baal brought by
     Elagabalus from Syria to Rome. In the context of Minoan Crete, such objects (called
     conventionally "baetyls" without proof that this was their Minoan name) have been
     tentatively identified in ritual scenes chiefly depicted on seals and signet rings, as
     well as on probable actual examples from Gournia, Kephala Vasilikis, Ayia Triada,
     and Malia on Crete, as well as Phylakopi on Melos.

4   *Prothesis* (πρόθεσις "exposition") represents the deceased lying in state on a bed/
     bier, surrounded by mourning figures; *ekphora* indicates the next stage, where the
     dead (still on a bed/bier) is transported to the burial ground, where interment,
     usually following cremation, is to take place. For Geometric (chiefly eighth century
     BCE) imagery, see Ahlberg (1971).

5   Furniture representations are scarce in Cyprus before the Late Bronze Age. Besides
     the "throne" on the Vounous model (see Chapter 5 in this volume), terracotta *models*
     of cradles occur in Cypriote burials between *c.* 2200–1900 BCE (Theodossiadou
     1996: 74–5, fig. 2). Rather than "genre" scenes, they could indicate some belief
     in rebirth, possibly (but hardly certainly) associated with the "tomb as womb"
     metaphor. As these are chronologically restricted, there is no likely association with
     the terracotta figurines of *kourotrophoi* (female figures holding infants) that appear
     again in the Late Bronze Age and the Cypro-Archaic periods.

6   Ziffer 2005: figs. 2–3; cf. Xenophon, *Anabasis* 4.5.26–7, on drinking Armenian "barley
     wine" with straws; this beverage appears similar to that which accompanied the funerary
     banquet in Gordion Tumulus MM (see Chapter 6, endnote 2 in this volume).

7   The myth of Danae and Perseus is rarely depicted on Attic vase painting. Danae was
     the daughter of Akrisios, king of Argos, who, according to an oracle would be killed
     by Danae's son. Although Akrisios imprisoned his daughter, Zeus who desired
     Danae, came to her in the form of golden rain and so their offspring Perseus was
     born. Then Akrisios confined Danae and Perseus in a wooden chest and cast them
     into the sea. In most of the narrative scenes of the myth a carpenter is depicted
     holding the tools for the manufacture of the chest. For the iconography of the
     myth, see LIMC s.v. *Danae* (331–2, 336, nos. 41–52, plate 247), LIMC s.v. *Akrisios*
     (450–1, nos. 1–9, plates 342–4), and Christopoulos (1990: 101–10).

Chapter 9

*   The part of this chapter that deals with evidence up to the early first millennium BCE
     is accompanied by Table 9.1 that includes a selection of main furniture terms used
     in Egypt, the Near East and the Aegean during the Bronze and the Early Iron Ages.

1   Cf. also Cypriot θόρναξ, "footstool." Greek θρόνος, "throne," might have had the
     original meaning of "support" (the exclusive elite connotations may not date before
     the Classical period), if the derivation from the root *d^her- is accepted (note that
     suffix *-onos* is very rare in the inherited Greek lexicon).

2   Palaima has observed that the sum of chairs plus "footstools" on the Ta tablets gives
     twenty-two items (although the reading of one numeral following a record of chairs
     is ambiguous, see Shelmerdine 2012: 686), which is twice the number of tables,
     suggesting that "each table is meant to have two 'sitting' pieces" (Palaima 2000: 237).
     Acceptance of this would require that Mycenaean *thrānuwes* are not "footstools,"

but actually a type of canonical seat. Hittite ^(GIŠ)GÌR.GUB = ^{GIŠ}*hassalli-* (see above and Table 9.1), which could mean both "footstool" and "stool," supports Palaima's hypothesis, although this is difficult to reconcile with the form of the footstool sign (*220*, see Sakellarakis 1996: 106, fig. 1) and Aegean iconographic evidence (such as the Tiryns Treasure gold signet ring) (see Plate 9.2(a)-(b) and Chapter 8 in this volume).

3   Knossian tables: KN V(2) 280.5;. Pylian bedsteads: PY Un 1482.4; Vn 851.1; Wr 1326.γ; Linear B sign*169* "bedstead": PY Pa 49, 53, 889 and Pn 30 (*c.* 1200 BCE). Abbreviated adjunct *DE* accompanying *169* on PY Pa 49 and 53 may stand for *demi-ni-jo* (cf. δέμνιον "couch" or "bed" in Homer).

4   Laser (1968: 44) has argued that the semantic difference between them is indicated by ἑξείης (cf. ἑξῆς) ἕζοντο (*only* on Hom., *Od.* 1.145 and 3.389), that he interprets as indicating an age/rank distinction: "elders and people of high rank sit on θρόνοι, the younger on κλισμοί." But ἑξείης implies none of this with certainty; it only denotes sequence ("one after another"), simply conveying that they sat in an orderly manner (cf. κόσμῳ; Hom., *Od.* 13.77): no notion of hierarchy is certainly conveyed by ἑξείης.

5   Athenaeus (*Deipn.* 5.192e–f) discusses Homeric references to the terms θρόνος, κλισμός, and δίφρος and comments that these types refer to hierarchical divisions: ὁ γὰρ θρόνος αὐτὸ μόνον ἐλευθέριός ἐστιν καθέδρα σὺν ὑποποδίῳ [...] ὁ δὲ κλισμὸς περιττοτέρως κεκόσμηται ἀνακλίσει. τούτων δ᾽εὐτελέστερος ἦν ὁ δίφρος" (for the *thronos* taken by itself is a noble chair with a footstool [...]. The *klismos*, on the other hand, is provided more lavishly with an inclined back. Of them poorer was the *diphros*).

6   For example, *IG* II² 1388, lines 19, 20, 21, 23; 1393, lines 6, 7, 8, 9 (Attica); and *ID* 396B, 399B, 442B, 443Bb, 444B, 461Bb (Artemision Treasure C, Delos).

7   *Abaci* are possibly the slab-topped tables or sideboards (Juvenal, *Satires* III.204; Cato, *Agr.* 11.3; Cic., *Ver.* 4. 35; Liv. 39, 6. 7; Plin., *HN* 34.14); *monopodia* are the tables on one leg. The last two literary references mention *monopodia et abacos* together. The exact form of these tables is not known. *Abaci* are, in modern bibliography, the slabs forming the top of the table. Part of Vulso's booty might have been table-slabs and table-legs of one-legged table types. Certain scholars have identified the *abaci* of the literary sources with smaller one-legged tables (Stephanidou-Tiveriou 1993: 60, n. 255).

8   The references on papyroi were retrieved from http://www.columbia.edu/cu/lweb/projects/digital/apis/.

9   Retrieved from http://www.columbia.edu/cu/lweb/projects/digital/apis/. Specifically, for (a) seats, see *Sammelb.* 4292; *POxy.* 646; *SB* 8 9834 b, r40; *P.Masp.* 6 ii 63; *P.Cair.Masp.* 1 67006, v64; *PAntin.* 3 204, 7; *P.Cair.Masp.* 1 67006, 90; *P.Grenf.* 2 111; *POxy.*1146.6; *Book of Ceremonies* 407.3, 419.1, 431.18; *POxy.* 1288.16; *P.Masp.* 6 ii 47; *P.Cair.Masp.* 1 67006, v89; *PDura* 33, 12. For (b) footstools, see *P.Cair.Masp.* 1 67006, v47; *P.Grenf.* 2 111; *P.Masp.* 6 v 89; *PAntin.* 3 204, 5. For (c) beds, see *PAntin.* 3 204, 3; *PSI* 3 225, 5; *PFouad* 1 85, 4; *POxy.* 16 1925, 9; *POxy.* 56 3860, 18; *P.Berl.Sarisch.* 21, 46; *SB* 22 15249, 5; *POxy.* 77 5126, 6; *P.Leid.Inst.* 13, 27; *P.Cair.Masp.* 1 67006, v46, 89–90, 97; *POxy.* 16 1925, 15; *P.Gen.* 1 (2e éd.) 68, 10. For (d) tables, see *P.Prag.* 2 178, 4; *P.Grenf.* 2 111; *SB* 20 14379, 21; *P.Cair.Masp.* 1 67006, v46–7; *P.Leid.Inst.* 13, 16; *POxy.* 16 2058, 25. For (e) containers, see *P.Berl.Sarisch.* 21, 35; *P.Cair.Masp.* 1 67006, 65, v90; *P.Cair.Masp.* 3 67340, 79; *P.Cair.Masp.* 1 67006, 90. It should be noted that in a papyrus

dated 114 CE reference is made to three cases or chests with leather lining (κάμπτραι ἐσκυτωμέναι), cost per chest two drachmas, a total of six drachmas, *P.Wisc.* 2 80; on this papyrus, see Mayerson (1999: 189–92). *P.Masp.* 6 ii 90. The ebony one in *P.Cair.Masp.* 1 67006, v91, the ivory one *in P.Cair.Masp.* 1 67006, v91 (sixth century) and the three wooden ones, *P.Cair.Masp.* 1 67006, v92. *P.Berl.Sarisch.* 21, 34 (sixth century); *P.Leid.Inst.* 13, 11 (seventh to eighth century), where reference is made to *skrinia*, silver chests; *P.Cair.Masp.* 3 67340, 78 (sixth century). For (f) other furniture see, *P.Bodl.* 1 48 R, 7 (second to third century) and commentaries on the papyrus, see Kramer (1998: 38–41). *P.Berl.Sarisch.* 21, 45 (sixth century); *PAntin.* 3 204, 8 (sixth to seventh century). *SB 8 9834 b*, r40 (date 300–325).

BIBLIOGRAPHY

SELECTED PRIMARY SOURCES

Actes de Chilandar: Christophe Giros, Vassiliki Kravari, and Mirjana Zivojinovic (eds.), *Actes de Chilandar I, Des origines à 1319*, Archives de l'Athos XX, Paris: P. Lethielleux, 1998.

Actes de Xéropotamou: Jean Bompaire (ed.), *Actes de Xéropotamou*, Archives de l'Athos III, Paris: P. Lethielleux, 1964.

Alexander Romance: L. Bergson (ed.), *Der griechische Alexanderroman. Rezension β*, Stockholm: Almqvist & Wiksell, 1965.

Apokaukos, John, *Letters*: A. Papadopoulos-Kerameus (ed.), "Συνοδικὰ γράμματα Ἰωάννου τοῦ Ἀποκαύκου, μητροπολίτου Ναυπάκτου," *Βυζαντίς*, 1 (1909–10): 8–30.

Basilika Series A: H.J. Scheltema and N. Van der Wal (eds.), *Basilicorum libri LX. Series A*, vols. 1–8, Groningen: Wolters et al., 1955–88.

Basilika Series B: D. Holwerda and H.J. Scheltema (eds.), *Basilicorum libri LX.*, Series B, vols. 1–9, Groningen: Wolters et al., 1953–85.

Belthandros and Chrysantza: J. Egea (ed.), *Historia extraordinaria de Beltandro y Crisanza*, Granada: Athos Pérgamos, 1998.

The Book of Ceremonies: J.J. Reiske (ed.), *Constantini Porphyrogeniti imperatoris de cerimoniis aulae Byzantinae libri duo* [*Corpus scriptorum historiae Byzantinae*], Bonn: Weber, 1829.

Callimachos and Chrysorrhoe: M. Pichard (ed.), *Le Roman de Callimaque et de Chrysorrhoé*, Paris: Les Belles Lettres, 1956.

Commentary on Aristophanes: F. Dübner (ed.), *Scholia Graeca in Aristophanem*, Paris: Georg Olms, 1877 (repr. Hildesheim, 1969).

Commentary on Klemes of Alexandria: O. Stählin and U. Treu (eds.), *Clemens Alexandrinus*, vol. 1, 3rd edn., Berlin: Berlin Akademie Verlag, 1972.

Commentary on Lucian: H. Rabe (ed.), *Scholia in Lucianum*, Leipzig: B.G. Teubner, 1906 (repr. Stuttgart, 1971).

Dagron et al. 2020: Gilbert Dagron, Bernard Flusin, and Denis Feissel (eds.), *Constantin VII Porphyrogénète: Le livre des cérémonies*, Corpus fontium historiae byzantinae 52/ vols. 1–5, Paris: Association des Amis du Centre d'Histoire et Civilisations de Byzance, 2020.

The Escorial Taktikon: N. Oikonomidès (ed.), *Les listes de préséance byzantines des IXe et Xe siècles*, Paris: Éditions du centre national de la recherche scientifique, 1972.

Eusebios, *Church History*: G. Bardy (ed.), *Eusèbe de Césarée. Histoire ecclésiastique*, 3 vols. [*Sources chrétiennes* 31, 41, 55], Paris: Éditions du Cerf, 1952–8.

Eustathios of Thessalonike, *Commentary on Homer Iliad*: M. Van der Valk, *Eustathii archiepiscopi Thessalonicensis commentarii ad Homeri Iliadem pertinentes*, vols. 1–4, Leiden: Brill, 1971–87.

Eustathios of Thessalonike, *Commentary on Odyssey*: G. Stallbaum (ed.), *Eustathii archiepiscopi Thessalonicensis commentarii ad Homeri Odysseam*, 2 vols., Leipzig: Georg Olms, 1825–6 (repr. Hildesheim, 1970).

Hansen, P.A. (ed.), *Hesychii Alexandrini lexicon*, vol. 3 [*Sammlung griechischer und lateinischer Grammatiker (SGLG)*, vol. 11/3, Berlin: W. de Gruyter & Co, 2005.

Herodianos, *Partitiones*: J.F. Boissonade (ed.), *Herodiani partitiones*, London: A.M. Hakkert, 1819 (repr. Amsterdam, 1963).

Hesychios, *Lexicon*: K. Latte (ed.), *Hesychii Alexandrini lexicon*, vols. 1–2, Copenhagen: W. de Gruyter & Co, 1953–66.

Homer (1919), *Odyssey, Volume II: Books 13–24*, translated by A.T. Murray, revised by George E. Dimock, Cambridge, MA: Harvard University Press.

Isidore of Seville, *The Etymologies* (or *Origins*): W.M. Lindsay (ed.), *Isidori Hispalensis Episcopi Etymologiarum sive Originum Libri XX*, Oxford: Clarendon Press, 1911.

Kosmas Indikopleustes, *The Christian Topography*: W. Wolska-Conus (ed.), *Cosmas Indicopleustès. Topographie chrétienne*, 2 vols., Paris: Les éditions du Cerf, 1970.

Kyrillos of Alexandria, *Letter*: E. Schwartz, *Collectio Casinensis, Acta Conciliorum Oecumenicorum*, Tomus 1, vol. 4, Berlin: W. de Gruyter & Co, 1922–3: 224–5.

Kyrillos of Skythopolis, *Life of Euthymios*: E. Schwartz (ed.), *Kyrillos von Skythopolis* [Texte und Untersuchungen 49.2], Leipzig: J.C. Hinrichs Verlag, 1939.

Leontios of Neapolis, *The Life of Saint John Merciful*: A.-J. Festugière and L. Rydén (eds.), *Léontios de Néapolis, Vie de Syméon le Fou et Vie de Jean de Chypre*, Paris: Paul Geuthner, 1974.

The Life of Lazaros of Mt. Galesion: H. Delehaye (ed.), *Acta Sanctorum (Novembris)*, Tomus III, Brussels: Société des Bollandistes, 1910 (repr. 1965): 508–88.

The Life of Saint Nicholas of Sion: I. Sevcenko and N.P. Sevcenko (eds.), *The Life of Saint Nicholas of Sion*, Brookline, MA: Hellenic College Press, 1984.

Lydos, John, *On Powers*: A.C. Bandy (ed.), *Ioannes Lydus: On Powers or the Magistracies of the Roman State*, Philadelphia: American Philosophical Society, 1983.

Menandros Protector, *De legationibus*: C. De Boor (ed.), *Excerpta historica iussu imp. Constantini Porphyrogeniti confecta*, vol. 1, Berlin: Weidmann, 1903.

Metaphrasis of Alexias: H. Hunger (ed.), *Anonyme Metaphrase zu Anna Komnene, Alexias XI-XIII*, Vienna: Österreichische Akademie der Wissenschaften, 1981.

Oribasios: J. Raeder (ed.), *Oribasii collectionum medicarum reliquiae*, vols. 1–4, Leipzig: B.G. Teubner, 1928–33.

Paschal Chronicle: L. Dindorf (ed.), *Chronicon paschale*, vol. 1, Bonn: Weber, 1832.

Photios, *Lexicon*: C. Theodoridis (ed.), *Photii patriarchae lexicon*, vols. 1–3, Berlin: W. de Gruyter & Co, 1982–2013.

Ptochoprodromica: H. Eideneier (ed.), *Ptochoprodromos* [*Neograeca Medii Aevi 5*], Cologne: Romiosini, 1991.

Sophronios, *Miracles*: N. Fernández Marcos (ed.), *Sophronius, Narratio miraculorum sanctorum Cyri et Joannis*, Madrid: Instituto Antonio de Nebrija, 1975.

Story on the Construction of the Hagia Sophia: T. Preger (ed.), *Scriptores originum Constantinopolitanarum*, 1, Leipzig: B.G. Teubner, 1901.

Suda Lexicon: A. Adler (ed.), *Suidae lexicon*, 4 vols. [Lexicographi Graeci 1.1–1.4], Leipzig: B.G. Teubner, 1928–35.

Synesios, *Letters*: A. Garzya (ed.), *Synésios de Cyrène, Correspondance: Lettres I–CLVI*, vols. 2–3, Paris: Les Belles Lettres, 2000.

The Life of Saint Philaretos the Merciful: L. Rydén (ed.), *The Life of St. Philaretos the Merciful written by his grandson Niketas*, Uppsala: Uppsala University Library, 2002.

Theophanes, *Chronography*: C. De Boor (ed.), *Theophanis chronographia*, Leipzig: B.G. Teubner, 1883 (repr. Hildesheim, 1963).

Typikon of Pantocrator: P. Gautier (ed.), ""Le typikon du Christ Sauveur Pantocrator," *Revue des études byzantines*, 32 (1974): 27–131.

Vogt 1935: A. Vogt (ed.), *Le livre des cérémonies*, vols. 1–2, Paris: Les Belles Lettres, 1935–9 (repr. 1967).

SECONDARY SOURCES

ARV² = Beazley, J.D. (1963), *Attic Red-Figure Vase-Painters*, 2nd edition, Oxford: Clarendon Press.

BAPD = Beazley Archive Pottery Database, online (https://www.beazley.ox.ac.uk/carc/pottery)

LIMC = *Lexicon Iconographicum Mythologiae Classicae* (1981–2009), Zurich: Artemis.

Σίνδος. Κατάλογος της έκθεσης (1985), Thessaloniki: Archaeological Receipts Fund (TAP).

Acton, Peter Hampden (2014), *Poiesis: Manufacturing in Classical Athens*, Oxford: Oxford University Press.

Adriani, Achille (1936), *La Nécropole de Moustafa Pacha. Annuaire du Musée gréco-romain (1933–34 et 1934–35)*, Alexandria: Whitehead Morris.

Ahlberg, Gudrun (1971), *Prothesis and Ekphora in Greek Geometric Art*, Studies in Mediterranean Archaeology 32, Gothenburg: Paul Åströms Förlag.

Ajootian, Aileen (2000), "A Roman Table Support at Ancient Corinth," *Hesperia*, 69: 487–507.

Akamatis, Ioannis M. (2011), "Pella," in Robin J. Lane Fox (ed.), *Brill's Companion to Ancient Macedon, Studies in the Archaeology and History of Macedon, 650 BC–300 AD*, 393–408, Leiden: Brill.

Åkerström-Hougen, Gunilla (1974), *The Calendar and Hunting Mosaics of the Villa of the Falconer in Argos: A Study in Early Byzantine Iconography*, Acta Instituti Atheniensis Regni Sueciae XXIII, Stockholm: Paul Åströms Förlag.

Albertz, Rainer and Rüdiger Schmitt (2012), *Family and Household Religion in Ancient Israel and the Levant*, Winona Lake, IN: Eisenbrauns.

Aldred, Cyril (1954), "Fine Wood-Work," in Charles Singer, E.J. Holmyard, and A.R. Hall (eds.), *A History of Technology*, vol. 1, *From Early Times to the Fall of Ancient Empires*, 684–703, Oxford: Clarendon Press.

Al-Gailani Werr, Lamia (1996), "Domestic Furniture in Iraq, Ancient and Traditional," in Georgina Herrmann (ed.), *The Furniture of Western Asia: Ancient and Traditional: Papers of the Conference Held at the Institute of Archaeology, University College London, June 28 to 30, 1993*, 29–32, Mainz: Philipp von Zabern.

Allison, Penelope M. (1992), "The Distribution of Pompeian House Contents and its Significance," Ph.D. thesis, University of Sydney.

Allison, Penelope, ed. (1999), *The Archaeology of Household Activities*, London: Routledge.

Allison, Penelope M. (2001), "Using the Material and Written Sources: Turn of the Millennium Approaches to Roman Domestic Space," *American Journal of Archaeology*, 105 (2): 181–208.

Allison, Penelope M. (2006), "Engendering Roman Spaces," in Elizabeth C. Robertson,
    Jeffrey D. Seibert, Deepika C. Fernandez, and Marc U. Zender (eds.), *Space and Spatial
    Analysis in Archaeology*, 343–54, Albuquerque: University of New Mexico Press.
Amandry, Pierre (1986), "Sièges mycéniens tripodes et trépied pythique," in *Φίλια Έπη
    εις Γεώργιον Ε. Μυλωνάν*, vol. 1, Βιβλιοθήκη της Εν Αθήναις Αρχαιολογικής Εταιρείας
    103, 167–84, Athens: The Archaeological Society at Athens.
Amedick, Rita (1991), *Die Sarkophage mit Darstellungen aus dem Menschenleben*,
    Berlin: Gebr. Mann Verlag.
Amyx, D.A. (1958), "The Attic Stelai, Part III," *Hesperia*, 27: 163–310.
Andrianou, Dimitra (2006), "Late Classical and Hellenistic Furniture and Furnishings:
    The Epigraphic Evidence," *Hesperia*, 75: 561–84.
Andrianou, Dimitra (2009), *The Furniture and Furnishings of Ancient Greek Houses
    and Tombs*, New York: Cambridge University Press.
Andrianou, Dimitra (2010), "Κλίναι σφιγγόποδες, *lecti Deliaca specie and cenae
    Serapiacae*: Material and Epigraphic Evidence for Hellenistic Bed-Couches on
    Delos," in Sabine Ladstätter and Veronika Scheibelreiter (eds.), *Städtisches Wohnen
    im östlichen Mittelmeerraum 4. Jh. v.Chr.- 1. Jh. n. Chr.*, 595–604, Vienna:
    Academy of Sciences Press.
Andrianou, Dimitra (2012), "Eternal Comfort: Funerary Textiles in Late Classical and
    Hellenistic Greece," in Maureen Carroll and John Peter Wild (eds.), *Dressing the
    Dead in Classical Antiquity*, 42–61, Stroud, UK: Amberley.
Andrianou, Dimitra (2017), *Memories in Stone: Figured Grave Reliefs from Aegean
    Thrace*, Meletemata 75, Athens: National Hellenic Research Foundation.
Andrianou, Dimitra (2021), "Furniture Textiles in Classical and Hellenistic
    Iconography," in Susanna Harris, Cecilie Brøns, and Marta Zuchowska (eds.),
    Textiles in Ancient Mediterranean Iconography, 91–105, Oxford: Oxbow Books.
Andronikos, Manolis (1984), *Vergina: The Royal Tombs and the Ancient City*, Athens:
    Ekdotike Athenon.
Angar, Mabi (2015), "Furniture and Imperial Ceremony in the Great Palace: Revisiting
    the Pentapyrgion," in Michael Featherstone, Jean-Michel Spieser, Gülru Tanman,
    and Ulrike Wulf-Rheidt (eds.), *The Emperor's House: Palaces from Augustus to the
    Age of Absolutism*, 181–200, Berlin: de Gruyter.
Anguissola, Anna (2010), *Intimità a Pompei: Riservatezza, condivisione e prestigio negli
    ambienti ad alcova di Pompei*, Berlin: de Gruyter.
Arvanitaki, Anna (2006), *Ήρωας και πόλη. Το παράδειγμα του Ηρακλή στην αρχαϊκή
    εικονογραφία της Κορίνθου*, Thessaloniki: University Studio Press.
Arvanitopoulos, Apostolos S. (1928), *Γραπταί Στήλαι. Δημητριάδος– Παγασών*, Athens:
    The Archaeological Society at Athens.
Asouti, E. (2003), "Wood Charcoal from Santorini (Thera): New Evidence for Climate,
    Vegetation and Timber Imports in the Aegean Bronze Age," *Antiquity*, 77: 471–84.
Assante, Julia (2002), "Style and Replication in 'Old Babylonian' Terracotta Plaques:
    Strategies for Entrapping the Power of Images," in Oswald Loretz, Alexander
    Metzler, and Hanspeter Schaudig (eds.), *Ex Mesopotamia et Syria Lux: Festschrift
    für Manfried Dietrich zu seinem 65, Geburtstag*, 1–29, Münster: Ugarit-Verlag.
Aufleger, Michaela (1996), "Holzarbeiten und Holzbearbeitung," in Alfried Wieczorek,
    Patrik Périn, Karin Von Welck, and Wilfried Menghin (eds.), *Die Franken:
    Wegbereiter Europas (6.-8. Jahrhundert): Vor 1500 Jahren: König Chlodwig und
    seine Erben*, Katalog-Handbuch, 599–604, Mainz: von Zabern.
Ault, Bradley (1994), "Classical Houses and Households: An Architectural and
    Artifactual Case Study from Halieis, Greece," Ph.D. dissertation, Indiana University.

Ayalon, Etan (2005), *The Assemblage of Bone and Ivory Artifacts from Caesarea Maritima, Israel, 1st–13th Centuries CE*, BAR International series 1457, Oxford: Archaeopress.

Azéma, Yvan (1955), *Théodoret de Cyr. Correspondance I*, Introduction, texte critique, traduction et notes, Sources chrétiennes 40, Paris: Éditions du Cerf.

Bailey, Douglass W. (2005), *Prehistoric Figurines: Representation and Corporeality in the Neolithic*, London: Routledge.

Baker, Hollis S. (1966), *Furniture in the Ancient World: Origins and Evolution 3100–475 B.C.*, London: The Connoisseur.

Baldini Lippolis, Isabelle (1999), *L'oreficeria nell'impero di Costantinopoli tra IV. e VII. Secolo*, Bibliotheca archaeologica 7, Bari: Edipuglia.

Baldini, Isabella and Salvatore Cosentino (2021), "Rituali di corte. Il Triclinio dei XIX Letti del Grande Palazzo di Costantinopoli," *Byzantinische Zeitschrift*, 114: 65–110.

Baldwin Smith, E. (1917), "The Alexandrian Origin of the Chair of Maximianus," *American Journal of Archaeology*, 21 (1): 22–37.

Balty, Jean Charles (1984), "Notes sur l'habitat romain, byzantin et arabe d'Apamée. Rapport de synthèse," in Jean C. Balty (ed.), *Apamée de Syrie. Bilan des recherches archéologiques 1973–1979. Actes du 3e Colloque tenu à Bruxelles du 29 au 30 mai 1980: aspects de l'architecture domestique d'Apamée*, 471–501, Brussels: Centre belge de recherches archéologiques à Apamée de Syrie.

Balza, Maria Elena and Clelia Mora (2011), "'And I built this everlasting peak for him': The Two Scribal Traditions of the Hittites and the ᴺᴬ4ḫekur SAG.UŠ," *Altorientalische Forschungen*, 38: 213–25.

Bardet, Guillame, Francis Joannès, Bertrand Lafont, Denis Soubeyran, and Pierre Villard (1984), *Archives Royales de Mari XXIII*, Archives administratives de Mari 1, Paris: éditions Recherche sur les Civilisations.

Barr-Sharrar, Beryl (1985), "The Antikythera Fulcrum Bust: A Portrait of Arsinoe III," *American Journal of Archaeology*, 89: 689–92.

Barr-Sharrar, Beryl (1987), *The Hellenistic and Early Imperial Decorative Bust*, Mainz: Philipp von Zabern.

Barr-Sharrar, Beryl (1988), "The Bronze Fulcrum Attachment: Some Clarifications in the Chronology of Solutions to this Problematic Format," in Kurt Gschwantler and Alfred Bernhard-Walcher (eds.), *Griechische und römische Statuetten und Großbronzen: Akten der 9. Internationalen Tagung über Antike Bronzen, Wien 21.–25. April 1986*, 279–84, Vienna: Historisches Museum.

Barr-Sharrar, Beryl (1994), "The Bronze Appliques," in Gisela Hellenkemper Salies, Hans-Hoyer Von Prittwitz, and Gerhard Bauchhenß Gaffron (eds.), *Das Wrack: Der antike Schiffsund von Mahdia*, 559–72, Cologne: Rheinland Verlag.

Bartoloni, Gilda, ed. (2000), *Principi etruschi tra Mediterraneo ed Europa*, Bologna: Marsilio.

Batiffol, Pierre (1911), ""Les présents de saint Cyrille à la cour de Constantinople," *Bulletin d'ancienne littérature et d'archéologie chrétiennes*, 1: 247–64.

Baughan, Elizabeth (2013), *Couched in Death: Klinai and Identity in Anatolia and Beyond*, Madison: University of Wisconsin Press.

Bentini, Laura and Tullia Moretto (2002), "Arredi," in Patrizia von Eles (ed.), *Guerriero e sacerdote: Autorità e comunità nell'età del ferro a Verucchio. La Tomba del Trono*, 74–82, Florence: All'Insegna del Giglio.

Berger, Albrecht (2013), *Accounts of Medieval Constantinople: The Patria*, Dumbarton Oaks Medieval Library 24, Cambridge, MA: Harvard University Press.

Bethe, Erich (1967), *Pollucis onomasticon*, 2nd edn., 2 vols., Lexicographi Graeci 9.1–9.2, Stuttgart: Teubner.

Blanck, Horst and Giuseppe Proietti (1986), *La Tomba dei Rilievi di Cerveteri*, Rome: De Luca.

Blegen, Carl W. and Marion Rawson (1966), *The Palace of Nestor at Pylos in Western Messenia I: The Buildings and Their Contents*, Princeton, NJ: Princeton University Press.

Blondé, F., S. Dadaki, A. Muller, P. Pétridis, and G. Sanidas (2014), "Les abords Nord de l'Artemision (THANAR). Campagnes 2012–2013. Collaboration XVIIIe EPKA–12e EBA–EFA," *Bulletin de Correspondance Hellénique*, 138 (2): 613–61.

Boardman, John (1990), "Symposium Furniture," in Oswyn Murray (ed.), *Sympotica: A Symposium on the* Symposion, 122–31, Oxford: Oxford University Press.

Bonfante, Larissa (2005), "The Verucchio Throne and the Corsini Chair: Two Status Symbols of Ancient Italy," in John Pollini (ed.), *Terra Marique: Studies in Art History and Marine Archaeology in Honor of Anna Marguerite McCann*, 3–11, Oxford: Oxbow Books.

Bonini, Paolo (2006), *La Casa nella Grecia Romana. Forme et funzioni dello spazio private fra I e VI secolo*, Rome: Edizioni Quasar.

Bookidis Nancy and Joan E. Fisher (1972), "The Sanctuary of Demeter and Kore on Acrocorinth Preliminary Report IV: 1969–1970," *Hesperia*, 41: 283–331.

Bovini, Giuseppe (1970), *Edifici di culto d'età teodoriciana e giustinianea a Ravenna*, Bologna: Patron.

Breasted, James Henry (1906), *Ancient Records of Egypt*, vol. 1, Chicago: University of Chicago Press.

Breckenridge, James D. (1979), "Diptych Leaf with Justinian as Defender of the Faith," in Kurt Weitzmann (ed.), *Age of Spirituality: Late Antique and Early Christian Art, Third to Seventh Century, Catalogue of the exhibition at The Metropolitan Museum of Art, November 19, 1977 through February 12, 1978*, 33–5, New York: The Metropolitan Museum of Art; Princeton, NJ: Princeton University Press.

Brett, Gerard (1954), "The Automata in the Byzantine 'Throne of Salomon'," *Speculum*, 29: 477–87.

Briguet, Marie-Françoise and Dominique Briquel (2002), *Musée du Louvre: Département des antiquités grecques, étrusques et romaines. Les urnes cinéraires étrusques de l'époque hellénistique*, Paris: Réunion des Musées Nationaux.

British Museum (n.d.-a), "Cylinder Seal." Available online: https://www.britishmuseum.org/collection/object/W_1880-1009-1 (accessed April 17, 2021).

British Museum (n.d.-b), "Wall Panel; Relief." Available online: https://www.britishmuseum.org/collection/object/W_1850-1228-9 (accessed April 17, 2021).

British Museum (n.d.-c), "Wall Panel; Relief." Available online: https://www.britishmuseum.org/collection/object/W_1856-0909-53 (accessed April 17, 2021).

Brown, Peter (1992), *Power and Persuasion in Late Antiquity: Towards a Christian Empire*, Madison: University of Wisconsin Press.

Bruit, Louise (1990), "The Meals at the Hyakinthia," in Oswyn Murray (ed.), *Sympotica: A Symposium on the Symposium*, 162–74, Oxford: Clarendon Press.

Brümmer, Elfriede (1985), "Griechische Truhenbehälter," *Jahrbuch des Deutschen Archäologischen Instituts*, 100: 1–168.

Bruyne, Pieter de (1982), *Vorm en geometrie in de Oud-Egyptische meubelkunst: van 19 Juni tot 26 September 1982*, Gent: Museum voor Sierkunst, Stadsbestuur van Gent.

Bryce, Trevor (2002), *Life and Society in the Hittite World*, Oxford: Oxford University Press.

Burnyeat, M.F. (1999), "Culture and Society in Plato's Republic," *Tanner Lectures on Human Values*, 20: 215–324.

Cadogan, Gerald (1976), *Palaces of Minoan Crete*, London: Barrie and Jenkins.

Cahill, Nicholas D. (1991), "Olynthus: Social and Spatial Planning in a Greek City," Ph.D. dissertation, University of California, Berkeley.

Cahill, Nicholas D. (2002), *Household and City Organization at Olynthus*, New Haven, CT: Yale University Press.

Cailliaud, Frédéric (1831), *Recherches sur les arts et métiers, les usages de la vie civile et domestique des anciens peuples de l'Egypte, de la Nubie et de l'Ethiopie*, Paris: Lebure.

Calabi Limentani, I. (1960), "Eborarius," in *Enciclopedia dell'arte antica, classica e orientale*, vol. 3, 203, Rome.

Calmeyer, Peter (1996), "Achämenidische Möbel," in Georgina Herrmann (ed.), *The Furniture of Western Asia: Ancient and Traditional: Papers of the Conference Held at the Institute of Archaeology, University College London, June 28 to 30, 1993*, 223–31, Mainz: Philipp von Zabern.

Camp, John M., II (1986), *The Athenian Agora: Excavations in the Heart of Classical Athens*, London: Thames and Hudson.

Camp, John M., II. (1990), *The Athenian Agora: A Guide to the Excavations and Museum*, Athens: American School of Classical Studies at Athens.

Camporeale, G. (2011), *Gli Etruschi: Storia e Civiltà*, 3rd edn., Milan: UTET.

Canavas, Constantin (2003), "Automaten in Byzanz. Der Thron von Magnaura," in Klaus Grubmüller and Markus Stock (eds.), *Automaten in Kunst und Literatur des Mittelalters und der Frühen Neuzeit*, 49–72, Wiesbaden: Harrassowitz.

Canciani, Fulvio and Friedrich-Wilhelm von Hase (1979), *La Tomba Bernardini di Palestrina*, Rome: Consiglio Nazionale delle Ricerche.

Caracuta, Valentina and Girolamo Fiorentino (2013), "Forests Near and Far: An Anthracological Perspective on Ebla," in Paolo Matthiae and Nicolo Marchetti (eds.), *Ebla and its Landscape: Early State Formation in the Ancient Near East*, 403–12, Walnut Creek, CA: Left Coast Press.

Carrión, Yolanda and Pablo Rosser (2010), "Revealing Iberian Woodcraft: Conserved Wooden Artefacts from South-East Spain," *Antiquity*, 84: 747–64.

Cartwright, Caroline (2005), "The Bronze Age Wooden Tomb Furniture from Jericho: The Microscopical Reconstruction of a Distinctive Carpentry Tradition," *Palestine Exploration Quarterly*, 137(2): 99–138.

Caseau, Béatrice (2007a), "Objects in Churches: The Testimony of Inventories," in Luke Lavan, Ellen Swift, and Toon Putzeys (eds.), *Objects in Context, Objects in Use: Material Spatiality in Late Antiquity*, Late Antique Archaeology 5, 551–79, Leiden: Brill.

Caseau, Béatrice (2007b), "Ordinary Objects in Christian Healing Sanctuaries," in Luke Lavan, Ellen Swift, and Toon Putzeys (eds.), *Objects in Context, Objects in Use: Material Spatiality in Late Antiquity*, Late Antique Archaeology 5, 625–54, Leiden: Brill.

Çatalhöyük Research Project (n.d.). Available online: http://www.catalhoyuk.com/ (accessed December 4, 2021).

Cavanagh, William G. and Christopher Mee (1995), "Mourning Before and After the Dark Age," in Christine Morris (ed.), *Klados: Essays in Honour of J.N. Coldstream*, BICS Supplement 63, 45–61, London.

Čerškov, Toni, Gordana Jeremić and Selena Vitezović (2016), "Zoomorphic decorations from osseous materials from Naissus (Niš)," in Selena Vitezović (ed.), *Close to the Bone: Current Studies in Bone Technology*, 104–11, Belgrade: Institute of Archaeology.

Cerveteri (2013) = *Gli Etruschi e il Mediterraneo: La città di Cerveteri*, Paris: Somogy éditions d'art.

Chalkia, Eugenia (1991), *Le mense paleocristiane: Tipologia e funzioni delle mense secondarie nel culto paleocristiano*, Studi di antichità cristiana, Vatican City: Pontificio Istituto di Archeologia Cristiana.

Chatzidimitriou, Athina (2005), *Παραστάσεις εργαστηρίων και εμπορίου στην εικονογραφία των αρχαϊκών και κλασικών χρόνων*, Athens: Archaeological Receipts Fund (TAP).

Chatzidimitriou, Athina (2012), "Σκηνή διδασκαλίας σε αττικό ερυθρόμορφο αρύβαλλο," in Polyxeni Adam-Veleni and Katerina Tzanavari (eds.), *Δινήεσσα: Τιμητικός τόμος για την Κατερίνα Ρωμιοπούλου*, 277–88, Thessaloniki: Editions ZITI.

Cholakov, Ivo Dinchev (2010), *Roman and Early Byzantine Metal Tools on the Territory of Bulgaria (the 1st–the Beginning of the 7th Century)*, Sofia: Nous Publishers [in Bulgarian].

Cholidis, Nadja (1992), *Möbel in Ton: Untersuchungen zur archäologischen und religionsgeschichtlichen Bedeutung der Terrakottamodelle von Tischen, Stühlen und Betten aus dem Alten Orient*, Altertumskunde des Vorderen Orients 1, Münster: Ugarit Verlag

Christopoulos, M. (1990), "Κιβωτός: Une approche. L'idée de l'arche dans la mythologie hellénique," in Harry E. Tzalas (ed.), *Proceedings of the 2nd International Symposium on Ship Construction in Antiquity, Delphi, August 27–29, 1987*, 101–10, Athens: Hellenic Institute for the Preservation for Nautical Tradition.

Chrysostomou, Pavlos (2011), "The Palace at Pella," in Maria Lilimbaki-Akamati, Ioannis Akamatis, Anastasia Chrysostomou, and Pavlos Chrysostomou (eds.), *The Archaeological Museum of Pella*, 58–65, Athens: John S. Latsis Public Benefit Foundation.

Claridge, Amanda (2015), "Marble Carving Techniques, Workshops, and Artisans," in Elise A. Friedland, Melanie Grunow Sobocinski, and Elaine K. Gazda (eds.), *The Oxford Handbook of Roman Sculpture*, 107–15, New York: Oxford University Press.

Clarke, D.V. and N. Sharples (1990), "Settlement and Subsistence in the Third Millennium BC," in Colin Renfrew (ed.), *The Prehistory of Orkney*, 54–82, Edinburgh: Edinburgh University Press.

Claude, Dieter (1981), "Die Handwerker der Merowingerzeit nach erzählenden und urkundlichen Quellen," in Herbert Jankuhn, Walter Janssen, Ruth Schmidt-Wiegand and Heinrich Tiefenbach (eds.), *Das Handwerk in vor–und frühgeschichtlicher Zeit. Teil I: Historische und rechtshistorische Beiträge und Untersuchungen zur Frühgeschichte der Gilde*, Abhandlungen der Akademie der Wissenschaften in Göttingen III 122, 204–65, Göttingen: Vandenhoeck & Ruprecht.

Cline, Eric H. (2014), *1177 B.C.: The Year Civilization Collapsed: Turning Points in the Ancient World*, Princeton, NJ: Princeton University Press.

Corsten, Thomas (1991), *Die Inschriften von Prousa ad Olympum*, 2 vols., Bonn: R. Habelt.

Cova, Elisabetta (2013), "Cupboards, Closets and Shelves: Storage in the Pompeian House," *Phoenix*, 67 (3/4): 373–91.

Cranz, Galen (1998), *The Chair: Rethinking Culture, Body and Design*, New York: W.W. Norton and Co.

Cranz, Galen (2000), "The Alexander Technique in the World of Design: Posture and the Common Chair, Part I: The Chair as Health Hazard," *Journal of Bodywork and Movement Therapies*, 4 (2): 90–8.

Crawford, Harriet (1996), "The Earliest Evidence from Mesopotamia," in Georgina Herrmann (ed.), *The Furniture of Western Asia: Ancient and Traditional: Papers of the Conference Held at the Institute of Archaeology, University College London, June 28 to 30, 1993*, 33–9, Mainz: Philipp von Zabern.

Crawford, J. Stephens, et al. (1990), *The Byzantine Shops at Sardis*, Sardis Monographs 9, Cambridge, MA: Harvard University Press.

Croom, Alexandra T. (2007), *Roman Furniture*, Stroud, UK: Tempus Publishing.

Curtis, John (1996), "Assyrian Furniture: The Archaeological Evidence," in Georgina Herrmann (ed.), *The Furniture of Western Asia: Ancient and Traditional: Papers of the Conference Held at the Institute of Archaeology, University College London, June 28 to 30, 1993*, 167–80, Mainz: Philipp von Zabern.

Cutler, Anthony (1993), "Five Lessons in Late Roman Ivory," *Journal of Roman Archaeology*, 6: 167–92 (=Anthony Cutler, *Late Antique and Byzantine Ivory Carving*, Aldershot, UK: Ashgate Variorum, 1998, vol. 2, pp. 1–23).

Cutler, Anthony (1994), *The Hand of the Master: Craftsmanship, Ivory, and Society in Byzantium*, Princeton, NJ: Princeton University Press.

Dagron, Gilbert (2003), "*Trônes* pour un empereur," in Anna Avramea et al. (ed.), Βυζάντιο κράτος και κοινωνία: Μνήμη Ν. Οικονομίδη [Byzantium: State and Society, in Memory of Nikos Oikonomides], 179–204, Athens: National Hellenic Research Foundation.

Dagron, Gilbert (2005), "Architecture d'intérieur: le Pentapyrgion," *Travaux et Mémoires*, 15: 109–17.

Dauterman Maguire, Eunice, Henry P. Maguire, and Maggie Duncan Flowers (1989), *Art and Holy Powers in the Early Chistian House*, Urbana: Krannert Art Museum, University of Illinois at Urbana–Champaign.

David, Rosalie A. (1997), *The Pyramid Builders of Ancient Egypt: A Modern Investigation of Pharaoh's Workforce*, London: Routledge.

Davies, W. Vivian (1995), "Ancient Egyptian Timber Imports: Analysis of Wooden Coffins in the British Museum," in W. Vivian Davies and Louise Schofield (eds.), *Egypt, Aegean and the Levant: Interconnections in the Second Millennium BC*, 146–56, London: British Museum Publications.

De Carolis, Ernesto (2007), *Il mobile a Pompei ed Ercolano: Lette, tavoli, sede e armadi: Contributo alla tipologia dei mobili della prima eta imperiale*, Rome: "L'Erma" di Bretschneider.

Decker, Michael (2008), "Everyday Technologies," in Elizabeth Jeffreys, John Haldon, and Robin Cormack (eds.), *The Oxford Handbook of Byzantine Studies*, 492–502, Oxford: Oxford University Press.

De Cupere, B., W. Van Neer, and A. Lentacker (1993), "Some Aspects of the Bone-Working Industry in Roman Sagalassos," in Marc Waelkens and Jeroen Poblome (eds.), *Sagalassos II*, Acta Archaeologica Lovaniensia Monographiae 6, 269–87, Leuven: Leuven University Press.

De Grummond, Nancy (1986), "Rediscovery," in Larissa Bonfante (ed.), *Etruscan Life and Afterlife*, 18–46, Detroit, MI: Wayne State University Press.

De Grummond, Nancy (1996), "Etruscan Italy Today," in John Franklin Hall (ed.), *Etruscan Italy*, 149–89, Provo, UT: Brigham Young University.

Delemen, Inci (2006), "An Unplundered Chamber Tomb on Ganos Mountain in Southeastern Thrace," *American Journal of Archaeology*, 110: 251–73.

De Morgan, Jacques Jean Marie (1897), *Tombeau Royal de Négadah*, Paris: E. Leroux.

Dennis, George (1985), *Three Byzantine Military Treatises*, Corpus Fontium Historiae Byzantinae 25, Washington, DC: Dumbarton Oaks Research Library and Collection.

Déonna, Waldemar (1938), *Exploration archéologique de Délos*, vol. 18, *Le mobilier Délien*, Paris: de Boccard.

Déroche, Vincent, Platon Pétridis, and Alain Badie (1995), "Villa Sud-Est: Travaux de l'École française d'Athènes en Grèce en 1994," *BCH*, 119: 649–50.

Déroche, Vincent, Platon Pétridis, and Alain Badie (2014), *Le Secteur au Sud-Est du Péribole*, Fouilles de Delphes II. Topographie et Architecture 15, Paris-Athènes: De Boccard- École française d'Athènes.

Despoini, Aikaterini (2016), *Σίνδος. Το νεκροταφείο. Ανασκαφικές έρευνες 1980–1982*, vols. 1–3, Athens: The Archaeological Society at Athens.

Dietz, Søren and Ioannis Papachristodoulou (1988), *Archaeology in the Dodecanese*, Copenhagen: National Museum of Denmark.

Dinkler, Erich (1979), "Abbreviated Representations," in Kurt Weitzmann (ed.), *Age of Spirituality: Late Antique and Early Christian Art, Third to Seventh Century, Catalogue of the exhibition at The Metropolitan Museum of Art, November 19, 1977 through February 12, 1978*, 396–403, New York: The Metropolitan Museum of Art; Princeton, NJ: Princeton University Press.

Dittemore, Margaret R. (1983), "Zemzemiye: An Ethnoarchaeological Study of a Turkish Village," Ph.D. dissertation, University of Chicago.

Docter, Roald F. (2002–3), "The Topography of Archaic Carthage. Preliminary Results of Recent Excavations and some Prospects," *Talanta*, 34–5: 113–33.

Doumas, Christos G. (1983), *Thera: Pompeii of the Ancient Aegean*, London: Thames & Hudson.

Doumas, Christos G. (1993), "Ἀνασκαφὴ Ἀκρωτηρίου Θήρας," *Praktika tes en Athenais Archaiologikes Etaireias*: 164–87.

Doumas, Christos G. (1994), "Ἀνασκαφὴ Ἀκρωτηρίου Θήρας," *Praktika tes en Athenais Archaiologikes Etaireias*: 155–66.

Doumas, Christos G. (1999), "Ἀνασκαφὴ Ἀκρωτηρίου Θήρας," *Praktika tes en Athenais Archaiologikes Etaireias*: 155–202.

Doumas, Christos G. (2000), "Ἀνασκαφὴ Ἀκρωτηρίου Θήρας," *Praktika tes en Athenais Archaiologikes Etaireias*: 169–72.

Downey, Glanville and Henricus Schenkl (1965), *Themistii orationes quae supersunt*, vol. 1, Leipzig: Teubner.

Drescher, J. (1944), "A Widow's Petition. With Two Plates," *Bulletin de la Société d'Archéologie Copte*, 10: 91–6.

Drougou, Stella (2018), "The Gold-Threaded Textile of Vergina-Aigai," in Taner Korkut and Britta Özen-Kleine (eds.), *Festschrift für Heide Froning*, 81–92, Istanbul: E. Yayınları.

Dunbabin, Katherine M.D. (1998), "Ut Graeco more biberatur: Greeks and Romans on the Dining Couch," in Inge Nielsen and Hanne Sigismund Nielsen (eds.), *Meals in a Social Context: Aspects of the Communal Meal in the Hellenistic and Roman World*, 81–101, Aarhus: Aarhus University Press.

Dunbabin, Katherine M.D. (2003), *The Roman Banquet: Images of Conviviality*, Cambridge: Cambridge University Press.

Eaton–Krauss, Marianne (2008), *The Thrones, Chairs, Stools, and Footstools from the Tomb of Tutankhamun*, Oxford: Griffith Institute.

Egberts, Arno (2001), "Wenamun," in Donald B. Redford (ed.), *The Oxford Encyclopedia of Ancient Egypt*, vol. 3, 495–6, Oxford: Oxford University Press.

Ellis, Simon P. (1997), "Late-Antique Dining: Architecture, Furnishings and Behaviour," in Ray Laurence and Andrew Wallace-Hadrill (eds.), *Domestic Space in the Roman World: Pompeii and Beyond*, JRA Supplementary Series 22, 41–51, Portsmouth, RI: Journal of Roman Archaeology.

Emery, Walter B. (1949), *Great Tombs of the First Dynasty*, vol. 1, Cairo: Government Press.

Emiliozzi, Adriana (2013),"Princely Chariots and Carts," in Jean M. Turfa (ed.), *The Etruscan World*, 778–97, London: Routledge.

Étienne, Roland (1990), *Ténos et les Cyclades du milieu du IVe siècle av. J.-C. au milieu du IIIe siècle ap. J.-C.*, Athens: École Française d' Athènes.

Evans, Arthur J. (1935), *The Palace of Minos*, vol. 4, pt. 2, London: Macmillan and Co.

Evely, R. Doniert G. (1993–2000), *Minoan Crafts, Tools and Techniques: An Introduction*, Studies in Mediterranean Archaeology 92, vols. 1–2, Gothenberg: P. Åström.

Fabricius, Johanna (1999), *Die hellenistischen Totenmahlreliefs: Grabrepräsentation und Wertvorstellungen in ostgriechischen Städten*, Munich: Pfeil.

Faust, Sabine (1994), "Die Klinen," in Gisela Hellenkemper Salies, Hans-Hoyer von Prittzwitz, and Gerhard Bauchhenß Gaffron (eds.), *Das Wrack: Der antike Schiffsfund von Mahdia*, 573–606, Cologne: Rheinland Verlag.

Faust, Sabine (1989), *Fulcra: figürliche und ornamentaler Schmuck an antiken Betten*, Mainz: Philipp von Zabern.

Feissel, Denis (2006), *Chroniques d'épigraphie byzantine 1987–2004*, Centre de Recherche d'Histoire et Civilisation de Byzance, Monographies 20, Paris: Association des Amis du Centre d'Histoire et Civilisation de Byzance.

Feldman, Marian H. (2006), *Diplomacy By Design: Luxury Arts and an "International Style" in the Ancient Near East, 1400–1200 BCE*, Chicago: University of Chicago Press.

Feldman, Marian H. (2009), "Hoarded Treasures: The Megiddo Ivories and the End of the Bronze Age," *Levant*, 41 (2): 175–94.

Feuser, Stefan (2013), *Monopodia: Figürliche Tischfüße aus Kleinasien*, Istanbul: Ege Yayınları.

Filow, Bogdan Dimitrov (1934), *Die Grabhügelnekropole bei Duvanlij in Südbulgarien*, Sofia: Bulgarian Archaeological Institute.

Finley, Moses I. (1952), *Studies in Land and Credit in Ancient Athens, 500–200 BC: The Horos Inscriptions*, New Brunswick, NJ: Rutgers University Press.

Frantz, Alison (1988), *Late Antiquity 267–700*, The Athenian Agora 24, Princeton, NJ: American School of Classical Studies.

French, Valerie (1987), "Midwives and Maternity Care in the Roman World," *Helios*, 13: 69–84.

Fuchs, Werner (1963), *Der Schiffsfund von Mahdia*, Tübingen: W. Wasmuth.

Furtwängler, Adolf (1881), "Marmore von der Akropolis," *Mitteilungen des Deutschen Archäologischen Instituts, Athenische Abteilung*, 6: 174–90.

Gadolou, Anastasia (2011), "A Late Geometric Architectural Model with Figure Decoration from Ancient Helike, Achaea," *Annual of the British School at Athens*, 106: 247–73.

Gale, Rowena, Peter Gasson, Nigel Hepper, and Geoffrey Killen (2000), "Wood," in Paul T. Nicholson and Ian Shaw (eds.), *Ancient Egyptian Materials and Technology*, 334–71, Cambridge: Cambridge University Press.

Galestin, Marjan C. (2001), "The Simpelveld Sarcophagus: A Unique Monument in a Provincial Roman Context," in Titus A.S.M. Panhuysen (ed.), *Die Maastrichter Akten des 5. Internationalen Kolloquiums über das provinzialrömische Kunstschaffen im Rahmen des CSIR*, 63–76, Maastricht: Goossens.

Galinsky, Karl (1996), *Augustan Culture: An Interpretive Introduction*, Princeton, NJ: Princeton University Press.

Gaultier, Françoise (2013), "La scultura funeraria in età arcaica," in *Cerveteri* 2013: 185–9.

Gerontas, A. (2004), "Αποκάλυψη και συντήρηση κρεβατιών στο Ακρωτήρι Θήρας/ Exposure and Conservation of Beds at Akrotiri, Thera," *ΑΛΣ*, 4: 39–52 [in English, pp. 47–52].

Ginouvès, René and Roland Martin (1985), *Dictionnaire méthodique de l'architecture grecque et romaine*, vol. 1, *Matériaux, techniques de construction, techniques et formes du décor*, Publications de l'École française de Rome 84, Rome: École Française de Rome.

Giouni, Maria (1991), "Ὠναί Μακεδονίας I," *Αρμενόπουλος, Επιστημονική Επετηρίδα Δικηγορικού Συλλόγου Θεσσαλονίκης*, 12: 25–50.

Glare, P.G.W., ed. (1982), *Oxford Latin Dictionary*, Oxford: Clarendon Press.

Goldberg, Marilyn Y. (1999), "Spatial and Behavioural Negotiation in Classical Athenian City Houses," in Penelope Allison (ed.), *The Archaeology of Household Activities*, 142–61, London: Routledge.

Goldfus, Haim and Kim Bowes (2000), "New Late Roman Bone Carvings from Halusa and the Problem of Regional Bone Carving Workshops in Palestine," *Israel Exploration Journal*, 50: 185–202.

Goodman, William Louis (1964), *The History of Woodworking Tools*, Baltimore: Johns Hopkins University Press and the Society for the History of Technology; London: G. Bell and Sons.

Goudineau, Christian (1967), "Ἱεραῖ Τράπεζαι," *Mélanges d'archéologie et d'histoire de l'École Française de Rome, Antiquité (MEFRA)*, 79: 77–134.

Grayson, Kirk A. and Jamie Novotny (2014), *The Royal Inscriptions of Sennacherib, King of Assyria (704–681 BC), Part 2, The Royal Inscriptions of the Neo-Assyrian Period*, vol. 3/2, Winona Lake, IN: Eisenbrauns.

Grosdidier de Matons, José (1979a), "Notes sur le sens médiéval du mot κλίνη," *Travaux et mémoires*, 7: 363–73.

Grosdidier de Matons, José (1979b), "Le sens byzantin de 'kline'," *Revue des études grecques*, 92 (fasc. 438–9): 17–18.

Gruen, Erich (2016), *Constructs of Identity in Hellenistic Judaism*, Berlin: de Gruyter.

Gubel, Eric (1987), *Phoenician Furniture: A Typology Based on Iron Age Representations with Reference to the Iconographical Context*, Leuven: Peeters.

Gubel, Eric (1996), "The Influence of Egypt on Western Asiatic Furniture and Evidence from Phoenicia," in Georgina Herrmann (ed.), *The Furniture of Western Asia: Ancient and Traditional: Papers of the Conference Held at the Institute of Archaeology, University College London, June 28 to 30, 1993*, 139–51, Mainz: Philipp von Zabern.

Guimier-Sorbets, Ann-Marie (2001), "Mobilier et décor des tombes macédoniennes," in Regula Frei-Stolba and Kristine Gex (eds.), *Recherches récentes sur le monde hellénistique, Actes du colloque international organisé à l'occasion du 60ᵉ anniversaire de Pierre Ducrey, Lausanne, November 20–21, 1998*, 217–29, Bern: Peter Lang.

Guimier-Sorbets, Ann-Marie (2002), "Architecture et décors funéraires, de la Grèce à l'Égypte: l'expression du statut héroïque du défunct," in Christel Müller and Francis Prost (eds.), *Identités et cultures dans le monde méditerranéen antique. Études en l'honneur de Francis Croissant (Histoire ancienne et médievale)*, 159–80, Paris: Sorbonne.

Guimier-Sorbets, Ann-Marie and Demetrios Michaelides (2009), "Alexandrian Influences on the Architecture and Decoration of the Hellenistic Tombs of Cyprus," in Demetrios Michaelides, Vassiliki Kassianidou, and Robert S. Merrillees (eds.), *Proceedings of the International Conference Egypt and Cyprus in Antiquity, Nicosia, April 3–6, 2003*, 216–33, Oxford: Oxbow Books.

Guimier-Sorbets, Ann-Marie and Yvette Morizot (2006), "Construite l'identité du mort: l'architecture funéraire en Macédoine," in Ann-Marie Guimier-Sorbets, Miltiade B. Hatzopoulos, and Yvette Morizot (eds.), *Rois, Cités, Nécropoles: Institutions, Rites et Monuments en Macédoine*, Meletemata 45, 117–30, Athens: National Hellenic Research Foundation.

Guimier-Sorbets, Ann-Marie and Marie-Dominique Nenna (2003), "Le lit funéraire dans les nécropoles alexandrines," in Jean-Yves Empereur and Marie-Dominique Nenna (eds.), *Nécropolis 2*, Études alexandrines 7, 533–75, Cairo: Institut Francais d'Archéologie Orientale du Caire.

Haldon, John F. (1990), *Constantine Porphyrogenitus: Three Treatises on Imperial Military Expeditions*, Vienna: Österreichischen Akademie der Wissenschaften.

Hansen, Günther Christian and Joseph Bidez (1960), *Sozomenus, Kirchengeschichte*, Berlin: Akademie-Verlag.

Harrison, Martin R. (1986), *Excavations at Sarachane in Istanbul*, vol. 1, *The Excavations, Structures, Architectural Decoration, Small Finds, Coins, Bones, and Molluscs*, Princeton, NJ: Princeton University Press; Washington, DC: Dumbarton Oaks Research Library and Collection.

Hatzopoulos, Miltiades B. (1988), *Actes de vente de la Chalcidique centrale*, Meletemata 6, Athens: Research Center for Greek and Roman Antiquity; Paris: de Boccard.

Haynes, Sybille (2000), *Etruscan Civilization: A Cultural History*, Los Angeles: Getty Museum.

Heinrich, Ernst (1982), *Die Tempel und Heiligtümer im Alten Mesopotamien: Typologie, Morphologie und Geschichte*, Berlin: de Gruyter.

Hendel, Ronald (1997), "Aniconism and Anthropomorphism in Ancient Israel," in Karel van der Toorn (ed.), *The Image and the Book: Iconic Cults, Aniconism, and the Veneration of the Holy Book in Israel and the Ancient Near East*, 205–28, Leuven: Peeters.

Hennig, Dieter (1987), "Kaufverträge über Häuser und Ländereien aus der Chalkidike und Amphipolis," *Chiron*, 17: 143–69.

Henning, Joachim (2007), "Early European Towns: The Development of the Economy in the Frankish Area between Dynamism and Deceleration AD 500–1100," in Joachim Henning (ed.), *Post-Roman Towns, Trade and Settlement in Europe and Byzantium*, vol. 1, *The Heirs of the Roman West*, Millennium Studien 5/1, 3–40, Berlin: de Gruyter.

Hepper, F. Nigel (2001), "The Cedar of Lebanon in History," *Archaeology and History of Lebanon*, 14: 2–7.

Hepper, Nigel F. (2009), *Pharaoh's Flowers: The Botanical Treasures of Tutankhamun*, 2nd edn., Chicago: KWS Publishers.

Herrmann, Georgina (1996a), "Ivory Furniture Pieces from Nimrud: North Syrian Evidence for a Regional Tradition of Furniture Manufacture," in Georgina

Herrmann (ed.), *The Furniture of Western Asia: Ancient and Traditional: Papers of the Conference Held at the Institute of Archaeology, University College London, June 28 to 30, 1993*, 153–64, Mainz: Philipp von Zabern.

Herrmann, Georgina, ed. (1996b), *The Furniture of Western Asia: Ancient and Traditional: Papers of the Conference Held at the Institute of Archaeology, University College London, June 28 to 30, 1993*, Mainz: Philipp von Zabern.

Herrmann, John, Jr. and Robert H. Tykot (2009), "Some Products from the Dokimeion Quarries: Craters, Tables, Capitals, and Statues," in Yannis Maniatis (ed.), *ASMOSIA VII: Actes du VIIe colloque international de l' ASMOSIA*, Bulletin de Correspondance Hellénique Supplement 51, 59–75, Athens: École française d'Athènes, Éditions De Boccard.

Hill, Dorothy K. (1963), "Ivory Ornaments of Hellenistic Couches," *Hesperia*, 32: 293–300.

Hodder, Ian and Lynn Meskell (2010), "The Symbolism of Çatalhöyük in Its Regional Context," in Ian Hodder (ed.), *Religion in the Emergence of Civilization: Çatalhöyük as a Case Study*, 32–72, Cambridge: Cambridge University Press.

Hodder, Ian (2020), "Twenty-Five Years of Research at Çatalhöyük," *Near Eastern Archaeology* 83.2: 72–9.

Hoepfner, Wolfram, ed. (1999), *Geschichte des Wohnens*, vol. 1, *5000 v.Chr.–500 n.Chr. Vorgeschichte, Frühgeschichte, Antike*, Stuttgart: Deutsche Verlags-Anstalt.

Houston, George W. (2014), *Inside Roman Libraries: Book Collections and Their Management in Antiquity*, Chapel Hill: University of North Carolina.

Huguenot, Caroline (2006), "Les trônes dans les tombes macédoniennes: Réflexions sur les coutumes funéraires de l'élite macédonienne," in Brigitte Boissavit-Camus, François Chausson, and Hervé Inglebert (eds.), *La mort du souverain entre antiquité et haut Moyen Age*, 29–51, Paris: Picard.

Huguenot, Caroline (2008), *Eretria XIX: La tombe aux érotes et la tombe d' Amarynthos, Architecture funéraire et présence macédonienne en Grèce centrale*, Eretria: Fouilles et recherches XIX, Lausanne: Infolio.

Humphreys, Sally C. (1995), "Women's Stories," in Ellen D. Reeder and Sally C. Humphreys (eds.), *Pandora: Women in Classical Greece*, 102–9, Baltimore: Walters Art Gallery; Princeton, NJ: Princeton University Press.

Hurwitt, Jeffrey M. (1999), *The Athenian Acropolis: History, Mythology, and Archaeology from the Neolithic Era to the Present*, Cambridge: Cambridge University Press.

Immerwahr, Sara A. (1971), *The Neolithic and Bronze Ages*, The Athenian Agora 13, Princeton, NJ: American School of Classical Studies at Athens.

Jagiełło, Mieszek (2018) "Zur Herkunft des griechischen Wortes σφίγξ," *Classica Cracoviensia* 21, 71–82.

Jameson, Michael (1990), "Domestic Space in the Greek City State," in Susan Kent (ed.), *Domestic Architecture and the Use of Space: An Interdisciplinary, Cross-Cultural Study*, 92–113, Cambridge: Cambridge University Press.

Jansen, Mark D. (2013), "The Iconography of Humiliation: The Depiction and Treatment of Bound Foreigners in New Kingdom Egypt," unpublished Ph.D. thesis, University of Memphis.

Janssen, Jac J. (2009), *Furniture at Deir el-Medîna, Including Wooden Containers of the New Kingdom, and Ostracon Varille 19*, London: Golden House Publications.

Jantzen, Ulf (1972), *Ägyptische und orientalische Bronzen aus dem Heraion von Samos*, Samos VIII, Bonn: R. Habelt.

Jashemski, Wilhelmina F. (1993), *The Gardens of Pompeii, Herculaneum and the Villas Destroyed by Vesuvius I*, New Rochelle, NY: Caratzas Bros.

Jeppesen, Kristian (2007), "A Fresh Approach to the Problems of the Parthenon Frieze," in Erik Hallager and Jesper Tae Jensen (eds.), *Proceedings of the Danish Institute at Athens V*, 101–72, Athens: Aarhus University Press.

Jilek, Sonja (2003), "Mobiliar aus den Hanghäusern von Ephesos," in Beatrix Asamer and Wolfgang Wohlmayr (eds.), *Akten des 9. Österreichischen Archäologentages in Salzburg 2001 am Institut für Klassische Archäologie der Paris-Lodron–Universität Salzburg vom 6. bis 8. Dezember 2001*, 87–91, Vienna: Phoibos.

Kaltsas, Nikolaos (2001), *Εθνικό Αρχαιολογικό Μουσείο: Τα γλυπτά*, Athens: Editions Kapon.

Kaplan, Michel (1999), "The Producing Population," in John Haldon (ed.), *The Social History of Byzantium*, 143–67, Oxford: Wiley Blackwell Publishing.

Karageorghis, Vassos (1968), "Die Elfenbein–Throne von Salamis, Zypern," *Laser*: 99–103.

Karageorghis, Vassos (1973–4), *Excavations in the Necropolis of Salamis III*, Salamis 5, Nicosia: Department of Antiquities.

Karageorghis, Vassos (2006), "Homeric Cyprus," in Sigrid Deger-Jalkotzy and Irene Lemos (eds.), *Ancient Greece from the Mycenaean Palaces to the Age of Homer*, Edinburgh Leventis Studies 3, 665–75, Edinburgh: Edinburgh University Press.

Kavvadias, Giorgos (2000), *O ζωγράφος του Sabouroff*, Athens: Archaeological Receipts Fund (TAP).

Kazhdan, Alexander and Anthony Cutler (1991a), "Artisan," in Alexander Kazhdan (ed.), *The Oxford Dictionary of Byzantium*, vol. 1, 196–201, Oxford: Oxford University Press.

Kazhdan Alexander and Antony Cutler (1991b), "Carpenter," in Alexander Kazhdan (ed.), *The Oxford Dictionary of Byzantium*, vol. 1: 382–3, Oxford: Oxford University Press.

Killen, Geoffrey (1980), *Ancient Egyptian Furniture*, vol. 1, *4000–1300 BC*, Warminster, UK: Aris and Phillips.

Killen, Geoffrey (1994a), *Ancient Egyptian Furniture*, vol. 2, *Boxes, Chests and Footstools*, Warminster, UK: Aris and Phillips.

Killen, Geoffrey (1994b), *Egyptian Woodworking and Furniture*, Princes Risborough, UK: Shire Publications.

Killen, Geoffrey (1997), "Wood Turning in Ancient Egypt," *Tools and Trades*, 10: 10–25.

Killen, Geoffrey (2000), "Chapter 15: Wood [Technology]," in Paul T. Nicholson and Ian Shaw (eds.), *Ancient Egyptian Materials and Technology*, 353–71, Cambridge: Cambridge University Press.

Killen, Geoffrey (2017a), *Ancient Egyptian Furniture*, vol. 1, *4000–1300 BC*, 2nd edn., Oxford: Oxbow Books.

Killen, Geoffrey (2017b), *Ancient Egyptian Furniture*, vol. 2, *Boxes, Chests and Footstools*, 2nd edn., Oxford: Oxbow Books.

Killen, Geoffrey (2017c), *Ancient Egyptian Furniture*, vol. 3, *The Ramesside Period*, Oxford: Oxbow Books.

Killen, Geoffrey and Lara Weiss (2009), "Markings on Objects of Daily Use from Deir el-Medîna: Ownership Marks or Administrative Aids?" in Petra Andrássy, Julia Budka, and Frank Kammerzell (eds.), *Non-Textual Marking Systems, Writing and Pseudo Script from Prehistory to Modern Times*, Lingua Aegyptia 8, 137–58, Göttingen: Seminar für Ägyptologie und Koptologie.

Killen, John T. (1998), "The Pylos Ta Tablets Revisited," *Bulletin de Correspondance Hellénique*, 122: 421–2.

Kiourtzian, Georges (2003), "L'époque protobyzantine à travers les monuments épigraphiques," in Bernard Geyer and Jacques Lefort (eds.), *La Bithynie au Moyen Age*, Réalités Byzantines 9, 43–64, Paris: P. Lethielleux.

Knigge, Ursula (1976), *Die Südhügel*, Kerameikos IX, Berlin: Walter de Gruyter.

Kock, Theodor (1880–8), *Comicorum Atticorum Fragmenta*, Leipzig: B.G. Teubner.

Koder, Johannes (1991), *Das Eparchenbuch Leons des Weisen*, Corpus Fontium Historiae Byzantinae, Series Vindobonensis 33, Vienna: Österreichische Akademie der Wissenschaften.

Kolias, Taxiarchis G. and Maria Chroni (2010), *Το Επαρχικόν Βιβλίον Λέοντος Στ΄ του Σοφού*, Athens: Kanaki.

Kopaka, Katerina (1987), "Πήλινο ομοίωμα ανακλίντρου από τη Φαιστό," in *ΕΙΛΑΠΙΝΗ: Τόμος Τιμητικός για τον Καθηγητή Νικόλαο Πλάτωνα*, 93–100, Herakleion: Βικελαία Βιβλιοθήκη/ Δήμος Ηρακλείου.

Kopanias, Konstantinos (2009), "Some Ivories from the Geometric Stratum of Artemis Orthia, Sparta: Interconnections between Sparta, Crete and the Orient during the Late Eighth Century BC," in William Cavanagh, Chrysanthi Gallou and Mercourios Georgiadis (eds.), *Sparta and Laconia: From Prehistory to Pre-Modern*, BSA Studies 16, 123–31, London: The British School at Athens.

Kopcke, Günter (1967), "Neue Holzfunde aus Samos," *Athenische Mitteilungen*, 82: 100–48.

Kottaridi, Angeliki (2011), "The Palace of Aegae," in Robin J. Lane Fox (ed.), *Brill's Companion to Ancient Macedon, Studies in the Archaeology and History of Macedon, 650 BC–300 AD*, 297–333, Leiden: Brill.

Kotzias, Nikolaos (1937), "Ο παρά το αεροδρόμιον της Θεσσαλονίκης (Σέδες) Γ΄ τάφος," *Αρχαιολογική Εφημερίς* (3): 866–95.

Kougeas, S. (1912–13), "Αἰ ἐν τοῖς σχολίοις Ἀρέθα λαογραφικαί εἰδήσεις," *Λαογραφία*, 4: 237–73.

Koukoulès, Phédon (1948), *Βυζαντινῶν Βίος καί Πολιτισμός*, vol. 2.2, Athens: Institut français d'Athènes.

Koukoulès, Phédon (1951), *Βυζαντινῶν Βίος καί Πολιτισμός*, vol. 4, Athens: Institut français d'Athènes.

Koukoulès, Phédon (1952), *Βυζαντινῶν Βίος καί Πολιτισμός*, vol. 5, Athens: Institut français d'Athènes.

Koutsouflakis, George (2017), "Bronzes from the Aegean Sea: A Reassessment of Old and New Finds," in Jens Daehner, Kenneth Lapatin, and Ambra Spinelli (eds.), *Artistry in Bronze: The Greeks and Their Legacy, XIXth International Congress on Ancient Bronzes*, 28–39, Los Angeles: J. Paul Getty Museum and Getty Conservation Institute.

Kramer, Johannes (1998), "Bemerkungen zu einer Liste von Haushaltsgegenständen (P. Bodl. I. 48)," *Archiv für Papyrusforschung und verwandte Gebiete*, 44: 38–41.

Kreeb, Martin (1988), *Untersuchungen zur figürlichen Ausstattung delischer Privathäuser*, Chicago: Ares Publications.

Krzyszkowska, Olga (1996), "Furniture in the Aegean Bronze Age," in Georgina Herrmann (ed.), *The Furniture of Western Asia: Ancient and Traditional: Papers of the Conference Held at the Institute of Archaeology, University College London, June 28 to 30, 1993*, 85–103, Mainz: Philipp von Zabern.

Krzyszkowska, Olga and Robert Morkot (2000), "Ivory and Related Materials," in Paul T. Nicholson and Ian Shaw (eds.), *Ancient Egyptian Materials and Technology*, 320–31, Cambridge: Cambridge University Press.

Kübler, Karl (1976), *Die Nekropole der Mitte des 6. bis Ende des 5. Jahrhunderts*, Kerameikos VII.1, Berlin: de Gruyter.

Kuhlmann, Klaus P. (1977), *Der Thron im Alten Ägypten: Untersuchungen zu Semantik, Ikonographie und Symbolik eines Herrschaftszeichens*, Abhandlungen des Deutschen Archäologischen Instituts Kairo, Ägyptologische Reihe 10, Glückstadt: Augustin.

Kuniholm, Peter I. and Cecil L. Striker (1983), "Dendrochronological Investigations in the Aegean and Neighboring Regions, 1977–1982," *Journal of Field Archaeology*, 10: 411–20.

Küpper, Jean-Robert (1983), *Documents Administratifs de la Salle 135 du Palais de Mari Transcrits et Traduits*, Archives royales de Mari 22:2, Paris: Éditions Recherche sur les Civilisations.

Kyriakou, Athanasia (2005), "Η στενόμακρη τούμπα της Βεργίνας: Συμβολή στη μελέτη της ταφικής διαδικασίας στη Μακεδονία των ύστερων κλασσικών και πρώιμων ελληνιστικών χρόνων," Ph.D. dissertation, Aristotle University of Thessaloniki, Thessaloniki.

Kyrieleis, Helmut (1969), *Throne und Klinen: Studien zur Formgeschichte altorientalischer in griechischer Sitz– und Liegemöbel vorhellenistischer Zeit*, Jahrbuch des Deutschen Archäologischen Instituts Ergänzungsheft 24, Berlin: de Gruyter.

Kyrieleis, Helmut (1980), "Archaische Holzfunde aus Samos," *Athenische Mitteilungen*, 95: 87–147.

Lapatin, Kenneth D.S. (2001), *Chryselephantine Statuary in the Ancient Mediterranean World*, Oxford: Oxford University Press.

Lapatin, Kenneth D.S. (2015), *Luxus: The Sumptuous Arts of Greece and Rome*, Los Angeles: J. Paul Getty Museum.

Lapinkivi, Pirjo (2004), *The Sumerian Sacred Marriage in the Light of Comparative Evidence*, State Archives of Assyria Studies 15, Helsinki: Neo-Assyrian Text Corpus Project.

Laser, Siegfried (1968), *Hausrat*, Archaeologia Homerica II:P, Göttingen: Vandenhoeck and Ruprecht.

Lauffer, Siegfried (1971), *Diokletians Preisedikt*, Texte und Kommentare 5, Berlin: Walter de Gruyter and Co.

Lavan, Luke (2007a), "Political Space in Late Antiquity," in Luke Lavan, Ellen Swift, and Toon Putzeys (eds.), *Objects in Context, Objects in Use: Material Spatiality in Late Antiquity*, Late Antique Archaeology 5, 111–28, Leiden: Brill.

Lavan, Luke (2007b), "Religious Space in Late Antiquity," in Luke Lavan, Ellen Swift, and Toon Putzeys (eds.), *Objects in Context, Objects in Use: Material Spatiality in Late Antiquity*, Late Antique Archaeology 5, 159–201, Leiden: Brill.

Lavan, Luke, Lale Özgenel, and Alexander Sarantis (2007), *Housing in Late Antiquity: From Palaces to Shops*, Late Antique Archaeology 3.2, Leiden: Brill.

Lavan, Luke, Ellen Swift, and Toon Putzeys, eds. (2007), *Objects in Context, Objects in Use: Material Spatiality in Late Antiquity*, Late Antique Archaeology 5, Leiden: Brill.

Lev-Yadun, Simcha (2007), "Wood Remains from Archaeological Excavations: A Review with a Near Eastern Perspective," *Israel Journal of Earth Sciences*, 56: 139–62.

Lev-Yadun, Simcha, Michal Artzy, Ezra Marcus, and Ragna Stidsing (1996), "Wood Remains from Tel Nami, a Middle Bronze Age IIA and Late Bronze Age IIB Port, Local Exploitation of Trees and Levantine Cedar Trade," *Economic Botany*, 50 (3): 310–17.

Lewis, D.M. (1966), "After the Profanation of the Mysteries," in Ernst Badian (ed.), *Ancient Society and Institutions: Studies Presented to Victor Ehrenberg on His 75th Birthday*, 177–91, Oxford: Blackwell.

Lezzi-Hafter, Adrienne (1988), *Der Eretria-maler: Werke und Weggefährten*, Mainz am Rhein: Philipp von Zabern.

Lilimbaki–Akamati, Maria (1979), "An Inventory in the Agora," *Zeitschrift für Papyrologie und Epigraphik*, 36: 131–4.

Lilimbaki-Akamati, Maria and Ioannis Akamatis (2015), *Πέλλα: Ο αρχαιολογικός χώρος και το Μουσείο*, Athens: Archaeological Receipts Fund (TAP).

Ling, Roger (1991), *Roman Painting*, Cambridge: Cambridge University Press.

Lissarrague, Francois (1995), "Women, Boxes, Containers: Some Signs and Metaphors," in Ellen D. Reeder (ed.), *Pandora: Women in Classical Greece*, 91–101, Princeton, NJ: Princeton University Press.

Loud, Gordon (1939), *The Megiddo Ivories*, Chicago: University of Chicago Press.

Loverance, Rowena (2004), *Byzantium*, London: The British Museum Press.

Lucas, Alfred (1936), "The Wood of the Third Dynasty Plywood Coffin from Saqqara," *Annales du Service des antiquités de l'Égypte*, 36: 1–4.

Lynch, Kathleen M. (2015), "Drinking Cups and the Symposium at Athens in the Archaic and Classical Periods," in Kevin F. Daly and Lee Ann Riccardi (eds.), *Cities Called Athens: Studies Honoring John McK. Camp II*, 231–71, Lewisburg, PA: Bucknell University Press.

Lynch, Kathleen M. (2007), "More Thoughts on the Space of the Symposium," in Ruth Westgate, Nick Fisher, and James Whitley (eds.), *Building Communities: House, Settlement and Society in the Aegean and Beyond*, British School at Athens Studies 15, 243–9, London: British School of Archaeology.

McCallum, Lucinda Rasmussen (1987), "Decorative Program in the Mycenaean Palace of Pylos: The Megaron Frescoes," unpublished Ph.D. thesis, University of Pennsylvania.

McCrindle, John W. ([1897] 2010), *The Christian Topography of Cosmas, an Egyptian Monk*, Calcutta, repr. Cambridge Library Collection-Hakluyt First Series.

McEnerney, John I. (2007), *St Cyril of Alexandria, Letters 51–110*, The Fathers of the Church 76, Washington, DC: Catholic University of America Press.

McGovern, Patrick E. (2004), "The History and Archaeology of Jordan: The Second Millennium BC," *Studies in the History and Archaeology of Jordan*, 8: 285–99.

McIntosh, Jane R. (2005), *Ancient Mesopotamia: New Perspectives*, Santa Barbara, CA: ABC Clio.

MacIntosh, Jean (1974), "Representations of Furniture on the Frieze Plaques from Poggio Civitate Murlo," *Römische Mitteilungen*, 81: 15–40.

Magness, Jodi (2001), "A Near Eastern Ethnic Element among the Etruscan Elite?" *Etruscan Studies*, 8: 79–117.

Makaronas, Charalambos (1956), "Ανασκαφική έρευνα 'μακεδονικού' τάφου εν Δίω Πιερίας," *Praktika tes en Athenais Archaiologikes Etaireias*: 131–8.

Makaronas, Charalambos (1961–2), "Ανασκαφαί Πέλλης," *ADeltion*, 17 Chron. B¹: 209–13.

Mallowan, Max E.L. (1975), *Nimrud and Its Remains*, London: Collins.

Malmberg, Simon (2007), "Dazzling Dining: Banquets as an Expression of Imperial Legitimacy," in Leslie Brubaker and Kallirroe Linardou (eds.), *Eat, Drink and Be Merry (Luke 12:19)—Food and Wine in Byzantium, Papers of the 37th Annual Spring Symposium of Byzantine Studies in Honour of Professor A.A.M. Bryer*, 75–92, Aldershot, UK: Ashgate.

Mango, Cyril A. (1972), *The Art of the Byzantine Empire 312–1453*, Sources and Documents in History of Art, Englewood Cliffs, NJ: Prentice Hall.

Mango, Cyril A., Robert Scott, and Geoffrey Greatrex (1997), *The Chronicle of Theophanes Confessor: Byzantine and Near Eastern History A.D. 284–813*, Oxford: Oxford University Press.

Marangou, Lila (1976), *Bone carvings from Egypt: I. Graeco – Roman period*, Athens: Benaki Museum; Tübingen: Ernst Wasmuth Publishers.

Marinatos, Spyridon N. (1971), *Excavations at Thera IV (1970 Season)*, Athens: The Archaeological Society at Athens.

Mayerson, Philip (1999), "Measures (μετρηταί) and Donkeyloads of Oil in P. Wisc. II. 80," *Zeitschrift für Papyrologie und Epigraphik*, 127: 189–92.

Meiggs, Russell (1982), *Trees and Timber in the Ancient Mediterranean World*, Oxford: Clarendon Press.

Mellaart, James (1967), *Çatal Hüyük: A Neolithic Town in Anatolia*, New York: McGraw-Hill.

Merhav, Rivka (1991), "Secular and Cultic Furniture: Thrones, Footrests, and Tables," in Rivka Merhav (ed.), *Urartu: A Metalworking Center in the First Millennium* BCE, 245–71, Jerusalem: Israel Museum.

Mettinger, Tryggve N.D. (1995), *No Graven Image? Israelite Aniconism in Its Ancient Near Eastern Context*, Coniectanea Biblica 42, Stockholm: Almqvist and Wiksell International.

Metzger, Martin (1985), *Königsthron und Gottesthron: Thronformen und Throndarstellungen in Ägypten und im Vorderen Orient im dritten und zweiten Jahrtausend v.Chr. und deren Bedeutung für das Verständnis von Aussagen über den Thron im Alten Testament*, AOAT 15, Kevelaer: Verlag Butzon und Bercker; Neukirchen-Vluyn: Neu Kirchener Verlag.

Michaelides, Demetrios (2004), "Cypriot Painted Tombs and Their Ceilings," in László Borhy (ed.), *Plafonds et voûtes à l'époque antique: Actes du VIIIe Colloque International de l'Association Internationale pour la Peinture Murale Antique, Budapest-Veszprém, Mai 15–19, 2001*, 89–96, Budapest: Pytheas.

Michel, Vincent (2007), "Furniture, Fixtures, and Fittings in Churches: Archaeological Evidence from Palestine (4th–8th c.) and the Role of the Diakonikon," in Luke Lavan, Ellen Swift and Toon Putzeys (eds.), *Objects in Context, Objects in Use: Material Spatiality in Late Antiquity*, Late Antique Archaeology 5, 581–606, Leiden: Brill.

Miller, Frank Justus (1972), *Ovid in Six Volumes. III. Metamorphoses*, vol. 1, Books 1–8, translated by Frank Justus Miller, Revised by G.P. Goold, The Loeb Classical Library 42, Cambridge, MA: Harvard University Press.

Miller, Stella (1993), *The Tomb of Lyson and Kallikles: A Painted Macedonian Tomb*, Mainz am Rhein: Philipp von Zabern.

Mitchell, T.C. (1996), "Furniture in the West Semitic Texts," in Georgina Herrmann (ed.), *The Furniture of Western Asia: Ancient and Traditional: Papers of the Conference Held at the Institute of Archaeology, University College London, June 28 to 30, 1993*, 49–60, Mainz: Philipp von Zabern.

Mols, Stephan T.A.M. (1999), *Wooden Furniture in Herculaneum: Form, Technique and Function*, Amsterdam: Gieben. (Reprint Leiden: Brill, 2020.)

Mols, Stephan T.A.M. (2007–8), "Ancient Roman Household Furniture and its Use: From Herculaneum to the Rhine," in Alicia Fernández Díaz and Alejandro Quevedo Sánchez (eds.), *La arquitectura doméstica romana en ámbito urbano y rural*, 145–60, Murcia: Universidad de Murcia.

Moorey, Roger (1996), "Concluding Remarks," in Georgina Herrmann (ed.), *The Furniture of Western Asia: Ancient and Traditional: Papers of the Conference Held at the Institute of Archaeology, University College London, June 28 to 30, 1993*, 253–8, Mainz: Philipp von Zabern.

Moran, William L. (1992), *The Amarna Letters, Edited and Translated*, Baltimore: Johns Hopkins University Press.

Moretti Sgubini, Anna Maria, ed. (2004), *Eroi Etruschi e Miti Greci gli affreschidella Tomba François tornano a Vulci*, Florence: Edizioni Cooperativa Archeologia.

Morpurgo-Davies, Anna (1979), "Terminology of Power and Terminology of Work in Greek and Linear B," in Ernst Risch and Hugo Mühlestein (eds.), *Colloquium Mycenaeum: Actes du Sixiéme Colloque International sur les Textes Mycéniens et Égéens*, 87–108, Geneva: Université de Neuchâtel.

Muhly, Polymnia (1996), "Furniture from the Shaft Graves: The Occurrence of Wood in Aegean Burials of the Bronze Age," *Annual of the British School at Athens*, 91: 197–211.

Mundell Mango, Marlia (2008), "Metalwork," in Elizabeth Jeffreys, John Haldon, and Robin Cormack (eds.), *The Oxford Handbook of Byzantine Studies*, 444–52, Oxford: Oxford University Press.

Murray, Oswyn (2009), "The Culture of the *Symposion*," in Kurt A. Raaflaub and Hans van Wees (eds.), *A Companion to Archaic Greece*, 508–23, London: Wiley.

Murray, Oswyn, ed. (1990), *Sympotica: A Symposium on the Symposium*, Oxford: Clarendon Press.

Mylonas, George E. (1972–3), *Ο Ταφικός Κύκλος Β των Μυκηνών*, Βιβλιοθήκη της εν Αθήναις Αρχαιολογικής Εταιρείας 73, Athens: The Archaeological Society at Athens.

Naeh, Liat and Dana Brostowsky Gilboa eds. (2020), *The Ancient Throne: The Mediterranean, Near East, and Beyond, From the 3rd Millennium BCE to the 14th century CE*. Proceedings of the workshop held at the 10th ICAANE in Vienna, April 2016. Vienna: Austrian Academy of Sciences Press.

Nakamura, Carolyn and Lynn Meskell (2009), "Articulate Bodies: Forms and Figures at Çatalhöyük," *Journal of Archaeological Method and Theory*, 16: 205–30.

Nakassis, Dimitri (2015), "Labor and Individuals in Late Bronze Age Pylos," in Piotr Steinkeller and Michael Hudson (eds.) *Labor in the Ancient World*, vol. 5: 583–615, Dresden: ISLET-Verlag.

Naso, Alessandro (2012), "Etruskische und italische Funde in der Ägäis," in Petra Amann (ed.), *Kulte-Riten- religiöse Vorstellungen bei den Etruskern und ihr Verhältnis zu Politik und Gesellschaft*, 317–33, Vienna: Österreichischen Akademie der Wissenschaften.

Neesen, Lutz (1989), *Demiourgoi und Artifices: Studien zur Stellung freier Handwerker in den antiken Städten*, Frankfurt: Peterlang.

Netolitzky, Fritz (1934), "Pflanzliche Nahrungsmittel und Hölzer aus dem prähistorischen Kreta und Kephallonia," *Buletinui Facultatu de Stunfe din Cernauti*, 8: 172–8.

Nevett, Lisa C. (1999), *House and Society in the Ancient Greek World*, Cambridge: Cambridge University Press.

Nevett, Lisa C. (2010), *Domestic Space in Classical Antiquity*, Cambridge: Cambridge University Press.

Newman, Richard and Margaret Serpico (2000), "Adhesives and Binders," in Paul T. Nicholson and Ian Shaw (eds.), *Ancient Egyptian Materials and Technology*, 475–94, Cambridge: Cambridge University Press.

Nicholson, Paul T. and Ian Shaw, eds. (2000), *Ancient Egyptian Materials and Technology*, Cambridge: Cambridge University Press.

Niemeier, Wolf-Dietrich (2005), "Minoans, Mycenaeans, Hittites and Ionians in Western Asia Minor: New Excavations in Bronze Age Miletus-Millawanda," in Alexandra Villing (ed.), *The Greeks in the East*, 1–36, London: British Museum.

Nordbladh, Jarl (2013), "A Choreography of Furniture, the Art of Sitting, Standing Up and Lying Down," in Sophie Bergerbrant and Serena Sabatini (eds.), *Counterpoint: Essays in Archaeology and Heritage Studies in Honour of Kristian Kristiansen*, 421–8, Oxford: Oxford University Press.

Nowicka, Maria (1984), "Théophilos, peintre alexandrin, et son activité," in Nicola Bonacasa and Antonino Di Vita (eds.), *Alessandria e il mondo hellenistico–romano: Studi di onore di Achille Adriani*, 256–9, Rome: "L'Erma" di Bretschneider.

Oakley, John H. (2004), *Picturing Death in Classical Athens*, Cambridge: Cambridge University Press.

Oakley, John H. and Rebecca H. Sinos (1993), *The Wedding in Ancient Athens*, Madison: University of Wisconsin Press.

Oikonomides, Nicolas (1990), "The Contents of the Byzantine House from the Eleventh to the Fifteenth Century," *Dumbarton Oaks Papers*, 44: 205–14.

Oikonomos, George (1926), "Bronzen von Pella," *Athenische Mitteilungen*: 75–97.

Olch-Stern, Wilma and Danae Hadjilazaro-Thimme (2007), *Kenchreai: East Port of Corinth Results of Inverstigations by the University of Chicago and Indiana University for the American School of Classical Studies at Athens*, vol. 6, *Ivory, Bone and Related Wood Finds*, Leiden: Brill.

Olivier, Jean-Pierre (1967), "Le *damokoro*: un fonctionnaire mycénien," *Minos*, 8: 118–22.

Olson, Douglas S. and Alexander Sens (2000), *Archestratos of Gela: Greek Culture and Cuisine in the 4th c. BCE: Text, Translation and Commentary*, Oxford: Oxford University Press.

Oppenheim, Leo A. (1977), *Ancient Mesopotamia. Portrait of a Dead Civilization*, rev. edn., completed by Erica Reiner, Chicago: University of Chicago Press.

Orlandos, Anastasios K. and Ioannis N. Travlos (1986), Λεξικόν αρχαίων αρχιτεκτονικών όρων, Βιβλιοθήκη της εν Αθήναις Αρχαιολογικής Εταιρείας 94, Athens: The Archaeological Society at Athens.

Ostia-Antica (2020), "Tomb 80." Available online: https://www.ostia-antica.org/valkvisuals/html/tombe_80_1.htm (accessed May 6, 2021).

Otto, Brinna (2011), "Das hohe und das erhöhte Thronen in der bronzezeitlichen Ikonographie der Ägäis," in Fritz Blakolmer, Claus Reinholdt, Jörg Weilhartner, and Georg Nightingale (eds.), *Österreichische Forschungen zur Ägäischen Bronzezeit 2009*, 229–40, Vienna: Phoibos.

Özgüç, Tahsin (1988), *Inandiktepe. An Important Cult Center in the Old Hittite Period*, Türk Tarih Kurumu Yayinlari 43, Ankara: TTK.

Özgüç, Tahsin and Mahmut Akok (1958), *Horoztepe: An Early Bronze Age Settlement and Cemetery*, Türk Tarih Kurumu Yayinlari 18, Ankara: TTK.

[Page, Denys L., ed.] (1968), *Lyrica Graeca Selecta*, Oxford: Clarendon Press.

Palaima, Thomas G. (2000), "The Pylos Ta Series from Michael Ventris to the New Millennium," *Bulletin of the Institute of Classical Studies of the University of London*, 44: 236–7.

Palaiokrassa, Nomiki (2012), "Small Metal Objects and Utensils," in Nikolaos Kaltsas, Elena Vlachogianni, and Polyxeni Bouyia (eds.), *The Antikythera Shipwreck: The Ship, the Treasures, the Mechanism*, 116–31, Athens: Hellenic Ministry of Culture and Tourism.

Palmer, Leonard Robert (1957), "A Mycenaean Tomb Inventory," *Minos*, 5: 58–92.

Palyvou, Clairy (2005), *Akrotiri Thera: An Architecture of Affluence 3,500 Years Old*, Prehistory Monographs 15, Philadelphia: INSTAP Academic Press.

Papanikola-Bakirtzis, Demetra (2013), "Household Furnishings," in Anastasia Drandaki, Demetra Papanikola-Bakirtzi, and Anastasia Tourta (eds.), *Heaven and Earth*, vol. 1, *Art of Byzantium from Greek Collection*, 218–22, Athens: Hellenic Ministry of Culture and Sports and the Benaki Museum.

Papazoglou-Manioudaki, Lena (2012), "Gold and Ivory Objects at Mycenae and Dendra Revealed: Private Luxury and/or *insignia dignitatis*," in Marie-Louise Nosch and Robert Laffineur (eds.), *Kosmos: Jewellery, Adornment and Textiles in the Aegean Bronze Age*, Aegaeum 33, 447–56, Leuven: Peeters.

Paradiso, Annalisa (1991), *Forme di dipendenza nel mondo greco: ricerche sul VI libro di Ateneo*, Bari: Edipuglia.

Parakenings, Birgit (1989), "Der Andron: Gastzimmer des griechischen Hauses und Ort des Symposion," in Norbert Kunisch, Birgit Parakenings, Ursula Peifer, Anita Reiche, and Hans-Joachim Schalles (eds.), *Symposion: Griechische Vasen aus dem Antikenmuseum der Ruhr–Universität Bochum*, 20–3, Cologne: Rheinland Verlag.

Parani, Maria G. (2003), *Reconstructing the Reality of Images. Byzantine Material Culture and Religious Iconography (11th–15th Centuries)*, The Medieval Mediterranean 41, Leiden: Brill.

Pareti, Luigi (1947), *La tomba Regolini–Galassi del Museo Gregoriano Etrusco e la civiltà dell' Italia central nel sec. VII a.C.*, Vatican City: Tipografia Poliglotta Vaticana.

Parr, Peter J. (1996), "Middle Bronze Age Furniture from Jericho and Baghouz," in Georgina Herrmann (ed.), *The Furniture of Western Asia: Ancient and Traditional: Papers of the Conference Held at the Institute of Archaeology, University College London, June 28 to 30, 1993*, 41–8, Mainz: Philipp von Zabern.

Paspalas, Stavros A. (2005), "Philip Arrhidaios at Court: An Ill-Advised Persianism? Macedonian Royal Display in the Wake of Alexander," *Klio*, 87: 72–101.

Paton, William Roger (1969), *The Greek Anthology, with an English Translation*, vol. 1, Books 1–6, The Loeb Classical Library 68, Cambridge, MA: Harvard University Press.

Pautasso, Antonella (2004), "Wooden Stools dall' Heraion di Samo. Alcune osservazioni," in Nicholas Stampolidis and Angeliki Giannikouri (eds.), *Το Αιγαίο στην Πρώιμη Εποχή του Σιδήρου. Πρακτικά του Διεθνούς Συμποσίου, Ρόδος 1–4 Νοεμβρίου 2002*, 197–205, Athens: University of Crete/Ministry of Culture.

Pestman, Pieter Willem (1961), *Marriage and Matrimonial Property in Ancient Egypt*, Papyrologica Lugduno-Batava 9, Leiden: Brill.

Petersen, Leif Inge Ree (2013), *Siege Warfare and Military Organization in the Successor States (400–800 AD), Byzantium, the West and Islam*, History of Warfare 91, Leiden: Brill.

Peterson, Bengt E.J. (1973), *Zeichnungen aus einer Totenstadt*, Medelhavsmuseet Bulletin 7–8, Stockholm: Medelhavsmuseet.

Petrain, David (2013), "Visual Supplementation and Metonymy in the Roman Public Library," in Jason Konig, Katerina Oikonomopoulou, and Greg Woolf (eds.), *Ancient Libraries*, 332–46, Cambridge: Cambridge University Press.

Petrakis, Vassilis P. (2002–3), "*to-no-e-ke-te-ri-jo* reconsidered," *Minos*, 37–8: 293–316.

Petridis, Platon (2008), "Παρατηρήσεις στις πόλεις και τις αστικές οικείες της ύστερης αρχαιότητας στον ελλαδικό χώρο," *Δελτίον της Χριστιανικής Αρχαιολογικής Εταιρείας*, Περίοδος Δ΄, 28: 247–58.

Pétridis, Platon (2010), *La céramique protobyzantine de Delphes: Une production et son contexte*, Fouilles de Delphes V, Monuments figurés 4, Paris: De Boccard; Athens: École française d'Athènes.

Petrie, Flinders W.M. (1890), *Kahun, Gurob, and Hawara*, London: Kegan Paul, Trench, Trübner.

Petrie, Flinders W.M. (1901), *The Royal Tombs of the Earliest Dynasties, Part II*, London: EEF.

Petrie, Flinders W.M. (1913), *Tarkhan I and Memphis V*, London: BSAE.

Peyronel, Luca and Agnese Vacca (2013), "Natural Resources, Technology and Manufacture Processes at Ebla: A Preliminary Assessment," in Paolo Matthiae and Nicolò Marchetti (eds.), *Ebla and Its Landscape: Early State Formation in the Ancient Near East*, 431–49, Walnut Creek, CA: Left Coast Press.

Pfuhl, Ernst and Hans Möbius (1979), *Die griechischen Grabreliefs*, vol. 2, Mainz: Philipp von Zabern.

Phillipson, David W. (2009), "Aksum, the Entrepot, and Highland Ethiopia, 3th–12th Centuries," in Marlia Mundell Mango (ed.), *Byzantine Trade, 4th–12th Centuries: The Archaeology of Local, Regional and International Exchange; Papers of the Thirty–Eighth Spring Symposium of Byzantine Studies, St John's College, University of Oxford, March 2004*, 353–70, Aldershot, UK: Routledge.

Pinch, Geraldine (1993), *Votive Offerings to Hathor*, Oxford: Griffith Institute.

Piraud-Fournet, Pauline (2010), "Les fouilles du 'Palais de Trajan' à Bosra (2007–2009): Rapport préliminaire et perspectives de recherche," *Syria*, 87: 281–300.

Platon, Lefteris (2012), "New Evidence on the Origins of the Late Minoan III Chest-Shaped Larnax," in Eleni Mantzourani and Philip P. Betancourt (eds.), *Philistor: Studies in Honor of Costis Davaras*, Prehistory Monographs 36, Philadelphia: 161–8.

Platon, Lefteris and Yiannis Pararas (1991), *Pedestalled Offering Tables in the Aegean World*, Studies in Mediterranean Archaeology Pocket-Book 106, Jonsered: P. Åström.

Polychronakou-Sgouritsa, Nagia (2001), "Έπιπλα και επιπλουργία στον προϊστορικό οικισμό του Ακρωτηρίου Θήρας," in Ioannis M. Danezis (ed.), *Σαντορίνη, Θήρα, Θηρασία, Ασπρονήσι, Ηφαιστεία*, 133–9, Athens: Adam.

Polychronakou-Sgouritsa, Nagia (2003), "Μυκηναϊκά πήλινα ομοιώματα επίπλων," in Eleni Konsolaki-Yannopoulou (ed.), Αργοσαρωνικός: Πρακτικά 1ου Διεθνούς Συνεδρίου Ιστορίας και Αρχαιολογίας του Αργοσαρωνικού, Πόρος, *26–29 Ιουνίου 1998*, vol. 1, 301–9, Athens: Municipality of Poros.

Polychronakou-Sgouritsa, Nagia (2008), "Πρόσφατα στοιχεία αποθήκευσης και φύλαξης αγαθών στον ΥΚ I οικισμό του Ακρωτηρίου Θήρας," in Christos G. Doumas (ed.), *Ακρωτήρι Θήρας, 30 Χρόνια Έρευνας 1967–1997*, 151–67, Athens: The Archaeological Society at Athens.

Popko, Maciej (1978), "Kultobjekte der hethitischen Religion nach keilschriftlichen Quellen," Ph.D. dissertation, University of Warsaw.

Poulsen, Birte (2005), "Möbel für das Kultmahl: Kline-lectus–stibas," in Jean C. Balty (ed.), *Thesaurus Cultus et Rituum Antiquorum (ThesCRA)*, 358–62, Los Angeles: Getty Publications.

Prayon, Friedhelm (1975), *Frühetruskische Grab- und Hausarchitektur*, Römische Mitteilungen Ergänzungsheft 22, Heidelberg: F.H. Kerle.

Pringle, Jacqueline Marie (1993), "Hittite Kinship and Marriage. A Study Based on the Cuneiform Texts from 2nd Millennium Boğazköy," unpublished Ph.D. thesis, University of London.

Pritchett, William Kendrick (1953), "The Attic Stelai. Part I," *Hesperia*, 22: 225–99.

Pritchett, William Kendrick (1956), "The Attic stelai. Part II," *Hesperia*, 25: 178–328.

Prückner, Helmut (1968), *Die lokrischen Tonreliefs: Beitrag zur Kultgeschichte von Lokroi Epizephyrioi*, Mainz am Rhein: Philipp von Zabern.

Putzeys, Toon (2007), "Domestic Space in Late Antiquity," in Luke Lavan, Ellen Swift, and Toon Putzeys (eds.), *Objects in Context, Objects in Use: Material Spatiality in Late Antiquity*, Late Antique Archaeology 5, 49–62, Leiden: Brill.

Putzeys, Toon and Luke Lavan (2007), "Commercial Space in Late Antiquity," in Luke Lavan, Ellen Swift, and Toon Putzeys (eds.), *Objects in Context, Objects in Use: Material Spatiality in Late Antiquity*, Late Antique Archaeology 5, 81–109, Leiden: Brill.

Putzeys, Toon, Marc Waelkens, Jeroen Poblome, Wim Van Neer, Bea De Cupere, Thijs Van Thuyne, and Nathalie Kellens (2007), "Contextual Analysis at Sagalassos," in Luke Lavan, Ellen Swift, and Toon Putzeys (eds.), *Objects in Context, Objects in Use: Material Spatiality in Late Antiquity*, Late Antique Archaeology 5, 205–37, Leiden: Brill.

Quatember, Ursula (2014), "Funde aus Marmor und anderen Gesteinen," in Hilke Thür and Elisabeth Rathmayr (eds.), *Hanghaus 2 von Ephesos, Die Wohneinheit 6; Baubefund, Ausstattung, Funde. Textband 1*, Forschungen in Ephesos 8:9, 707–17, Vienna: Austrian Academy of Sciences.

Rackham, Harris (1969), *Pliny Natural History in Ten Volumes*, vol. 2, Booksbooks III–VII, The Loeb Classical Library 394, Cambridge, MA: Harvard University Press; London: William Heinemann.

Ransom, Caroline W. (1905), *Studies in Ancient Furniture: Couches and Beds of the Greeks, Etruscans and Romans*, Chicago: University of Chicago Press.

Rapoport, Amos (1990), *The Meaning of the Built Environment: A Nonverbal Communication Approach to Social Space*, Tucson: University of Arizona.

Rastrelli, Anna (2000), "La tomba di Poggio alla Sala (Siena)," in Gilda Bartoloni (ed.), *Principi etruschi tra Mediterraneo ed Europa*, 196–8, Bologna: Marsilio.

Rathje, Annette (2013), "The Banquet through Etruscan History," in Jean M. Turfa (ed.), *The Etruscan World*, 823–30, London: Routledge.

Raubitschek, Antony Erich (1949), *Dedications from the Athenian Akropolis: A Catalogue of the Inscriptions of the Sixth and Fifth Centuries BC*, Cambridge, MA: Archaeological Institute of America.

Raven, Maarten J. (2014), "Women's Beds from Deir el-Medîna," in Ben J.J. Haring, Olaf E. Kaper, and René Van Walsem (eds.), *The Workman's Progress, Studies in the Village of Deir el-Medîna and Other Documents from Western Thebes in Honour of Rob Demarée*, 191–204, Leuven: Peeters.

Reber, Karl (1998), *Eretria: Ausgrabungen und Forschungen/ Fouilles et recherches X. Die klassischen und hellenistischen Wohnhäuser im Westquartier*, 191–204, Lausanne: Swiss Archaeological School in Greece.

Reisner, George A. and William S. Smith (1955), *A History of the Giza Necropolis, The Tomb of Hetep-heres the Mother of Cheops*, vol. 2, Cambridge, MA: Harvard University Press.

Rethemiotakis, G. (1995), "Μινωική λάρνακα από το Κλήμα Μεσαράς," *Archaiologike Ephemeris*: 163–83.

Rhomiopoulou, Katerina (1989), "Κλειστά ταφικά σύνολα υστεροκλασικών χρόνων από τη Θεσσαλονίκη," in Φίλια Έπη εις Γεώργιον Ε. Μυλωνάν, vol. 3, Βιβλιοθήκη της Εν Αθήναις Αρχαιολογικής Εταιρείας 103, 194–218, Athens: The Archaeological Society at Athens.

Rice, Ellen E. (1983), *The Grand Procession of Ptolemy Philadelphus*, Oxford: Oxford University Press.

Richter, Gisela M.A. (1926), *Ancient Furniture*, Oxford: Clarendon Press.

Richter, Gisela M.A. (1957), "Were there Greek *Armaria?*" *Hommages à Waldemar Déonna (=Latomus* 28): 418–23.

Richter, Gisela M.A. (1965), "Notes on the Furniture of the Locrian Pinakes," *Klearchos*, 7: 105–14.

Richter, Gisela M.A. (1966), *The Furniture of the Greeks, Etruscans, and Romans*, London: Phaidon Press.

Ricketts, Michael (1960), "Furniture from the Middle Bronze Age Tombs," in Kathleen Kenyon, *Excavations at Jericho I*, 527–34, London: British School of Archaeology in Jerusalem.

Ritter, Stefan (2003), "Zur Bildsprache römischer Alltagsszenen: Die Mahl- und Küchenreliefs am Pfeilergrab von Igel," *Bonner Jahrbücher*, 202/3: 149–70.

Rizzardi, Clementina (2009), "Massimiano a Ravenna: la Cattedra eburnea del Museo Arcivescovile alla luce di nuove ricerche," in Raffaella Farioli Campanati, Clementina Rizzardi, Paola Porta, Andrea Augenti, and Isabella Baldini Lippolis (eds.), *Ideologia e cultura artistica tra Adriatico e Mediterraneo orientale (IV–X secolo): Il Ruolo dell'Autorità Ecclesiastica alla Luce di Nuovi Scavi e Ricerche*, Studi e Scavi del Dipartimento di Archeologia 19, 229–43, Alma Mater Studiorum–Università di Bologna Dipartimento di Archeologia, Bologna: Ante Quem.

Roaf, Michael (1996), "Architecture and Furniture," in Georgina Herrmann (ed.), *The Furniture of Western Asia: Ancient and Traditional: Papers of the Conference Held at the Institute of Archaeology, University College London, June 28 to 30, 1993*, 21–8, Mainz: Philipp von Zabern.

Robert, Louis (1966), "Noms des métiers dans les documents byzantins," in Χαριστήριον εις Αναστάσιον Κ. Ορλάνδον, Βιβλιοθήκη της εν Αθήναις Αρχαιολογικής Εταιρείας 54, 324–47, Athens: The Archaeological Society at Athens.

Robert, Louis (1978), "Documents d'Asie Mineure," *Bulletin de Correspondance Hellénique*, 102: 395–543.

Robinson, David M. and J. Walter Graham (1938), *The Hellenic House: A Study of the Houses Found at Olynthus with a Detailed Account of those Excavated in 1931 and 1934*, Olynthus VIII, Baltimore: Johns Hopkins University Press.

Robsjohn-Gibbings, Terence Harold and Carlton Pullin (1963), *Furniture of Classical Greece*, New York: Alfred A. Knopf.

Rodziewicz, Elizabeth (2009), "Ivory, Bone, Glass and Other Production at Alexandria, 5th–9th Centuries," in Marlia Mundell Mango (ed.), *Byzantine Trade, 4th–12th Centuries: The Archaeology of Local, Regional and International Exchange. Papers of the Thirty-Eighth Spring Symposium of Byzantine Studies, St John's College, University of Oxford, March 2004*, 83–96, Oxford: Routledge, Taylor and Francis Group.

Roller, Lynn E. (1999), *In Search of God the Mother: The Cult of Anatolian Cybele*, Berkeley: University of California Press.

Röllig, W., H. Waetzoldt, J. Siegelová, and P. Calmeyer (1993), "Möbel," in Dietz Otto Edzard (ed.), *Reallexikon der Assyriologie und vorderasiatische Archäologie*, vol. 8, 325–37, Berlin: de Gruyter.

Roncalli, Francesco (2013), "Le lastre dipinte," in *Cerveteri*, 2013: 242–9.

Rotroff, Susan I. (1999), "How Did Pots Function within the Landscape of Daily Living?" in Marie-Christine Villanueva Puig, François Lissarrague, Pierre Rouillard, and Agnès Rouveret (eds.), *Céramique et peinture grecques: Modes d'emploi. Actes du colloque international. École du Louvre*, 63–74, Paris: La Documentation Française.

Roux, Georges (1973), "Tables chrétiennes en marbre découvertes à Salamine," in Gilbert Argoud (ed.), *Salamine de Chypre IV: Anthologie Salaminienne*, Mission archéologique Salamine de Chypre, 169–74, Paris: Éditions de Boccard.

Rudenko, Sergei (1970), *Frozen Tombs of Siberia: The Pazyryk Burials of Iron-Age Horsemen*, Berkeley: University of California Press.

Russell, James (2000), "Household Furnishings," in Christine Kondoleon (ed.), *Antioch: The Lost Ancient City. Exhibition Catalogue*, 79–90, Princeton, NJ: Princeton University Press.

Russell, James (2002), "Anemourion," in Angeliki E. Laiou (ed.), *The Economic History of Byzantium from Seventh through the Fifteenth Century*, vol. 2, 221–8, Washington, DC: Dumbarton Oaks Research Library and Collection.

Russo, Simona (1998), "Il corredo dotale di una giovane antinoita," in Loretta Del Francia Barocas (ed.), *Antinoe cent'anni dopo: Catalogo della mostra*, 149–53, Florence: Istituto Papirologico "G. Vitelli."

Sakellarakis, Yannis A. (1970), "Das Kuppelgrab A von Archanes und das kretisch-mykenische Tieropferritual," *Prähistorische Zeitschrift*, 45: 135–219.

Sakellarakis, Yannis A. (1996), "Mycenaean Footstools," in Georgina Herrmann (ed.), *The Furniture of Western Asia: Ancient and Traditional: Papers of the Conference Held at the Institute of Archaeology, University College London, June 28 to 30, 1993*, 105–10, Mainz: Philipp von Zabern.

Sakellarakis, Yannis A. (2006), "Με αφορμή κάποια λείψανα επίπλων στο Ιδαίο Άντρο," in Eirini Gavrilaki and Yannis Tzifopoulos (eds.), *Ο Μυλοπόταμος από την Αρχαιότητα ως Σήμερα*, vol. 3, 137–81, Rethymno: Ιστορική και Λαογραφική Εταιρεία Ρεθύμνου.

Salapata, Gina (2014), *Heroic Offerings: The Terracotta Plaques from the Spartan Sanctuary of Agamemnon and Kassandra*, Ann Arbor: University of Michigan Press.

Salonen, Armas (1963), *Die Möbel des alten Mesopotamien nach sumerisch-akkadischen Quellen*, Annales Academiae Scientiarum Fennicae B 127, Helsinki: Academia Scientiarum Fennica.

Sannibale, Maurizio (2013), "I corredi funerari. La Tomba Regolini–Galassi," in *Cerveteri* 2013: 104–6.

Schäfer, Thomas (1989), *Imperii Insignia. Sella Curulis und Fasces. Zur Repräsentation römischer Magistrate*, Römische Mitteilungen Ergänzungsheft 29, Mainz: Philipp von Zabern.

Schauenburg, Konrad (1976–7), "Unteritalische Kentaurenbilder," *Jahreshefte des Österreichischen archäologischen Instituts in Wien*, 51: 17–44.

Schiaparelli, Ernesto (1927), *Relazione sui lavori della Missione archeologica italiana in Egitto, anni 1903–1920, La tomba intatta dell'architetto Cha nella necropoli di Tebe*, Turin: Museo di antichità.

Seidl, Ursula (1996), "Urartian Furniture," in Georgina Herrmann (ed.), *The Furniture of Western Asia: Ancient and Traditional: Papers of the Conference Held at the*

Institute of Archaeology, University College London, June 28 to 30, 1993, 181–6, Mainz: Philipp von Zabern.

Seiterle, Gérard and Alfred Mutz (1982), "Ein hellenistisches Bronzebett im Baseler Antikenmuseum," *Antike Kunst*, 25: 62–5.

Sethe, Kurt (1903), *Urkunden des Alten Reiches: Urkunden des ägyptischen Altertums*, vol. 1, Leipzig: J.C. Hinrichs'sche Buchhandlung.

Shapiro, Meyer (1980), "The Joseph Scenes on the Maximianus Throne," in Meyer Shapiro (ed.), *Late Antique, Early Christian and Medieval Art: Selected Papers 3*, 34–48, London: Chatto and Windus.

Shaw, Ian (1992), "Ideal Homes in ancient Egypt: The Archaeology of Social Aspiration," *Cambridge Archaeological Journal*, 2 (2): 147–66.

Shaw, Ian (2012), *Ancient Egyptian Technology and Innovation: Transformations in Pharaonic Material Culture*, London: Bloomsbury.

Shear, T. Leslie (1940), "The American Excavations in the Athenian Agora: Eighteenth Report," *Hesperia*, 9: 261–308.

Shelmerdine, Cynthia W. (2012), "Mycenaean Furniture and Vessels: Text and Image," in Marie-Louise Nosch and Robert Laffineur (eds.), *Kosmos: Jewellery, Adornment and Textiles in the Aegean Bronze Age. Proceedings of the 13th International Aegean Conference*, Aegaeum 33, 685–95, Leuven: Peeters.

Siebert, Gérard (1973), "Mobilier délien en bronze," *Bulletin de correspondance hellénique, Supplément* 1: 555–87.

Siebert, Gérard (1976), "Délos: Le Quartier Skardhana," *Bulletin de correspondance hellénique*, 100: 799–821.

Sigrist, Marcel (1988), *Isin Year Names*, Berrien Springs, MI: Andrews University Press.

Simpson, Elizabeth (1995), "Furniture in Ancient Western Asia," in Jack M. Sasson (ed. in chief), *Civilizations of the Ancient Near East*, vol. 3, 1647–71, New York: Charles Scribner's Sons.

Simpson, Elizabeth (1996), "Phrygian Furniture from Gordion," in Georgina Herrmann (ed.), *The Furniture of Western Asia: Ancient and Traditional: Papers of the Conference Held at the Institute of Archaeology, University College London, June 28 to 30, 1993*, 187–209, Mainz: Philipp von Zabern.

Simpson, Elizabeth (1999), "Early Evidence for the Use of the Lathe in Antiquity," in Philip P. Betancourt, Vassos Karageorghis, Robert Laffineur, and Wolf-Dietrich Niemeier (eds.), *Meletemata: Studies in Aegean Archaeology Presented to Malcolm H. Wiener as He Enters His 65th Year*, vol. 3, Aegaeum 20:3, 781–6, Liège: Université de Liège.

Simpson, Elizabeth (2002), "The Andokides Painter and Greek Carpentry," in Andrew J. Clark and Jasper Gaunt with Benedicte Gilman (eds.), *Essays in Honor of Dietrich von Bothmer*, Allard Pierson Series 14, 303–16, Amsterdam: Allard Pierson Museum.

Simpson, Elizabeth (2010), *The Furniture from Tumulus MM, The Gordion Wooden Objects*, vol. 1, Leiden: Brill.

Simpson, Elizabeth (2013), "An Early Anatolian Ivory Chair: The Pratt Ivories in the Metropolitan Museum of Art," in Robert B. Koehl (ed.), *Amilla: The Quest for Excellence. Studies Presented to Guenter Kopcke in Celebration of His 75th Birthday*, Prehistory Monographs 43, 221–61, Philadelphia: INSTAP Academic Press.

Simpson, Elizabeth (2020), "The Throne of King Midas," in Liat Naeh and Dana Brostowsky Gilboa (eds.), *The Ancient Throne: The Mediterranean, Near East, and Beyond, from the 3rd Millennium BCE to the 14th Century CE*, 135–49, Vienna: Austrian Academy of Sciences Press.

Simpson, Elizabeth and Krysia Spirydowicz (1999), *Gordion Wooden Furniture: The Study, Conservation and Reconstruction of the Furniture and Wooden Objects from Gordion, 1981–1998*, Ankara: Museum of Anatolian Civilizations.

Simpson, Elizabeth, Krysia Spirydowicz, and Valerie Dorge (1992), *Gordion: Ahsap Eserler/Wooden Furniture*, Ankara: Museum of Anatolian Civilizations.

Sismanidis, Kostas (1997), Κλίνες και κλινοειδείς κατασκευές των Μακεδονικών τάφων, Athens: Archaeological Receipts Fund (TAP).

Smith, Dennis E. (2003), *From Symposium to Eucharist: The Banquet in the Early Christian World*, Minneapolis, MN: Fortress Press.

Smith, Stuart T. (1992), "Intact Tombs of the Seventeenth and Eighteenth Dynasties from Thebes and the New Kingdom Burial Systems," *Mitteilungen des Deutschen Archäologischen Instituts (Abteilung Kairo)*, 48: 193–231.

Snape, Steven (2011), *Ancient Egyptian Tombs: The Culture of Life and Death*, London: Wiley-Blackwell.

Snodgrass, Anthony M. (1998), *Homer and the Artists: Text and Picture in Early Greek Art*, Cambridge: Cambridge University Press.

Sparkes, Brian A. (1975), "Illustrating Aristophanes," *Journal of Hellenic Studies*, 95: 122–35.

Spatharakis, Ioannis (2004), *The Illustrations of the Cynegetica in Venice: Codex Marcianus graecus Z 139*, Leiden: Alexandros Press.

St. Clair Harvey, Archer (2003), *Carving as Craft: Palatine East and the Greco-Roman Bone and Ivory Carving*, Baltimore: Johns Hopkins University Press.

Speciale, Maria Stella (2000), "Furniture in Linear B: The Evidence from Tables," in Alexandra Karetsou, Theocharis Detorakis, and Alexis Kalokairinos (eds.), Πεπραγμένα Η΄ Διεθνούς Κρητολογικού Συνεδρίου, vol. A3, 227–39, Herakleion: Εταιρεία Κρητικών Ιστορικών Μελετών.

Stampolidis, Nikolaos C. and Yorgos Tassoulas, eds. (2014), ΙΑΣΙΣ. Υγεία, Νόσος, Θεραπεία. Από τον Όμηρο στον Γαληνό, Athens: Museum of Cycladic Art.

Steel, Louise (2013), "The Social World of Early-Middle Bronze Age Cyprus: Rethinking the Vounous Bowl," *Journal of Mediterranean Archaeology*, 26 (1): 51–73.

Steingräber, Stephan (1979), *Etruskische Möbel*, Rome: Giorgio Bretschneider.

Steingräber, Stephan (2002), "Ahnenkult und bildliche Darstellungen von Ahnen in etruskischen und unteritalischen Grabgemälden aus vorrömischer Zeit," in Jakob Munk Højte (ed.), *Images of Ancestors*, 127–58, Aarhus: Aarhus University Press.

Steingräber, Stephan (2013), "Worshiping with the Dead: New Approaches to the Etruscan Necropolis," in Jean M. Turfa (ed.), *The Etruscan World*, 655–71, London: Routledge.

Steingräber, Stephan, ed. (1986), *Etruscan Painting. Catalogue raisonné of Etruscan Wall Paintings*, New York: Johnson Reprint Corp.

Stephanidou-Tiveriou, Theodosia (1993), Τραπεζοφόρα με πλαστική διακόσμηση. Η αττική ομάδα, Δημοσιεύματα του Αρχαιολογικού Δελτίου 50, Athens: Archaeological Receipts Fund (TAP).

Stern, Wilma Olch and Danae Hadjilazaro Thimme (2007), *Kenchreai: Eastern Port of Corinth. Results of Investigations by the University of Chicago and Indiana University for the American School of Classical Studies at Athens*, vol. 6, *Ivory, Bone, and Related Wood Finds*, Leiden: Brill.

Stocker, Sharon R. and Jack L. Davis (2004), "Animal Sacrifice, Archives, and Feasting at the Palace of Nestor," *Hesperia*, 73: 179–95.

Symington, Dorit (1996), "Hittite and Neo-Hittite Furniture," in Georgina Herrmann (ed.), *The Furniture of Western Asia: Ancient and Traditional: Papers of the*

Conference Held at the Institute of Archaeology, University College London, June 28 to 30, 1993, 111–38, Mainz: Philipp von Zabern.

Teissier, Beatrice (1996), *Egyptian Iconography on Syro-Palestinian Cylinder Seals of the Middle Bronze Age*, Orbis Biblicus et Orientalis 11, Freiburg: Switzerland University Press/Vandenhoeck und Ruprecht.

Themelis, Petros (1979), "Ausgrabungen in Kallipolis (Ost-Aetolien) 1977–1978," *Athens Annals of Archaeology*, 12: 245–79.

Themelis, Petros (1994), "Ο τάφος της Ηλείας Φιλημήνας," in *Γ' Επιστημονική Συνάντηση για την Ελληνιστική Κεραμική, 24–27 Σεπτεμβρίου 1991, Θεσσαλονίκη*, 146–57, Athens: The Archaeological Society at Athens.

Themelis, Petros and Ioannis Touratsoglou (1997), *Οι τάφοι του Δερβενίου*, Athens: Archaeological Receipts Fund (TAP).

Theodossiadou, Maro (1995), "Representations of Furniture on Cylinder Seals from Late Bronze Age Cyprus," in Christine Morris (ed.), *Klados: Essays in Honour of J.N. Coldstream*, BICS Supplement 63, 249–60, London: Institute of Classical Studies.

Theodossiadou, Maro (1996), "Cypriote Furniture and its Representations from the Chalcolithic to the Cypro–Archaic," in Georgina Herrmann (ed.), *The Furniture of Western Asia: Ancient and Traditional: Papers of the Conference Held at the Institute of Archaeology, University College London, June 28 to 30, 1993*, 73–83, Mainz: Philipp von Zabern.

Thiersch, Hermann (1904), *Zwei antike Grabanlagen bei Alexandria*, Berlin: G. Reimer.

Thompson, Dorothy B. (2000), "Philadelphus' Procession," in Leon Mooren (ed.), *Politics, Administration and Society in the Hellenistic and Roman World: Proceedings of the International Colloquium, Bertinoro, July 19–24, 1997*, 365–88, Leuven: Peeters.

Thureau-Dangin, François and Maurice Dunand (1936), *Til-Barsib*, Bibliothèque Archéologique et Historique 23, Paris: P. Geuthner.

Tittmann, Johannes A.H. (1967), *Iohannis Zonarae Lexicon ex tribus codicibus manuscriptis*, 2nd edn., 2 vols., Amsterdam: Hakkert.

Tomlinson, Richard A. (1984), "The Ceiling of Anfushy II.2," in Nicola Bonacasa and Antonino Di Vita (eds.), *Alessandria e il mondo hellenistico-romano. Studi in onore di Achille Adriani*, 260–4, Rome: "L'Erma" di Bretschneider.

Travlos, John (1988), *Bildlexikon zur Topographie des antiken Attika*, Tübingen: Ernst Wasmuth.

Trendall, Arthur D. (1960), "The Cassandra Painter and His Circle," *Jahrbuch der Berliner Museen*, 2: 7–33.

Trianti, Ismene (1998), *The Acropolis Museum*, Athens: Latsis Group.

Trümper, Monika (1998), *Wohnen in Delos: Eine baugeschichtliche Untersuchung zum Wandel der Wohnkultur in hellenistischer Zeit*, Rahden: Verlag Marie Leidorf.

Tsakirgis, Barbara (forthcoming), *Morgantina Studies 7: The Domestic Architecture of Morgantina in the Hellenistic and Roman Periods*, Princeton, NJ: Princeton University Press.

Tsimbidou-Avloniti, Maria (2000), "Λάρνακα ες αργυρέην ... (Ιλ. Σ, 413)," in Polyxeni Adam-Veleni (ed.), *Μύρτος: Μνήμη Ιουλίας Βοκοτοπούλου*, 543–75, Thessaloniki: Aristotle University of Thessaloniki.

Tsimbidou-Avloniti, Maria (2005), *Μακεδονικοί Τάφοι στον Φοίνικα και στον Άγιο Αθανάσιο Θεσσαλονίκης*, Athens: Hellenic Ministry of Culture.

Tuck, Anthony S. (1994), "The Etruscan Seated Banquet: Villanovan Ritual and Etruscan Iconography," *American Journal of Archaeology*, 98: 617–28.

Türcoğlu, Inci (2004), "Byzantine Houses in Western Anatolia: An Architectural Approach," *Al–Masāq*, 16: 93–130.

Turfa, Jean M. (2005), *Catalogue of the Etruscan Gallery of the University of Pennsylvania Museum of Archaeology and Anthropology*, Philadelphia: University Museum Press.

Turfa, Jean M., ed. (2013), *The Etruscan World*, London: Routledge.

Tzachou-Alexandri, Olga (1989), "Αθηναϊκή λευκή λήκυθος από τον αρχαίο Ωρωπό," in *Φίλια Έπη εις Γεώργιον Μυλωνάν*, vol. 3, Βιβλιοθήκη της εν Αθήναις Αρχαιολογικής Εταιρείας 103, 83–107, Athens: The Archaeological Society at Athens.

Ulrich, Roger Bradley (2007), *Roman Woodworking*, New Haven, CT: Yale University Press.

Uytterhoeven, Inge (2007), "Housing in Late Antiquity: Thematic Perspectives," in Luke Lavan, Lale Özgenel, and Alexander Sarantis (eds.), *Housing in Late Antiquity: From Palaces to Shops*, LAA Supplementary Series 1, 25–66, Leiden: Brill.

Van Der Meer, L. Bouke (1984), "Kylikeia in Etruscan Tomb Paintings," in Herman A.G. Brijder (ed.), *Ancient Greek and Related Pottery: Proceedings of the International Vase Symposium, April 12–15, 1984*, Allard Pierson Series 5, 298–304, Amsterdam: Allard Pierson.

van de Mieroop, Marc (1987), *Crafts in the Early Isin Period. A Study of the Isin "Craft Archive" from the Reigns of Išbi-Erra and Šu-Ilišu*, Louvain: Peeters.

Van Straten, Folkert T. (1995), *Hierà Kalà: Images of Animal Sacrifice in Archaic and Classical Greece*, Leiden: Brill.

Varias García, Carlos (2008), "Observations on the Mycenaean Vocabulary of Furniture and Vessels," in Anna Sacconi, Maurizio del Freo, Louis Godart, and Mario Negri (eds.), *Colloquium Romanum: Atti del XII Colloquio Internationale di Micenologia, Roma 20–25 febbraio 2006*, vol. 2, Pasiphae 2, 775–93, Pisa: Fabrizio Serra.

Varner, Eric R. (2015), "Reuse and Recarving: Technical Evidence," in Elise A. Friedland, Melanie Grunow Sobocinski, and Elaine K. Gazda (eds.), *The Oxford Handbook of Roman Sculpture*, 123–38, New York: Oxford University Press.

Vasileiadou, Magda (2011), "The Ivory Plaques of Eleutherna, Crete and their Workshop," in Kyriakos Savvopoulos (ed.), *Second Hellenistic Studies Workshop, July 4–11, 2010*, Bibliotheca Alexandrina, 66–76, Alexandria: Alexandria Center for Hellenistic Studies.

Vass, Lóránt (2010), "Bone-Working in Roman Dacia," in Alexandra Legrand-Pineau, Isabelle Sidéra, Natacha Buc, Eva David, and Vivian Scheinsohn (eds.), *Ancient and Modern Bone Artefacts from America to Russia: Cultural, Technological and Functional Signature*, British Archaeological Reports International Series Volume 2136, 55–63, Oxford: BAR Publishing.

Venit, Marjorie Susan (2002), *Monumental Tombs of Ancient Alexandria, The Theater of the Dead*, Cambridge: Cambridge University Press.

Verboven, Koenraad (2007), "The Associative Order: Status and Ethos among Roman Businessmen in Late Republic and Early Empire," *Athenaeum*, 95: 861–93.

Verpoorten, J.M. (1962), "La 'stibas' ou l'image de la brousse dans la société grecque," *Revue de l'histoire des religions*, 162: 147–60.

Veyne, Paul (1987), "The Roman Home: A Foreword," in Paul Veyne (ed.), *A History of Private Life. I: From Pagan Rome to Byzantium*, translated by Arthur Goldhammer, 315–17, Cambridge, MA: Harvard University Press.

Vokotopoulou, Ioulia (1990), *Οι ταφικοί τύμβοι της Αίνειας*, Δημοσιεύματα του Αρχαιολογικού Δελτίου 41, Athens: Archaeological Receipts Fund (TAP).

Von Eles, Patrizia (2000), "Verucchio (Rimini), necropoli Lippi, tomba 85," in Gilda Bartoloni (ed.), *Principi etruschi tra Mediterraneo ed Europa*, 365–72, Bologna: Marsilio.

Von Eles, Patrizia (2002), *Guerriero e sacerdote: Autorità e comunità nell'età del ferro a Verucchio, La Tomba del Trono*, Florence: All'Insegna del Giglio.

Vroom, Joanita (2007), "The Archaeology of Late Antique Dining Habits in the Eastern Mediterranean: A Preliminary Study of the Evidence," in Luke Lavan, Ellen Swift, and Toon Putzeys (eds.), *Objects in Context, Objects in Use: Material Spatiality in Late Antiquity*, Late Antique Archaeology 5, 313–61, Leiden: Brill.

Wada, Koichiro (2007), "Provincial Society and Cemetery Organization in the New Kingdom," *Studien zur Altägyptischen Kultur*, 36: 347–89.

Walter-Karydi, Elena (1994), *Die Nobilitierung des Wohnhauses: Lebensform und Architektur im spätklassischen Griechenland*, Xenia: Konstanzer althistorische Vorträge und Forschungen 35, Konstanz: UVK- Universitätsverlag Konstanz.

Wanscher, Ole (1980), *Sella Curulis: The Folding Stool, an Ancient Symbol of Dignity*, Copenhagen: Rosenkilde and Bagger.

Ward-Perkins, Bryan (2001), "Specialization, Trade and Prosperity: An Overview of the Economy of the Late Antique Eastern Mediterranean," in Kingsley Sean and Michael Decker (eds.), *Economy and Exchange in the East Mediterranean during Late Antiquity*, 167–78, Oxford: Oxbow Books.

Wecowski, Marek (2014), *The Rise of the Greek Aristocratic Banquet*, Oxford: Oxford University Press.

Wedoff, Briget (2009), "World and Witness: A Reevaluation of the Function, Form and Imagery of the Cathedra of Maximian," MA thesis, Northern Illinois University.

Weitzmann-Fielder, Josepha (1979), "Representations of Daily Life," in Kurt Weitzmann (ed.), *Age of Spirituality: Late Antique and Early Christian Art, Third to Seventh Century, Catalogue of the exhibition at The Metropolitan Museum of Art, November 19, 1977 through February 12, 1978*, 273–85, New York: The Metropolitan Museum of Art; Princeton, NJ: Princeton University Press.

Wendrich, Willemina Z. (2000), "Basketry," in Paul T. Nicholson and Ian Shaw (eds.), *Ancient Egyptian Materials and Technology*, 254–67, Cambridge: Cambridge University Press.

Westgate, Ruth (2015), "Space and Social Complexity from the Early Iron Age to the Classical Period," *Hesperia*, 84: 47–95.

Wiegand, Theodor and Hans Schräder (1904), *Priene: Ergebnisse der Ausgrabungen und Untersuchungen in den Jahren 1895–1898*, Berlin: G. Reimer.

Wikipedia (2021), "Gordion Furniture and Wooden Artifacts," last edited February 25, 2021. Available online: https://en.wikipedia.org/wiki/Gordion_Furniture_and_Wooden_Artifacts (accessed April 17, 2021).

Winlock, Herbert E. (1955), *Models of Daily Life in Ancient Egypt from the Tomb of Meket-Re at Thebes*, Publications of the Metropolitan Museum of Art 18, Cambridge, MA: Harvard University Press.

Winter, Irene J. (1986), "The King and the Cup: Iconography of the Royal Presentation Scene of Ur III Seals," in Marilyn Kelly-Buccellati, Paolo Matthiae, and Maurits Nanning Van Loon (eds.), *Insight through Images: Studies in Honor of Edith Porada*, Bibliotheca Mesopotamica 21, 253–68, Malibu: Undenda.

Winter, Irene J. (1993), "'Seat of the Kingship'/ 'A Wonder to Behold': The Palace as Construct in the Ancient Near East," *Ars Orientalis*, 23: 27–55.

Wiseman, James (1969), "Excavations in Corinth, the Gymnasium Area, 1967–1968," *Hesperia*, 38: 64–106.

Woolley, Leonard C. (1934), *Ur Excavations II, The Royal Cemetery*, London: British Museum and University of Pennsylvania Museum.

Woolley, Leonard and Max Mallowan (1976), *Ur Excavations VII, The Old Babylonian Period*, London: British Museum and University of Pennsylvania Museum.

Worp, K.A., J. Diethart, P.J. Sijpesteijn, and H. Harrauer (1990), "Bemerkungen zu Papyri III. <Korr. Tyche>," *Tyche*, 5: 179–82.

Wright, F.A. (1930), *The Works of Liudprand of Cremona: Antapodosis*, Liber De Rebus Gestis Ottonis, Relatio De Legatione Constantinopolitana, London: George Routledge & Sons.

Younger, John G. (1995), "The Iconography of Rulership: A Conspectus," in Paul Rehak (ed.), *The Role of the Ruler in the Prehistoric Aegean*, Aegaeum 11, 151–211, Liège: Université de Liège.

Ziffer, Irit (2005), "From Acemhöyük to Megiddo: The Banquet Scene in the Art of the Levant in the Second Millennium BCE," *Tel Aviv*, 32: 133–67.

Zimmer, Gerhard (1982), *Römische Berufsdarstellungen*, Berlin: Gebr. Mann Verlag.

Zimmermann, Norbert (2010), "Die spätantike und byzantinische Malerei in Ephesos," in Falko Daim and Jörg Drauschke (eds.), *Byzanz—das Römerreich im Mittelalter. Teil 2.2 Schauplätze* Monographien des Römisch-Germanischen Zentralmuseums: 84 2.2, 615–62, Mainz: Verlag des Römisch-Germanischen Zentralmuseums.

Zonhoven, Ludovicus M.J. (1979), "The Inspection of a Tomb at Deir el-Medîna (O.Wien.Aeg. 1)," *Journal of Egyptian Archaeology*, 65: 89–98.

INDEX